D1621065

BUNNY DROP ❾

YUMI UNITA

Translation: Kaori Inoue • Lettering: Alexis Eckerman

This book is a work of fiction. Names, characters, places, and incidents
are the product of the author's imagination or are used fictitiously.
Any resemblance to actual events, locales, or persons, living or dead, is
coincidental.

BUNNY DROP Vol. 9 © 2011 by Yumi Unita. All rights reserved. First
published in Japan in 2011 by SHODENSHA PUBLISHING CO., LTD.,
Tokyo. English translation rights in USA, Canada, and UK arranged with
SHODENSHA PUBLISHING CO., LTD. and Yen Press, LLC through Tuttle-
Mori Agency, Inc., Tokyo.

English translation © 2013 by Yen Press, LLC

Yen Press, LLC supports the right to free expression and the value of
copyright. The purpose of copyright is to encourage writers and artists to
produce the creative works that enrich our culture.

The scanning, uploading, and distribution of this book without permission
is a theft of the author's intellectual property. If you would like permission
to use material from the book (other than for review purposes), please
contact the publisher. Thank you for your support of the author's rights.

Yen Press
1290 Avenue of the Americas
New York, NY 10104

Visit us at yenpress.com
facebook.com/yenpress
twitter.com/yenpress
yenpress.tumblr.com

Date: 4/10/18

GRA 741.5 BUN V.9
Unita, Yumi,
Bunny drop.

t are not

Printed in the United States of America

PALM BEACH COUNTY
LIBRARY SYSTEM
3650 Summit Boulevard
West Palm Beach, FL 33406-4198

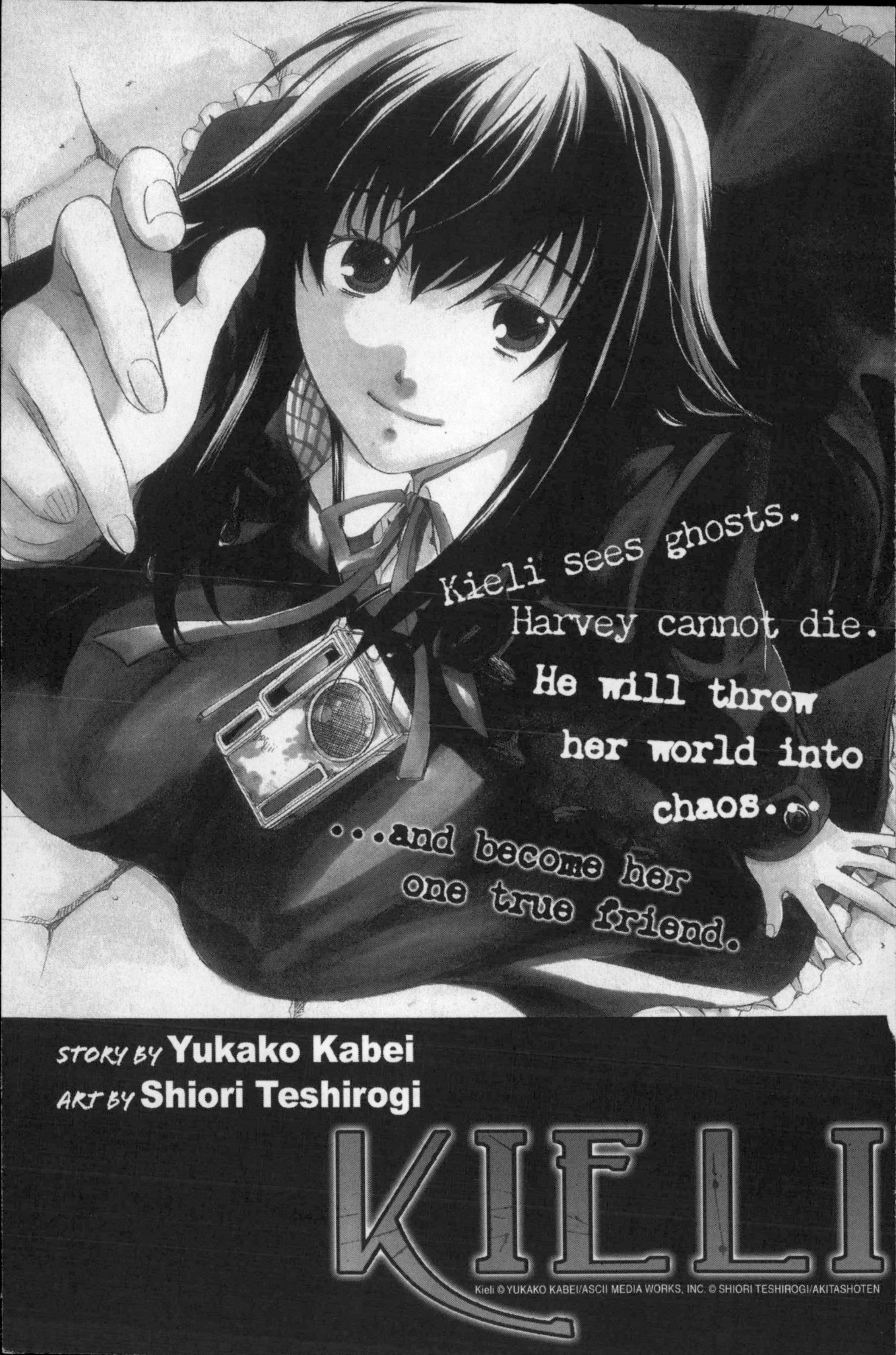
Kieli sees ghosts.
Harvey cannot die.
He will throw
her world into
chaos...
...and become her
one true friend.
STORY BY Yukako Kabei
ART BY Shiori Teshirogi
KIELI
Kieli © YUKAKO KABEI/ASCII MEDIA WORKS, INC. © SHIORI TESHIROGI/AKITASHOTEN

BUNNY**DROP** 9
yumi unita

MAIN CHARACTERS

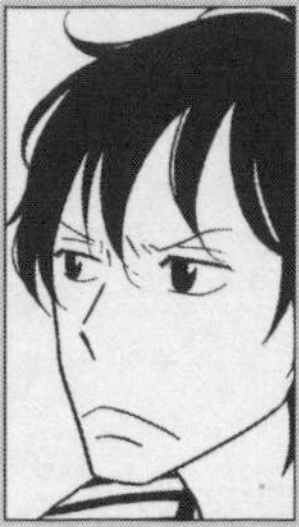

KOUKI NITANI
Rin's childhood friend from day-care. High school first-year. Because of one thing after another, he was rejected by Rin.

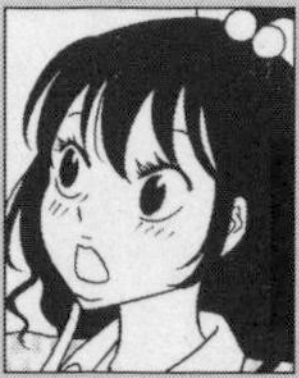

REINA
Daikichi's cousin Haruko's daughter. High school first-year. Rin's best friend.

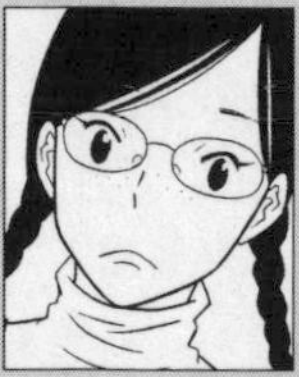

MASAKO YOSHII
Rin's birthmother. Manga artist. Recently had a second child.

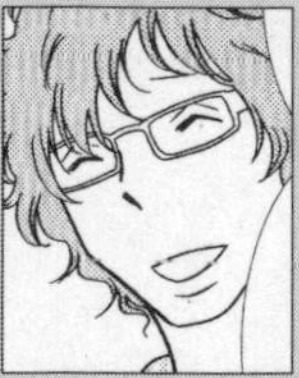

MASAKO'S HUSBAND
Also her chief assistant.

RIN KAGA
A smart and responsible high school first-year. Taken in by Daikichi when she was six. Secretly has feelings for Daikichi.

DAIKICHI KAWACHI
Forty years old and single. Has been Rin's guardian for ten years. His "romance" with Kouki's mother crashed and burned.

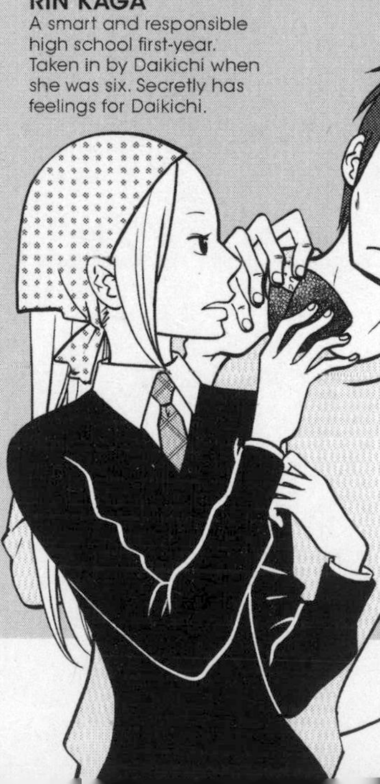

STORY

Ten years have passed since Daikichi made the decision to take in Rin, his grandfather's secret love child. As a single parent, he and Rin have survived these ten years by supporting each other.

Rin, in high school, reconnects with her birthmother, Masako. Rin is overjoyed with the impending birth of a little sister, but Daikichi and Masako are their usual combative selves. During all this, Rin grapples with her growing feelings of love for Daikichi...

contents

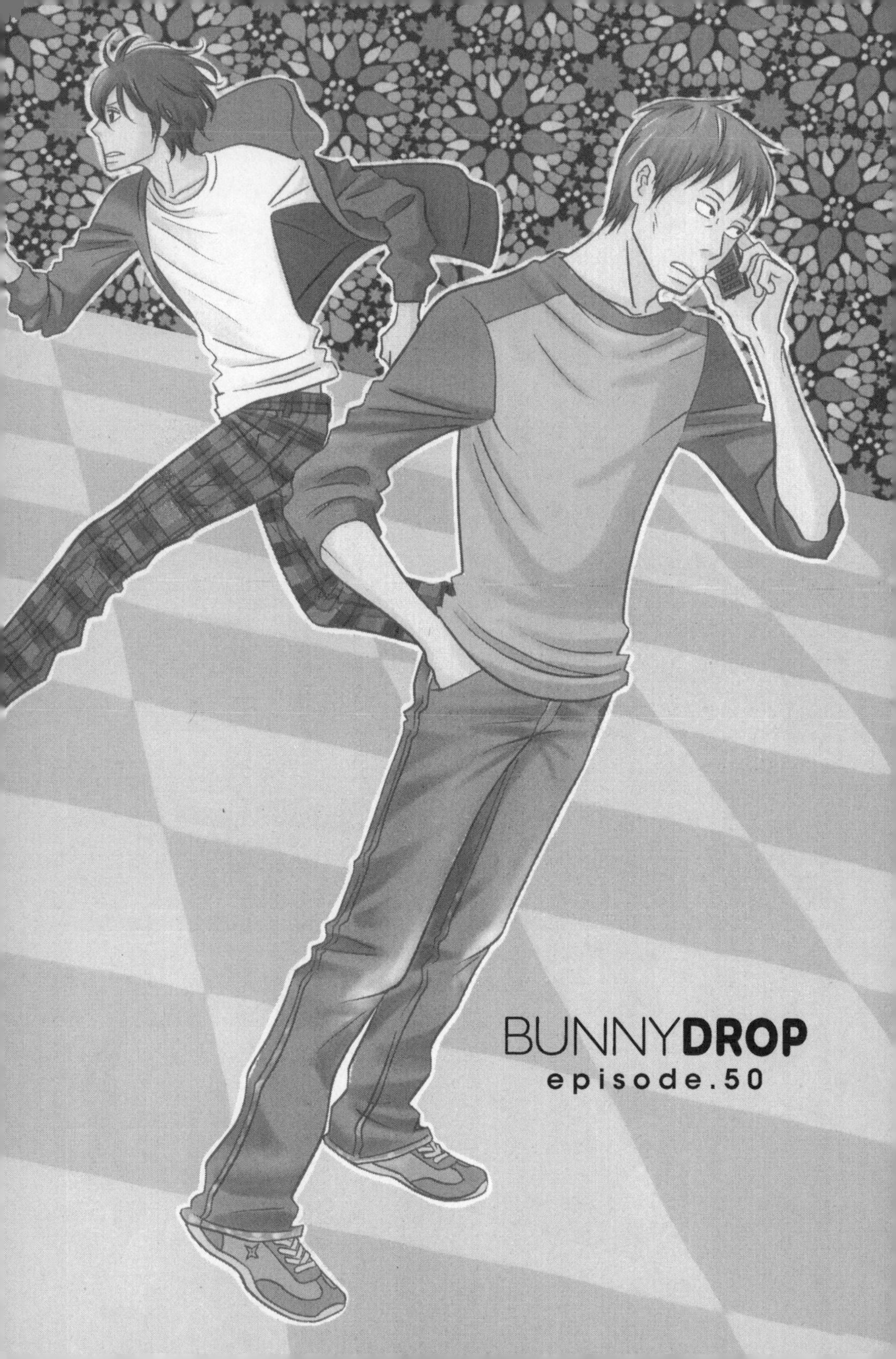

BUNNY DROP
episode.50

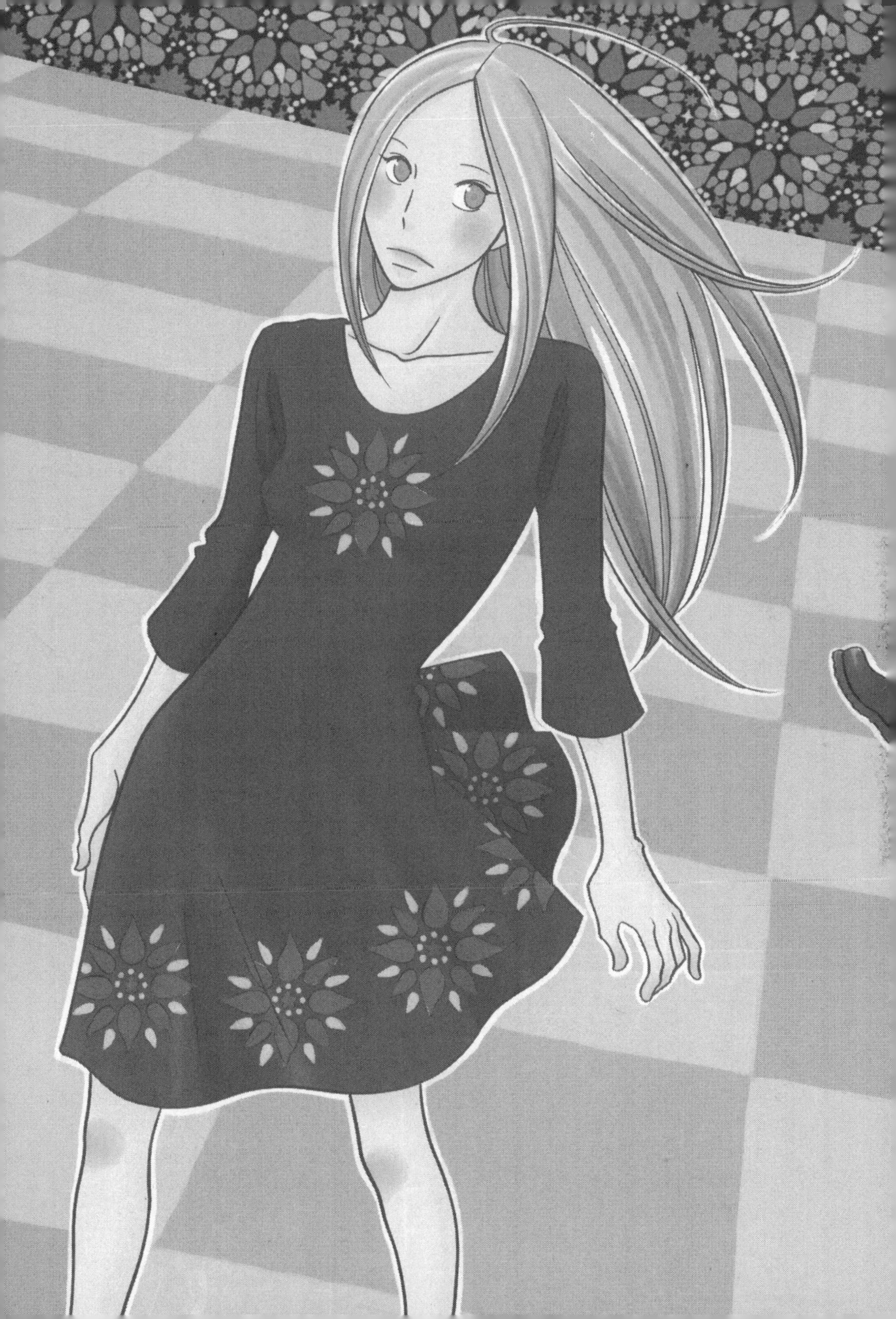

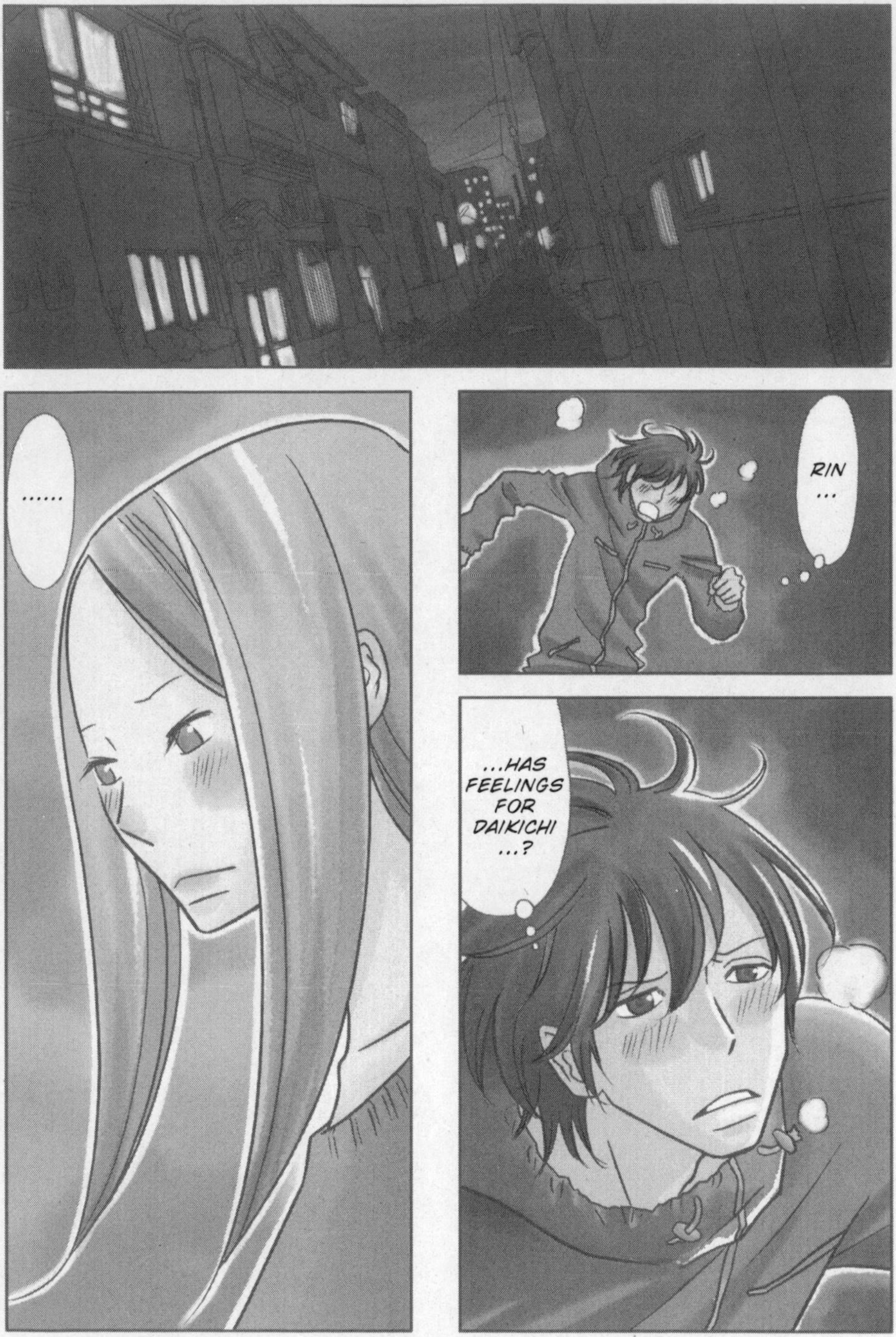
RIN ...
...HAS FEELINGS FOR DAIKICHI ...?
......

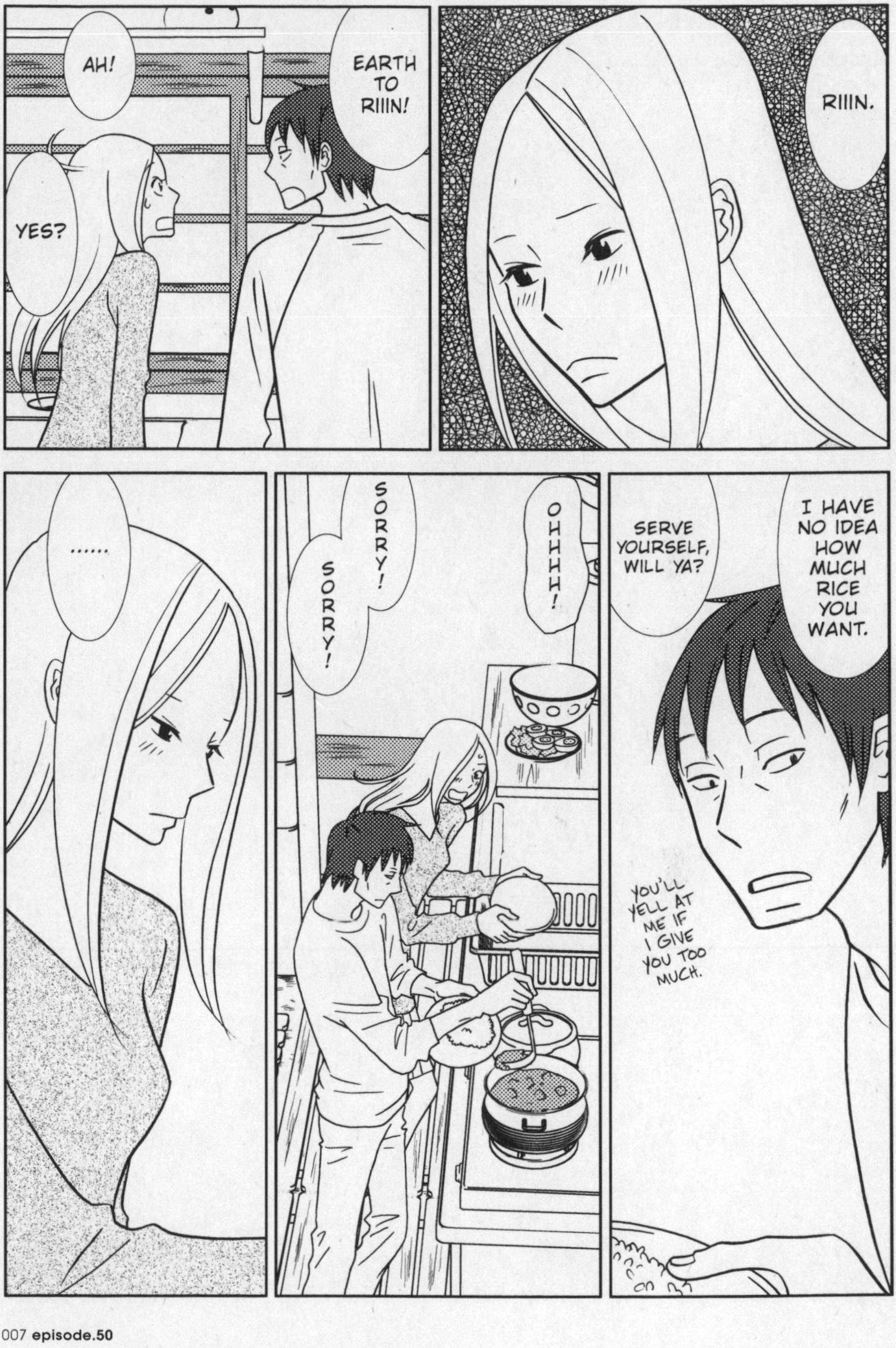
RIIIN.
EARTH TO RIIIN!
AH!
YES?
I HAVE NO IDEA HOW MUCH RICE YOU WANT.
SERVE YOURSELF, WILL YA?
YOU'LL YELL AT ME IF I GIVE YOU TOO MUCH.
OHHHH!
SORRY!
SORRY!
......

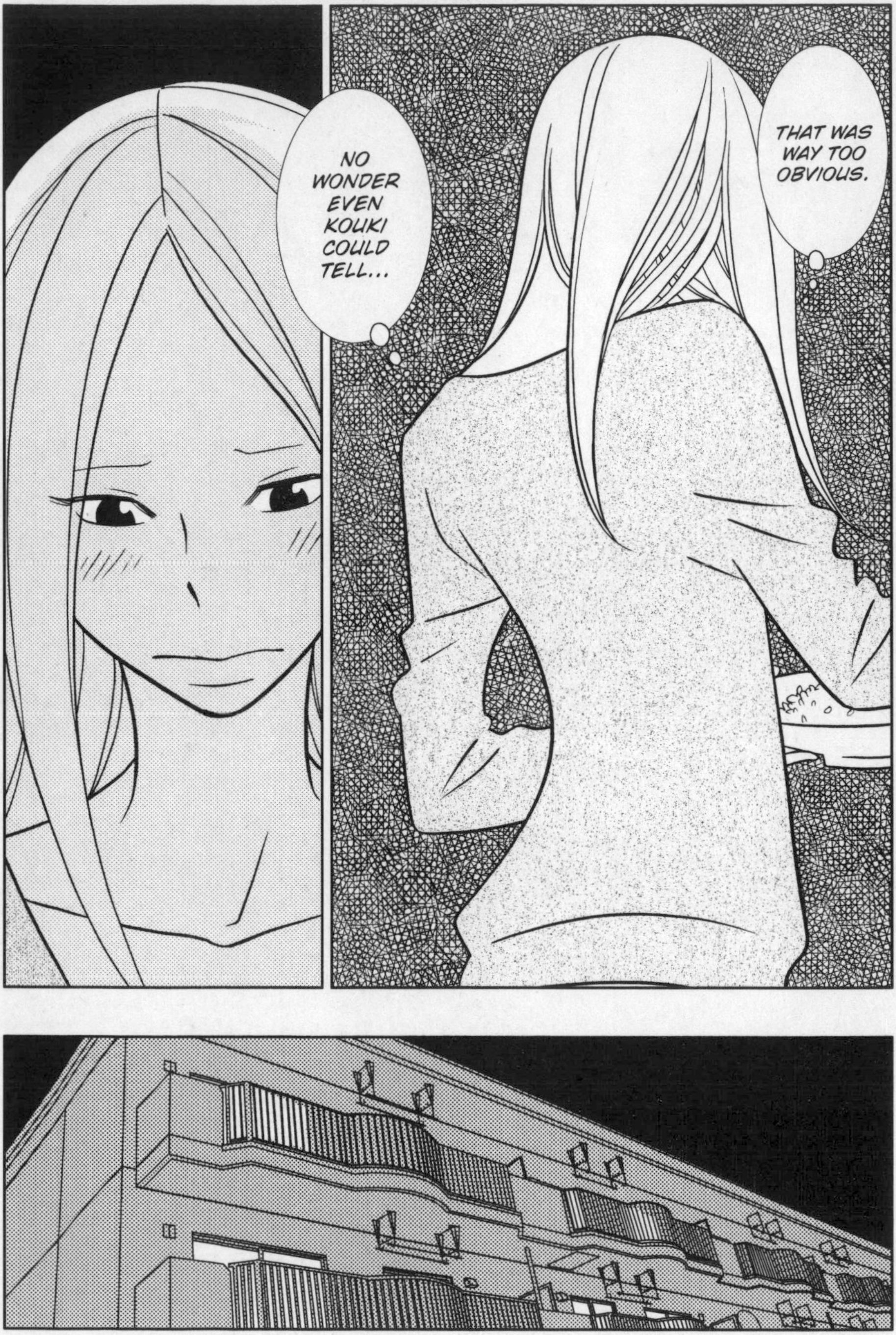
THAT WAS WAY TOO OBVIOUS.
NO WONDER EVEN KOUKI COULD TELL...

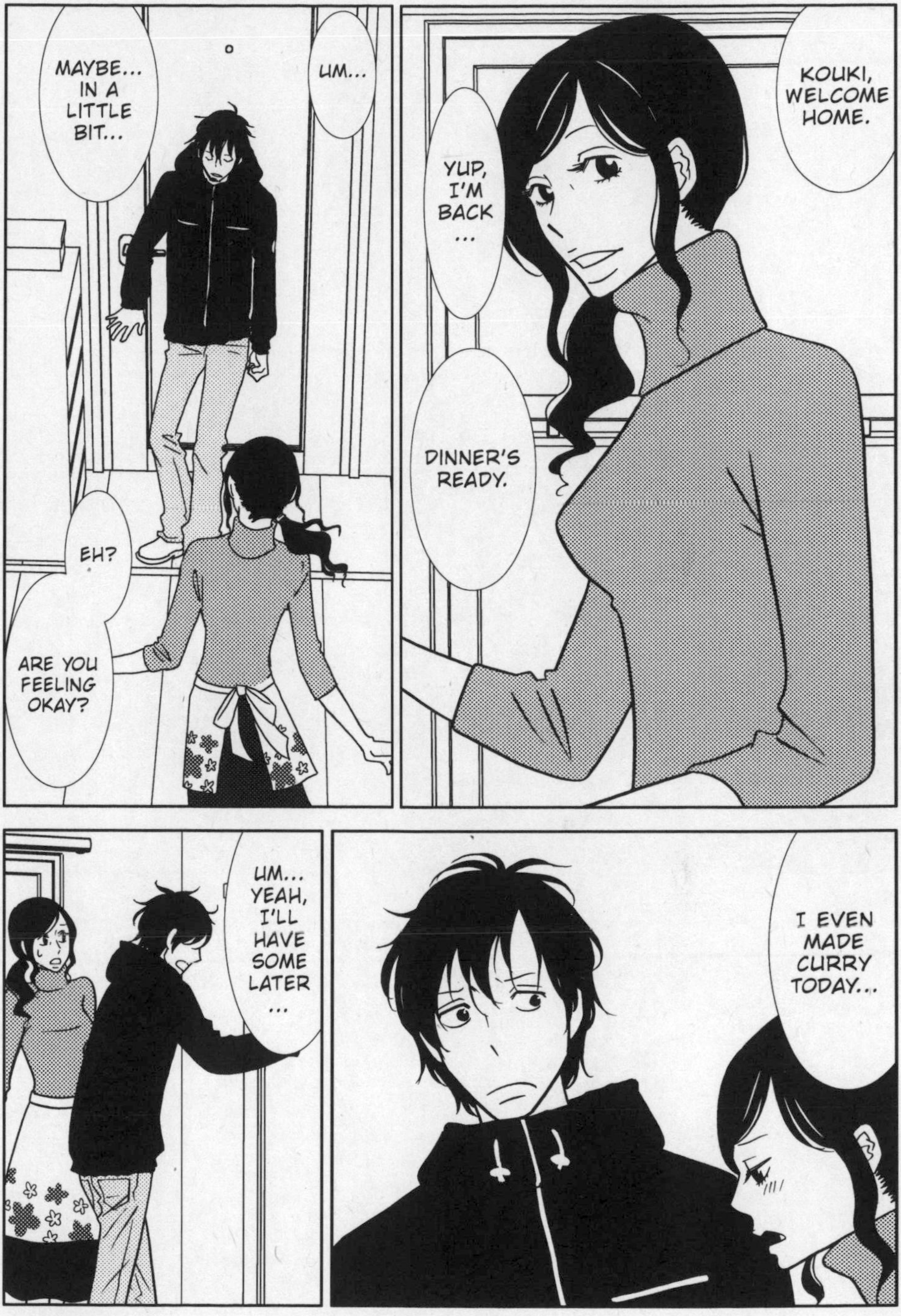
KOUKI, WELCOME HOME.
YUP, I'M BACK...
DINNER'S READY.
UM...
MAYBE... IN A LITTLE BIT...
EH?
ARE YOU FEELING OKAY?
I EVEN MADE CURRY TODAY...
UM... YEAH, I'LL HAVE SOME LATER...

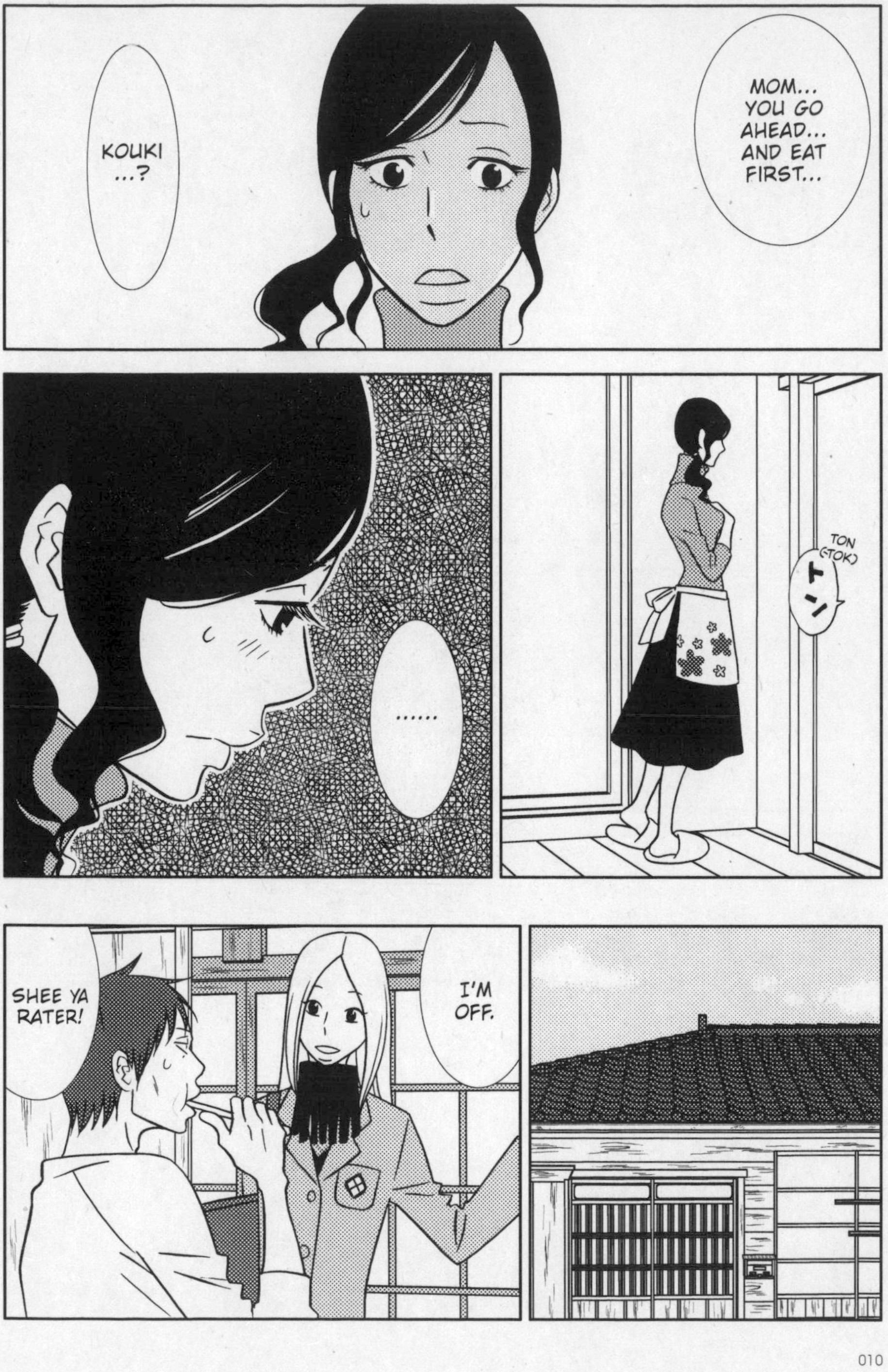
MOM... YOU GO AHEAD... AND EAT FIRST...
KOUKI ...?
トン
TON (TOK)
......
I'M OFF.
SHEE YA RATER!

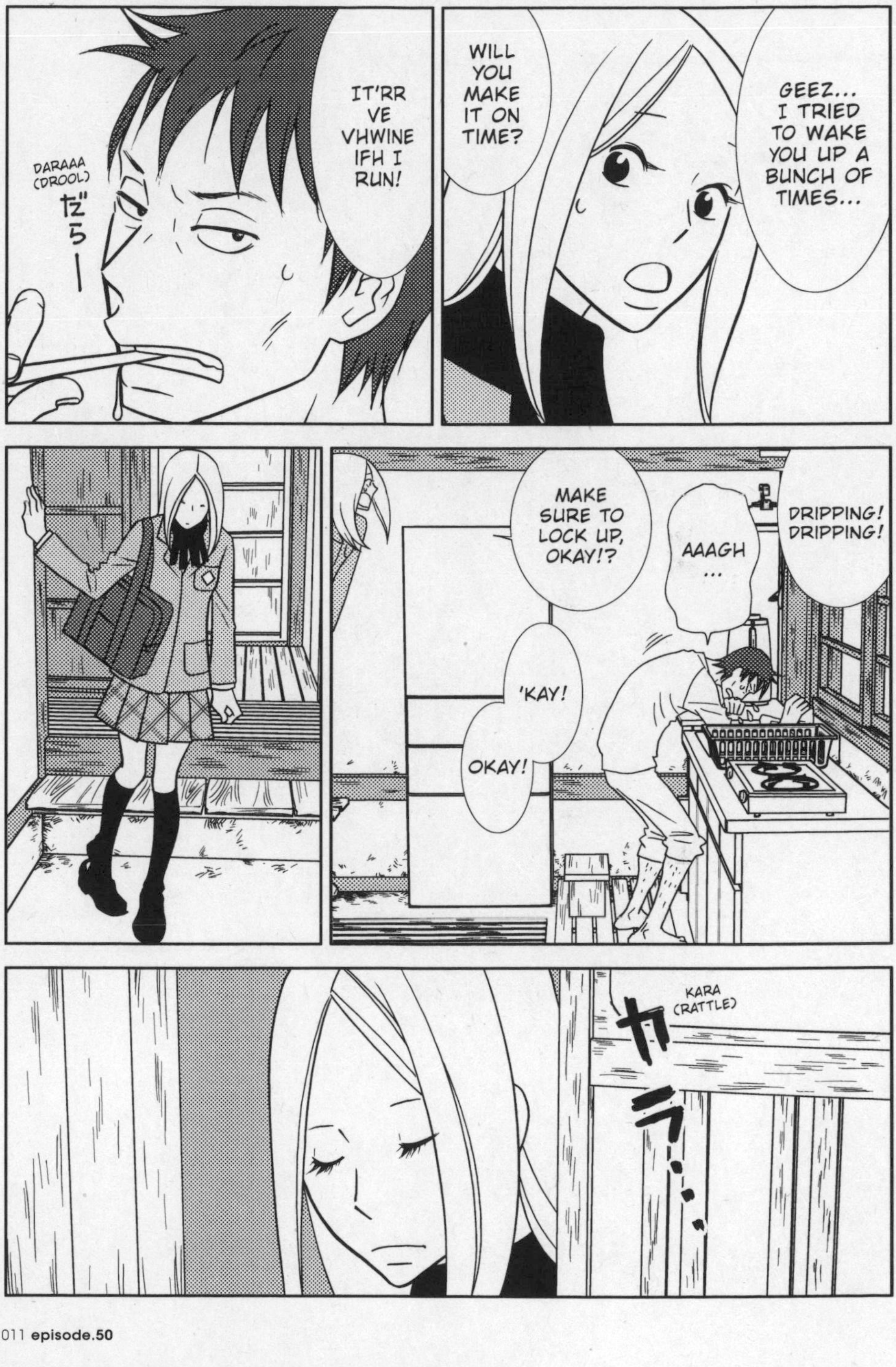
GEEZ... I TRIED TO WAKE YOU UP A BUNCH OF TIMES...
WILL YOU MAKE IT ON TIME?
IT'RR VE VHWINE IFH I RUN!
DARAAA (DROOL)
だらー
DRIPPING! DRIPPING!
AAAGH...
MAKE SURE TO LOCK UP, OKAY!?
'KAY!
OKAY!
KARA (RATTLE)
カラ...

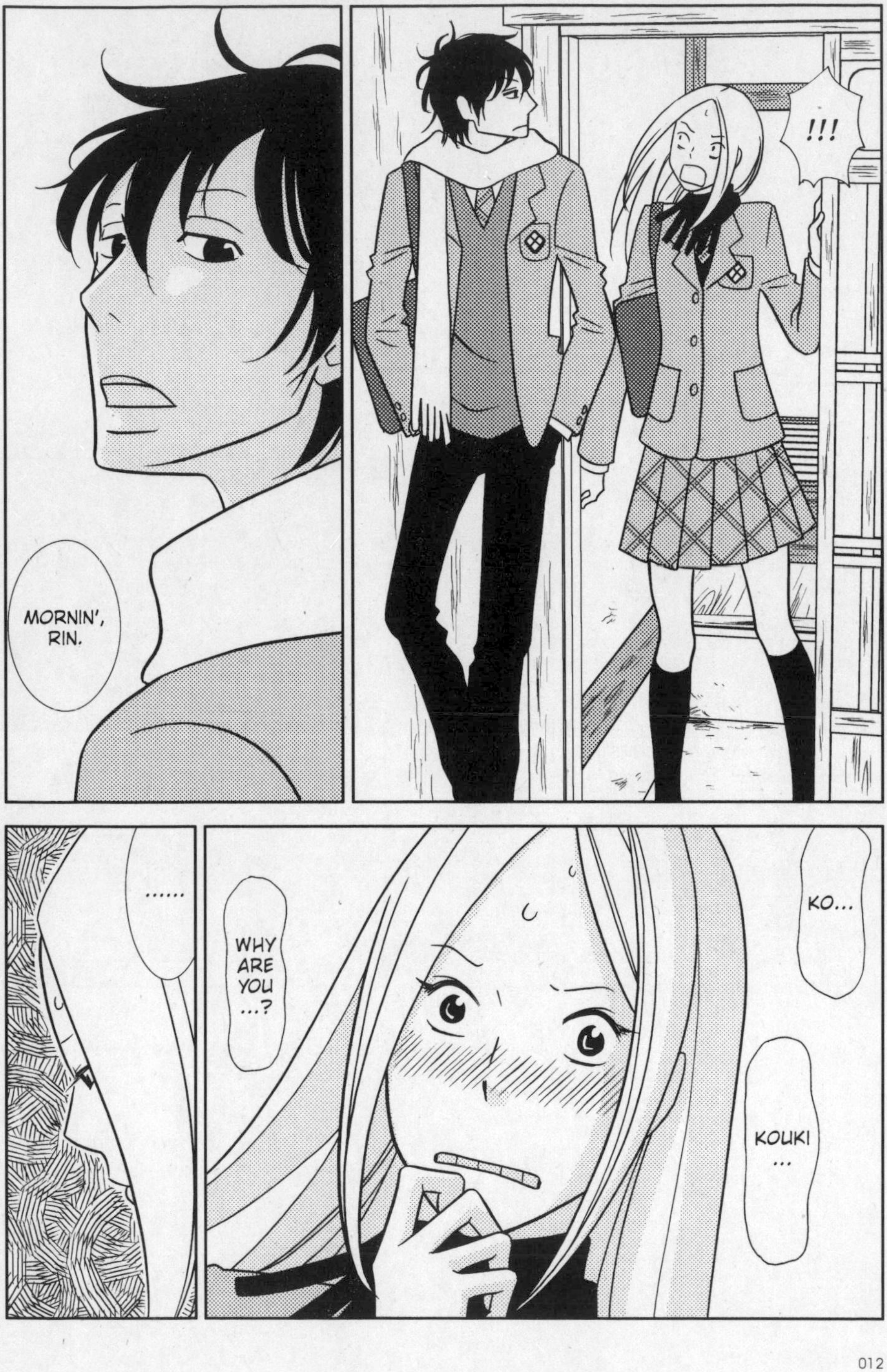
!!!
MORNIN', RIN.
KO...
KOUKI ...
WHY ARE YOU ...?
......

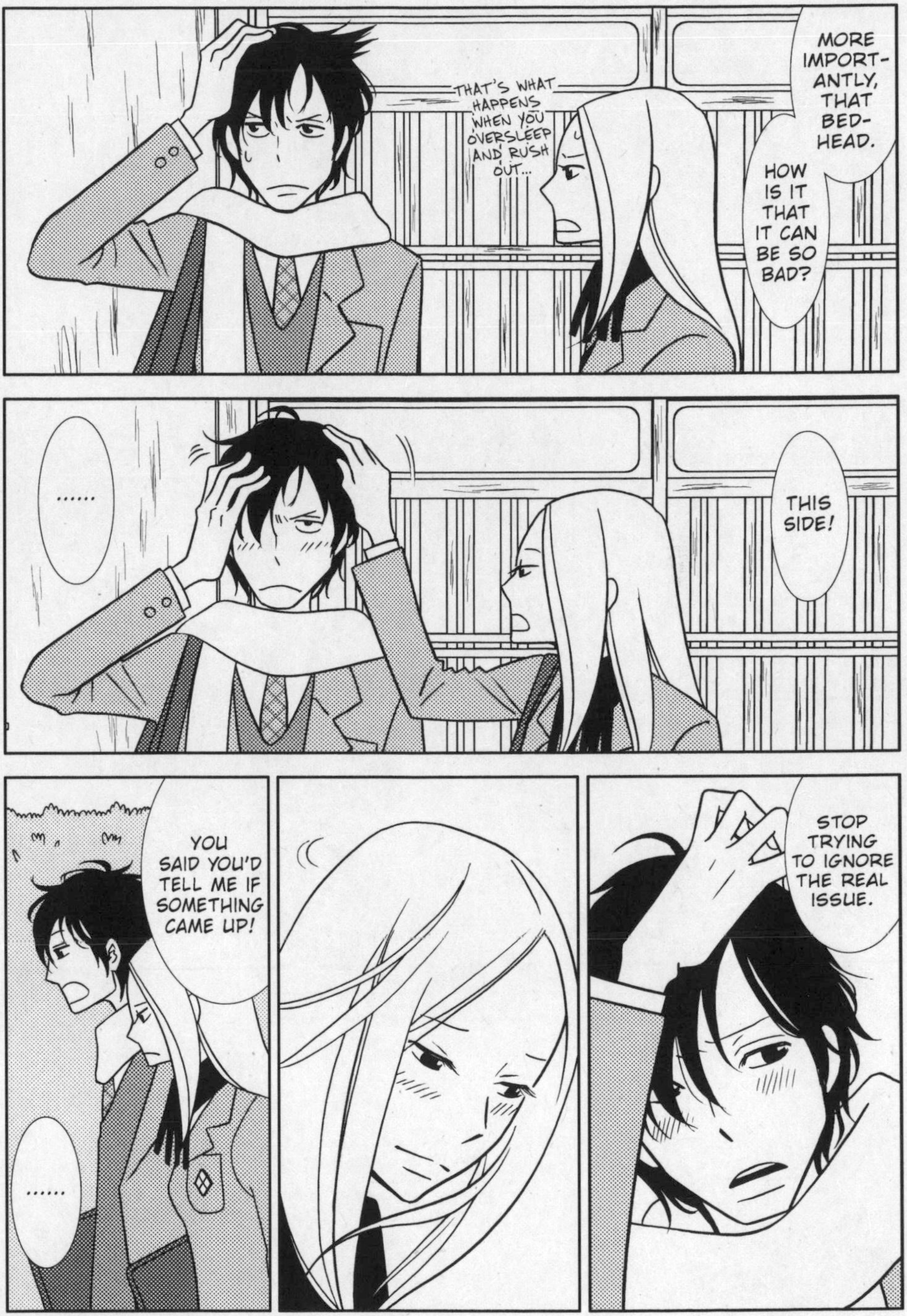
MORE IMPORT-ANTLY, THAT BED-HEAD.
HOW IS IT THAT IT CAN BE SO BAD?
THAT'S WHAT HAPPENS WHEN YOU OVERSLEEP AND RUSH OUT...
THIS SIDE!
......
STOP TRYING TO IGNORE THE REAL ISSUE.
YOU SAID YOU'D TELL ME IF SOMETHING CAME UP!
......

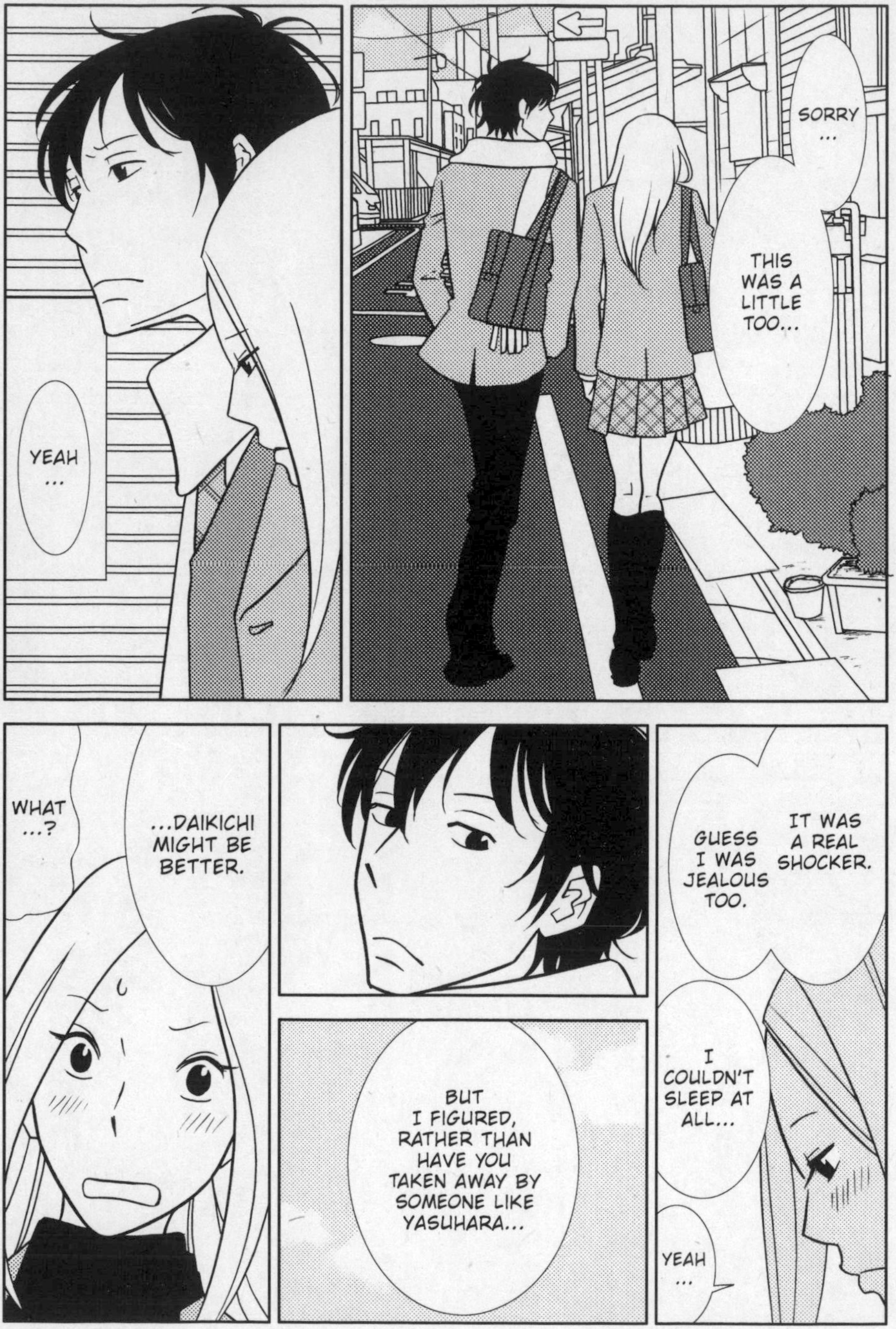
SORRY ...
THIS WAS A LITTLE TOO...
YEAH ...
IT WAS A REAL SHOCKER.
GUESS I WAS JEALOUS TOO.
I COULDN'T SLEEP AT ALL...
YEAH ...
BUT I FIGURED, RATHER THAN HAVE YOU TAKEN AWAY BY SOMEONE LIKE YASUHARA...
...DAIKICHI MIGHT BE BETTER.
WHAT ...?

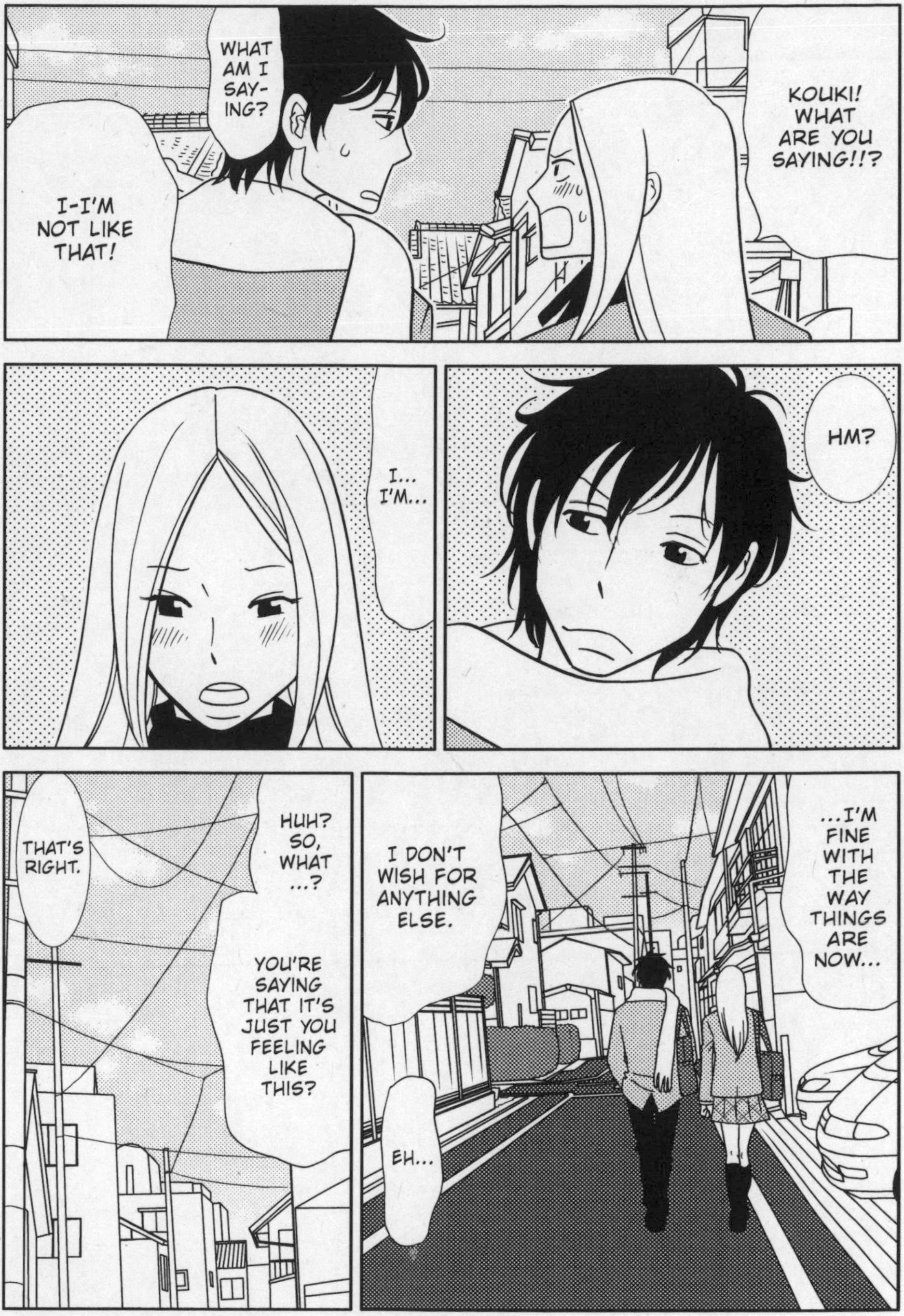
KOUKI! WHAT ARE YOU SAYING!!?
WHAT AM I SAY-ING?
I-I'M NOT LIKE THAT!
HM?
I... I'M...
...I'M FINE WITH THE WAY THINGS ARE NOW...
I DON'T WISH FOR ANYTHING ELSE.
EH...
HUH? SO, WHAT ...?
YOU'RE SAYING THAT IT'S JUST YOU FEELING LIKE THIS?
THAT'S RIGHT.

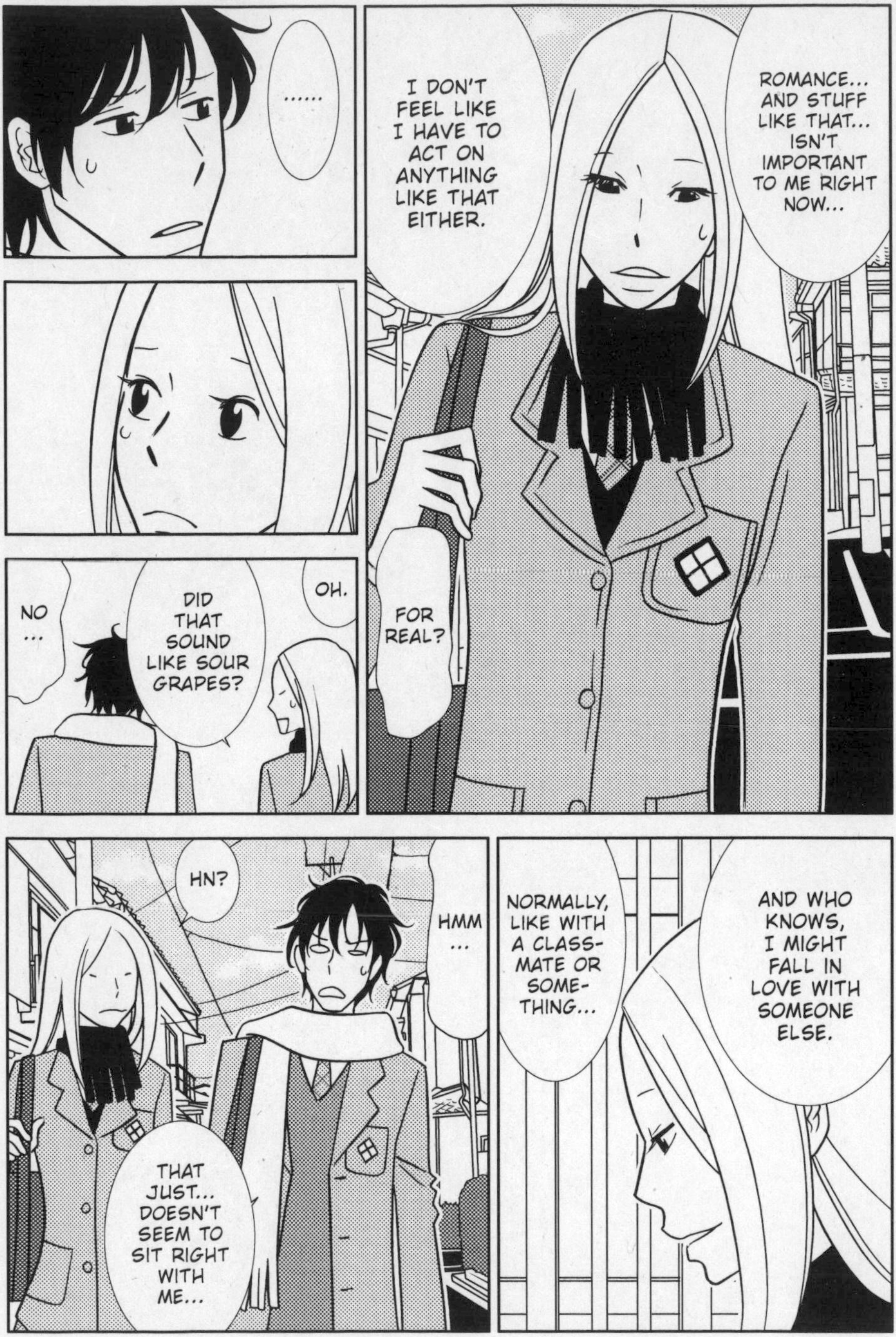
ROMANCE... AND STUFF LIKE THAT... ISN'T IMPORTANT TO ME RIGHT NOW...
I DON'T FEEL LIKE I HAVE TO ACT ON ANYTHING LIKE THAT EITHER.
FOR REAL?
......
OH.
DID THAT SOUND LIKE SOUR GRAPES?
NO ...
AND WHO KNOWS, I MIGHT FALL IN LOVE WITH SOMEONE ELSE.
NORMALLY, LIKE WITH A CLASSMATE OR SOME-THING...
HMM ...
HN?
THAT JUST... DOESN'T SEEM TO SIT RIGHT WITH ME...

RIN, YOU SAID YOURSELF THAT YOU WANTED TO GO TO A LOCAL UNIVERSITY WITH THE ULTIMATE GOAL OF BEING THERE TO TAKE CARE OF DAIKICHI IN HIS OLD AGE.
IF THOSE WORDS REFLECT WHAT YOU TRULY FEEL DEEP DOWN...
...THEN I DON'T THINK FALLING IN LOVE WITH SOMEONE ELSE...
...IS GONNA BE AN EASY THING TO DO.
......

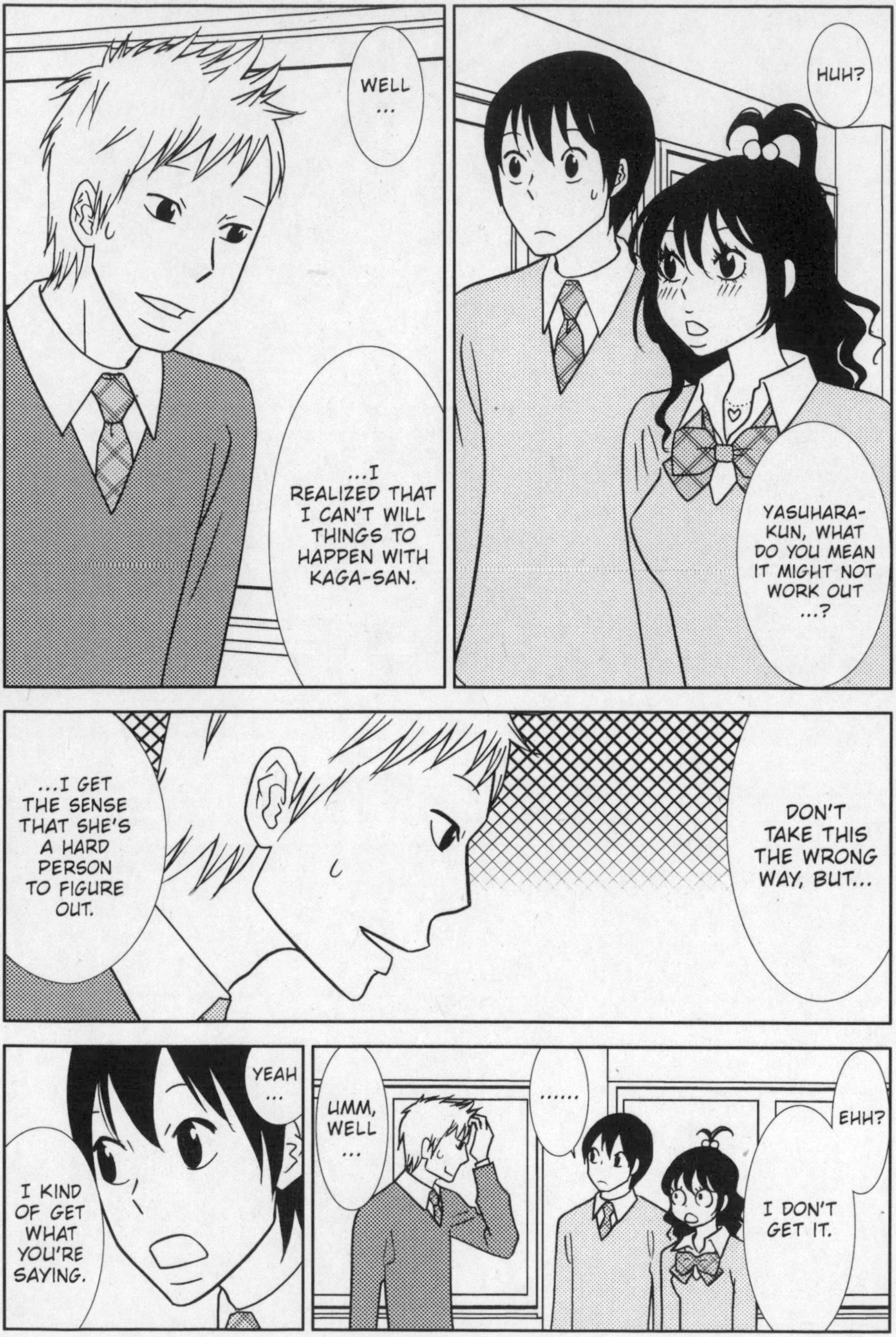
HUH?
YASUHARA-KUN, WHAT DO YOU MEAN IT MIGHT NOT WORK OUT ...?
WELL ...
...I REALIZED THAT I CAN'T WILL THINGS TO HAPPEN WITH KAGA-SAN.
DON'T TAKE THIS THE WRONG WAY, BUT...
...I GET THE SENSE THAT SHE'S A HARD PERSON TO FIGURE OUT.
EHH?
I DON'T GET IT.
......
UMM, WELL ...
YEAH ...
I KIND OF GET WHAT YOU'RE SAYING.

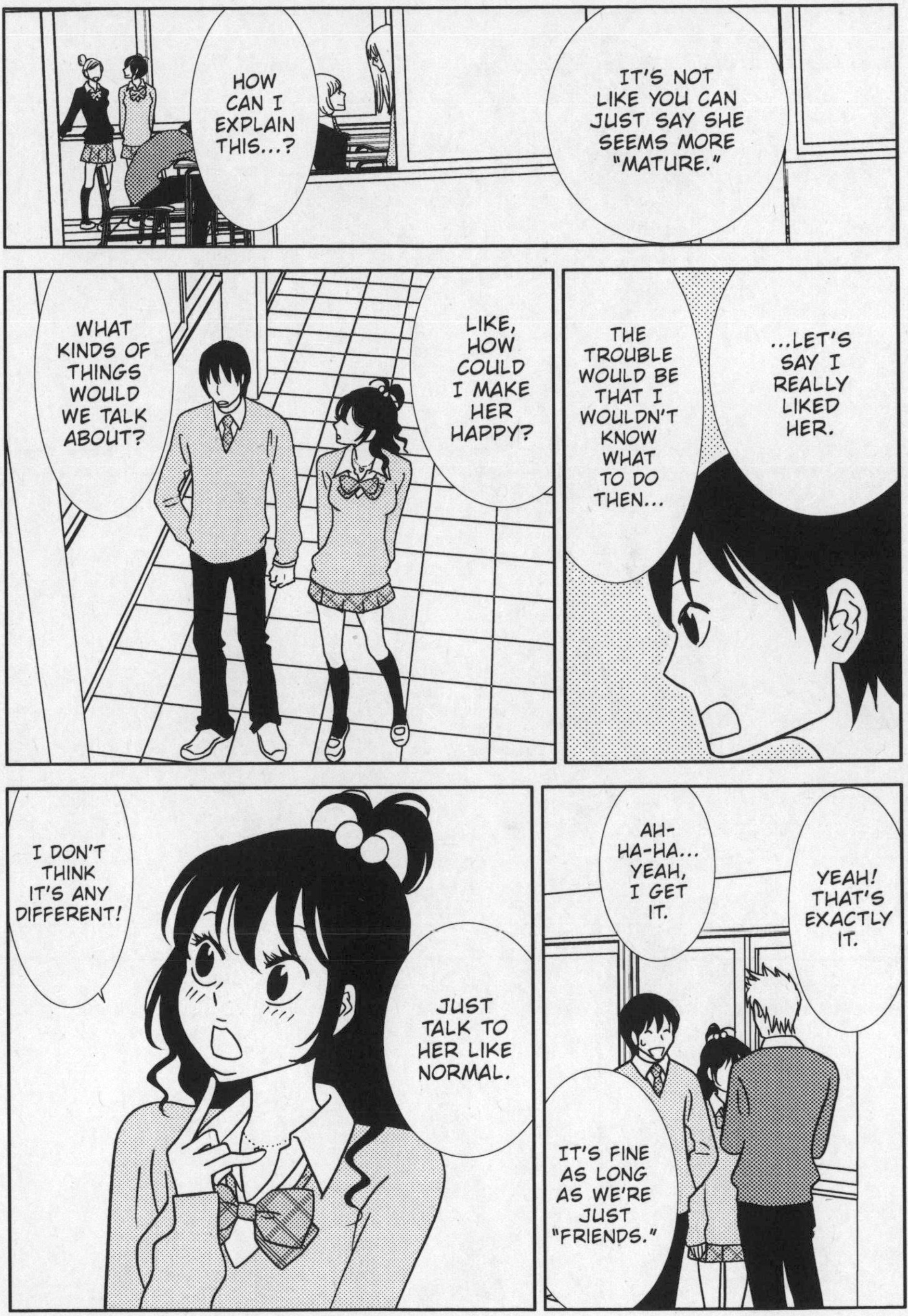
IT'S NOT LIKE YOU CAN JUST SAY SHE SEEMS MORE "MATURE."
HOW CAN I EXPLAIN THIS...?
...LET'S SAY I REALLY LIKED HER.
THE TROUBLE WOULD BE THAT I WOULDN'T KNOW WHAT TO DO THEN...
LIKE, HOW COULD I MAKE HER HAPPY?
WHAT KINDS OF THINGS WOULD WE TALK ABOUT?
YEAH! THAT'S EXACTLY IT.
AH-HA-HA... YEAH, I GET IT.
IT'S FINE AS LONG AS WE'RE JUST "FRIENDS."
I DON'T THINK IT'S ANY DIFFERENT!
JUST TALK TO HER LIKE NORMAL.

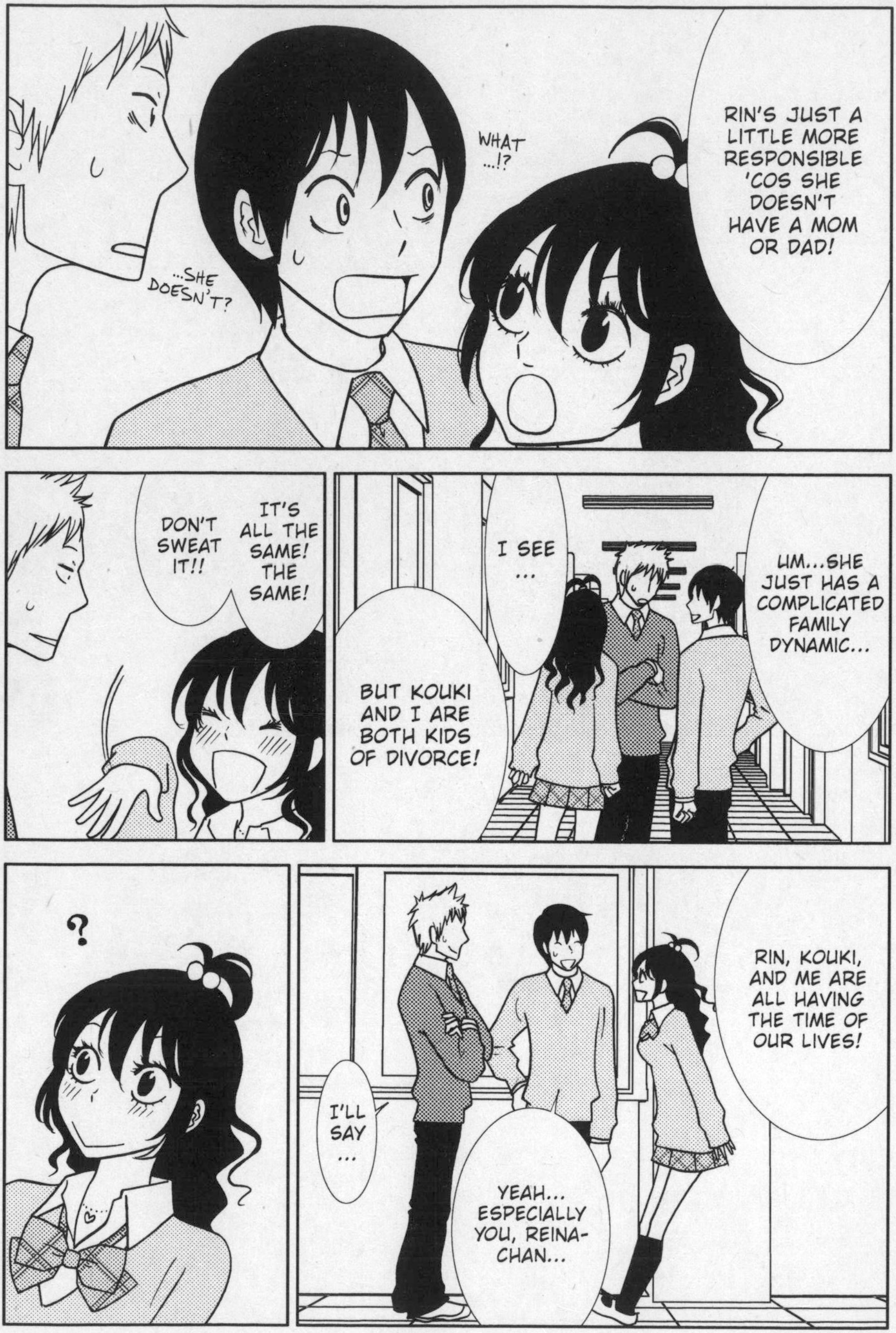
RIN'S JUST A LITTLE MORE RESPONSIBLE 'COS SHE DOESN'T HAVE A MOM OR DAD!
WHAT ...!?
...SHE DOESN'T?
UM...SHE JUST HAS A COMPLICATED FAMILY DYNAMIC...
I SEE ...
BUT KOUKI AND I ARE BOTH KIDS OF DIVORCE!
IT'S ALL THE SAME! THE SAME!
DON'T SWEAT IT!!
RIN, KOUKI, AND ME ARE ALL HAVING THE TIME OF OUR LIVES!
YEAH... ESPECIALLY YOU, REINA-CHAN...
I'LL SAY ...
?

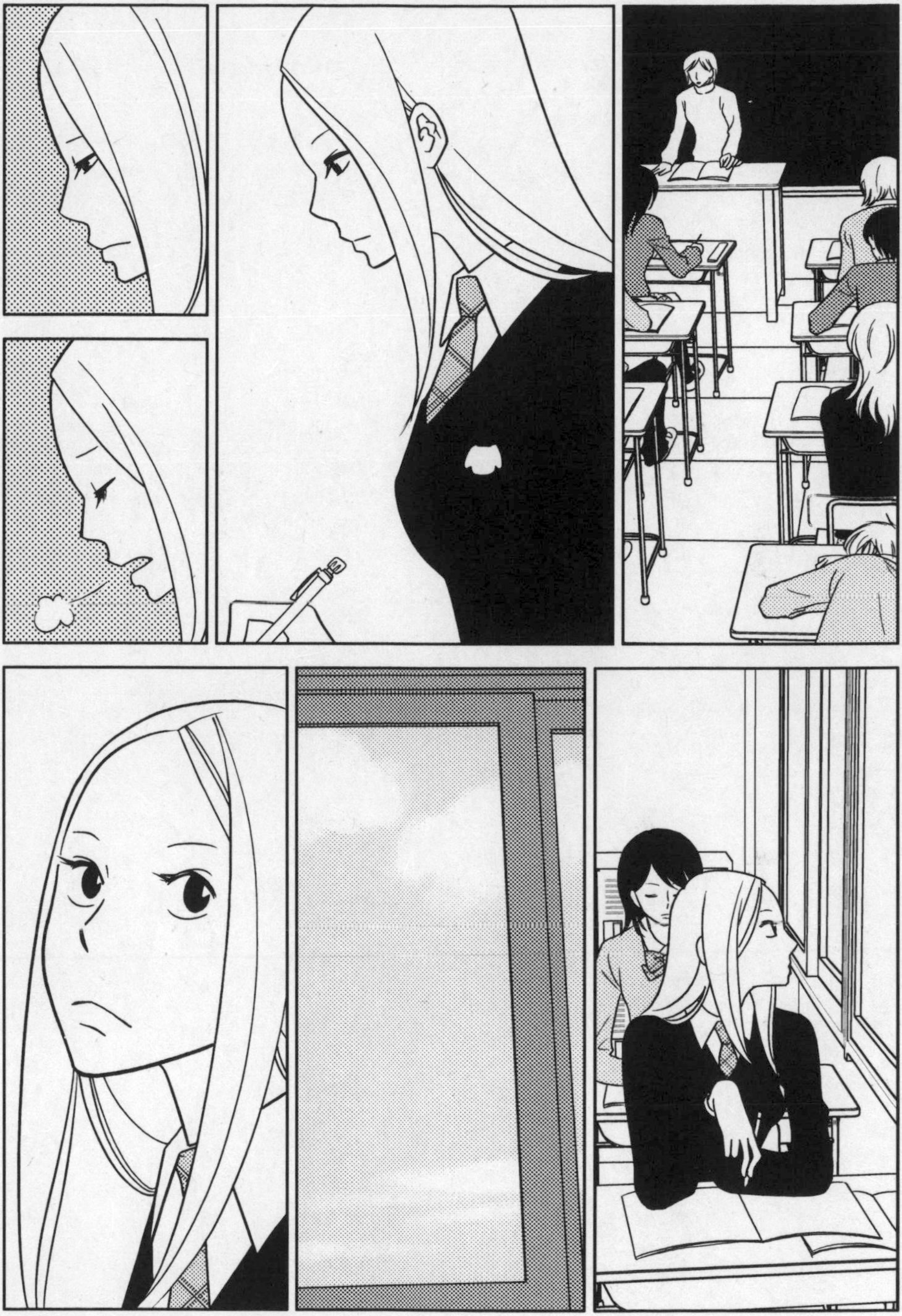

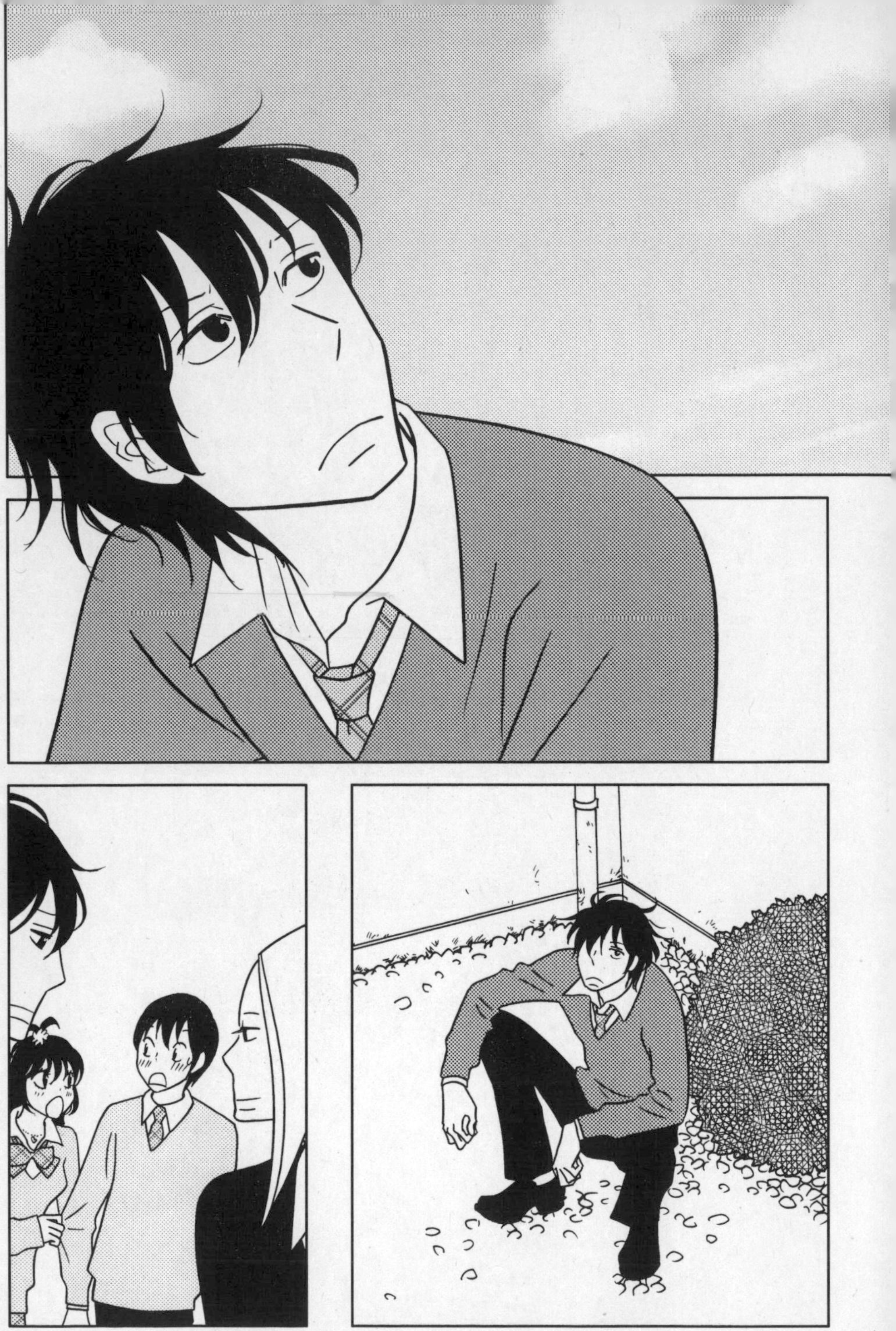

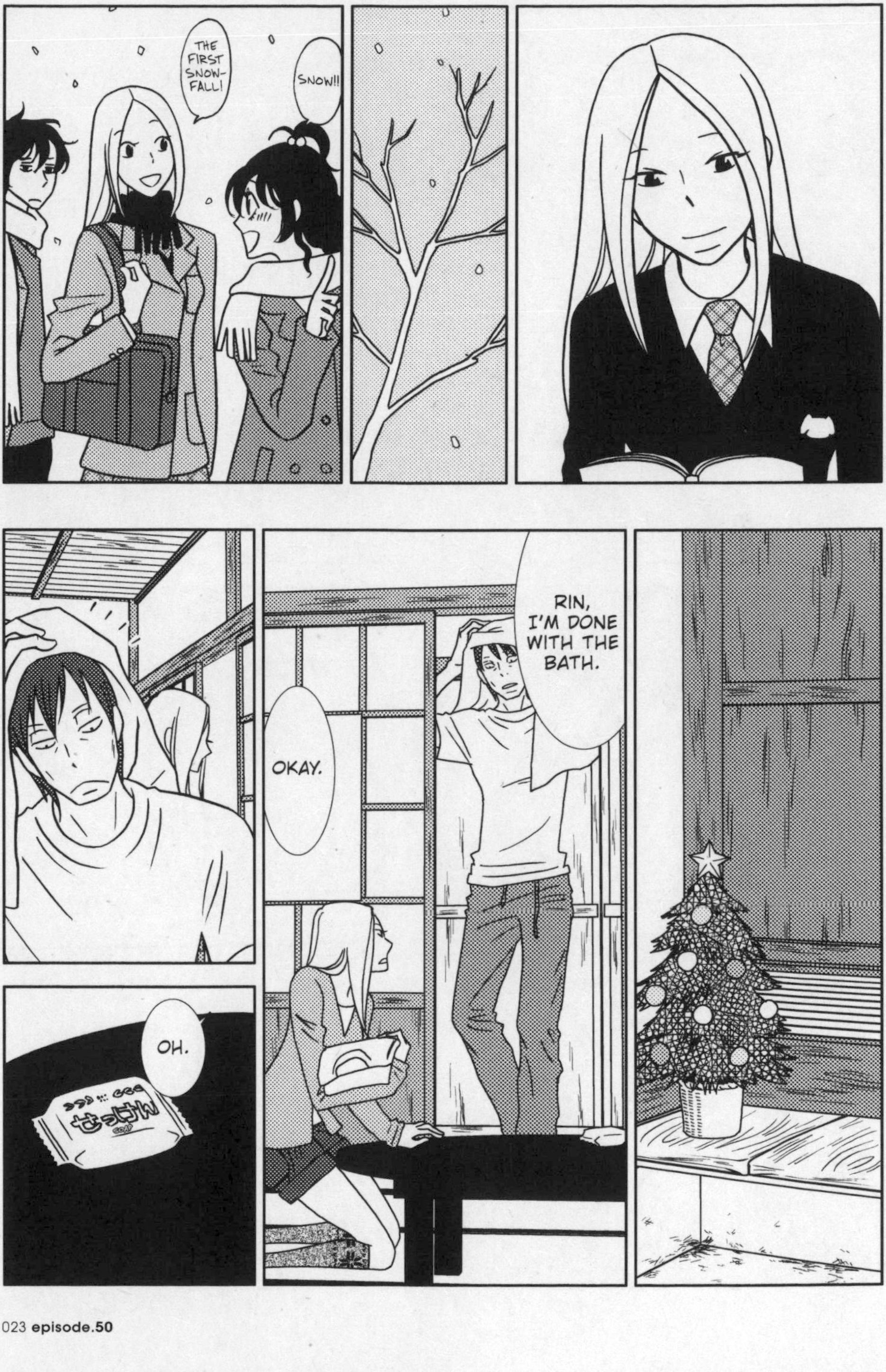
SNOW!!
THE FIRST SNOW-FALL!
RIN, I'M DONE WITH THE BATH.
OKAY.
OH.

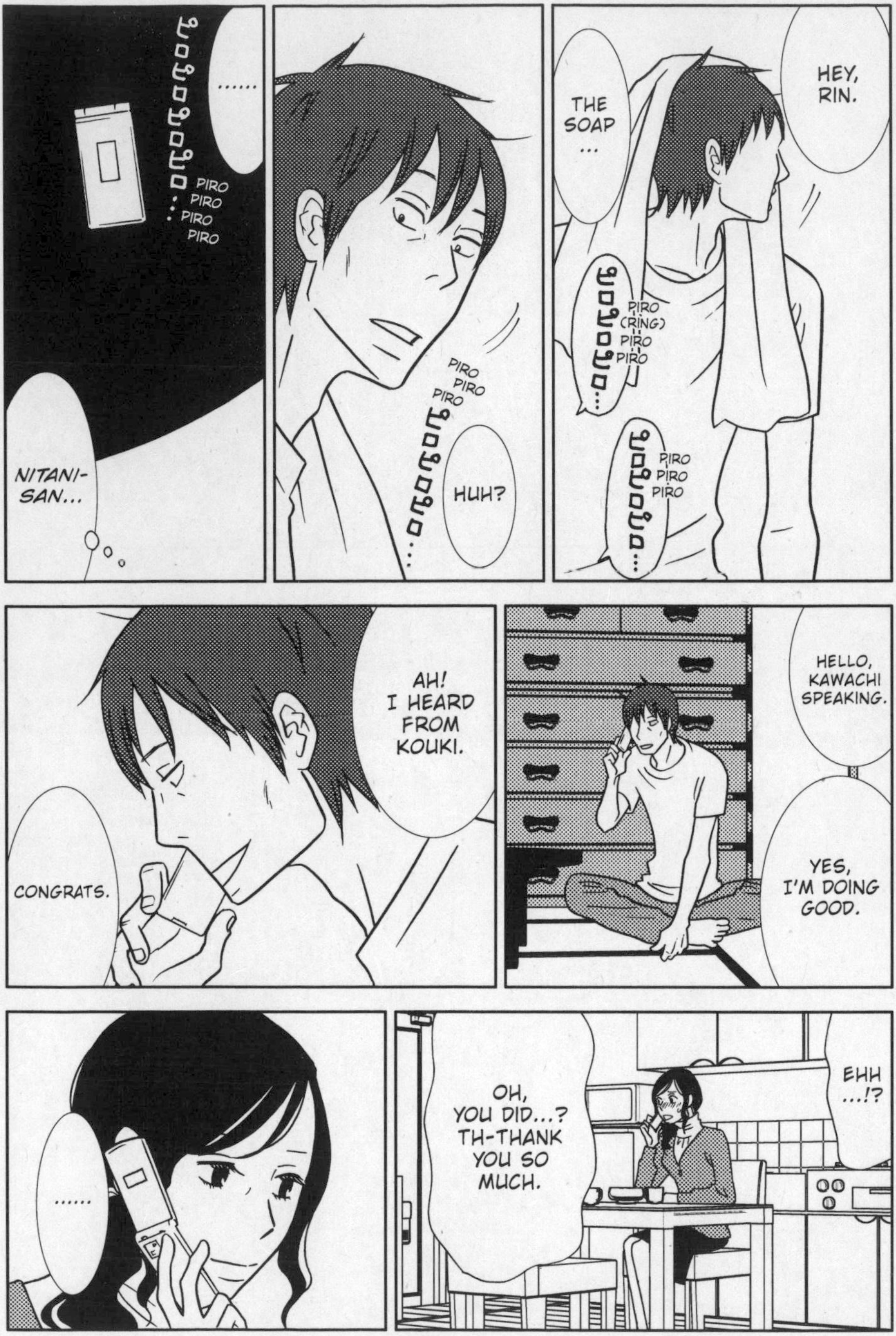
HEY, RIN.
THE SOAP ...
PIRO (RING) PIRO PIRO
PIRO PIRO PIRO
PIRO PIRO PIRO
HUH?
......
PIRO PIRO PIRO PIRO
NITANI-SAN...
HELLO, KAWACHI SPEAKING.
YES, I'M DOING GOOD.
AH! I HEARD FROM KOUKI.
CONGRATS.
EHH ...!?
OH, YOU DID...? TH-THANK YOU SO MUCH.
......

......
UM...
WAS THERE—?
Oh, I'm sorry... You caught me by surprise...
NO WORRIES.
Actually, Kouki isn't home yet...
Well, he's a big kid... I'm sure he'll be back soon.
......
HE'S BEEN DOING THIS MORE OFTEN LATELY...
I JUST...HAD FLASHBACKS TO WHEN HE WAS IN MIDDLE SCHOOL...
Nitani-san...
A little while ago... we went through... a rough patch with my getting remarried, but...
ガラ
GARA (CLATTER)
...things had calmed down.

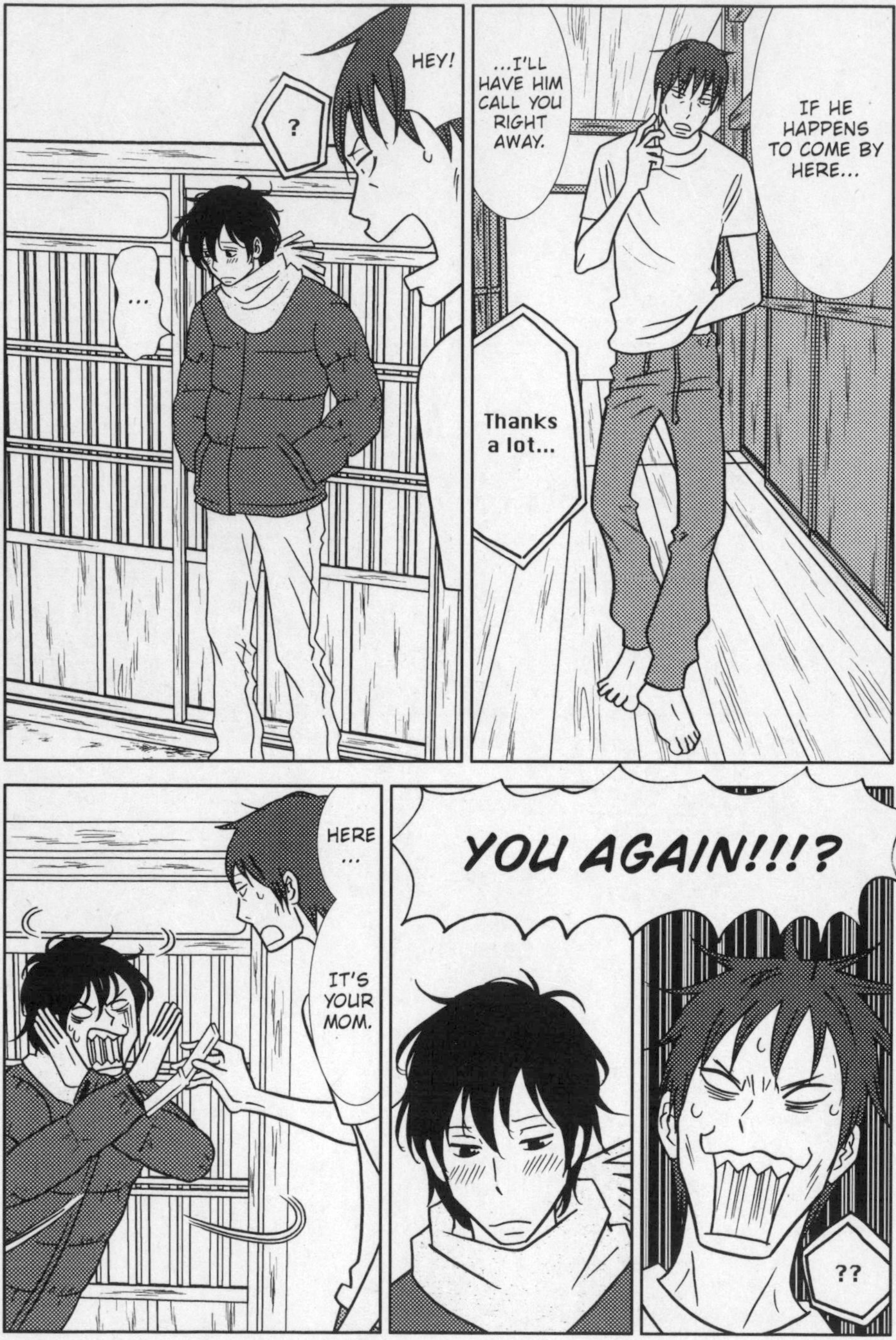
IF HE HAPPENS TO COME BY HERE...
...I'LL HAVE HIM CALL YOU RIGHT AWAY.
Thanks a lot...
HEY!
?
...
YOU AGAIN!!!?
??
HERE ...
IT'S YOUR MOM.

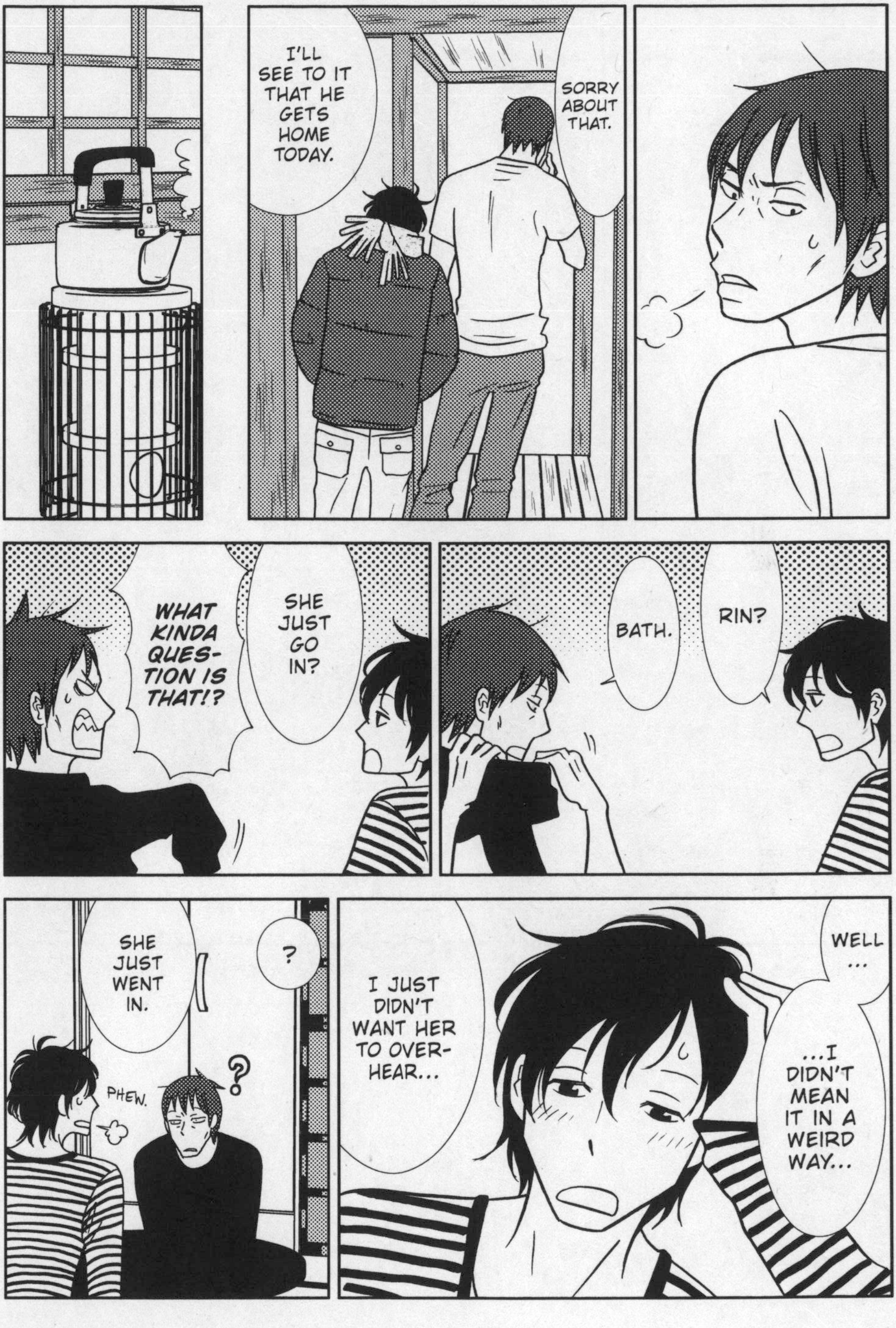
SORRY ABOUT THAT.
I'LL SEE TO IT THAT HE GETS HOME TODAY.
RIN?
BATH.
SHE JUST GO IN?
WHAT KINDA QUESTION IS THAT!?
WELL...
...I DIDN'T MEAN IT IN A WEIRD WAY...
I JUST DIDN'T WANT HER TO OVERHEAR...
?
SHE JUST WENT IN.
PHEW.

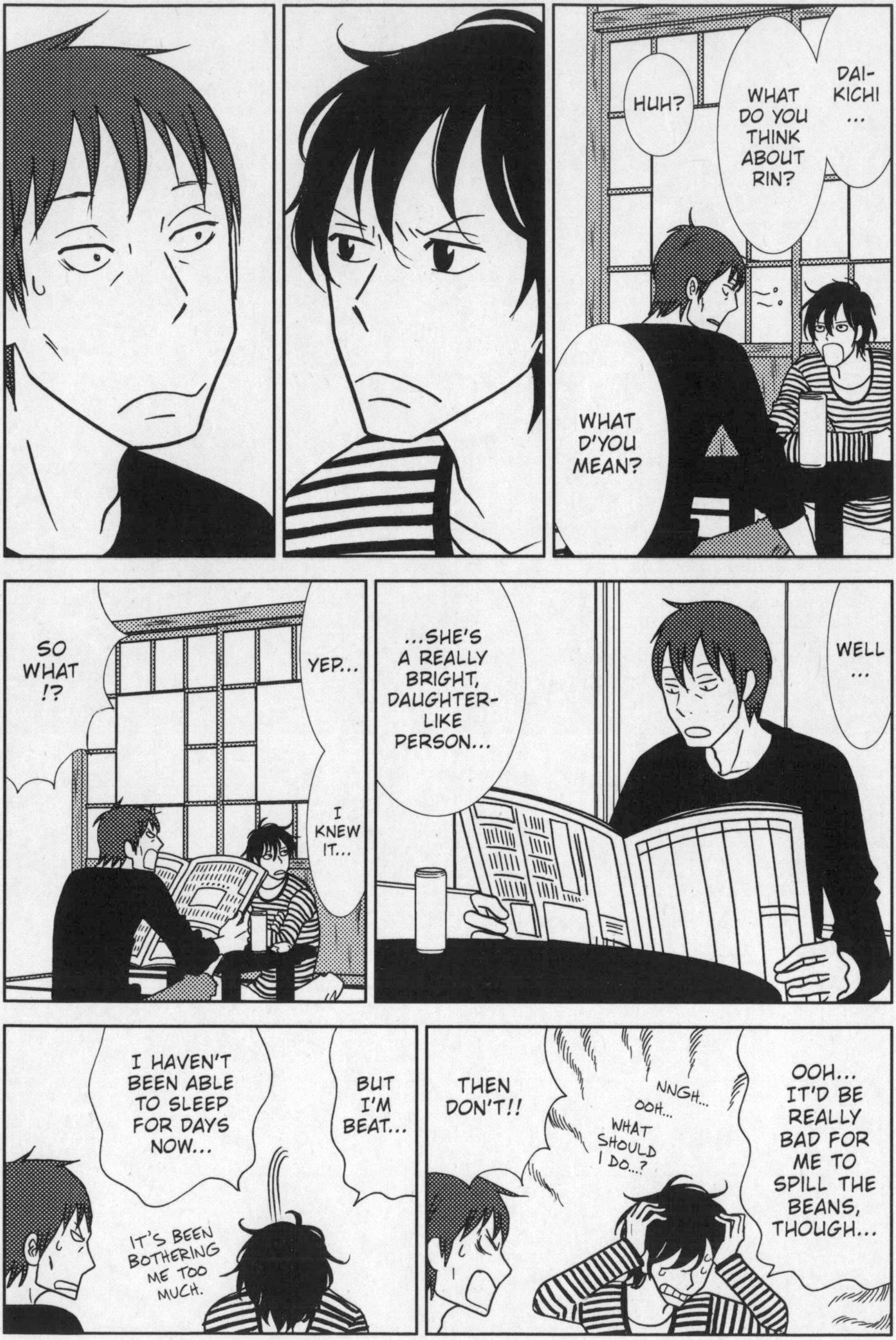
DAI-KICHI ...
WHAT DO YOU THINK ABOUT RIN?
HUH?
WHAT D'YOU MEAN?
WELL ...
...SHE'S A REALLY BRIGHT, DAUGHTER-LIKE PERSON...
YEP...
I KNEW IT...
SO WHAT !?
OOH... IT'D BE REALLY BAD FOR ME TO SPILL THE BEANS, THOUGH...
NNGH... OOH... WHAT SHOULD I DO...?
THEN DON'T!!
BUT I'M BEAT...
I HAVEN'T BEEN ABLE TO SLEEP FOR DAYS NOW...
IT'S BEEN BOTHERING ME TOO MUCH.

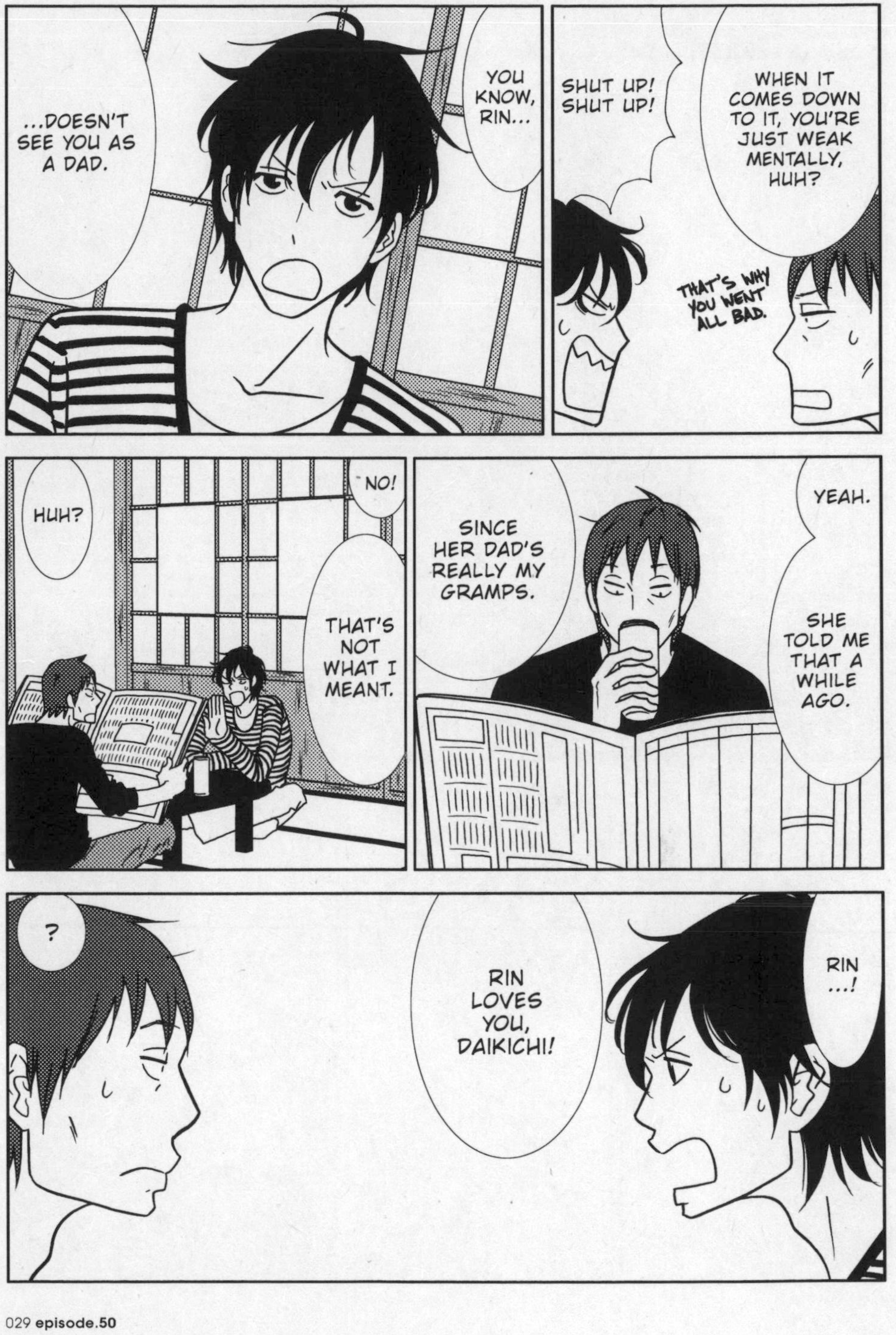
WHEN IT COMES DOWN TO IT, YOU'RE JUST WEAK MENTALLY, HUH?
SHUT UP! SHUT UP!
THAT'S WHY YOU WENT ALL BAD.
YOU KNOW, RIN...
...DOESN'T SEE YOU AS A DAD.
YEAH.
SHE TOLD ME THAT A WHILE AGO.
SINCE HER DAD'S REALLY MY GRAMPS.
NO!
THAT'S NOT WHAT I MEANT.
HUH?
RIN ...!
RIN LOVES YOU, DAIKICHI!
?

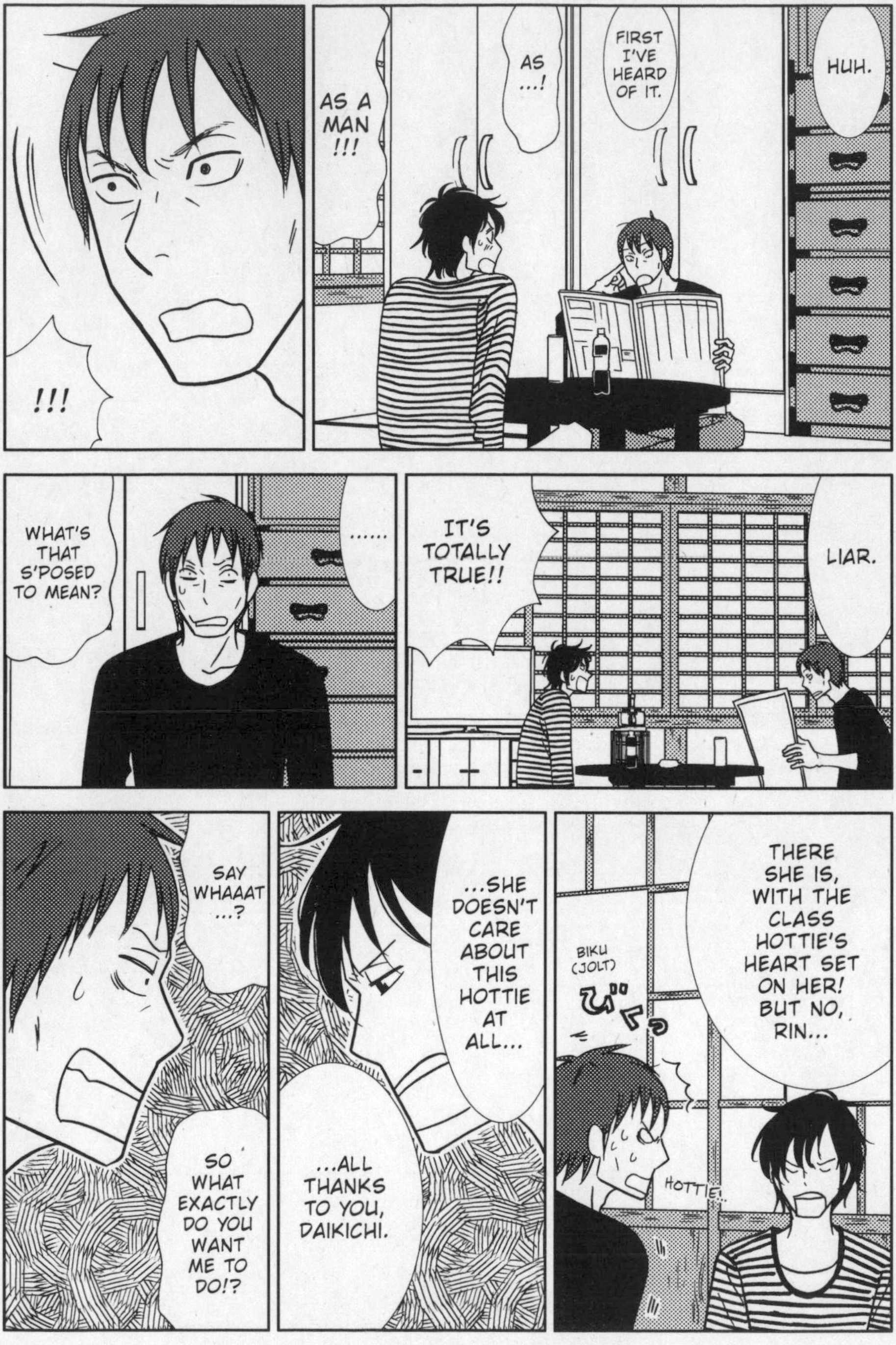
HUH.
FIRST I'VE HEARD OF IT.
AS ...!
AS A MAN!!!
!!!
LIAR.
IT'S TOTALLY TRUE!!
......
WHAT'S THAT S'POSED TO MEAN?
THERE SHE IS, WITH THE CLASS HOTTIE'S HEART SET ON HER! BUT NO, RIN...
BIKU (JOLT)
HOTTIE...
...SHE DOESN'T CARE ABOUT THIS HOTTIE AT ALL...
...ALL THANKS TO YOU, DAIKICHI.
SAY WHAAAT...?
SO WHAT EXACTLY DO YOU WANT ME TO DO!?

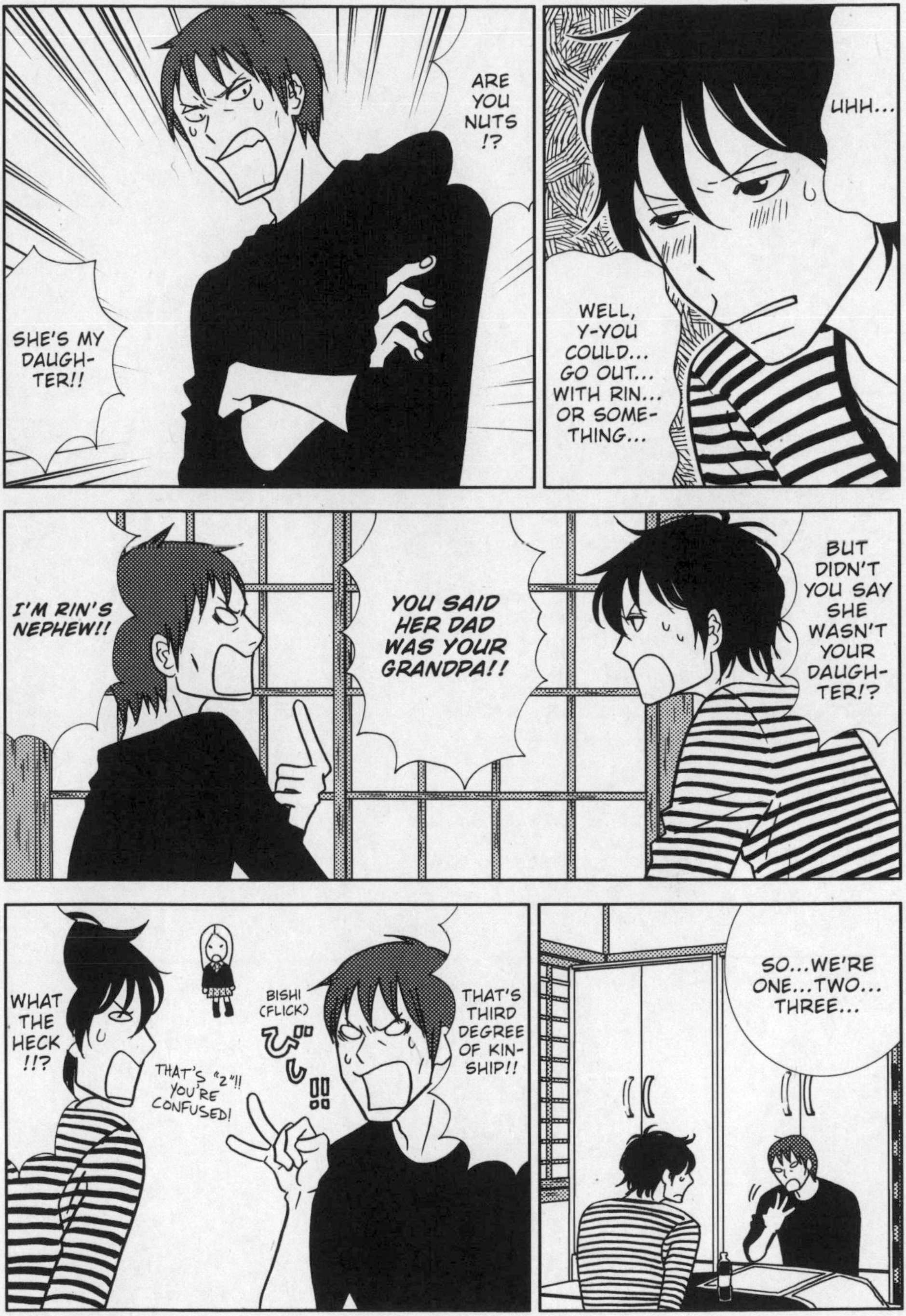
UHH...
WELL, Y-YOU COULD... GO OUT... WITH RIN... OR SOME-THING...
ARE YOU NUTS!?
SHE'S MY DAUGH-TER!!
BUT DIDN'T YOU SAY SHE WASN'T YOUR DAUGH-TER!?
YOU SAID HER DAD WAS YOUR GRANDPA!!
I'M RIN'S NEPHEW!!
SO...WE'RE ONE...TWO... THREE...
THAT'S THIRD DEGREE OF KIN-SHIP!!
BISHI (FLICK)
びし!!
THAT'S "2"!! YOU'RE CONFUSED!
WHAT THE HECK!!?

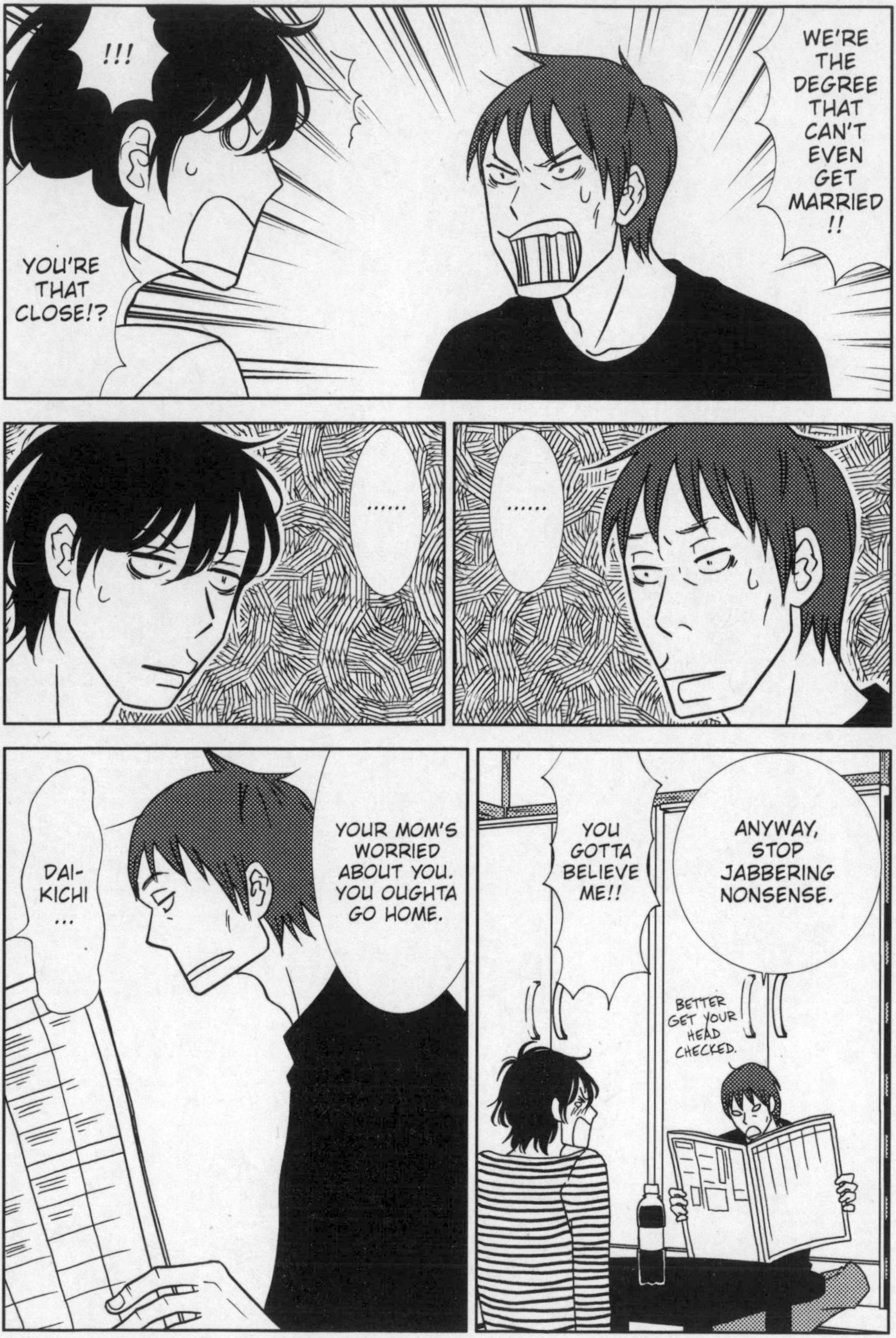
WE'RE THE DEGREE THAT CAN'T EVEN GET MARRIED!!
!!!
YOU'RE THAT CLOSE!?
......
......
ANYWAY, STOP JABBERING NONSENSE.
YOU GOTTA BELIEVE ME!!
BETTER GET YOUR HEAD CHECKED.
YOUR MOM'S WORRIED ABOUT YOU. YOU OUGHTA GO HOME.
DAI-KICHI ...

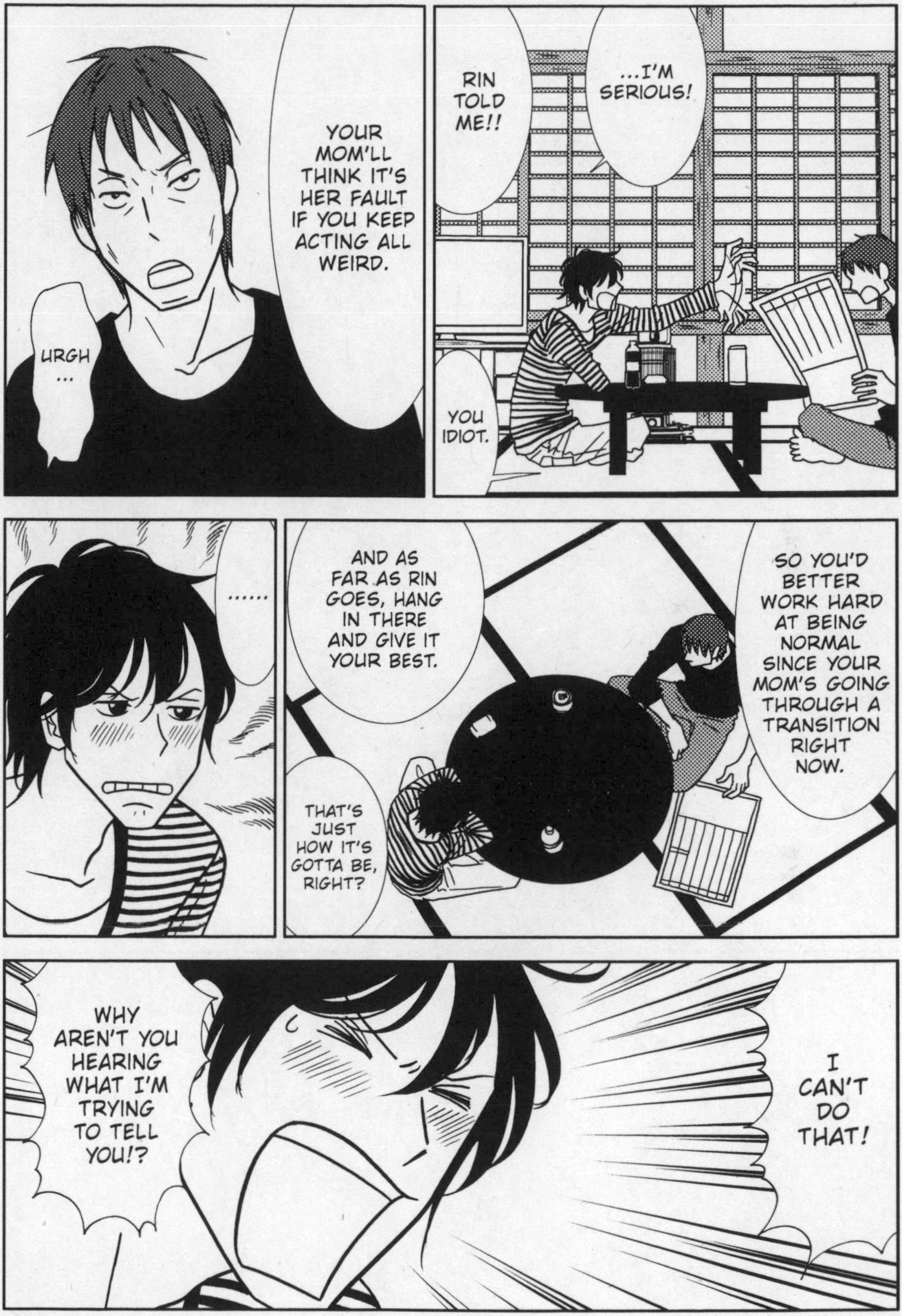
...I'M SERIOUS!
RIN TOLD ME!!
YOU IDIOT.
YOUR MOM'LL THINK IT'S HER FAULT IF YOU KEEP ACTING ALL WEIRD.
URGH ...
SO YOU'D BETTER WORK HARD AT BEING NORMAL SINCE YOUR MOM'S GOING THROUGH A TRANSITION RIGHT NOW.
AND AS FAR AS RIN GOES, HANG IN THERE AND GIVE IT YOUR BEST.
THAT'S JUST HOW IT'S GOTTA BE, RIGHT?
......
I CAN'T DO THAT!
WHY AREN'T YOU HEARING WHAT I'M TRYING TO TELL YOU!?

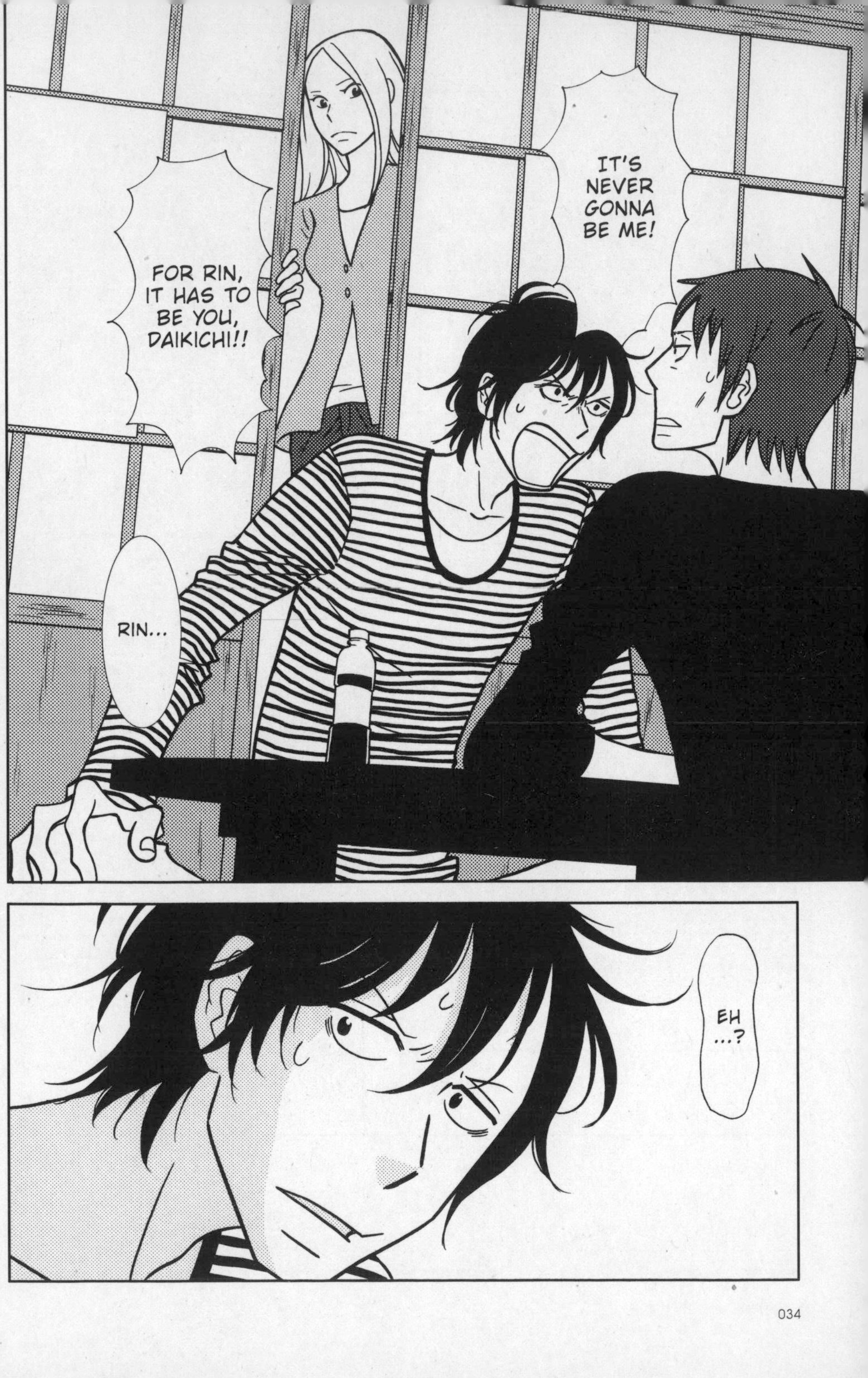
IT'S NEVER GONNA BE ME!
FOR RIN, IT HAS TO BE YOU, DAIKICHI!!
RIN...
EH ...?

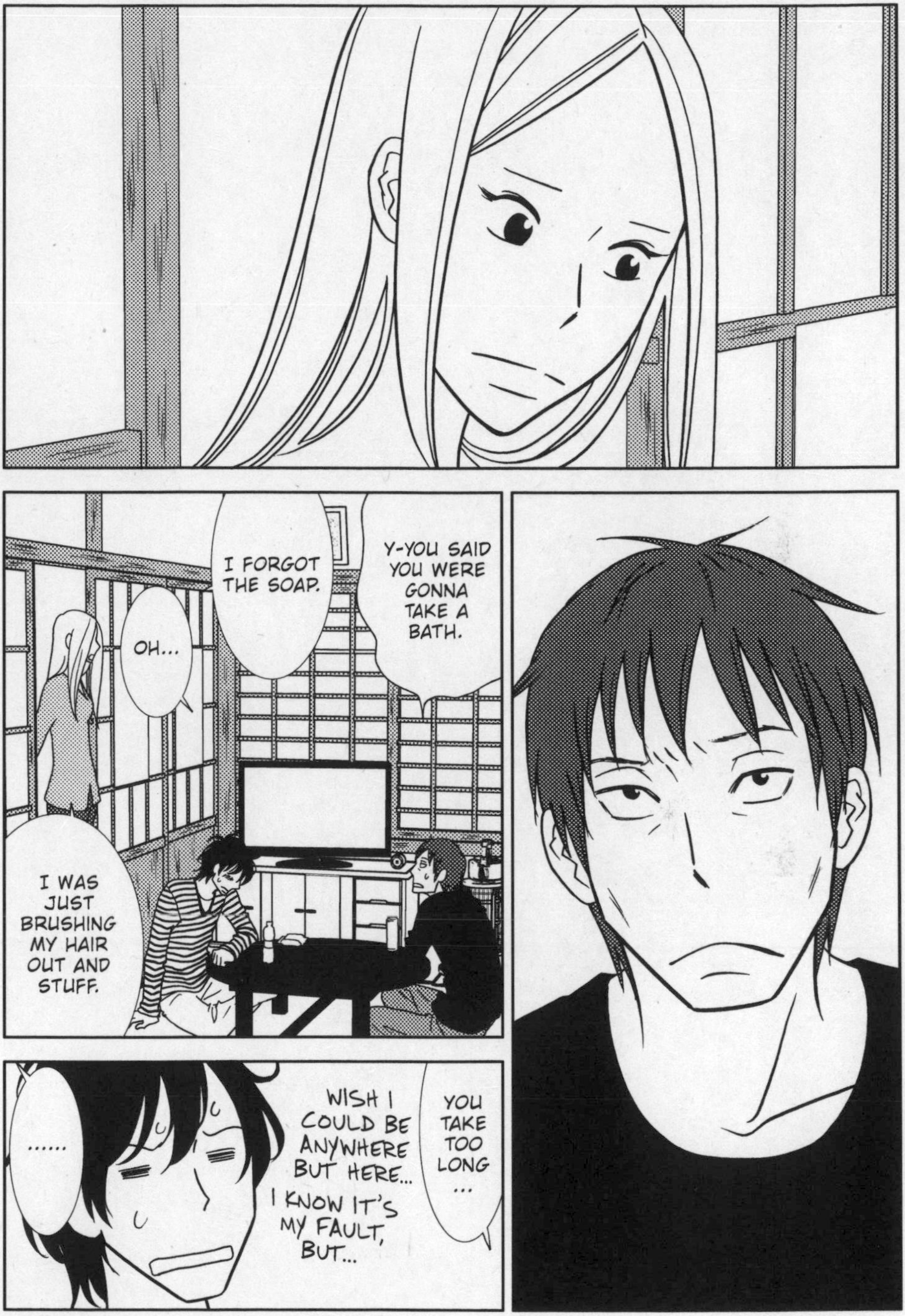
Y-YOU SAID YOU WERE GONNA TAKE A BATH.
I FORGOT THE SOAP.
OH...
I WAS JUST BRUSHING MY HAIR OUT AND STUFF.
YOU TAKE TOO LONG ...
WISH I COULD BE ANYWHERE BUT HERE...
I KNOW IT'S MY FAULT, BUT...
......

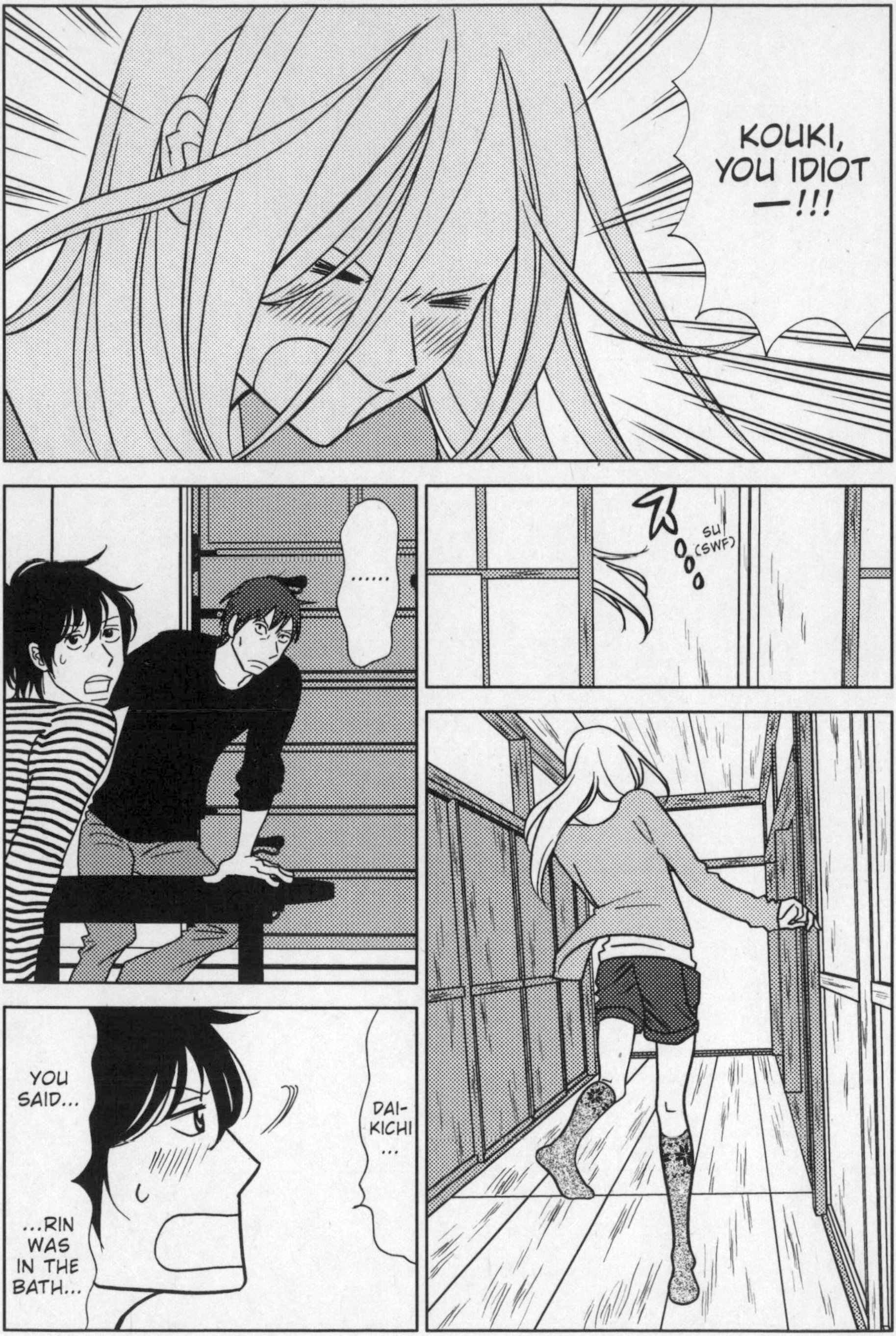
KOUKI, YOU IDIOT—!!!
SU (SWF)
......
DAI-KICHI...
YOU SAID...
...RIN WAS IN THE BATH...

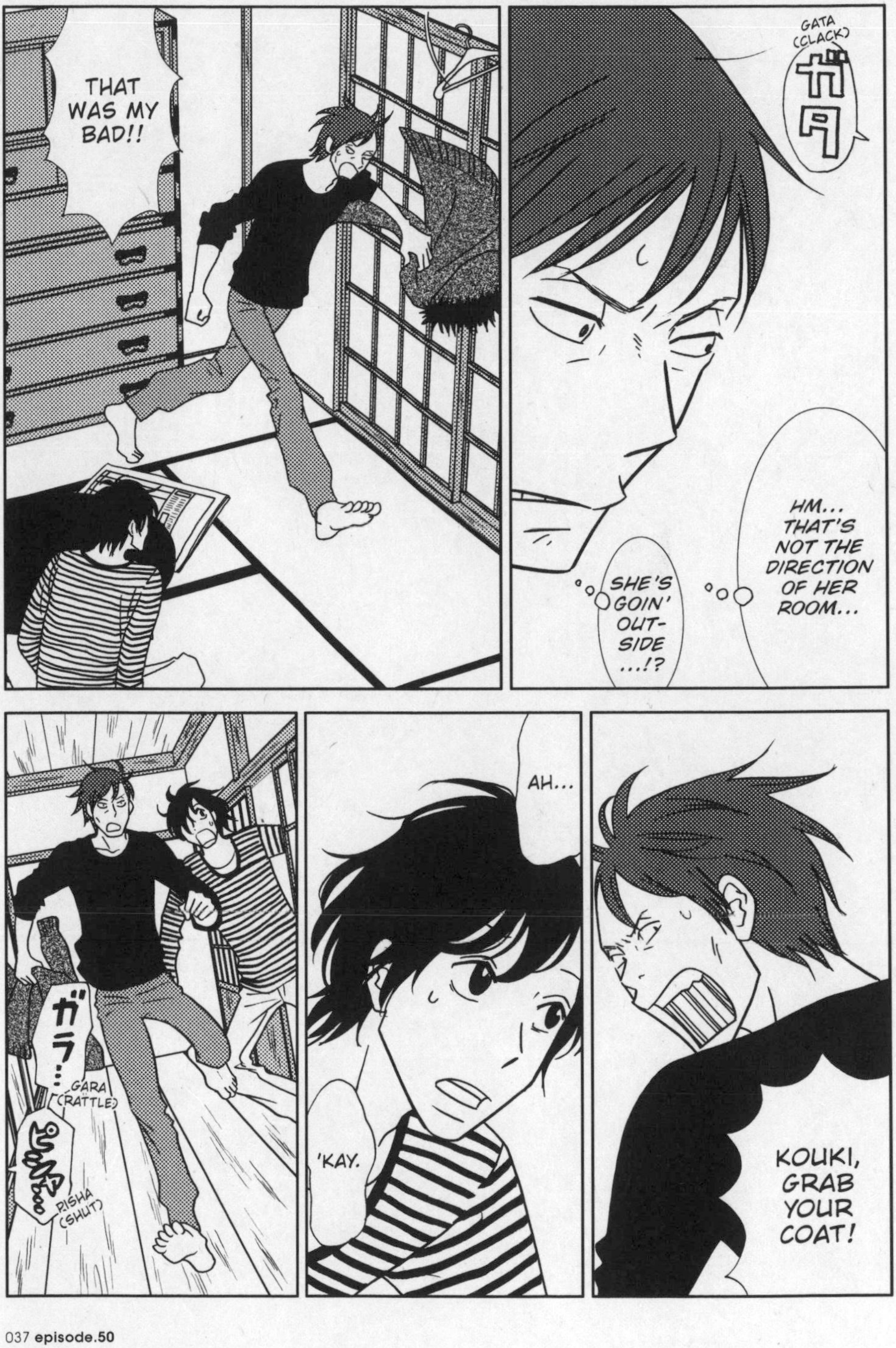
GATA (CLACK)
ガタ
HM... THAT'S NOT THE DIRECTION OF HER ROOM...
SHE'S GOIN' OUT-SIDE ...!?
THAT WAS MY BAD!!
KOUKI, GRAB YOUR COAT!
AH...
'KAY.
ガラ...
GARA (RATTLE)
PISHA (SHUT)

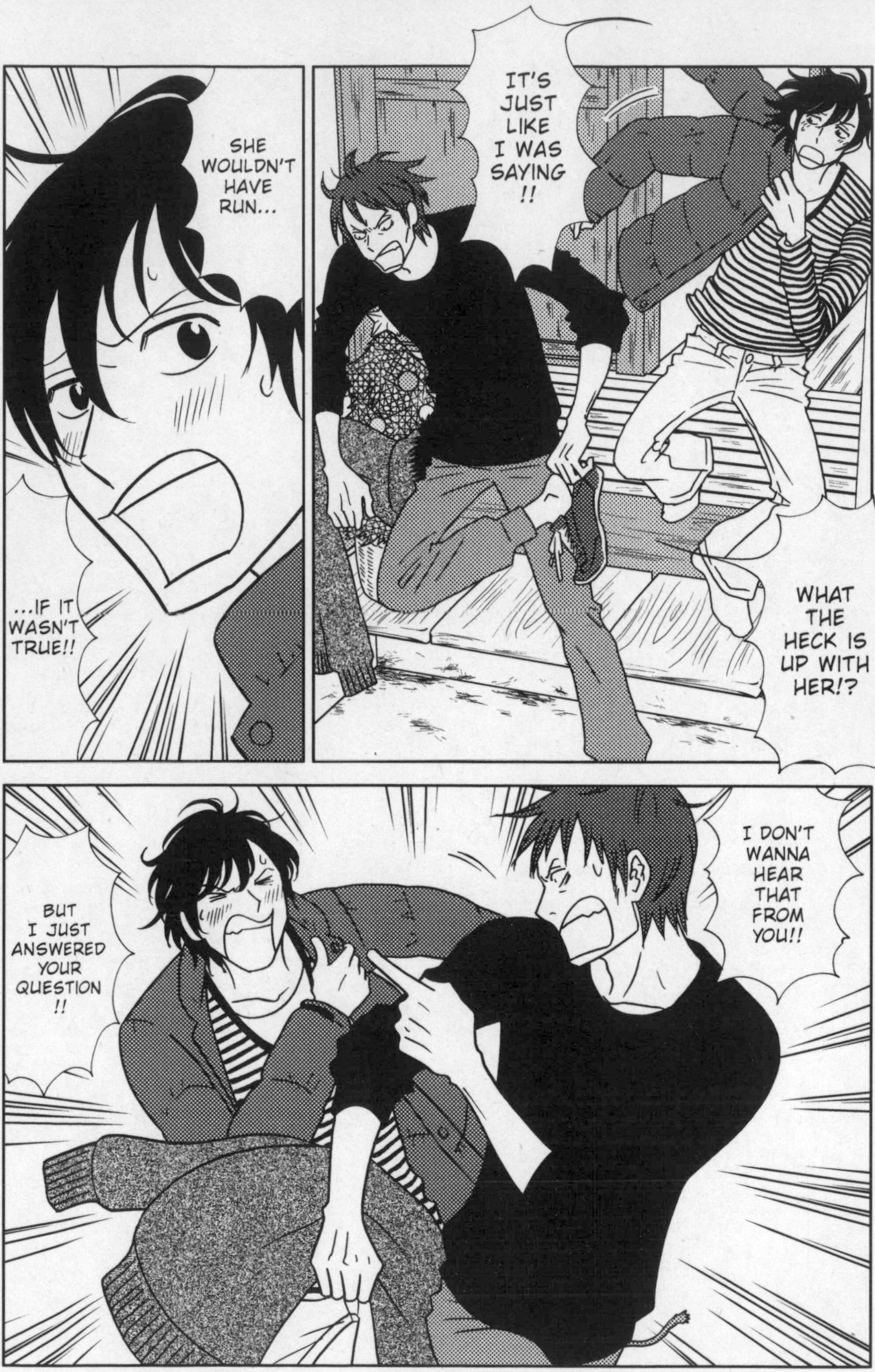
IT'S JUST LIKE I WAS SAYING!!
WHAT THE HECK IS UP WITH HER!?
SHE WOULDN'T HAVE RUN...
...IF IT WASN'T TRUE!!
I DON'T WANNA HEAR THAT FROM YOU!!
BUT I JUST ANSWERED YOUR QUESTION!!

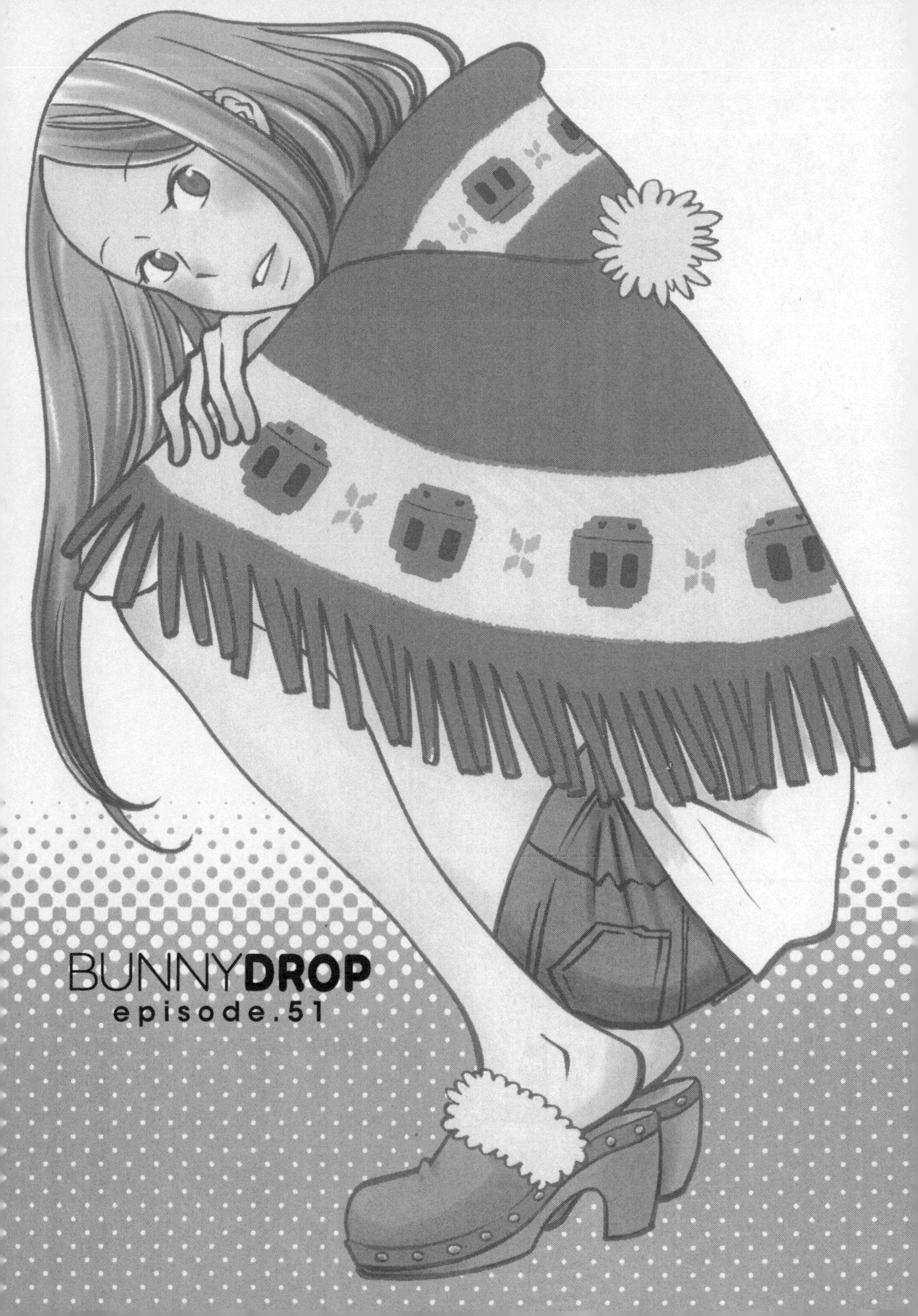
BUNNYDROP
episode.51

BUNNY**DROP**

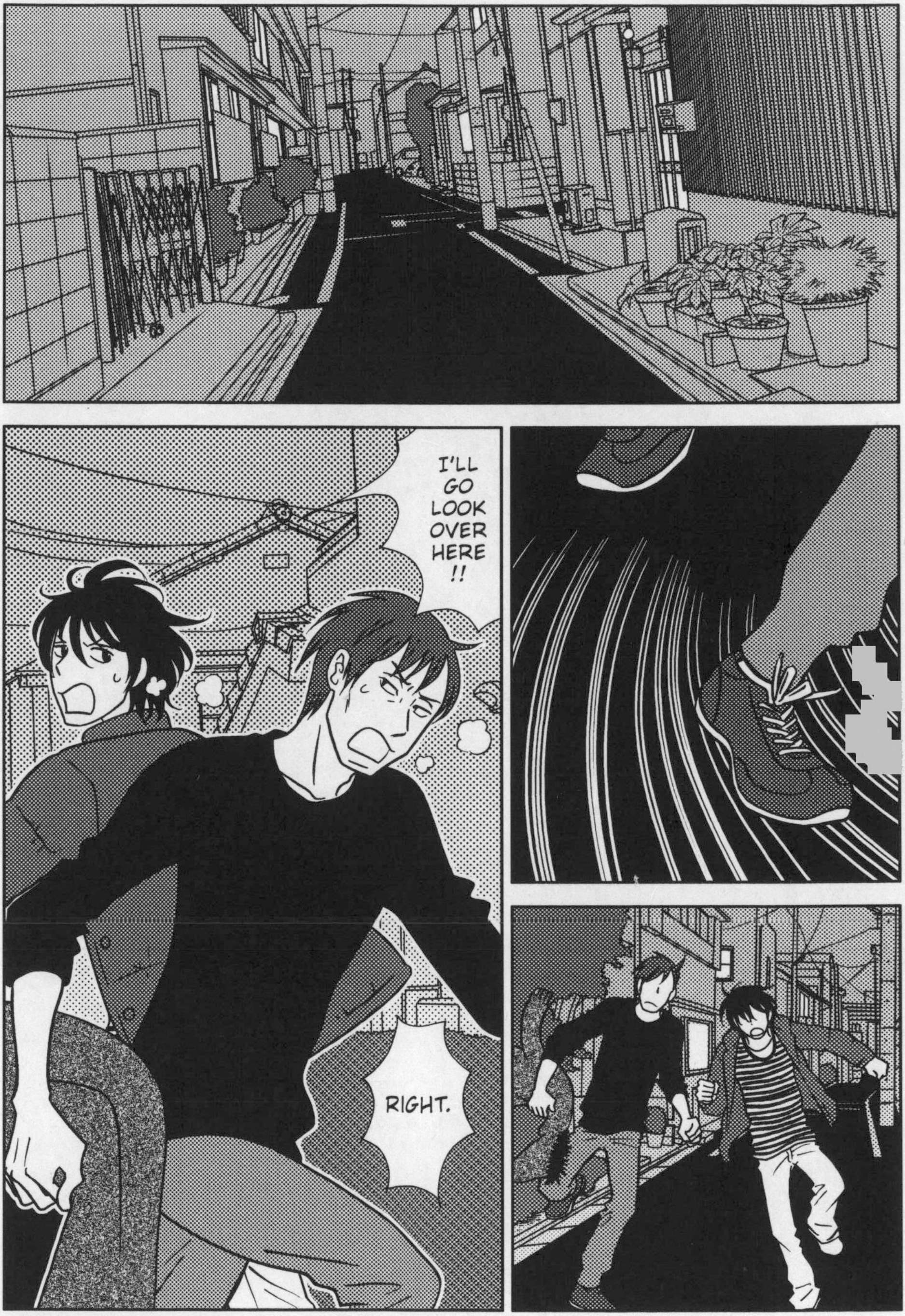
I'LL GO LOOK OVER HERE!!
RIGHT.

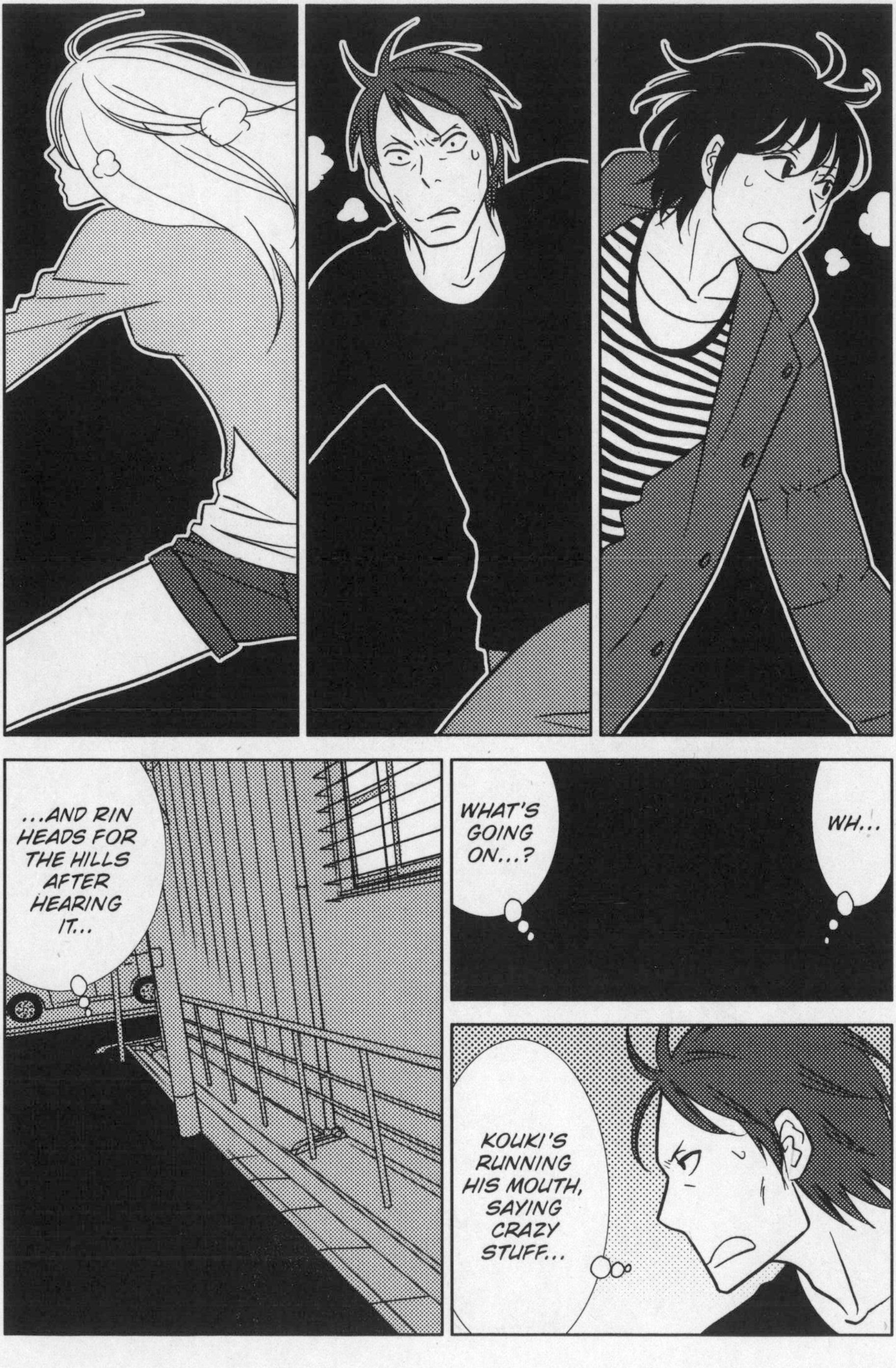
WH...
WHAT'S GOING ON...?
KOUKI'S RUNNING HIS MOUTH, SAYING CRAZY STUFF...
...AND RIN HEADS FOR THE HILLS AFTER HEARING IT...

FIND HER?

Nope... not at all.

WHAT THE HELL...

...IS WITH THEM...!!?

SFX: ZEE (WHEEZE) ZEE

SHUT UP!!

Rin can run fast, so don't strain yourself, Mister Forty-something!!

FOUND YA!!

AH.

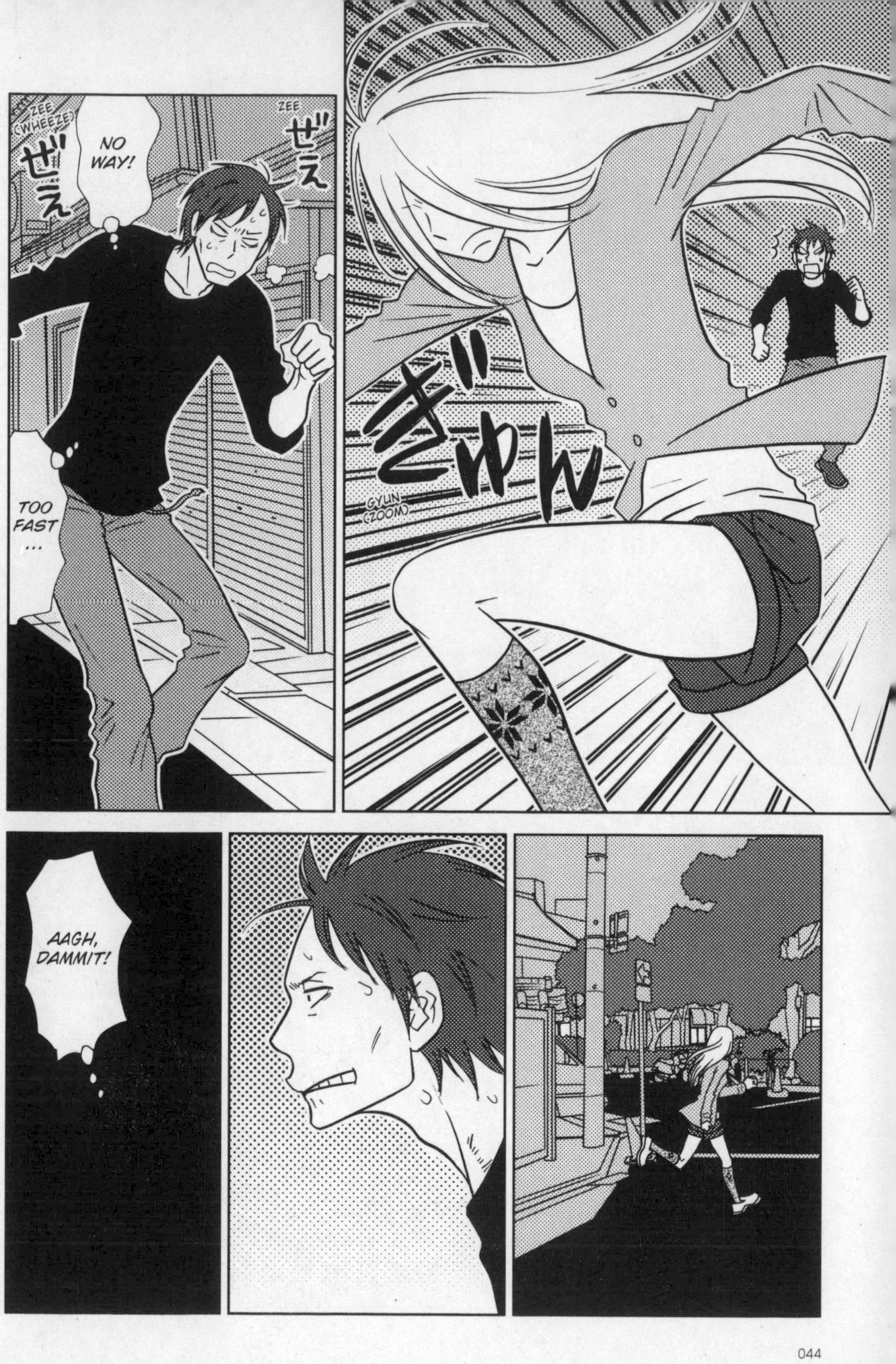
ぎゅん
GYUN (ZOOM)
ぜぇ
ZEE
ぜぇ
ZEE (WHEEZE)
NO WAY!
TOO FAST ...
AAGH, DAMMIT!

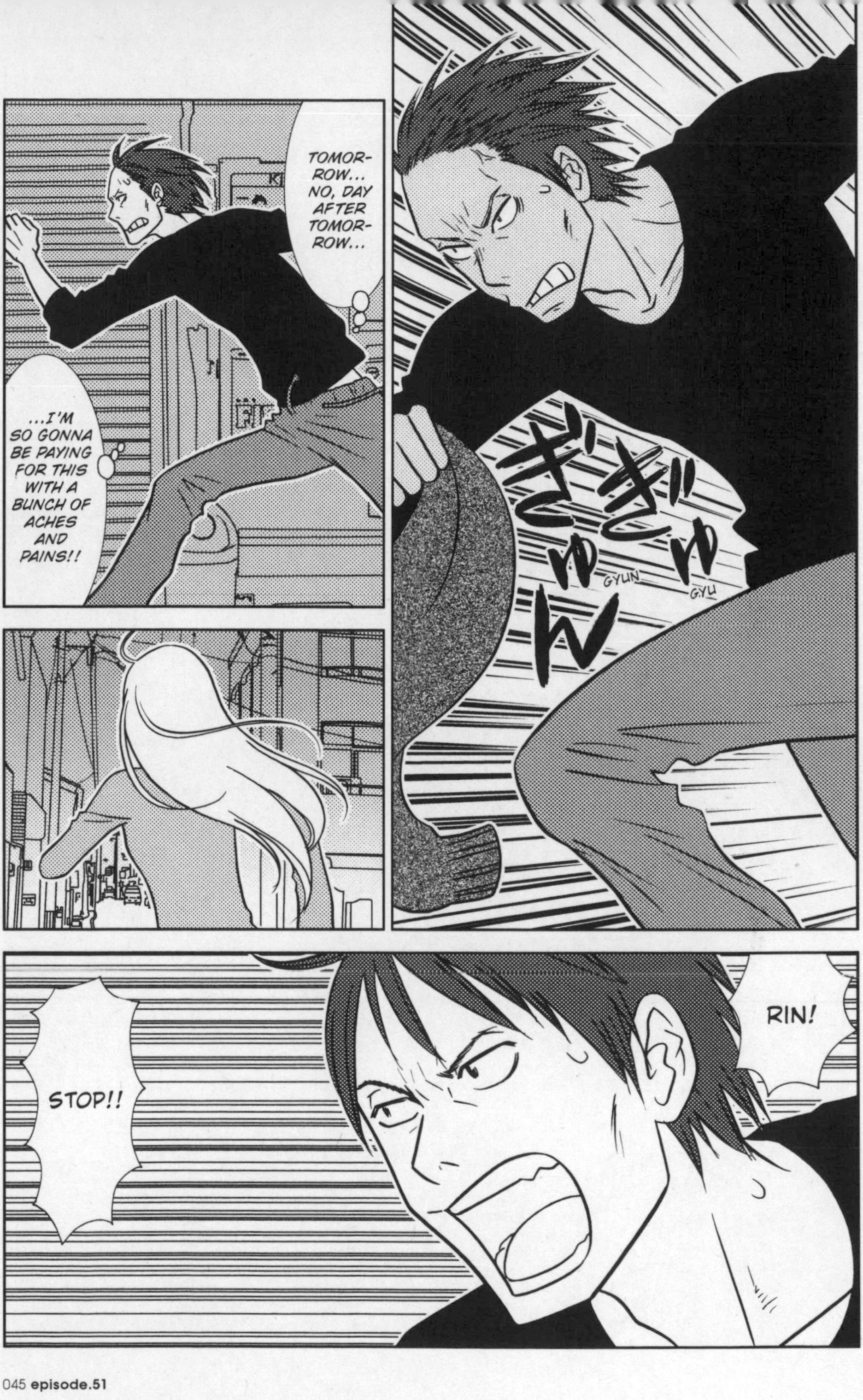
ぎゅ
GYU
ぎゅん
GYUN
TOMORROW... NO, DAY AFTER TOMORROW...
...I'M SO GONNA BE PAYING FOR THIS WITH A BUNCH OF ACHES AND PAINS!!
RIN!
STOP!!

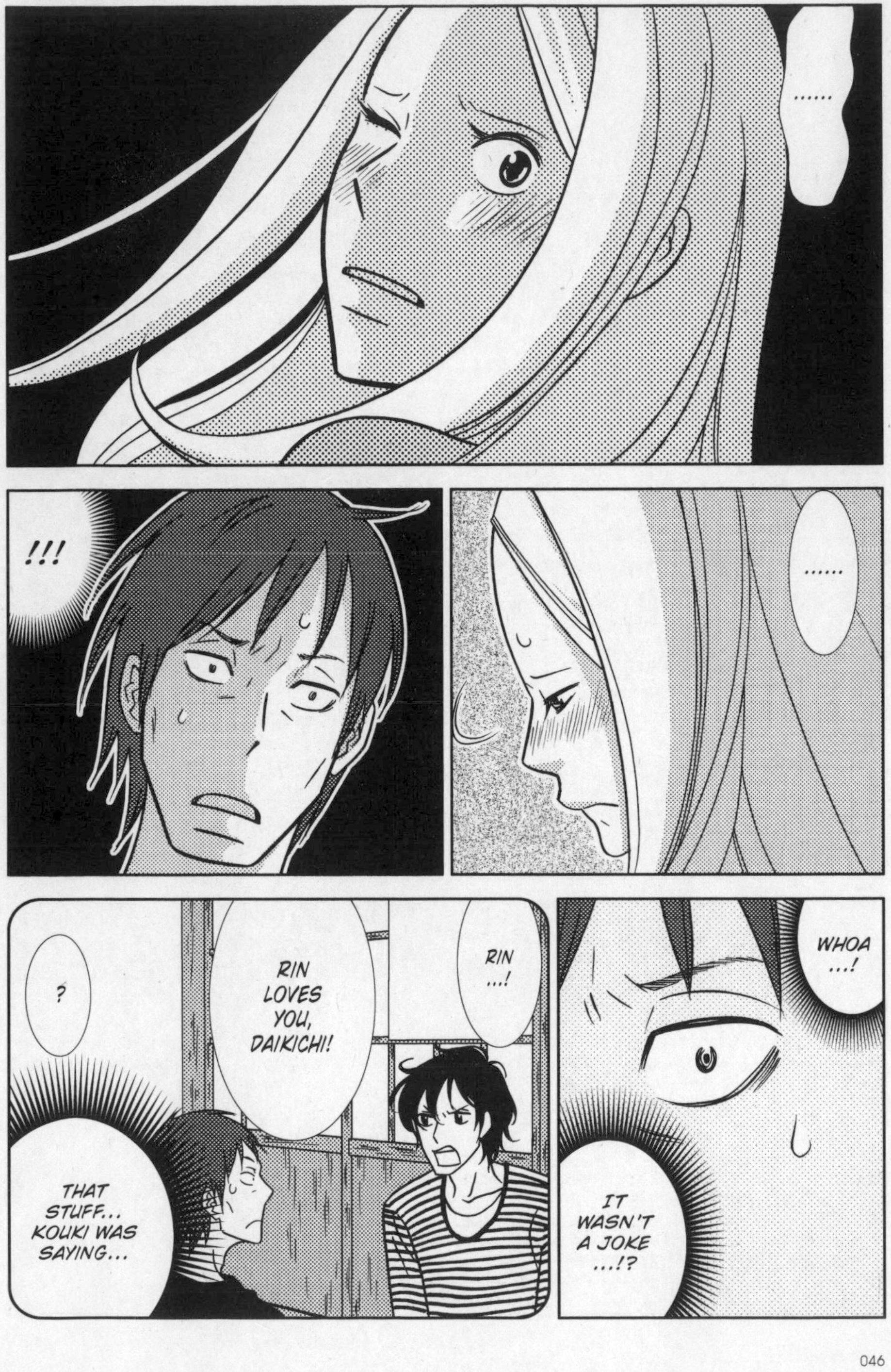
……
……
!!!
WHOA ...!
IT WASN'T A JOKE ...!?
RIN ...!
RIN LOVES YOU, DAIKICHI!
?
THAT STUFF... KOUKI WAS SAYING...

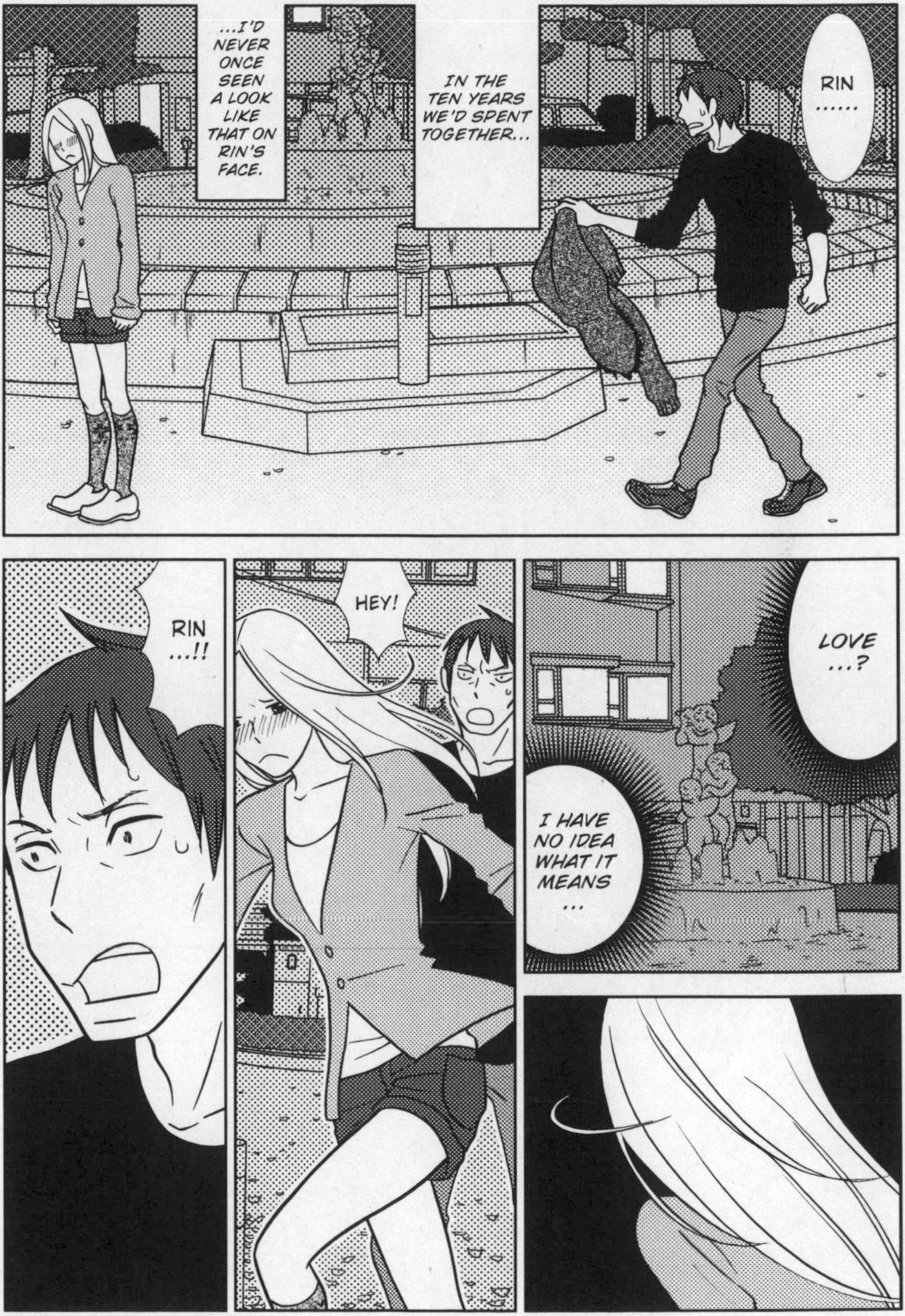
RIN ......
IN THE TEN YEARS WE'D SPENT TOGETHER...
...I'D NEVER ONCE SEEN A LOOK LIKE THAT ON RIN'S FACE.
LOVE ...?
I HAVE NO IDEA WHAT IT MEANS ...
HEY!
RIN ...!!

......

HOW IN THE WORLD DO I...

...HANDLE THIS ...?

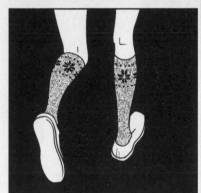

OH...

CRAP ...

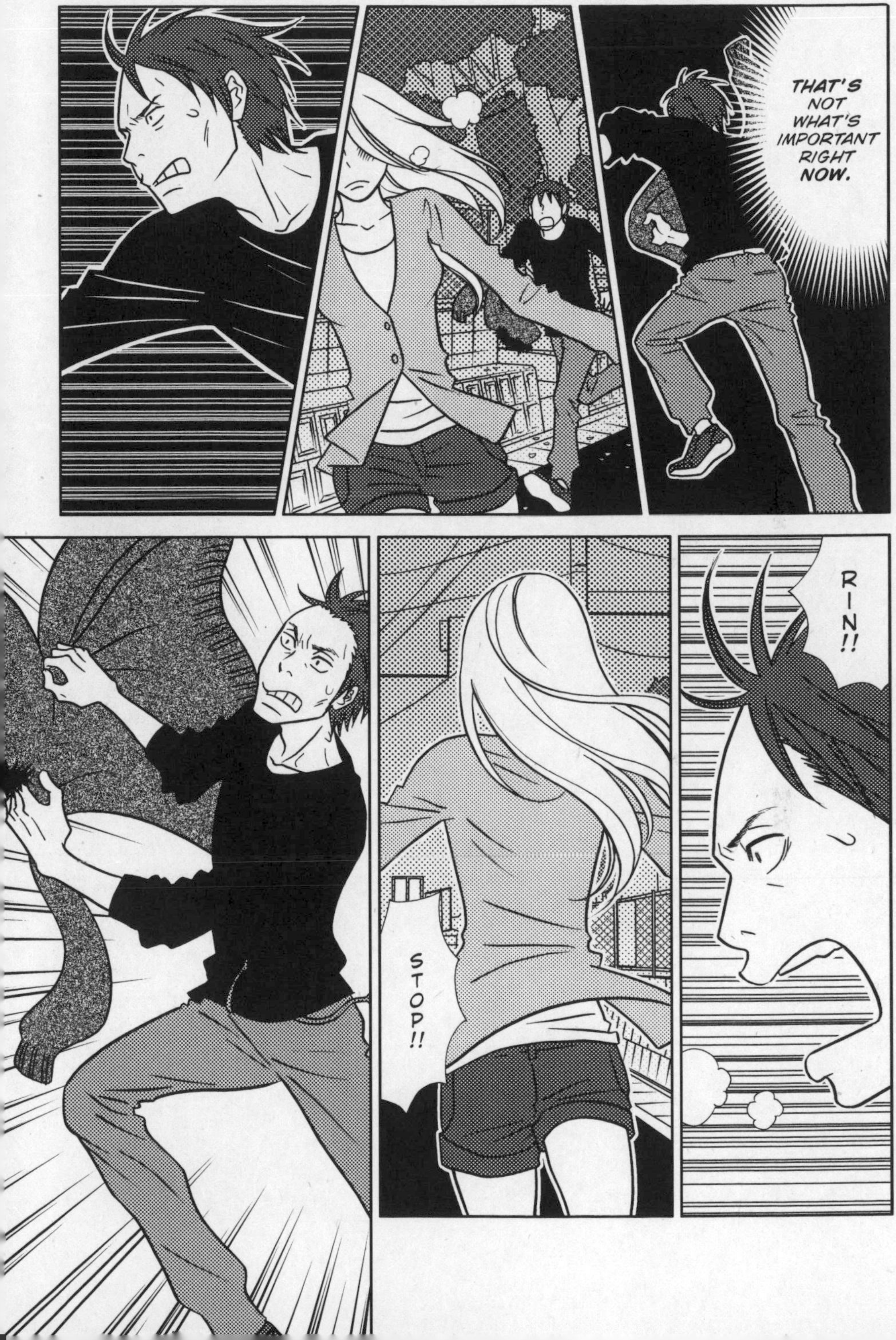
THAT'S NOT WHAT'S IMPORTANT RIGHT NOW.
RIN!!
STOP!!

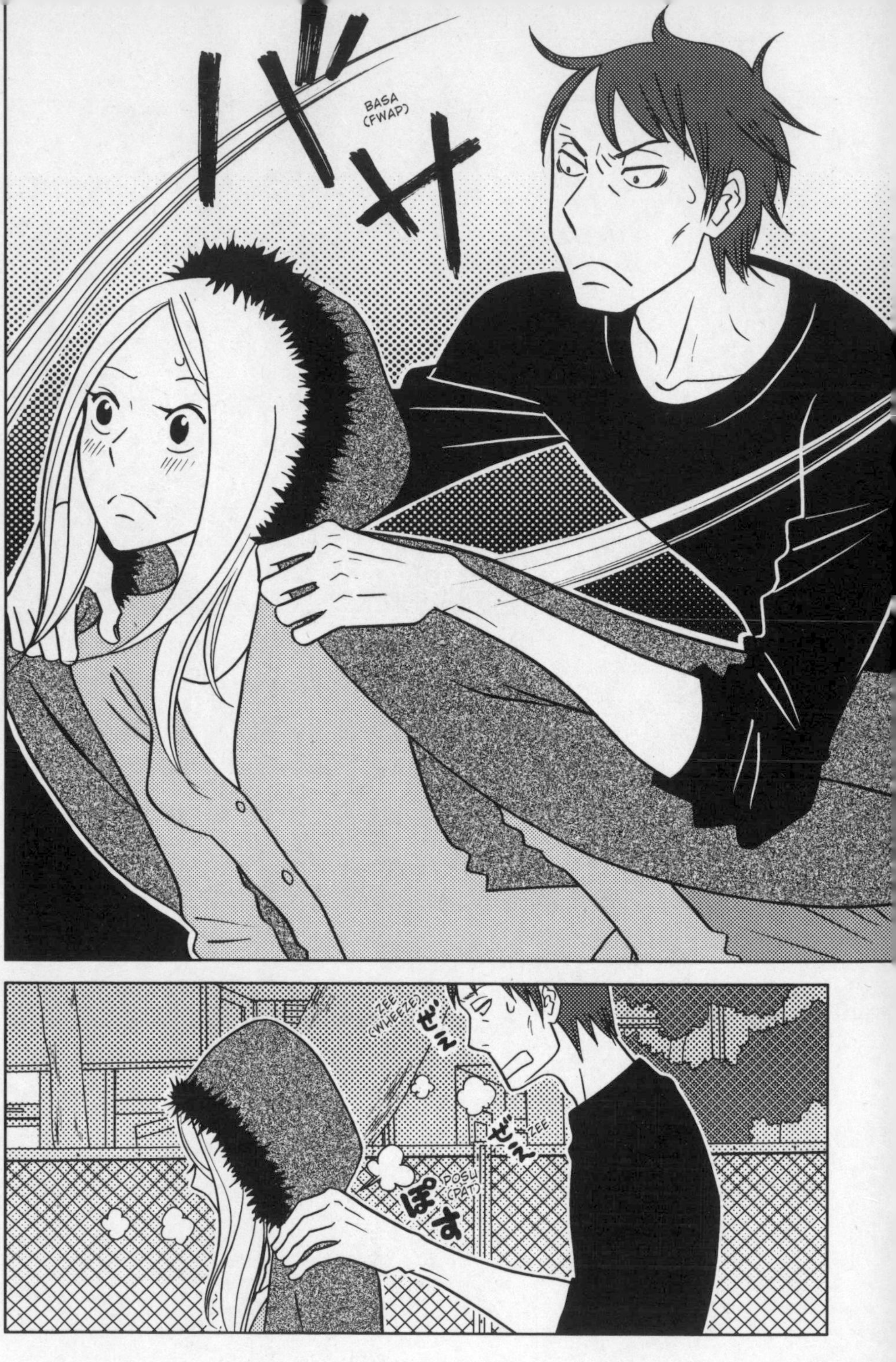
バサッ
BASA (FWAP)
ぜぇ
ZEE (WHEEZE)
ぜぇ
ZEE
ぽす
POSU (PAT)

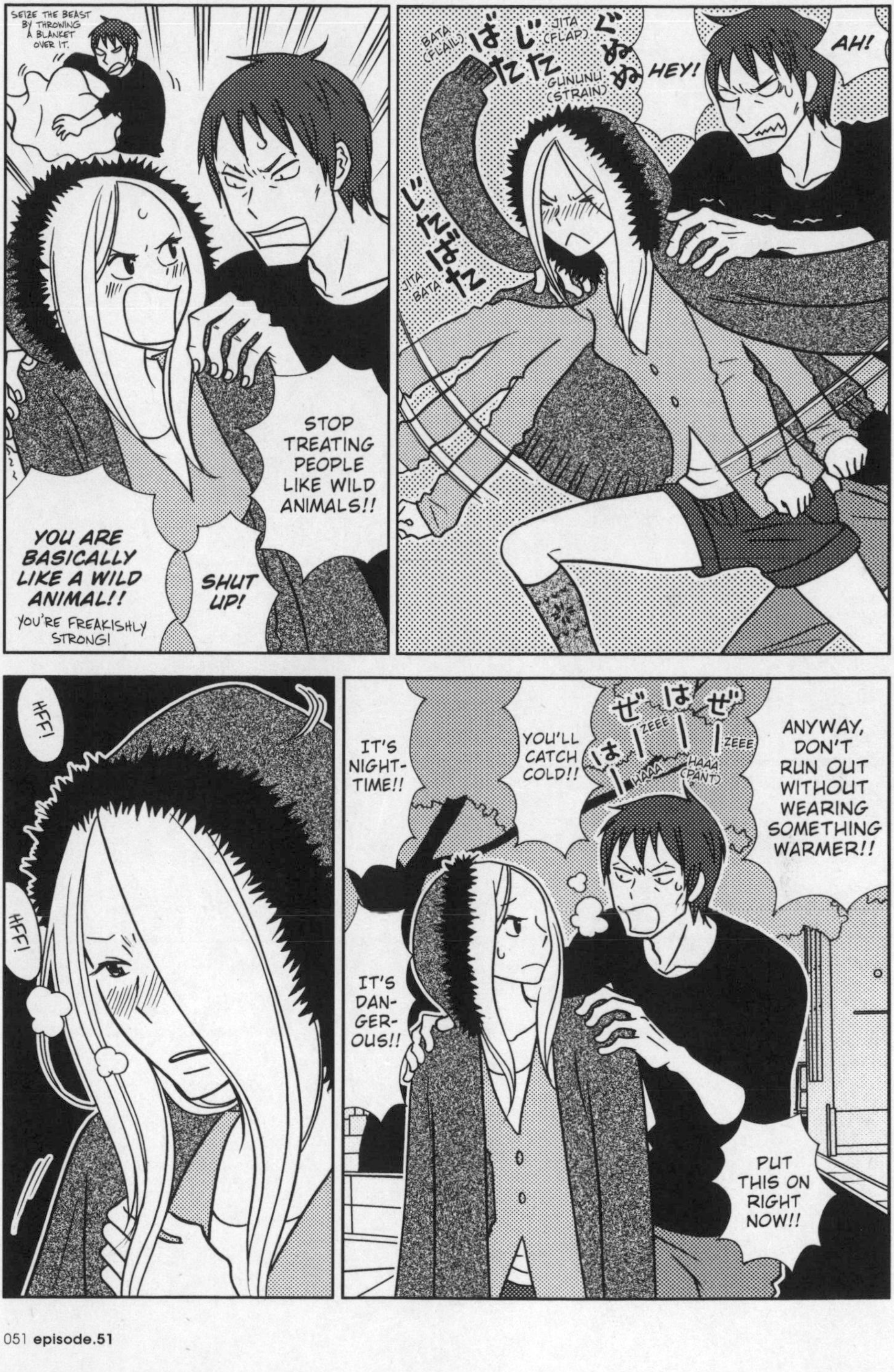
AH!
HEY!
ぐぬぬ
GUNUNU (STRAIN)
じ
JITA (FLAP)
ばたた
BATA (FLAIL)
じたばた
JITA BATA
SEIZE THE BEAST BY THROWING A BLANKET OVER IT.
STOP TREATING PEOPLE LIKE WILD ANIMALS!!
SHUT UP!
YOU ARE BASICALLY LIKE A WILD ANIMAL!!
YOU'RE FREAKISHLY STRONG!
ANYWAY, DON'T RUN OUT WITHOUT WEARING SOMETHING WARMER!!
ぜーはーぜーはー
ZEEE HAAA ZEEE HAAA (PANT)
YOU'LL CATCH COLD!!
IT'S NIGHT-TIME!!
PUT THIS ON RIGHT NOW!!
IT'S DAN-GER-OUS!!
HFF!
HFF!

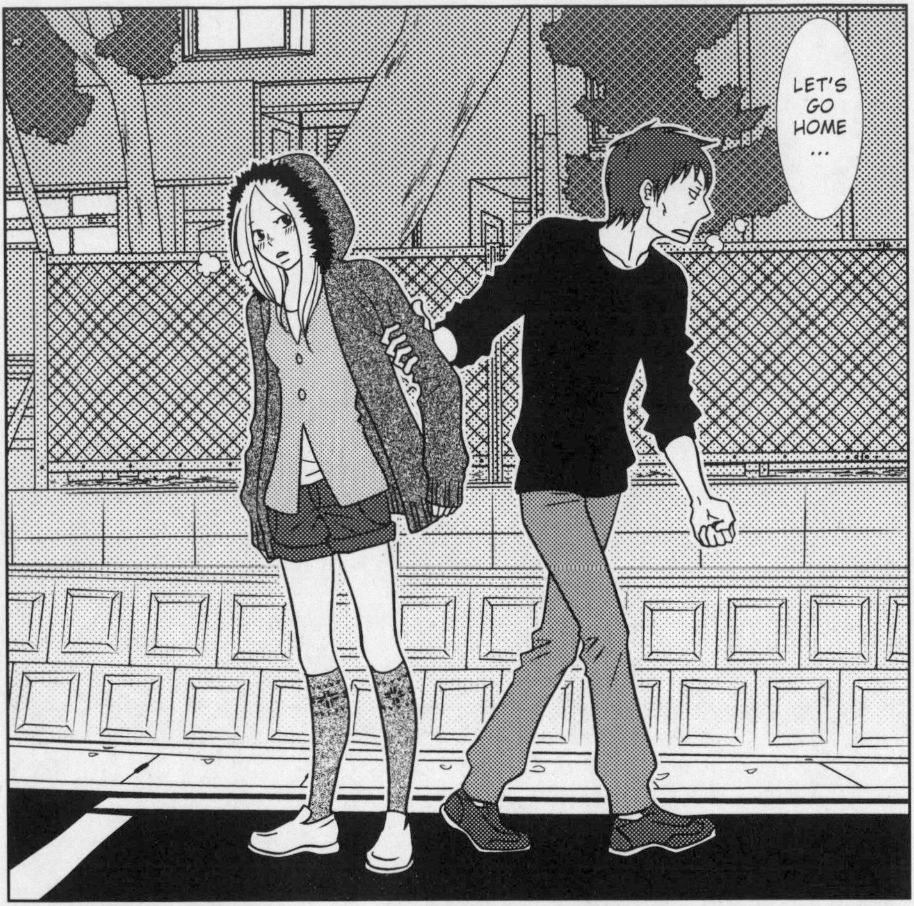
LET'S GO HOME ...
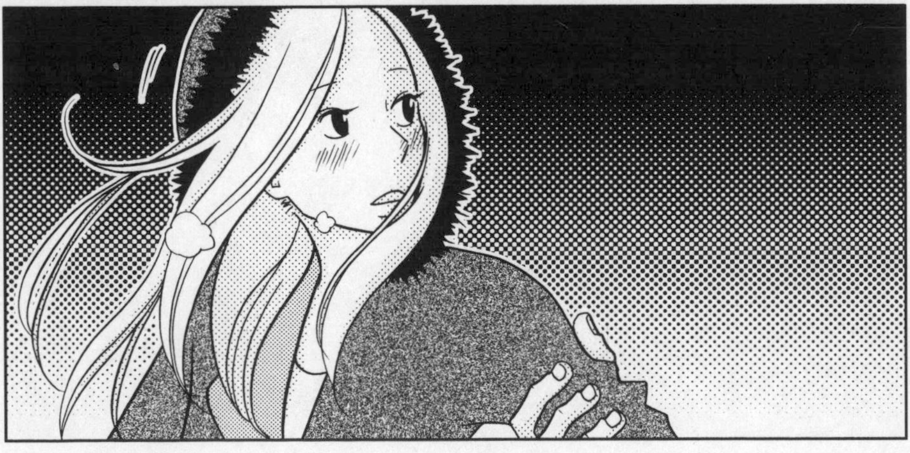

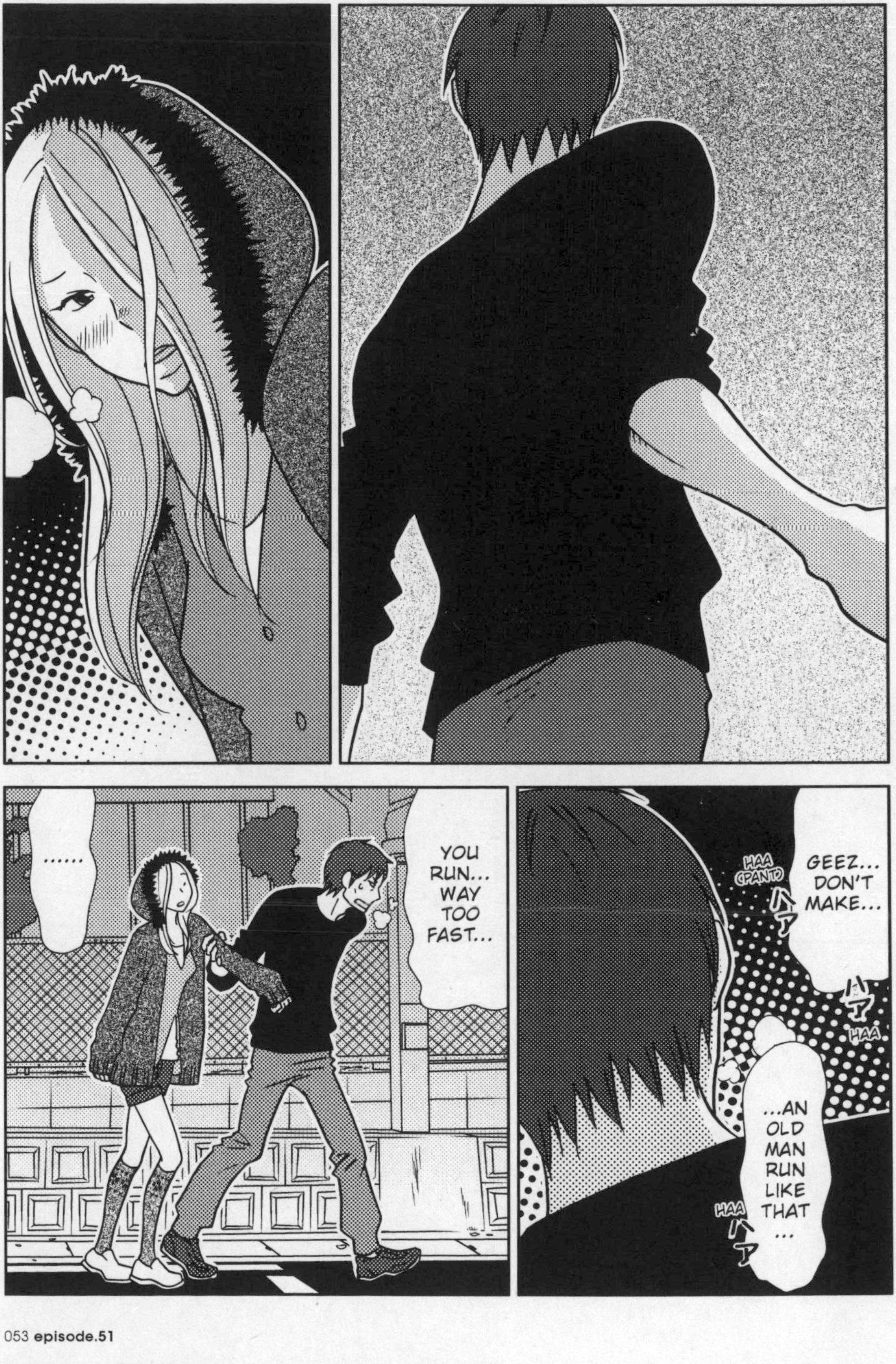
HAA (PANT)
GEEZ... DON'T MAKE...
HAA
...AN OLD MAN RUN LIKE THAT ...
HAA
YOU RUN... WAY TOO FAST...
......

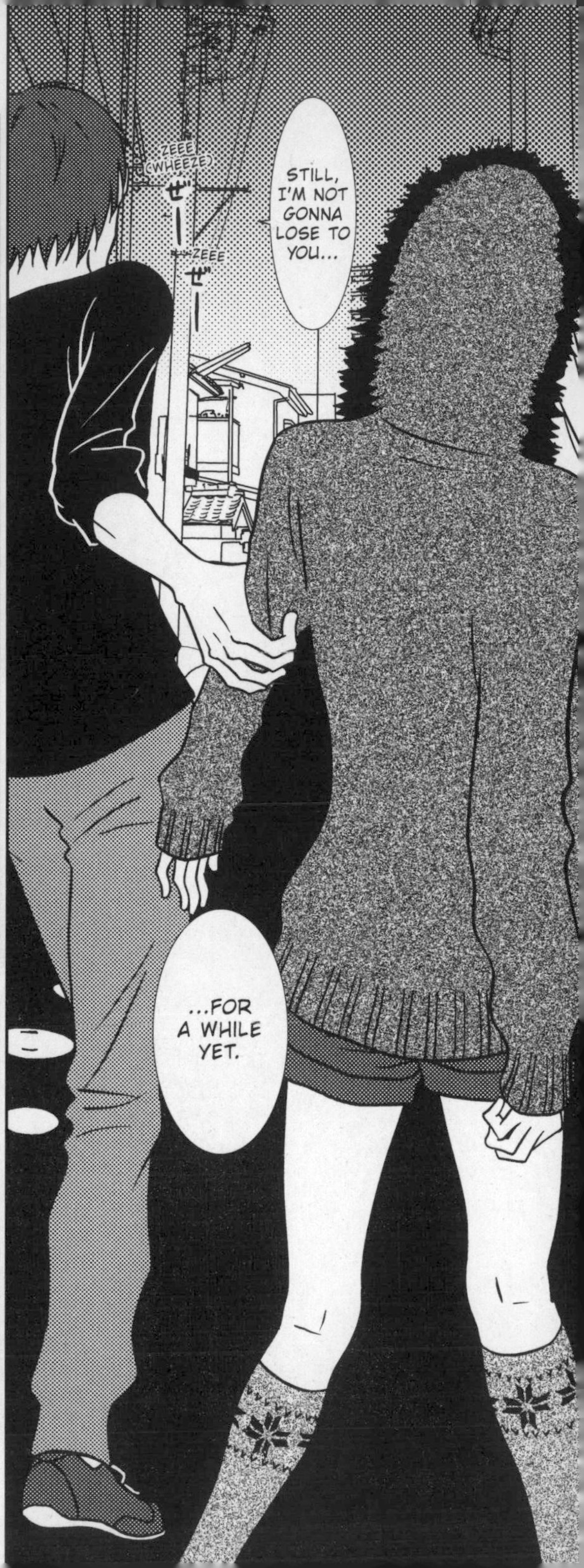
STILL, I'M NOT GONNA LOSE TO YOU...
ZEEE (WHEEZE) ゼー
ZEEE ゼー
...FOR A WHILE YET.
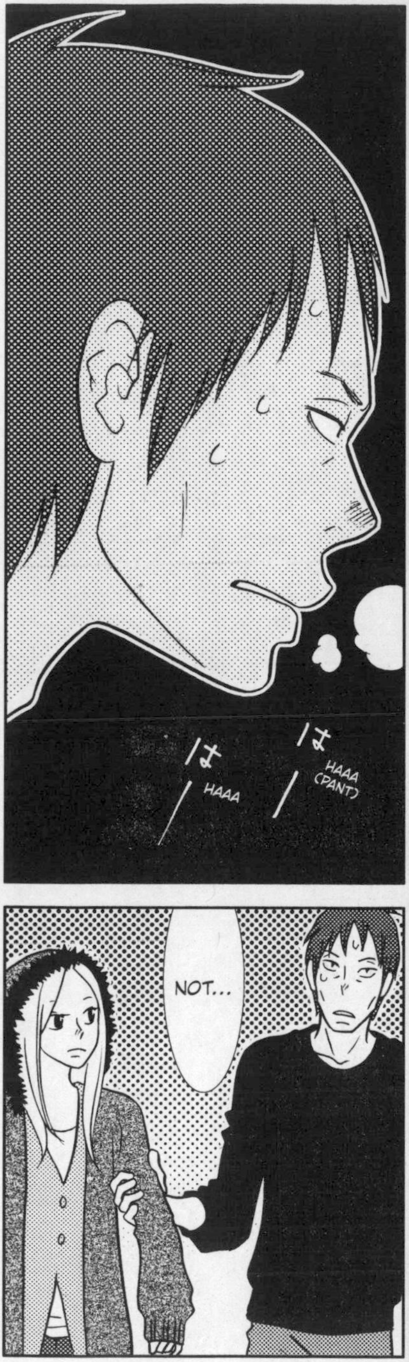
は HAAA (PANT)
は HAAA
NOT...

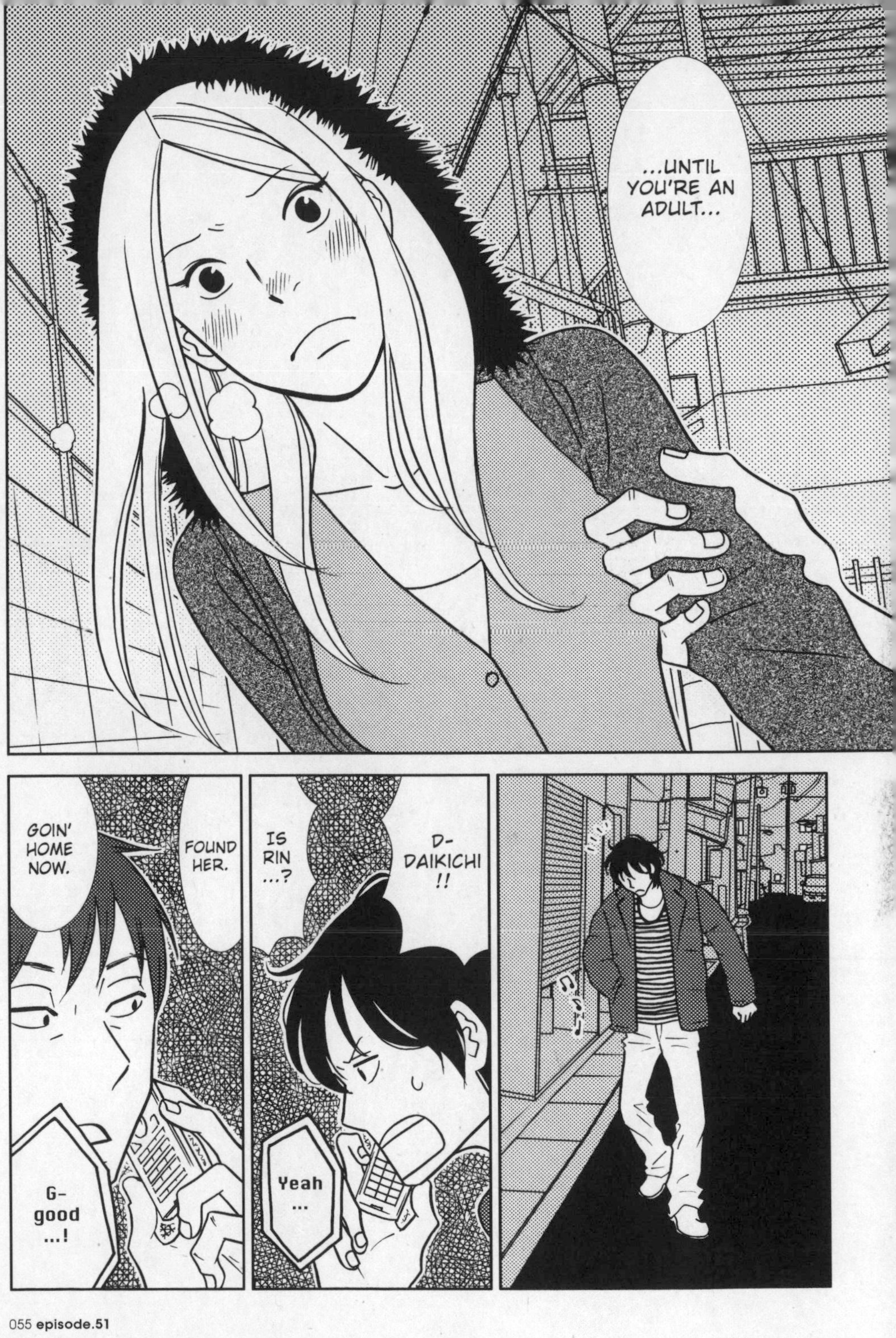
...UNTIL YOU'RE AN ADULT...
D- DAIKICHI !!
IS RIN ...?
Yeah ...
FOUND HER.
GOIN' HOME NOW.
G- good ...!

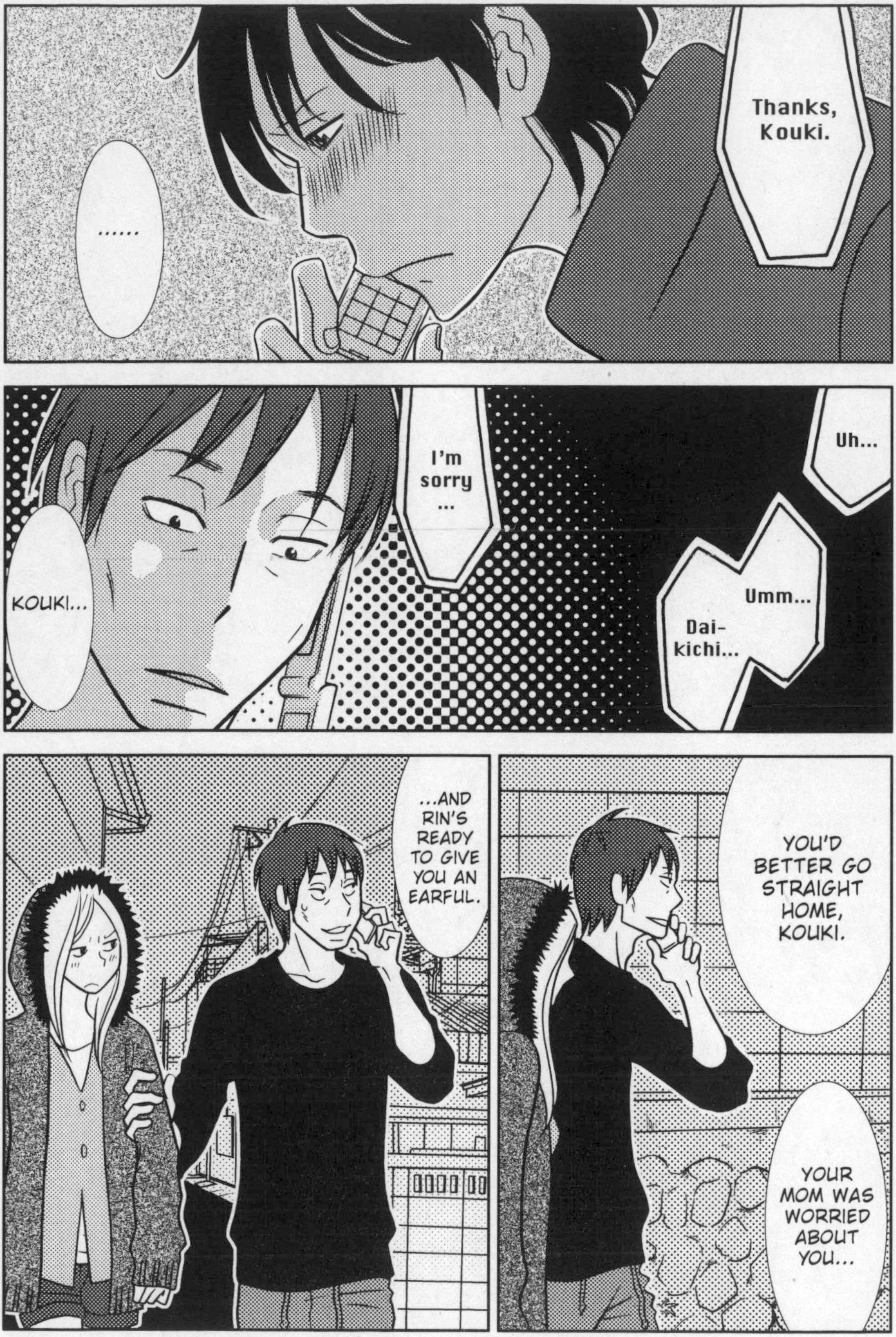
Thanks, Kouki.
......
Uh...
Umm... Dai-kichi...
I'm sorry ...
KOUKI...
YOU'D BETTER GO STRAIGHT HOME, KOUKI.
YOUR MOM WAS WORRIED ABOUT YOU...
...AND RIN'S READY TO GIVE YOU AN EARFUL.

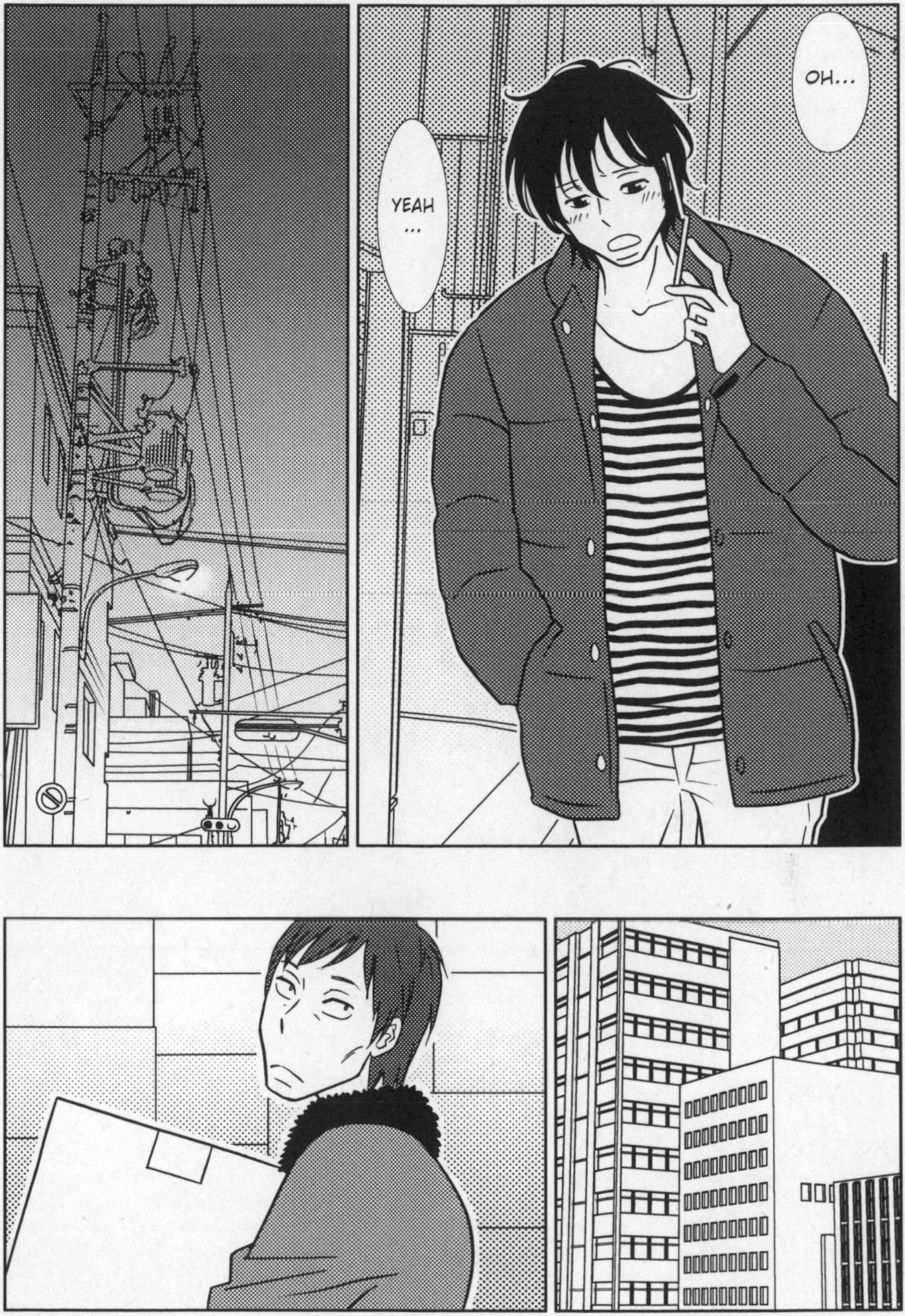
OH...
YEAH ...

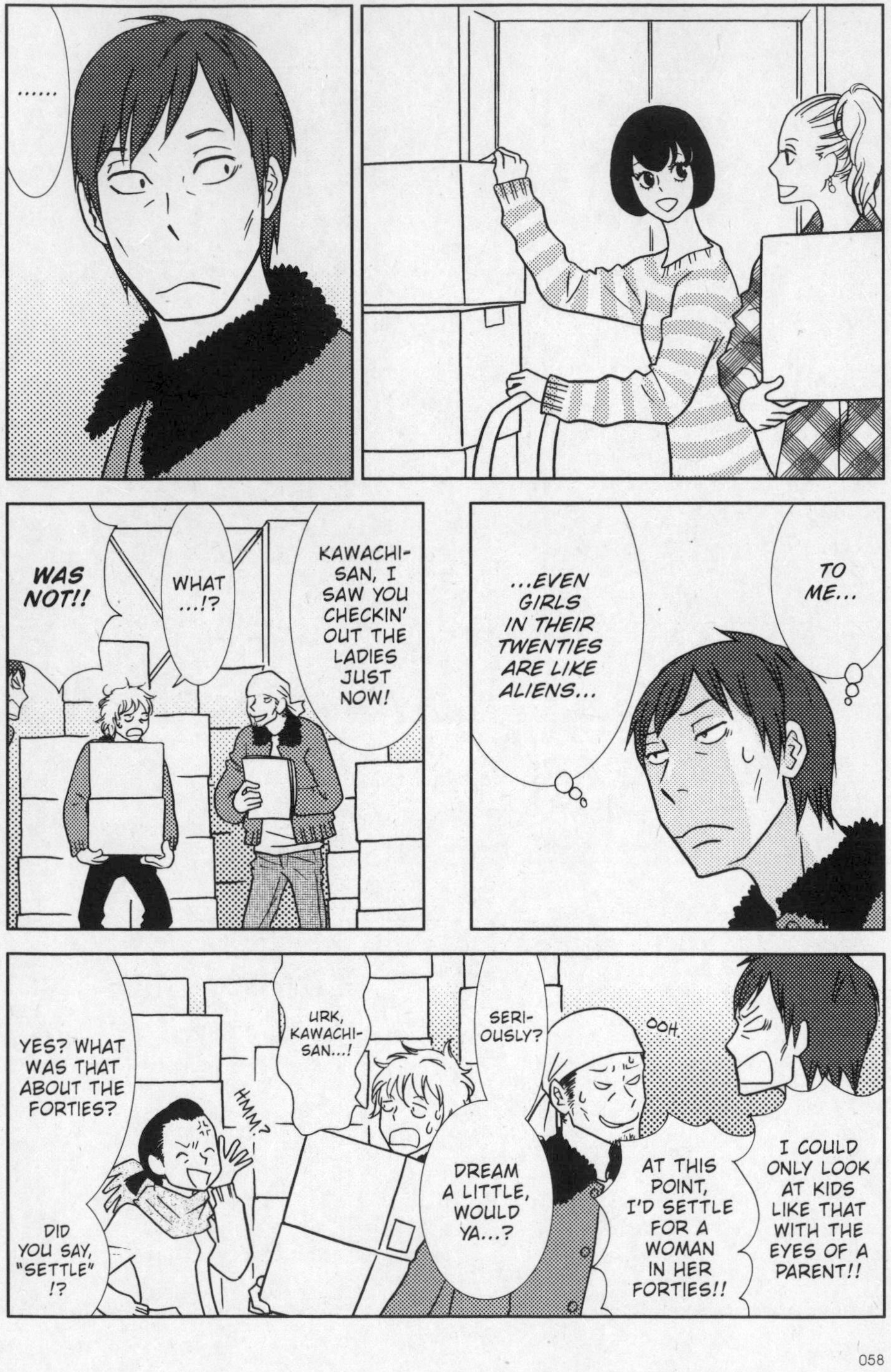
......
TO ME...
...EVEN GIRLS IN THEIR TWENTIES ARE LIKE ALIENS...
KAWACHI-SAN, I SAW YOU CHECKIN' OUT THE LADIES JUST NOW!
WHAT ...!?
WAS NOT!!
OOH.
I COULD ONLY LOOK AT KIDS LIKE THAT WITH THE EYES OF A PARENT!!
AT THIS POINT, I'D SETTLE FOR A WOMAN IN HER FORTIES!!
SERI-OUSLY?
DREAM A LITTLE, WOULD YA...?
URK, KAWACHI-SAN...!
HMM?
YES? WHAT WAS THAT ABOUT THE FORTIES?
DID YOU SAY, "SETTLE" !?

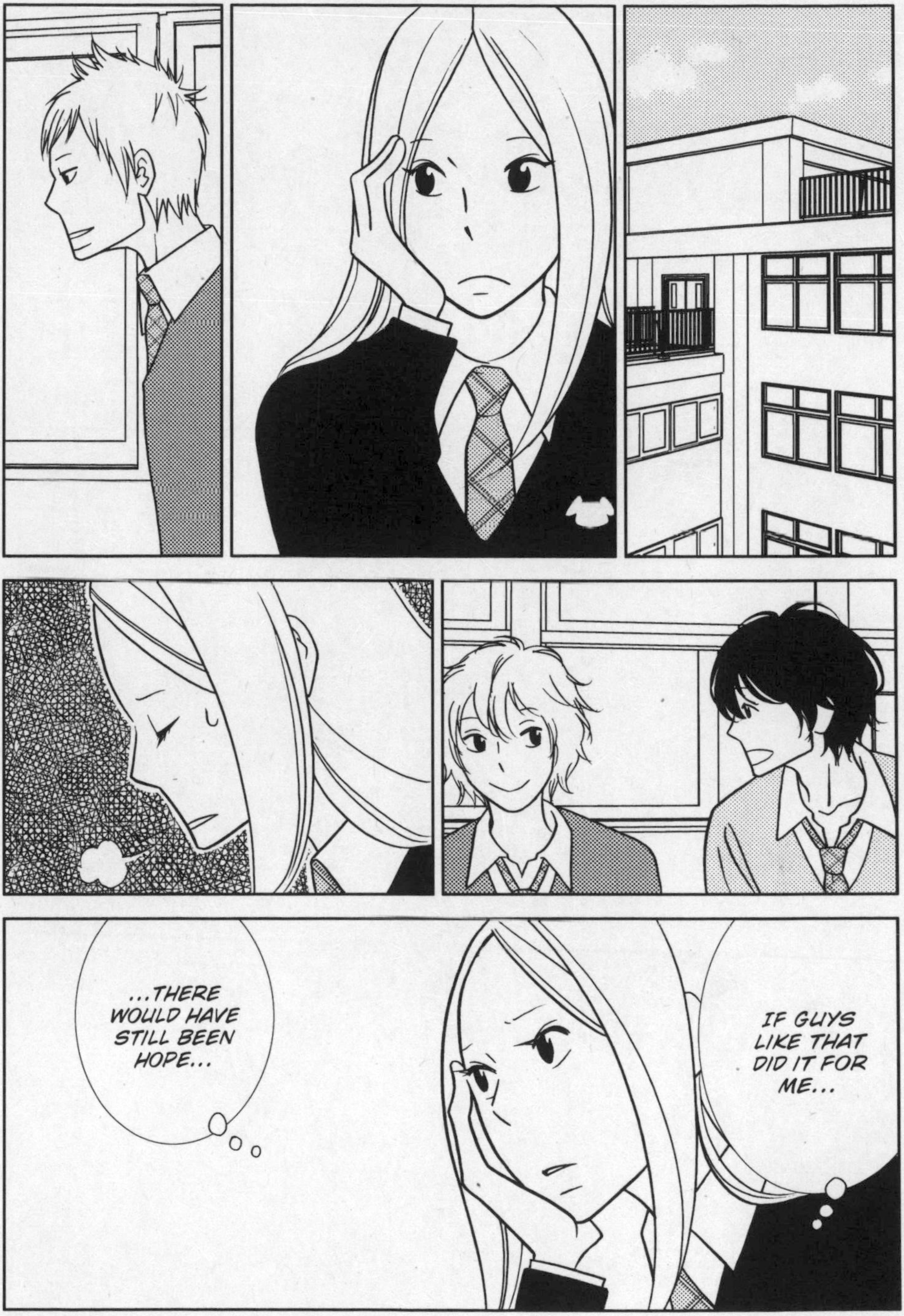
IF GUYS LIKE THAT DID IT FOR ME...
...THERE WOULD HAVE STILL BEEN HOPE...

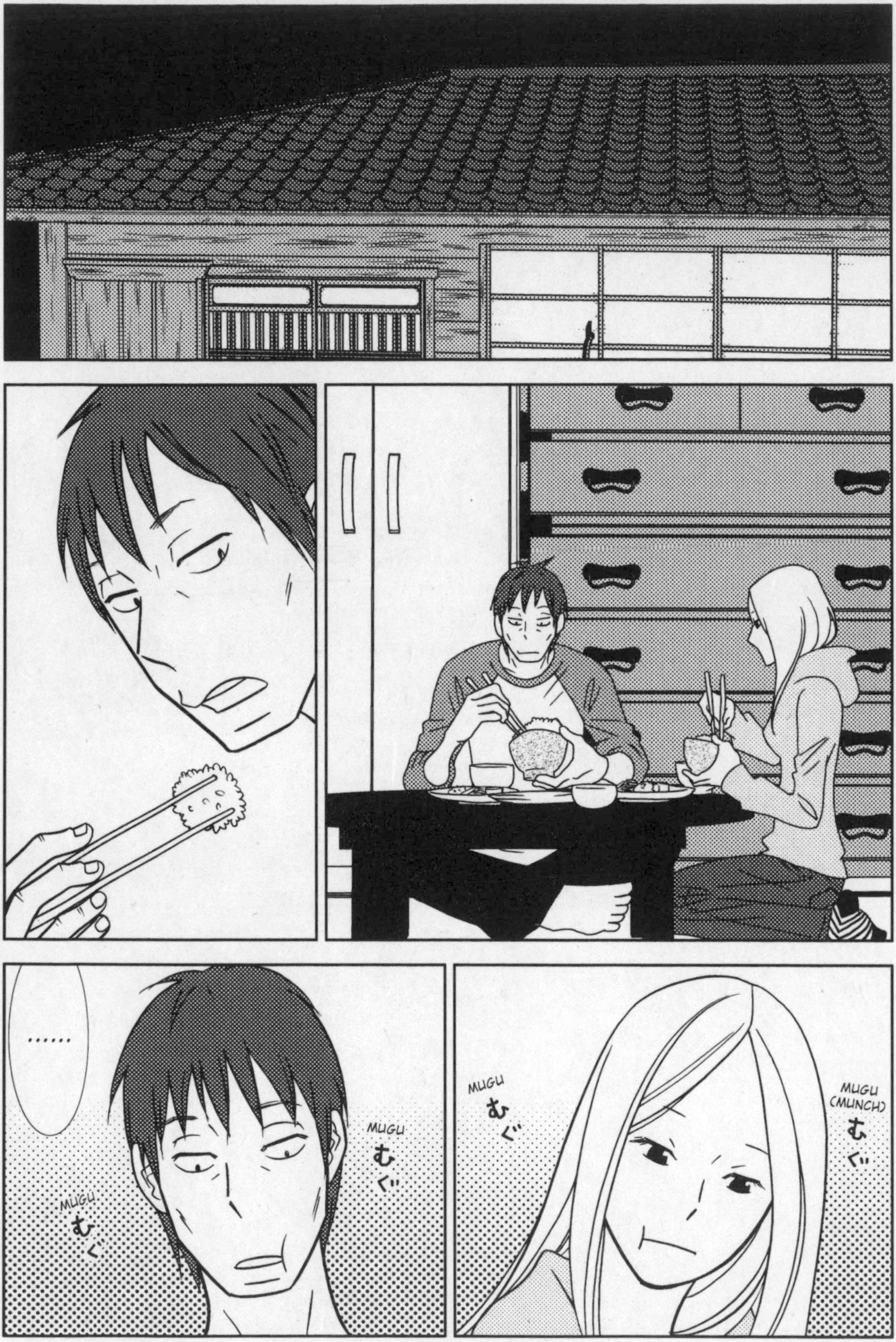
MUGU (MUNCH) むぐ
MUGU むぐ
......
MUGU むぐ
MUGU むぐ

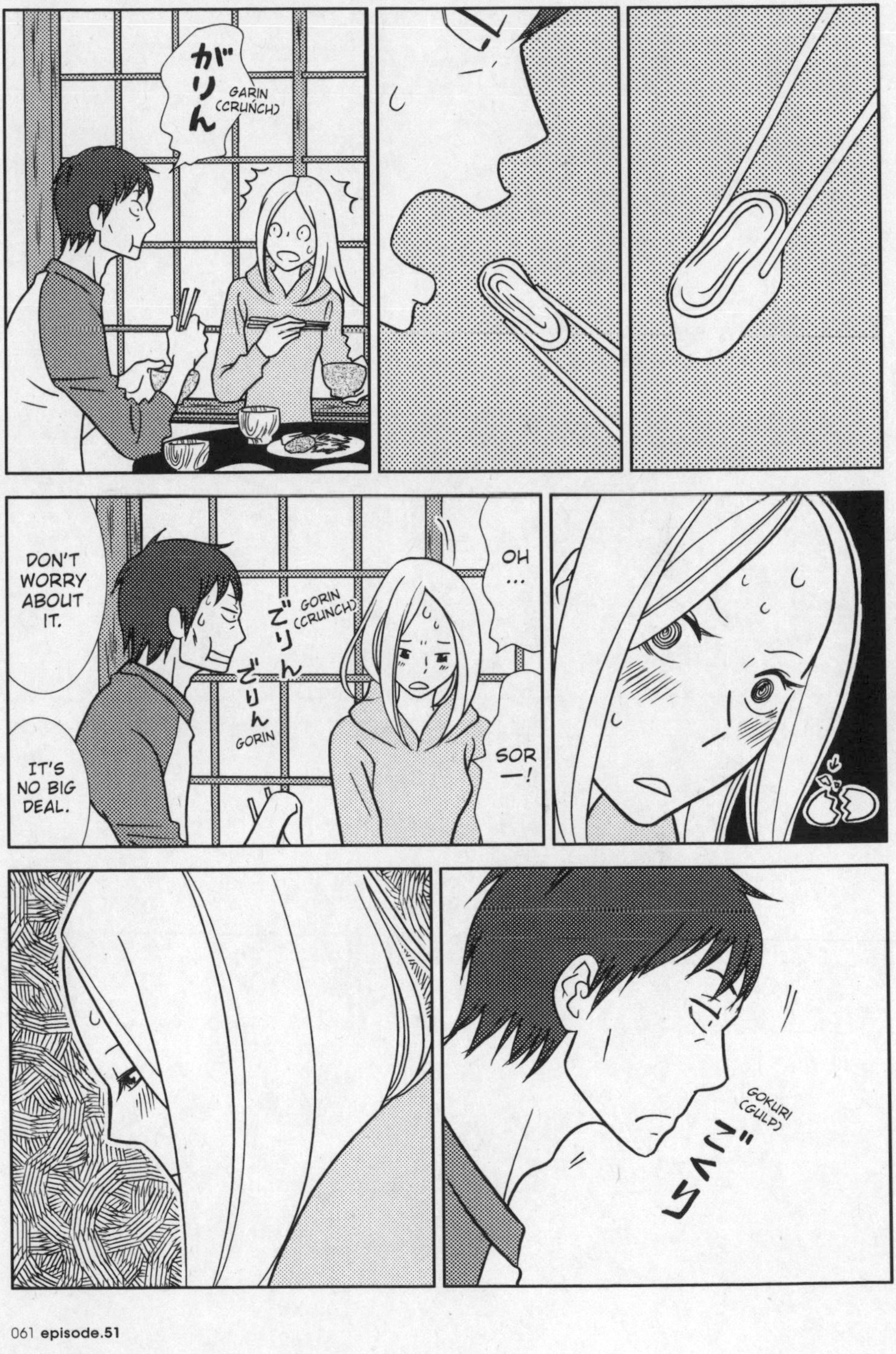
がりん
GARIN (CRUNCH)
OH ...
SOR—!
ごりん
GORIN (CRUNCH)
ごりん
GORIN
DON'T WORRY ABOUT IT.
IT'S NO BIG DEAL.
ごくり
GOKURI (GULP)

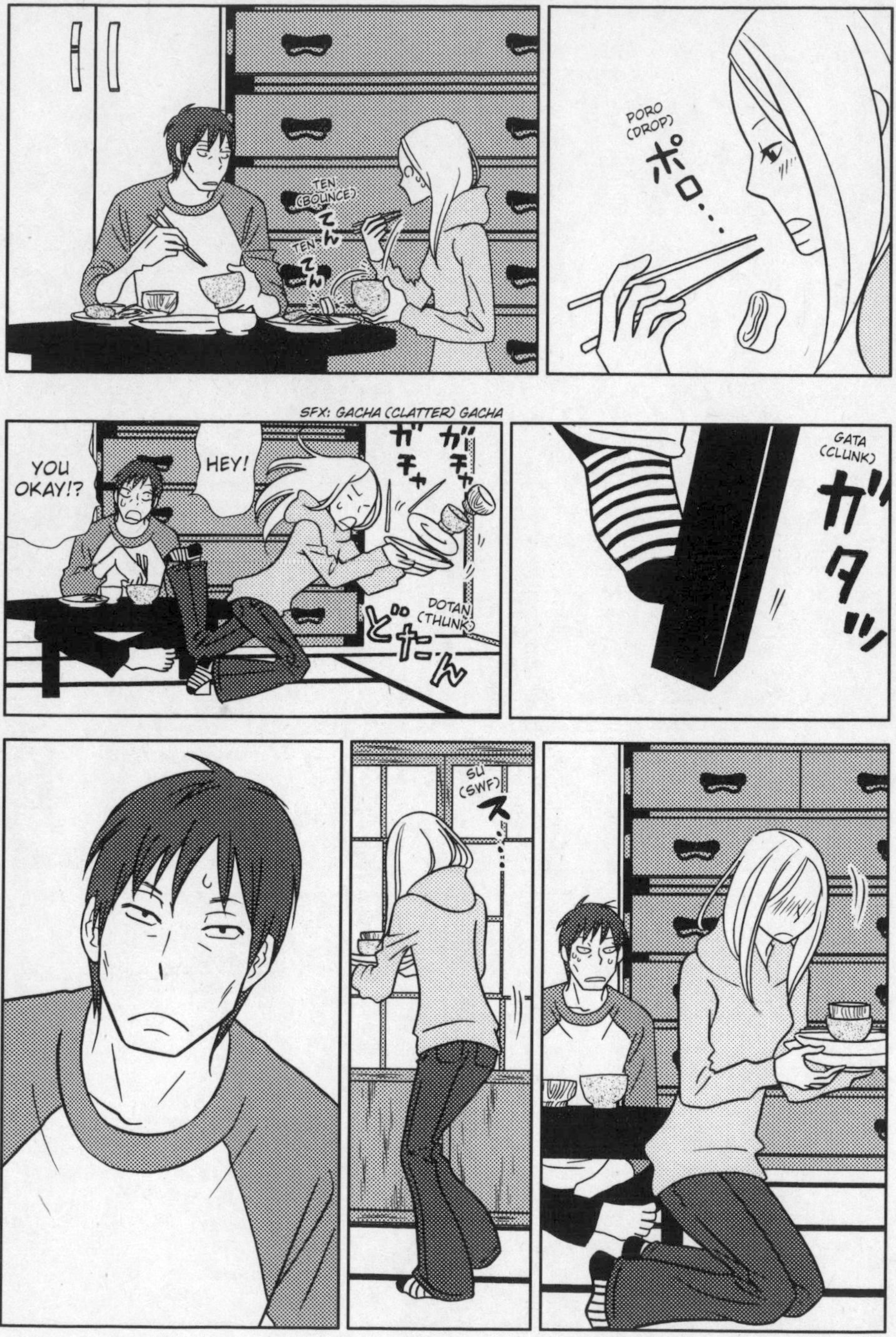

PORO (DROP)
ポロ…
TEN (BOUNCE)
てん
TEN
てん
GATA (CLUNK)
ガタッ
SFX: GACHA (CLATTER) GACHA
ガチャ
ガチャ
HEY!
YOU OKAY!?
DOTAN (THUNK)
どたーん
SU (SWF)
ス…

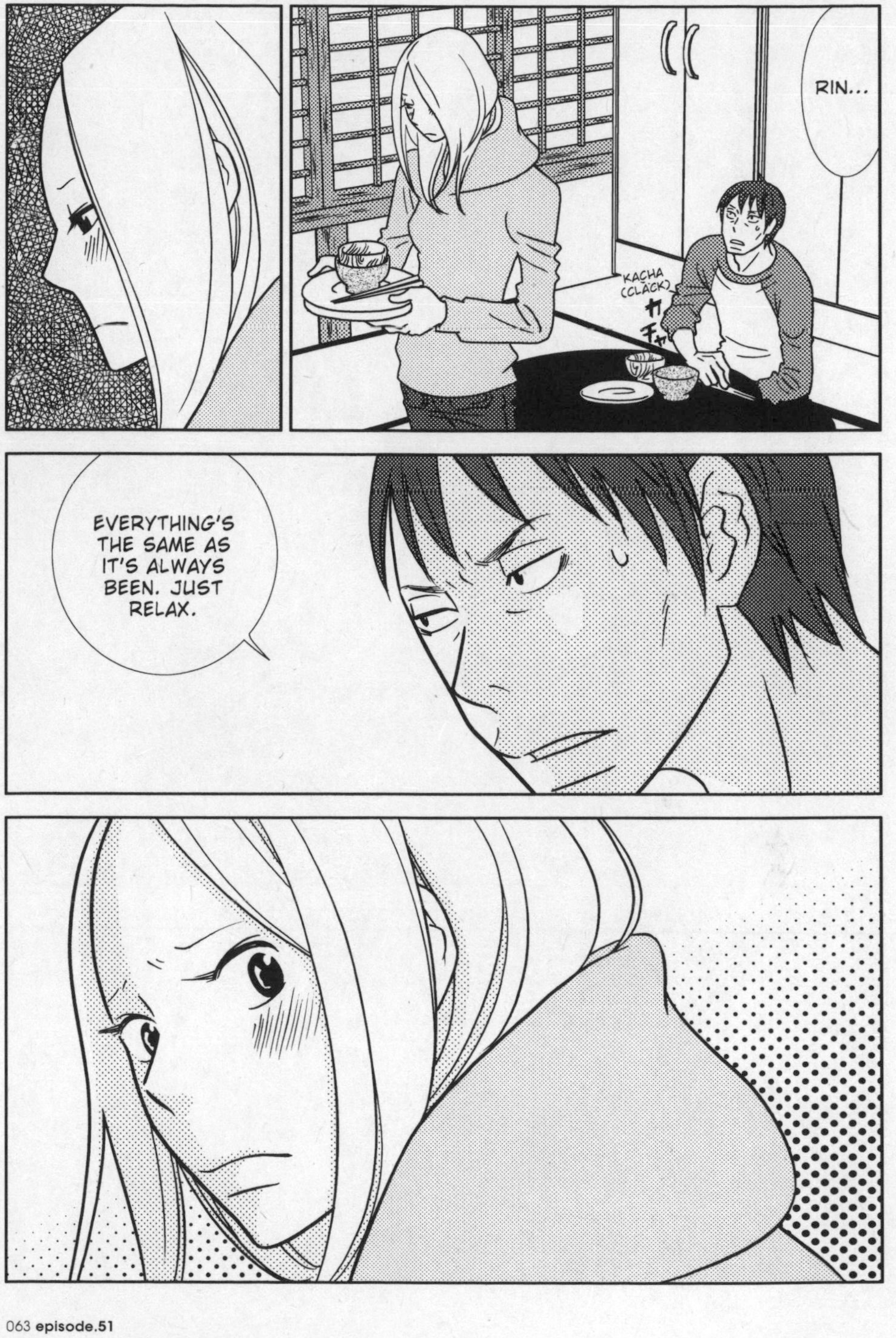
RIN...
KACHA (CLACK)
カチャ
EVERYTHING'S THE SAME AS IT'S ALWAYS BEEN. JUST RELAX.

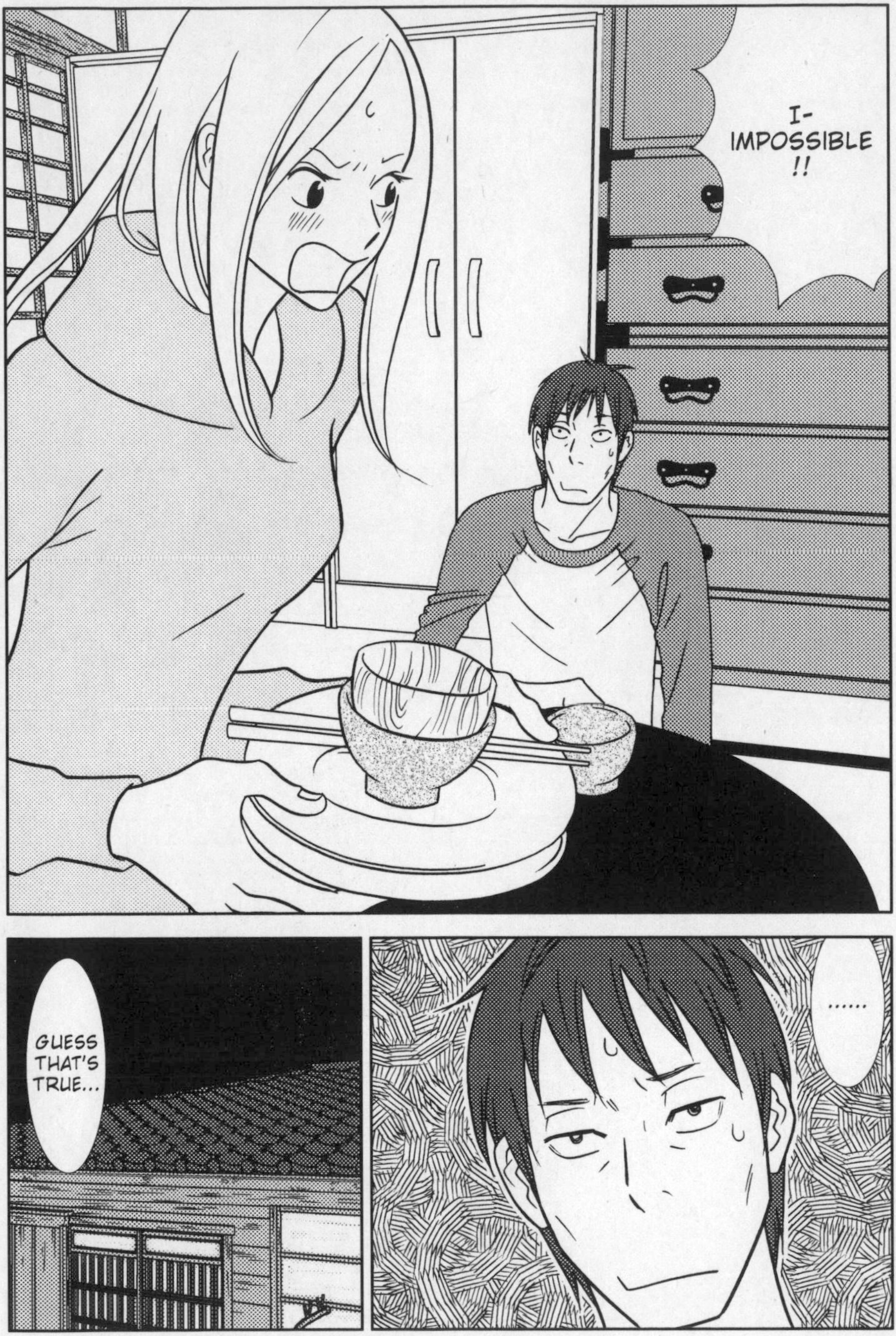
I-
IMPOSSIBLE
!!
......
GUESS THAT'S TRUE...

BUNNY**DROP**
episode.52

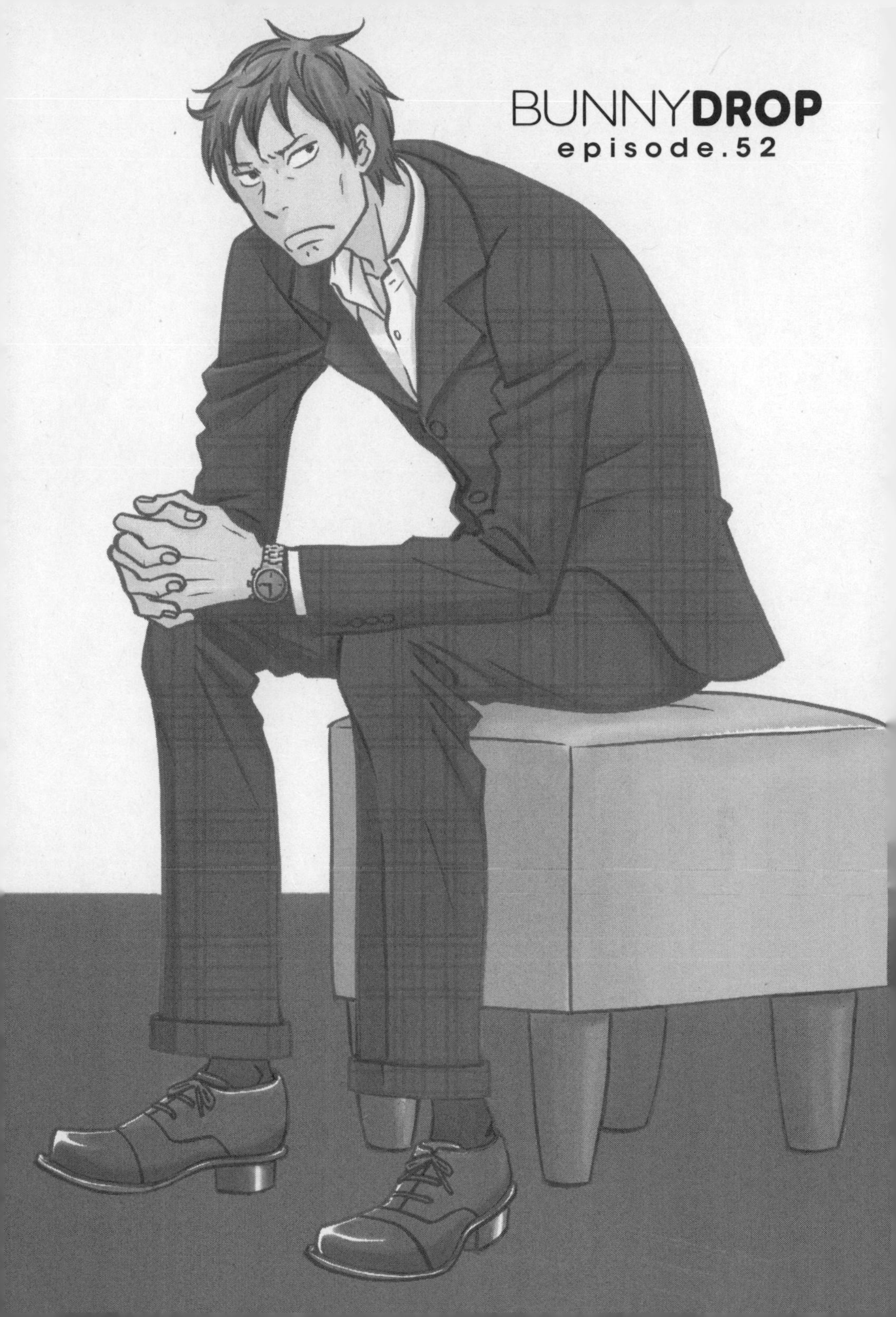

BUNNYDROP

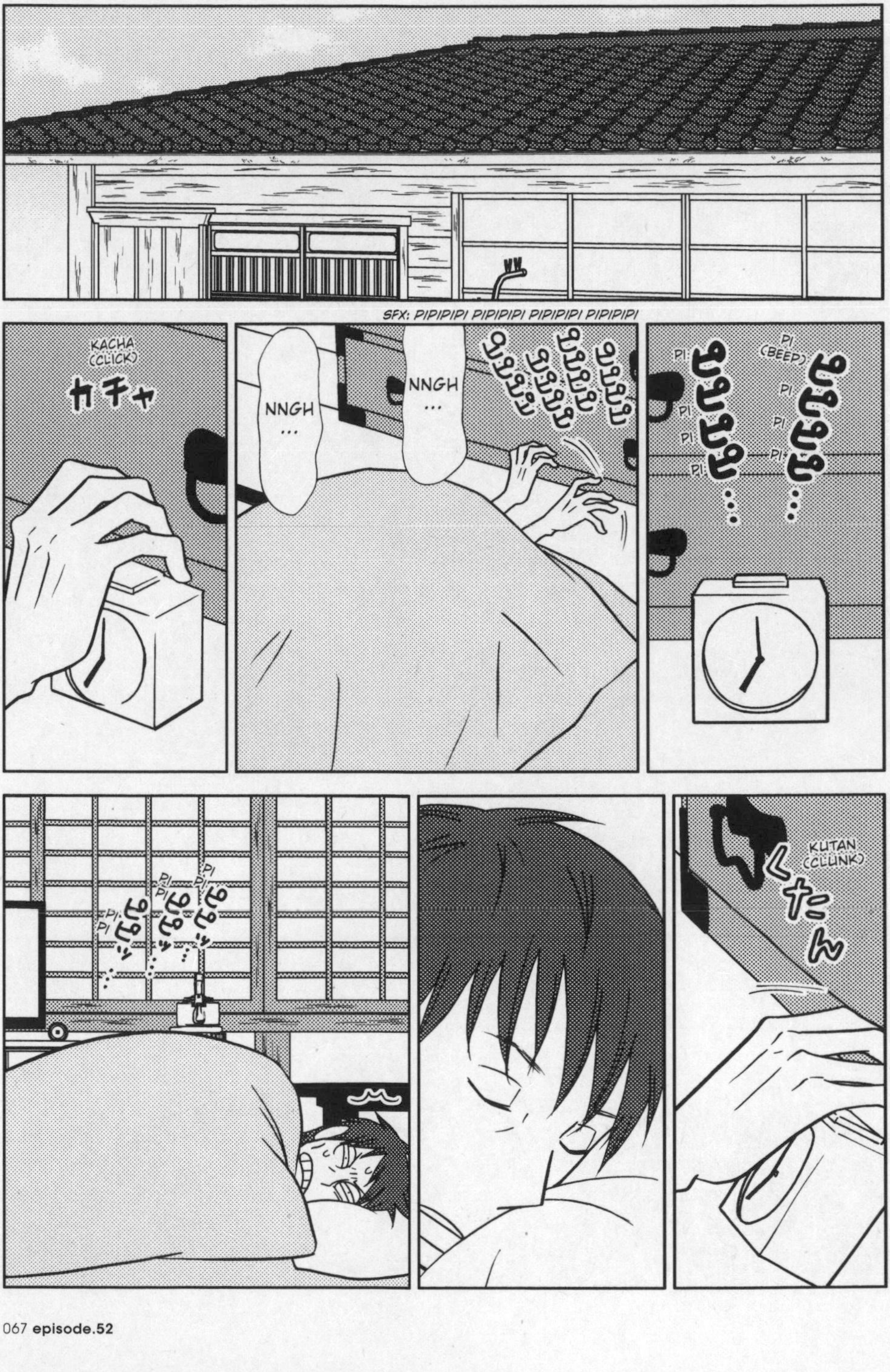
SFX: PIPIPIPI PIPIPIPI PIPIPIPI PIPIPIPI
ピピピピ…ピピピピ…
PI (BEEP)
PI PI PI PI PI PI PI
NNGH…
NNGH…
KACHA (CLICK)
カチャ
KUTAN (CLUNK)
くたん
PI PI PI PI PI

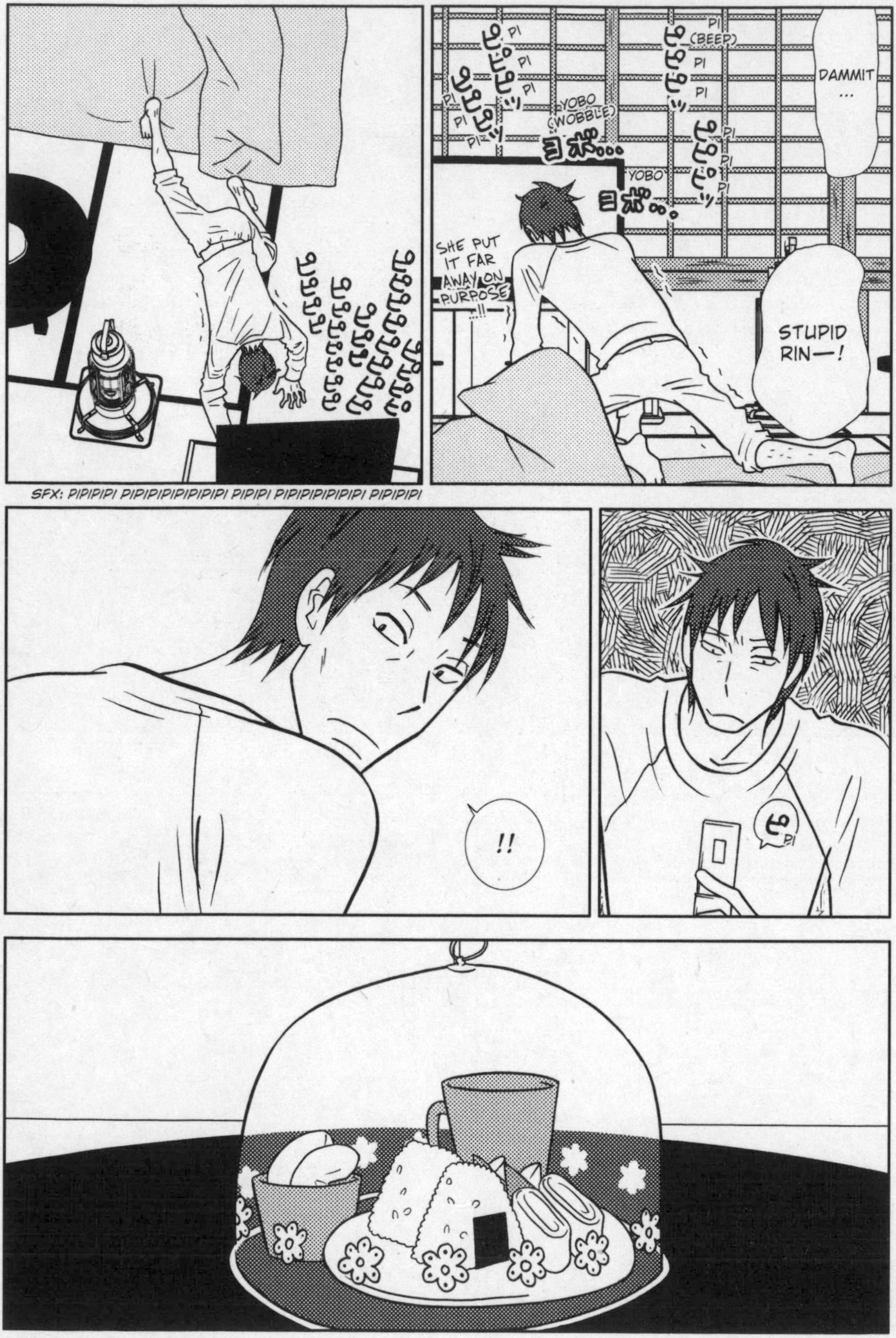
DAMMIT …
PI (BEEP) PI PI
PI PI PI
YOBO (WOBBLE)
YOBO
STUPID RIN—!
SHE PUT IT FAR AWAY ON PURPOSE …!!
PI PI PI
PI PI PI
SFX: PIPIPIPI PIPIPIPIPIPIPIPIPI PIPIPI PIPIPIPIPIPIPIPI PIPIPIPI
PI
!!

RIN
...?

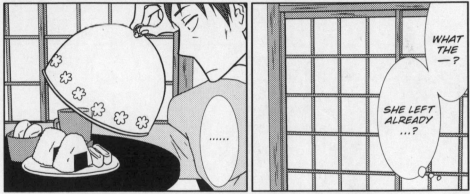

......

WHAT THE
—?

SHE LEFT
ALREADY
...?

WHAT,
LUNCH?

NOW?

SAME
OL' PROPER
BREAKFAST...

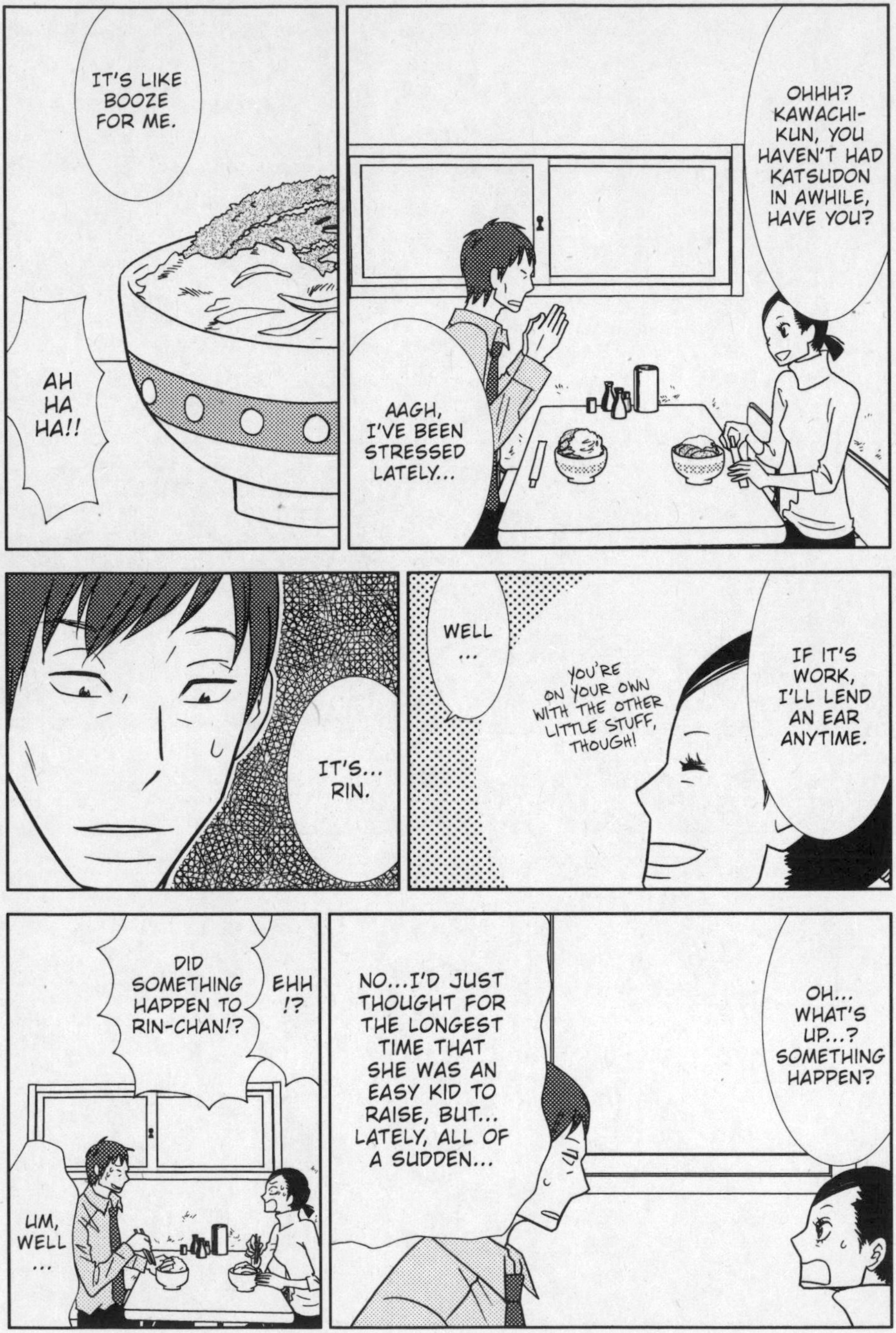
OHHH? KAWACHI-KUN, YOU HAVEN'T HAD KATSUDON IN AWHILE, HAVE YOU?
AAGH, I'VE BEEN STRESSED LATELY...
IT'S LIKE BOOZE FOR ME.
AH HA HA!!
IF IT'S WORK, I'LL LEND AN EAR ANYTIME.
YOU'RE ON YOUR OWN WITH THE OTHER LITTLE STUFF, THOUGH!
WELL ...
IT'S... RIN.
OH... WHAT'S UP...? SOMETHING HAPPEN?
NO...I'D JUST THOUGHT FOR THE LONGEST TIME THAT SHE WAS AN EASY KID TO RAISE, BUT... LATELY, ALL OF A SUDDEN...
EHH !?
DID SOMETHING HAPPEN TO RIN-CHAN!?
UM, WELL ...

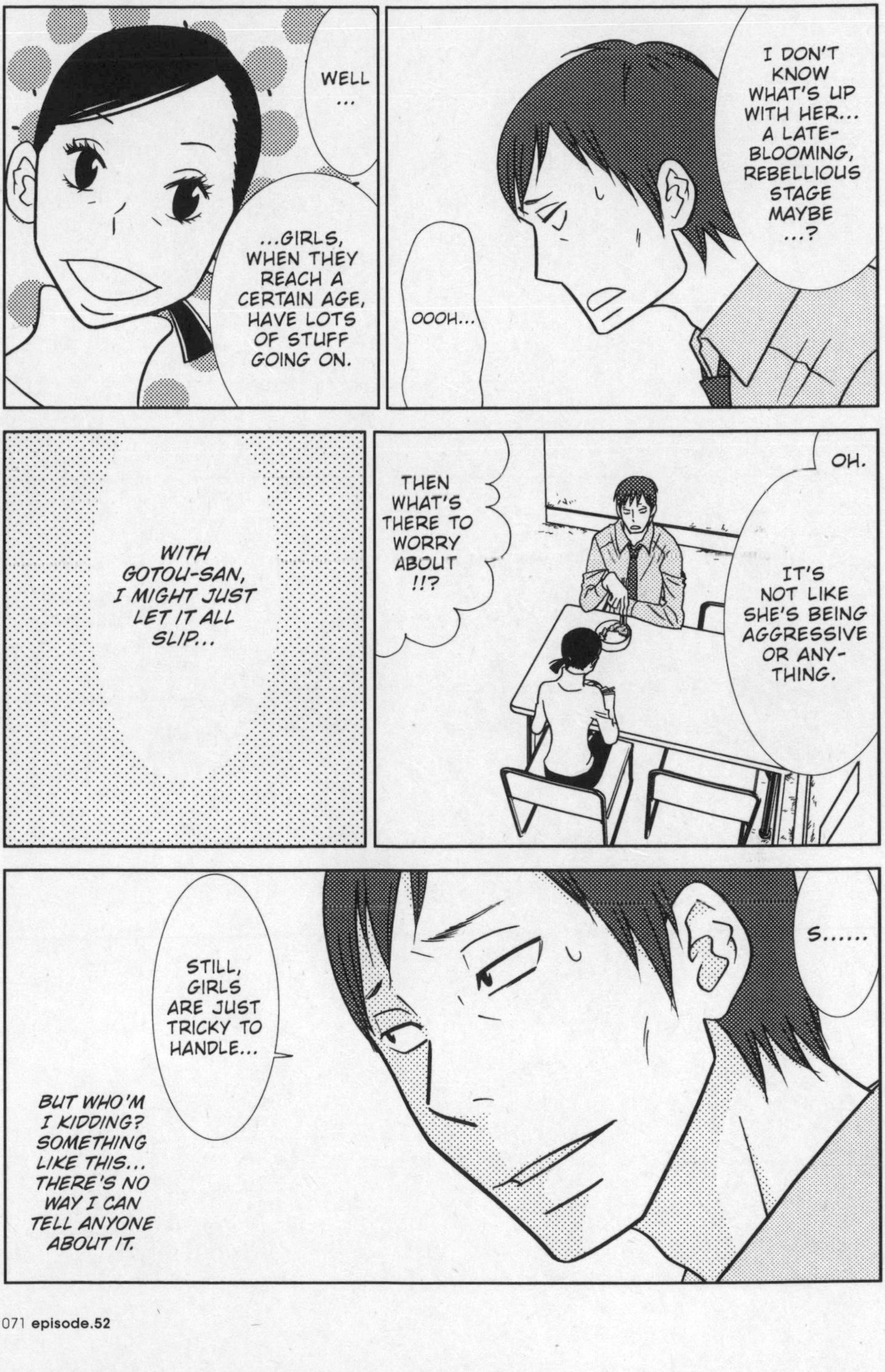
I DON'T KNOW WHAT'S UP WITH HER... A LATE-BLOOMING, REBELLIOUS STAGE MAYBE ...?
OOOH...
WELL ...
...GIRLS, WHEN THEY REACH A CERTAIN AGE, HAVE LOTS OF STUFF GOING ON.
OH.
IT'S NOT LIKE SHE'S BEING AGGRESSIVE OR ANY-THING.
THEN WHAT'S THERE TO WORRY ABOUT !!?
WITH GOTOU-SAN, I MIGHT JUST LET IT ALL SLIP...
S......
STILL, GIRLS ARE JUST TRICKY TO HANDLE...
BUT WHO'M I KIDDING? SOMETHING LIKE THIS... THERE'S NO WAY I CAN TELL ANYONE ABOUT IT.

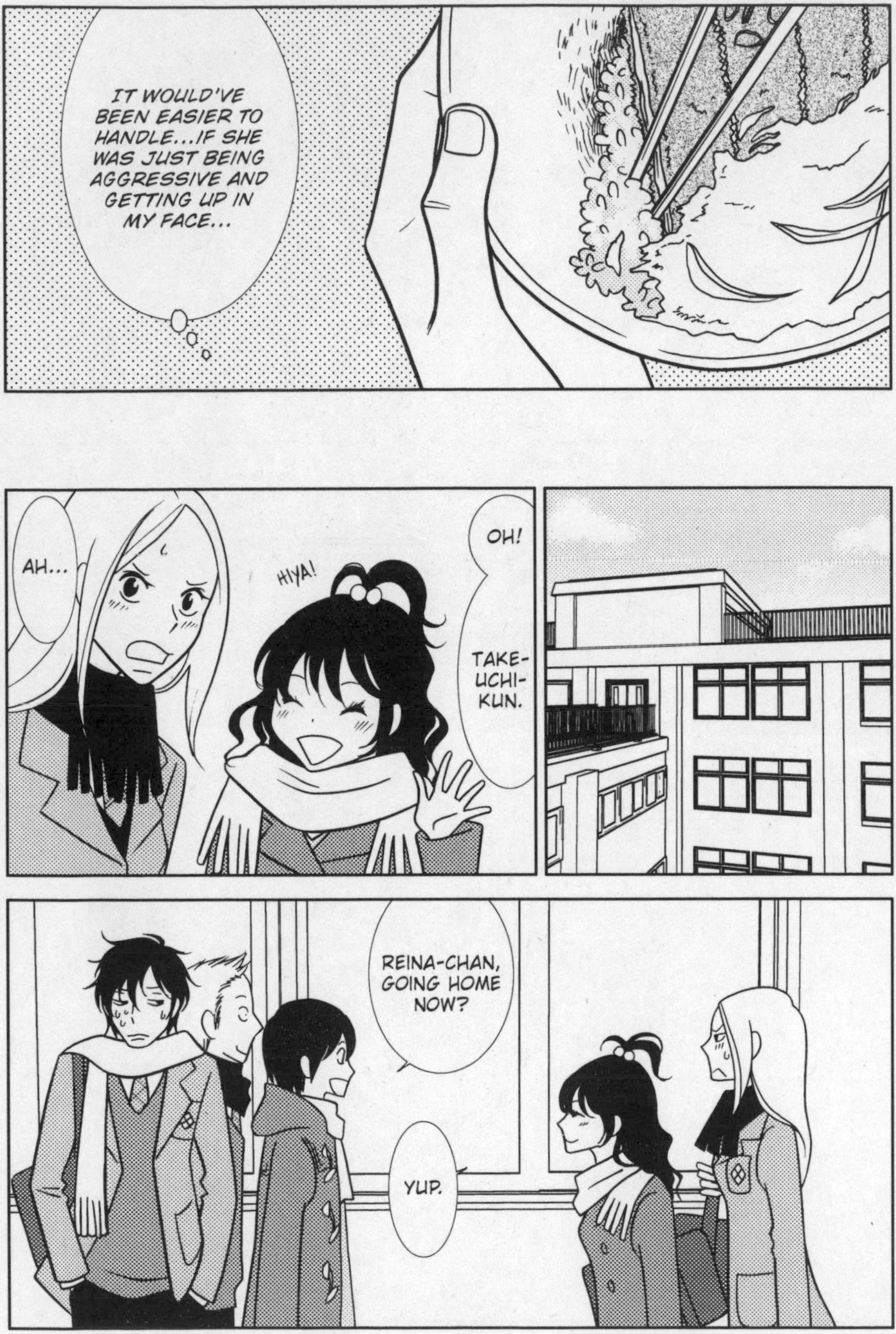
IT WOULD'VE BEEN EASIER TO HANDLE...IF SHE WAS JUST BEING AGGRESSIVE AND GETTING UP IN MY FACE...
OH! TAKE-UCHI-KUN.
HIYA!
AH...
REINA-CHAN, GOING HOME NOW?
YUP.

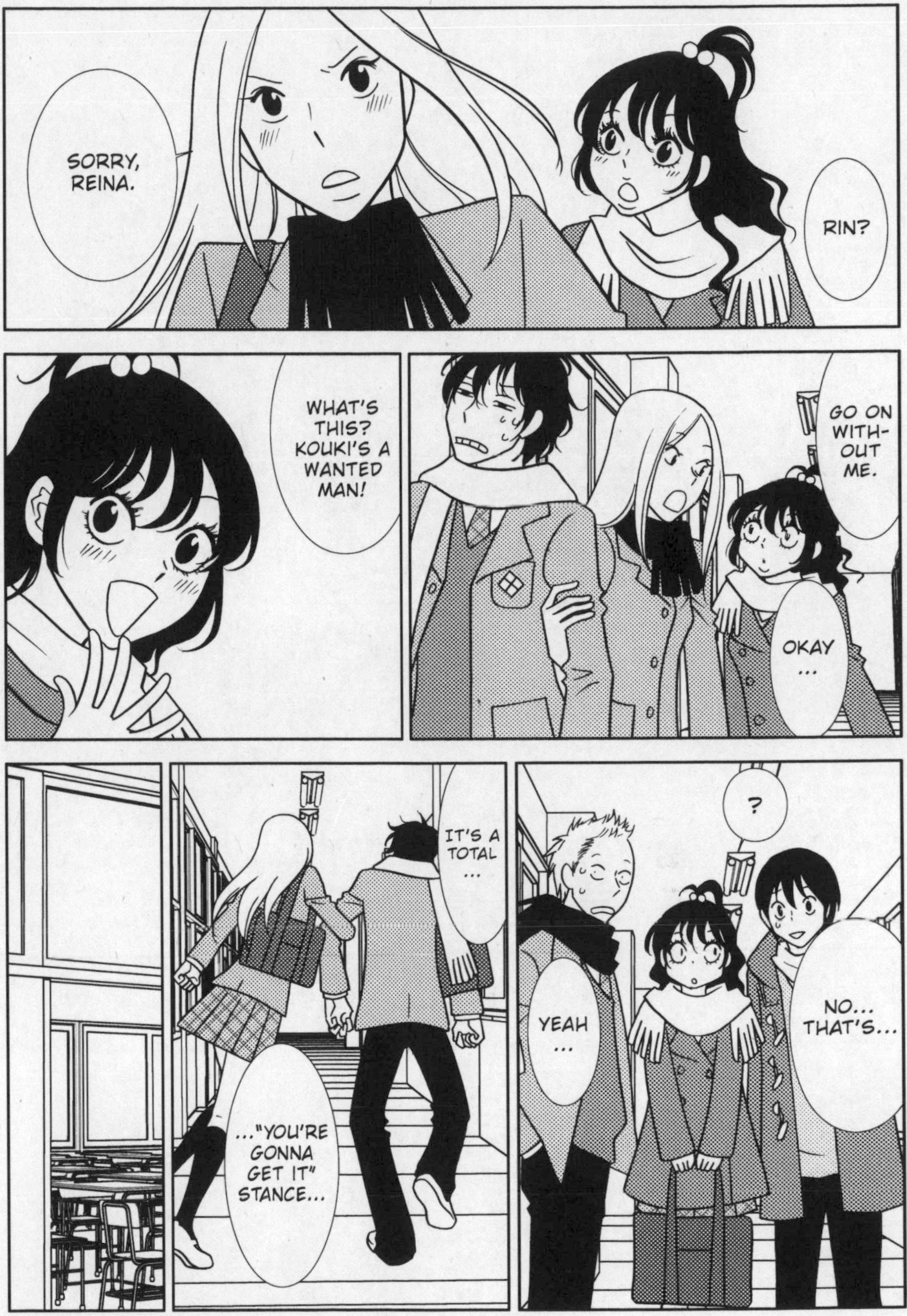
RIN?
SORRY, REINA.
GO ON WITH-OUT ME.
OKAY ...
WHAT'S THIS? KOUKI'S A WANTED MAN!
?
NO... THAT'S...
YEAH ...
IT'S A TOTAL ...
..."YOU'RE GONNA GET IT" STANCE...

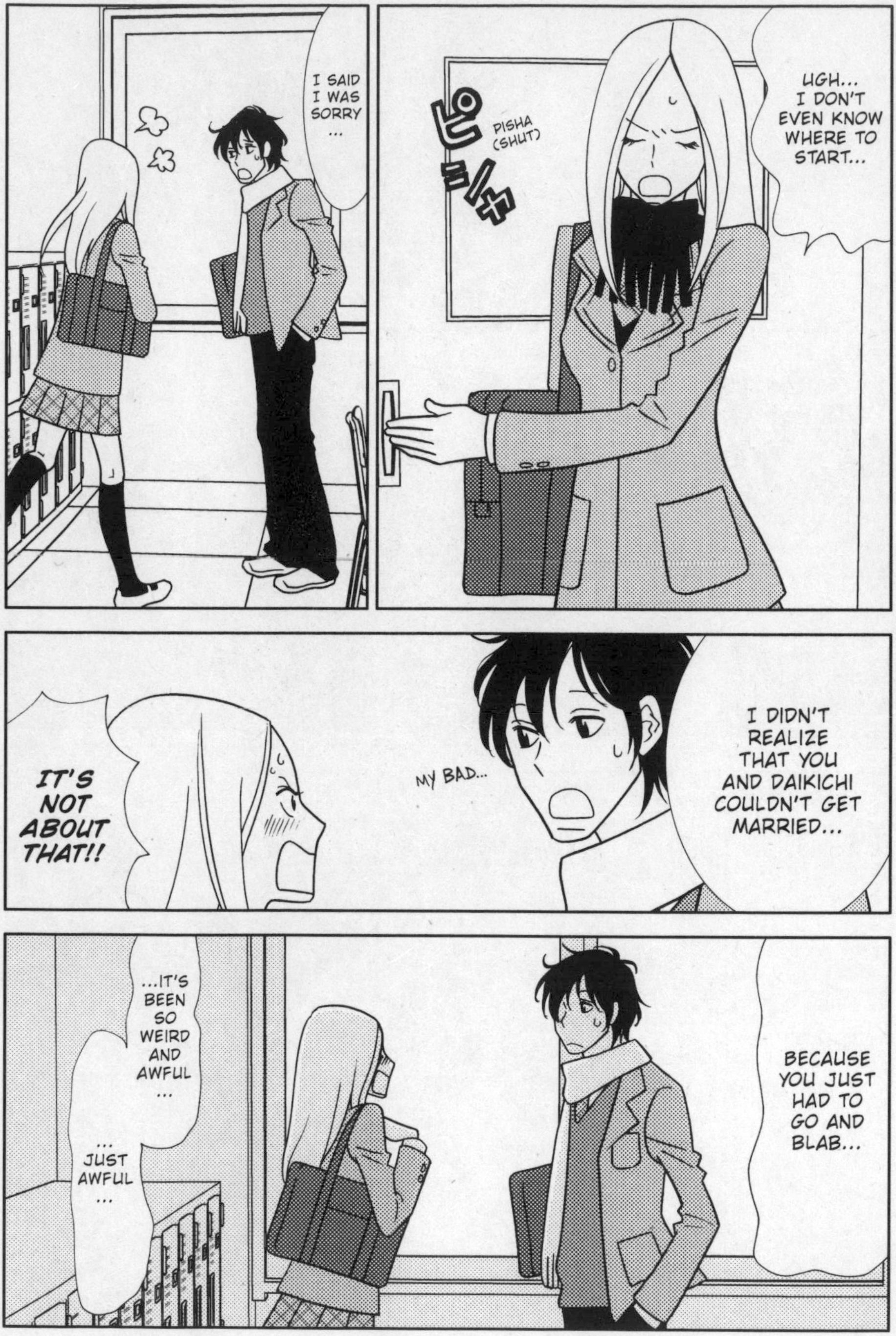
UGH... I DON'T EVEN KNOW WHERE TO START...
ピシャ
PISHA (SHUT)
I SAID I WAS SORRY ...
I DIDN'T REALIZE THAT YOU AND DAIKICHI COULDN'T GET MARRIED...
MY BAD...
IT'S NOT ABOUT THAT!!
BECAUSE YOU JUST HAD TO GO AND BLAB...
...IT'S BEEN SO WEIRD AND AWFUL ...
... JUST AWFUL ...

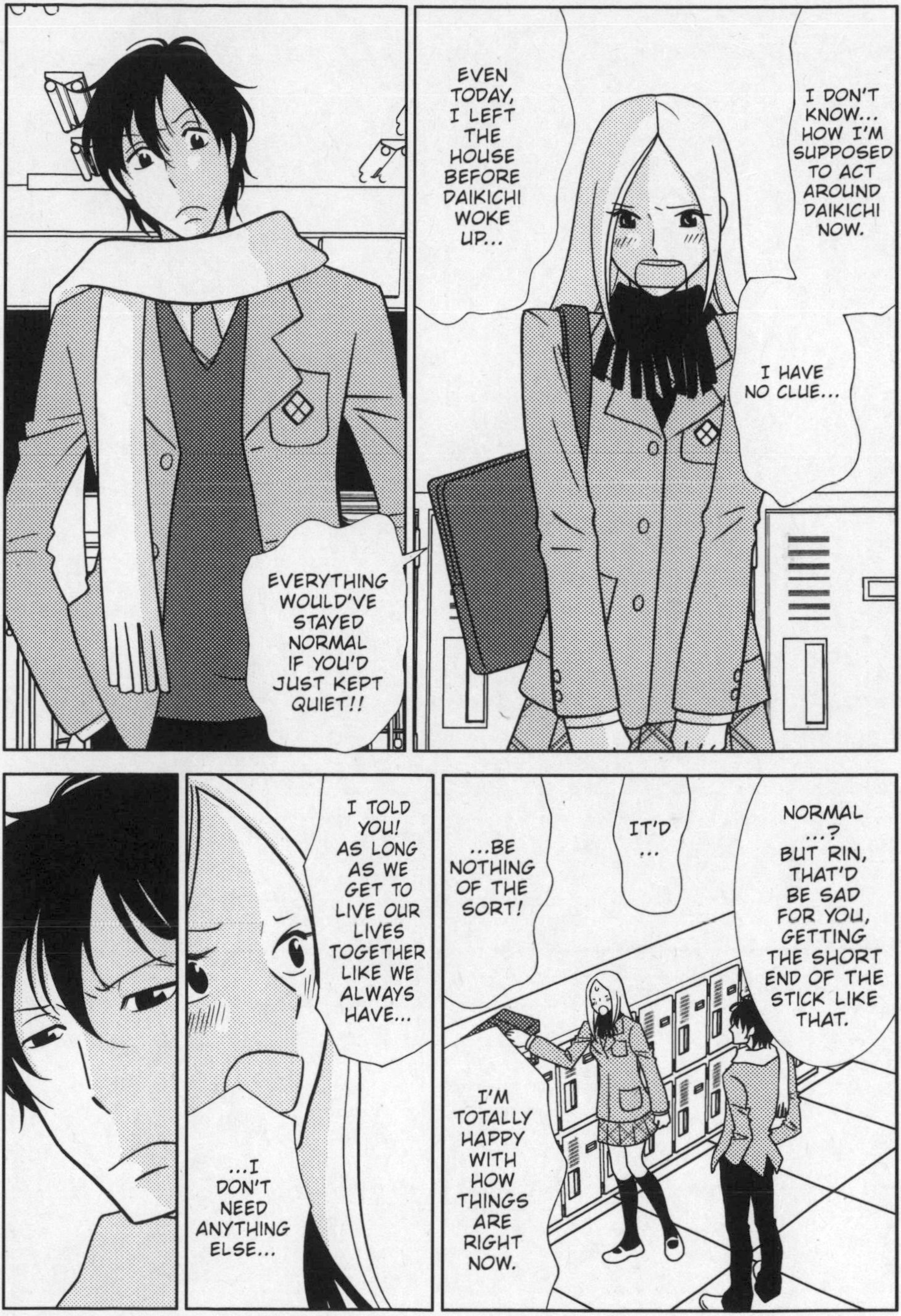
I DON'T KNOW... HOW I'M SUPPOSED TO ACT AROUND DAIKICHI NOW.
EVEN TODAY, I LEFT THE HOUSE BEFORE DAIKICHI WOKE UP...
I HAVE NO CLUE...
EVERYTHING WOULD'VE STAYED NORMAL IF YOU'D JUST KEPT QUIET!!
NORMAL ...? BUT RIN, THAT'D BE SAD FOR YOU, GETTING THE SHORT END OF THE STICK LIKE THAT.
IT'D ...
...BE NOTHING OF THE SORT!
I'M TOTALLY HAPPY WITH HOW THINGS ARE RIGHT NOW.
I TOLD YOU! AS LONG AS WE GET TO LIVE OUR LIVES TOGETHER LIKE WE ALWAYS HAVE...
...I DON'T NEED ANYTHING ELSE...

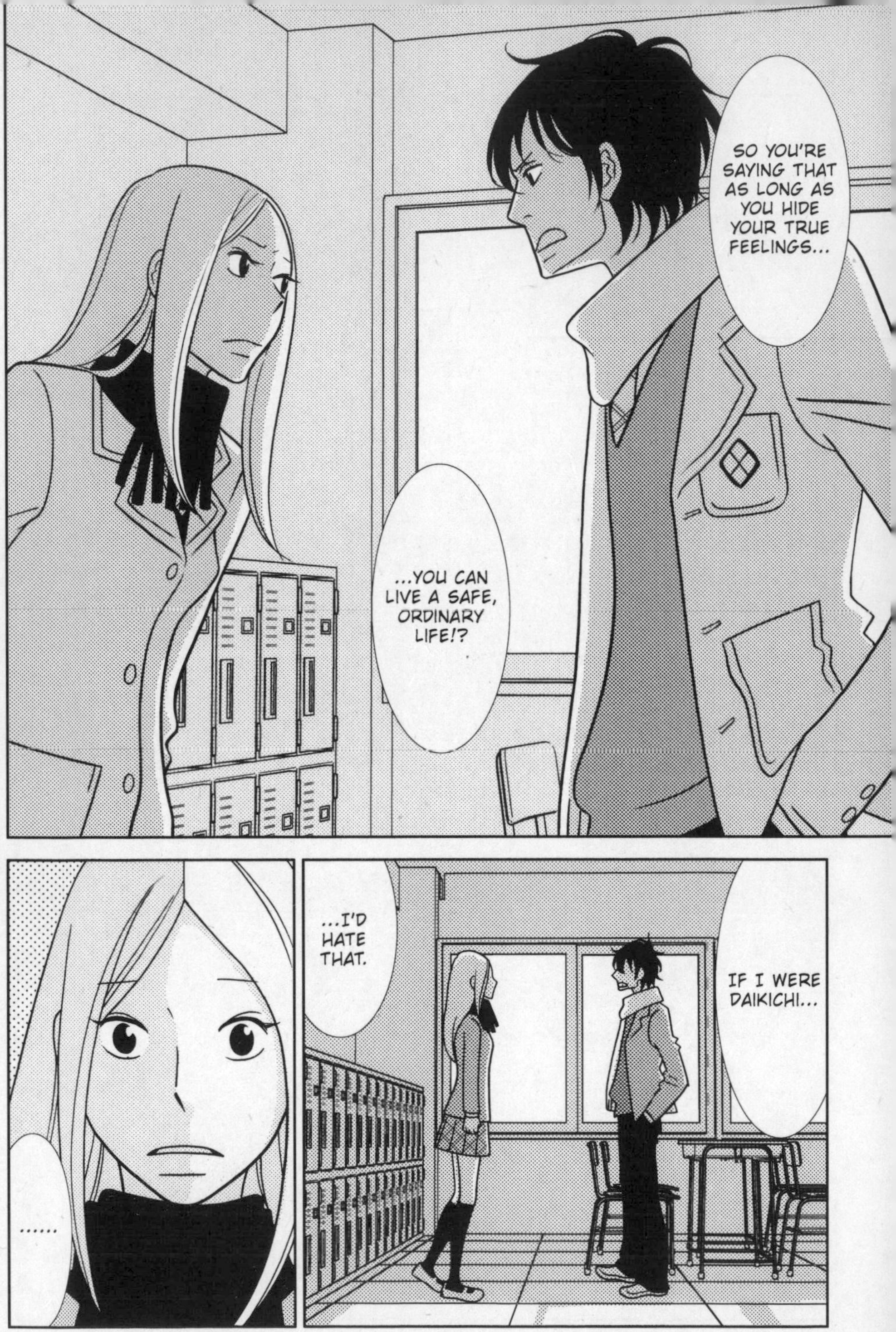
SO YOU'RE SAYING THAT AS LONG AS YOU HIDE YOUR TRUE FEELINGS...
...YOU CAN LIVE A SAFE, ORDINARY LIFE!?
IF I WERE DAIKICHI...
...I'D HATE THAT.
......

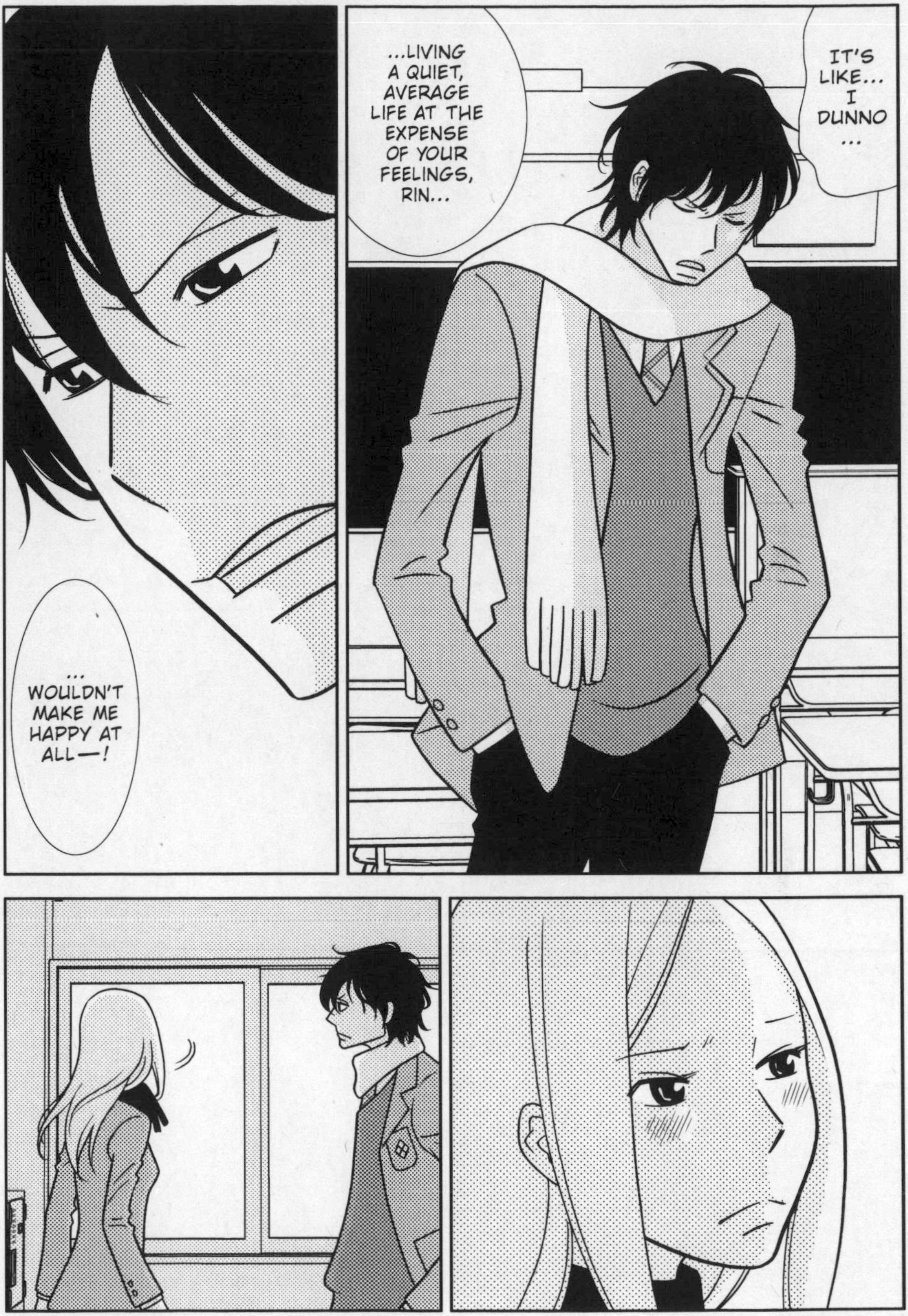
IT'S LIKE... I DUNNO ...
...LIVING A QUIET, AVERAGE LIFE AT THE EXPENSE OF YOUR FEELINGS, RIN...
... WOULDN'T MAKE ME HAPPY AT ALL—!

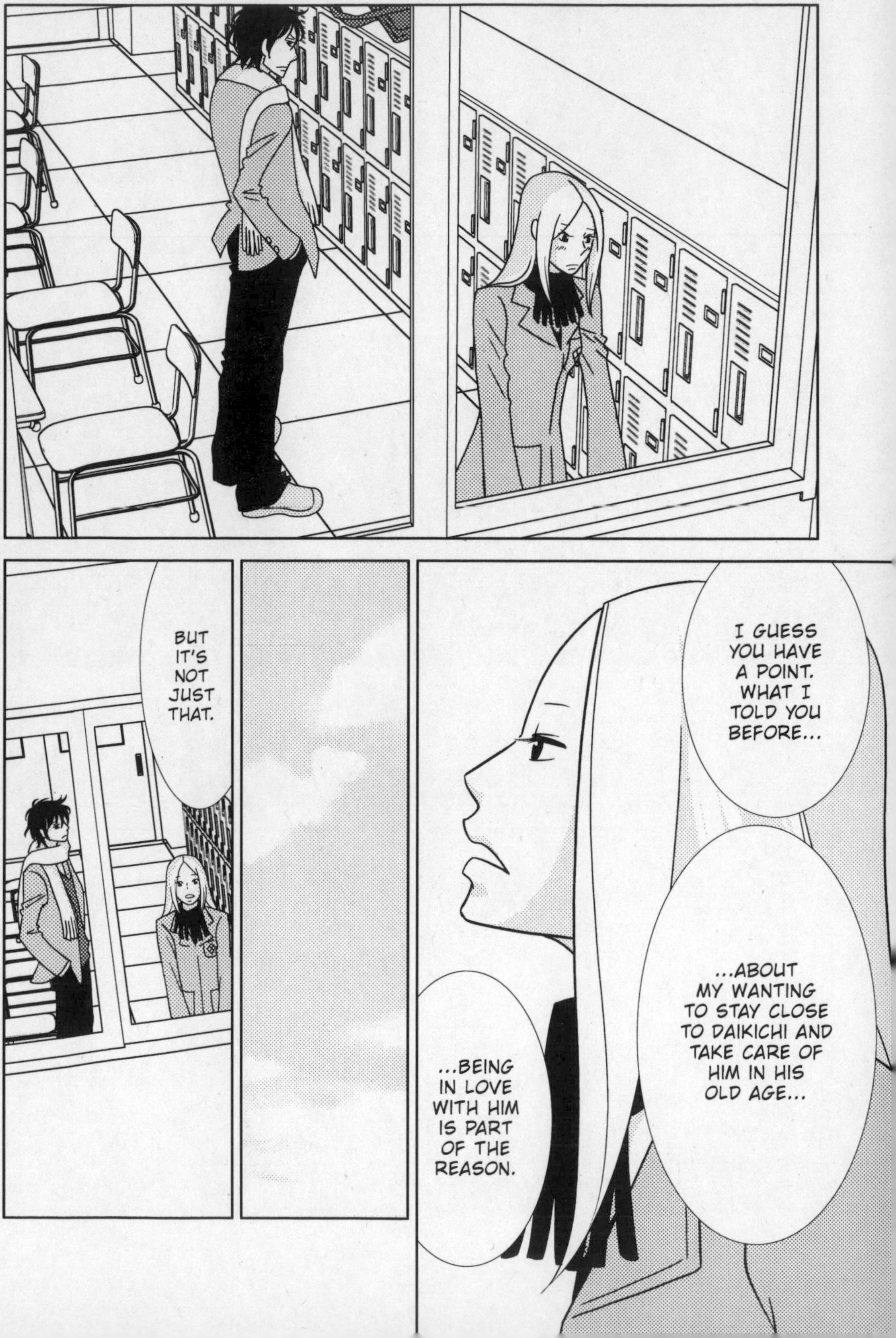
I GUESS YOU HAVE A POINT. WHAT I TOLD YOU BEFORE...
...ABOUT MY WANTING TO STAY CLOSE TO DAIKICHI AND TAKE CARE OF HIM IN HIS OLD AGE...
...BEING IN LOVE WITH HIM IS PART OF THE REASON.
BUT IT'S NOT JUST THAT.

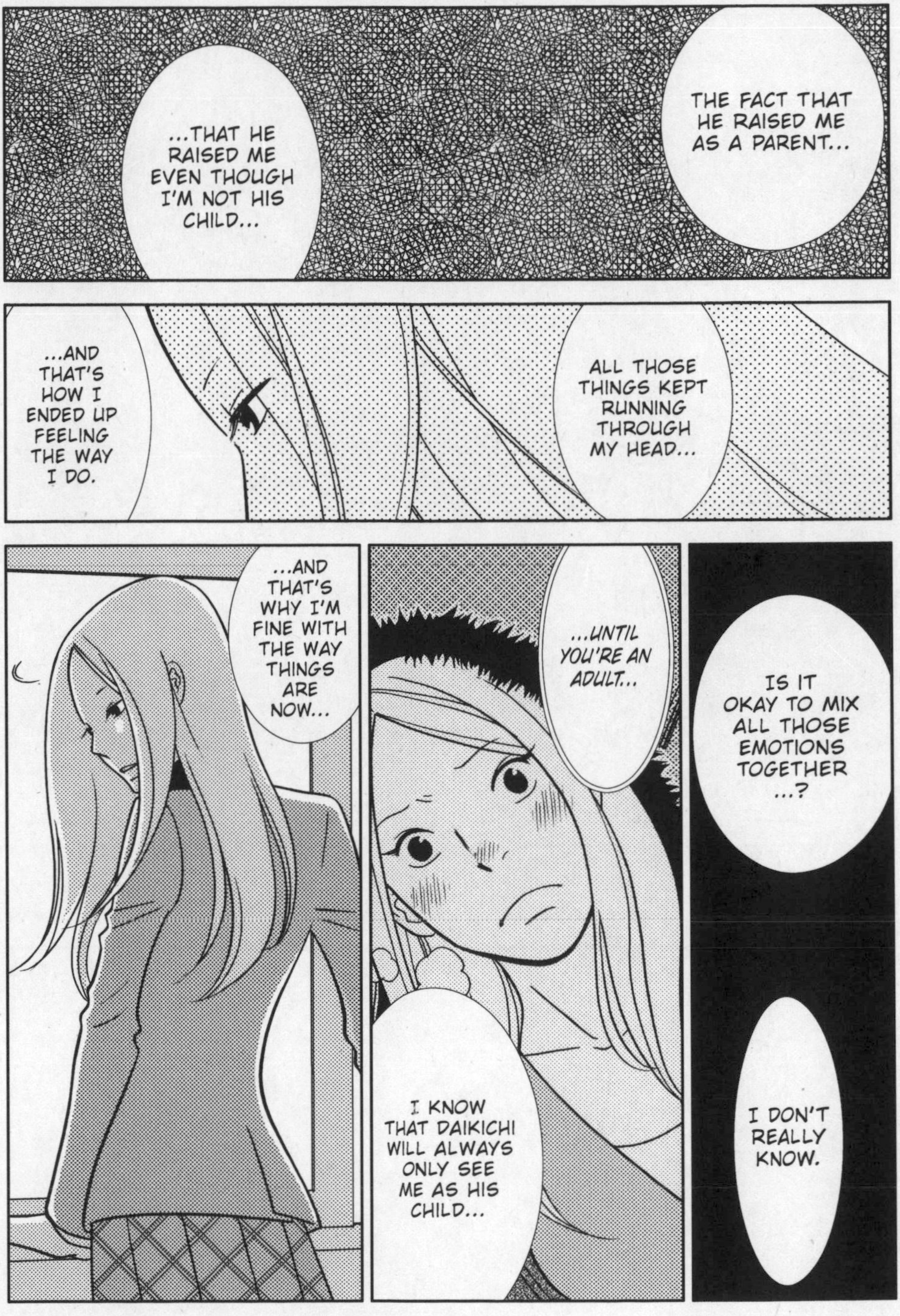
THE FACT THAT HE RAISED ME AS A PARENT...
...THAT HE RAISED ME EVEN THOUGH I'M NOT HIS CHILD...
ALL THOSE THINGS KEPT RUNNING THROUGH MY HEAD...
...AND THAT'S HOW I ENDED UP FEELING THE WAY I DO.
IS IT OKAY TO MIX ALL THOSE EMOTIONS TOGETHER ...?
I DON'T REALLY KNOW.
...UNTIL YOU'RE AN ADULT...
I KNOW THAT DAIKICHI WILL ALWAYS ONLY SEE ME AS HIS CHILD...
...AND THAT'S WHY I'M FINE WITH THE WAY THINGS ARE NOW...

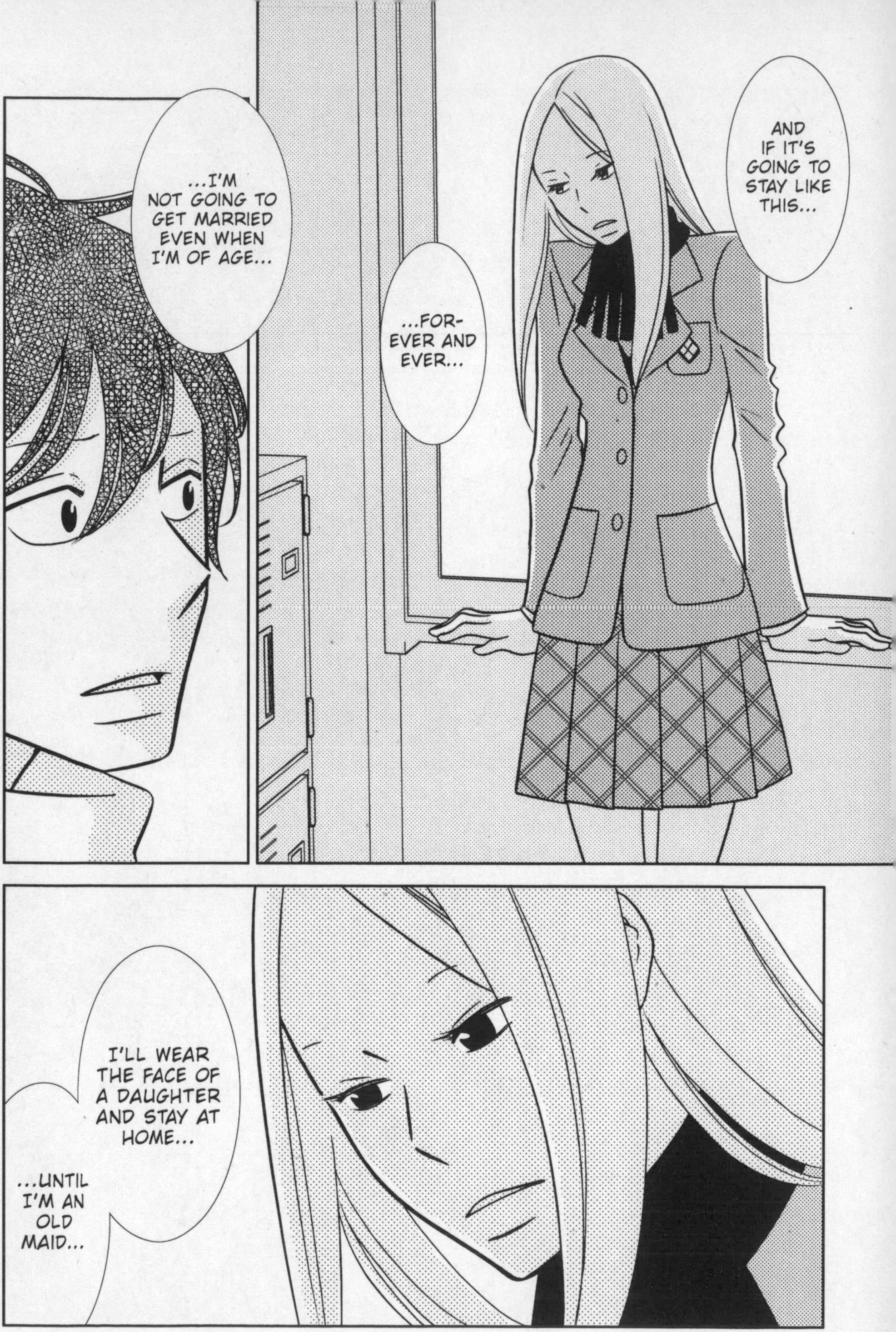
AND IF IT'S GOING TO STAY LIKE THIS...
...FOR-EVER AND EVER...
...I'M NOT GOING TO GET MARRIED EVEN WHEN I'M OF AGE...
I'LL WEAR THE FACE OF A DAUGHTER AND STAY AT HOME...
...UNTIL I'M AN OLD MAID...

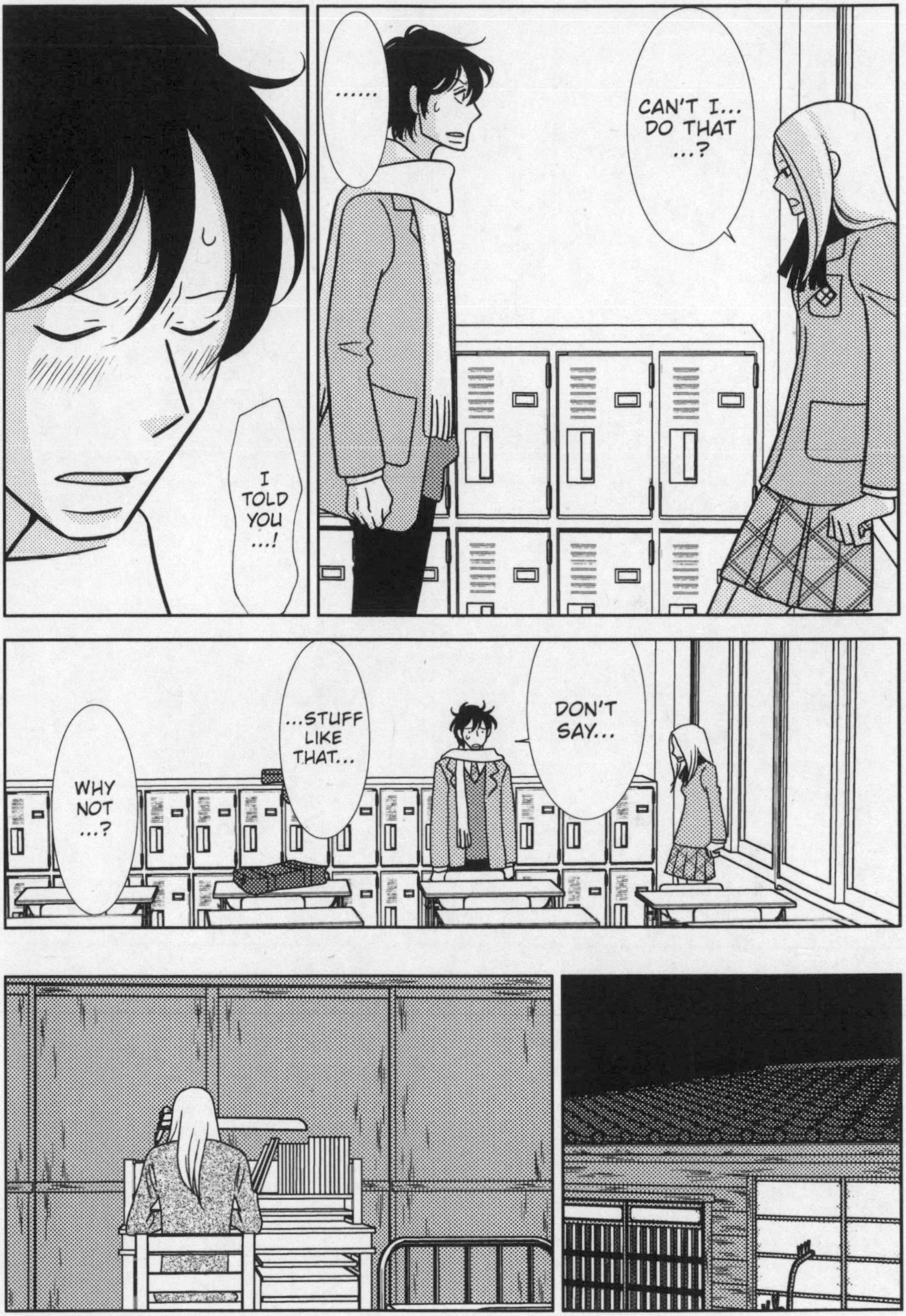
CAN'T I... DO THAT ...?
......
I TOLD YOU ...!
DON'T SAY...
...STUFF LIKE THAT...
WHY NOT ...?

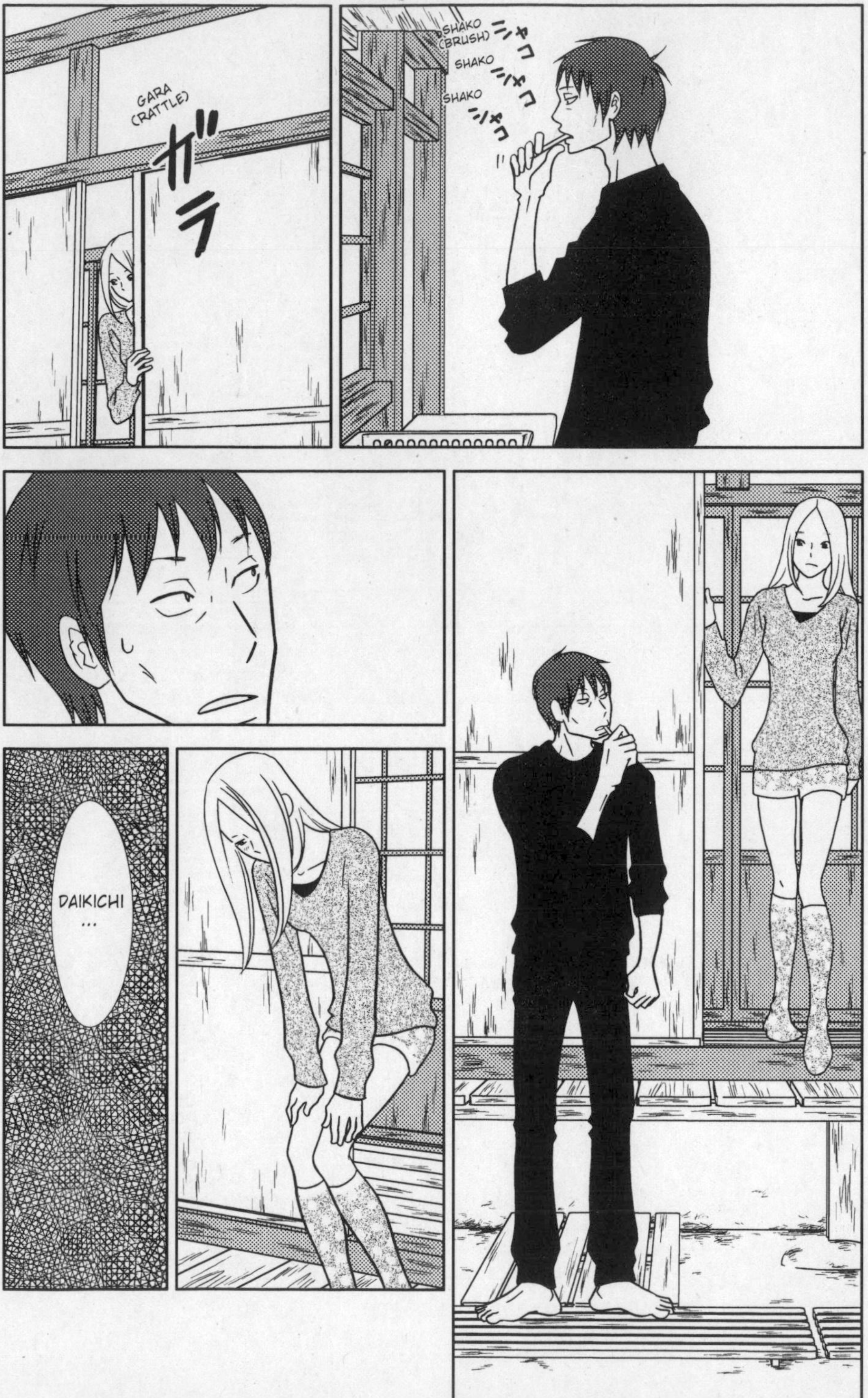
SHAKO (BRUSH)
シャコ
SHAKO
シャコ
SHAKO
シャコ
GARA (RATTLE)
ガラ
DAIKICHI ...

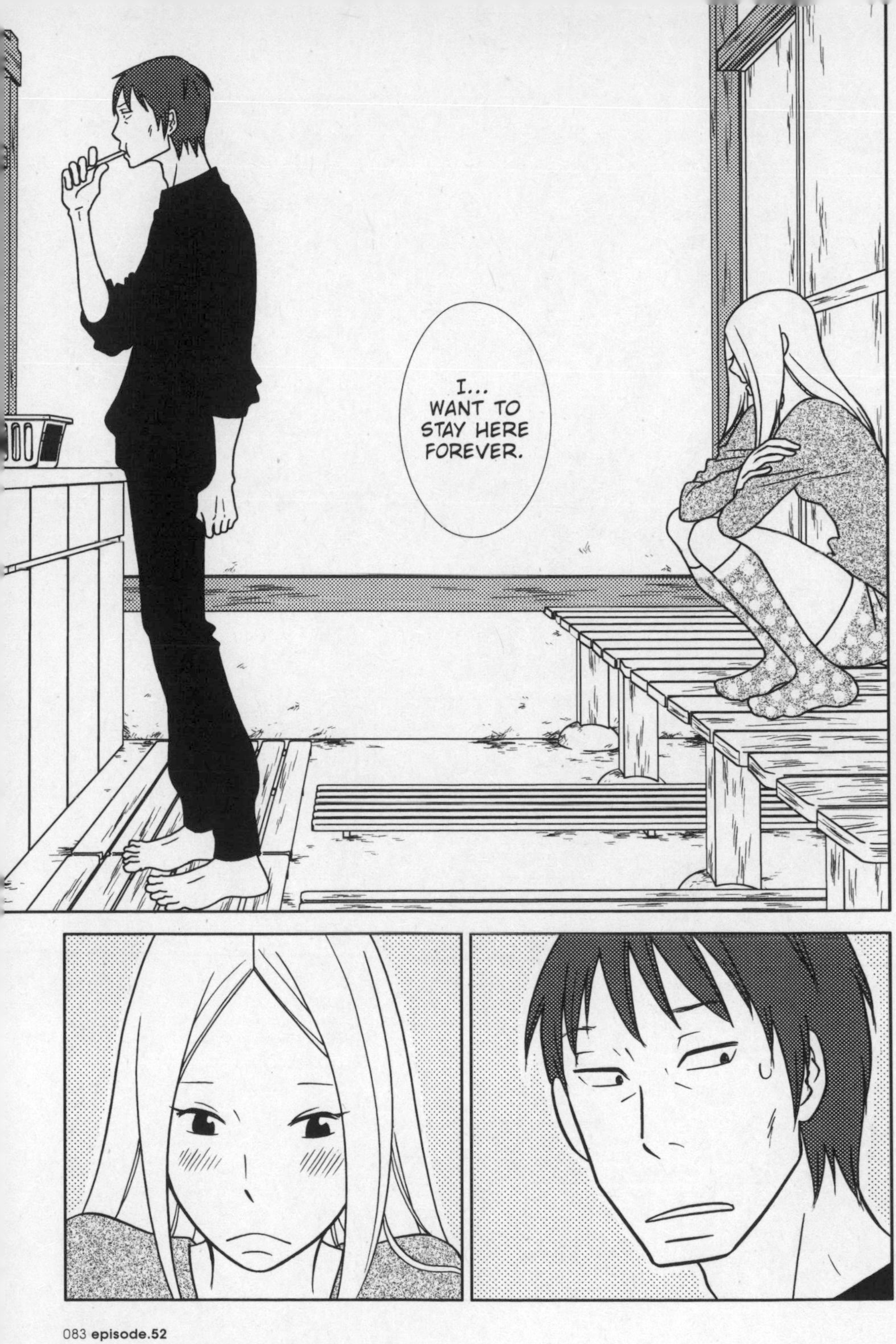
I...
WANT TO
STAY HERE
FOREVER.

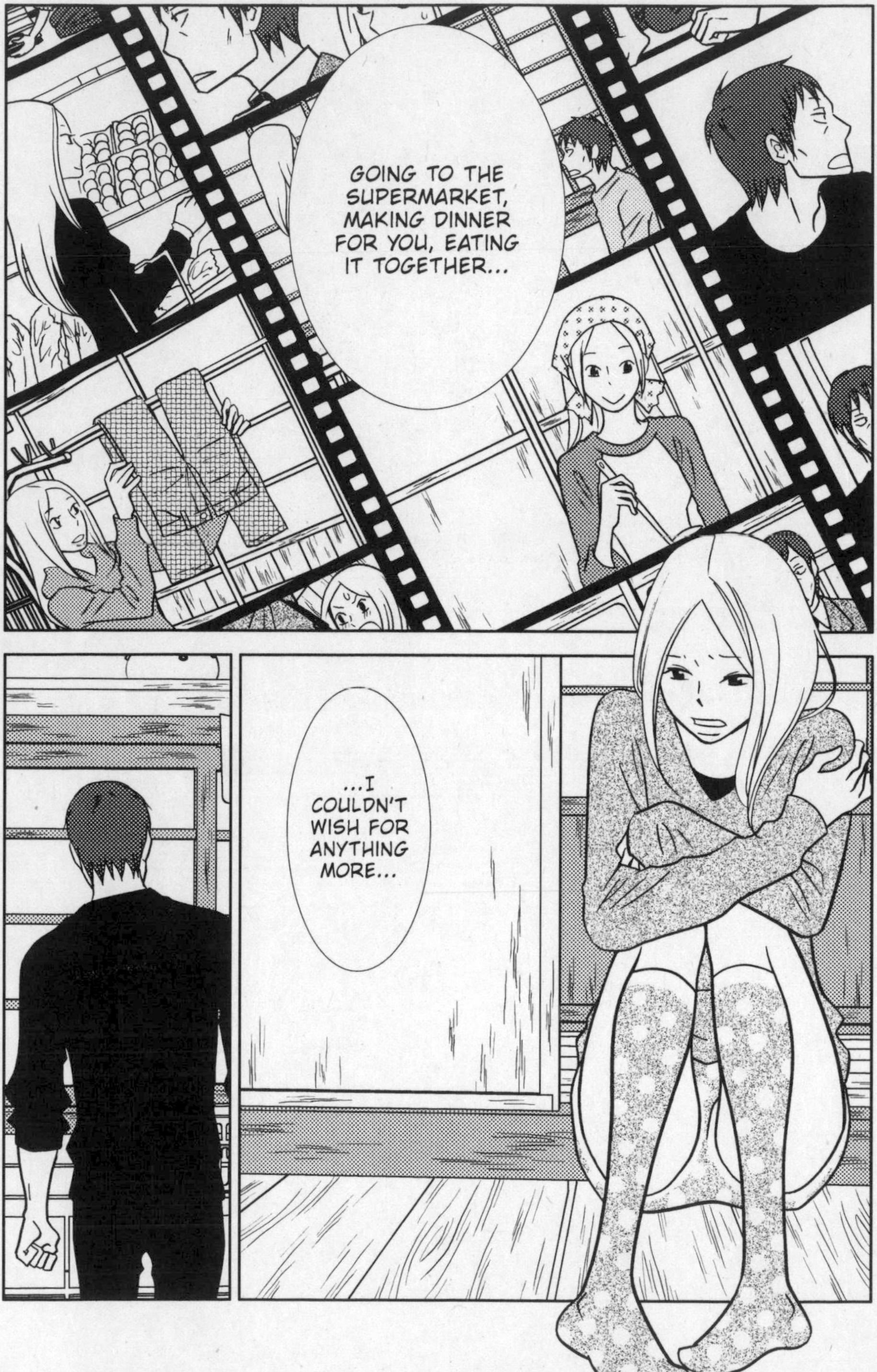
GOING TO THE SUPERMARKET, MAKING DINNER FOR YOU, EATING IT TOGETHER...
...I COULDN'T WISH FOR ANYTHING MORE...

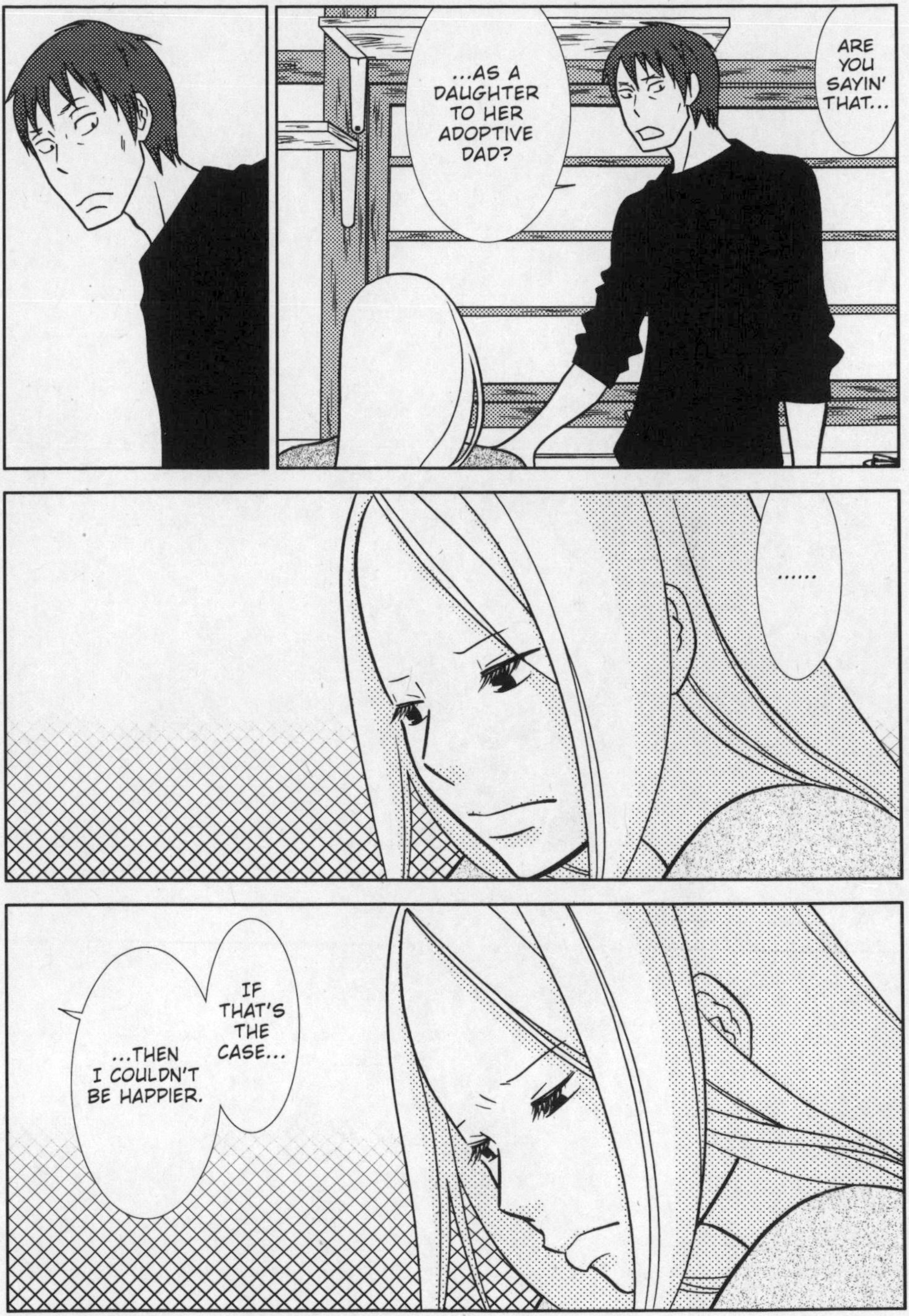
ARE YOU SAYIN' THAT...
...AS A DAUGHTER TO HER ADOPTIVE DAD?
......
IF THAT'S THE CASE...
...THEN I COULDN'T BE HAPPIER.

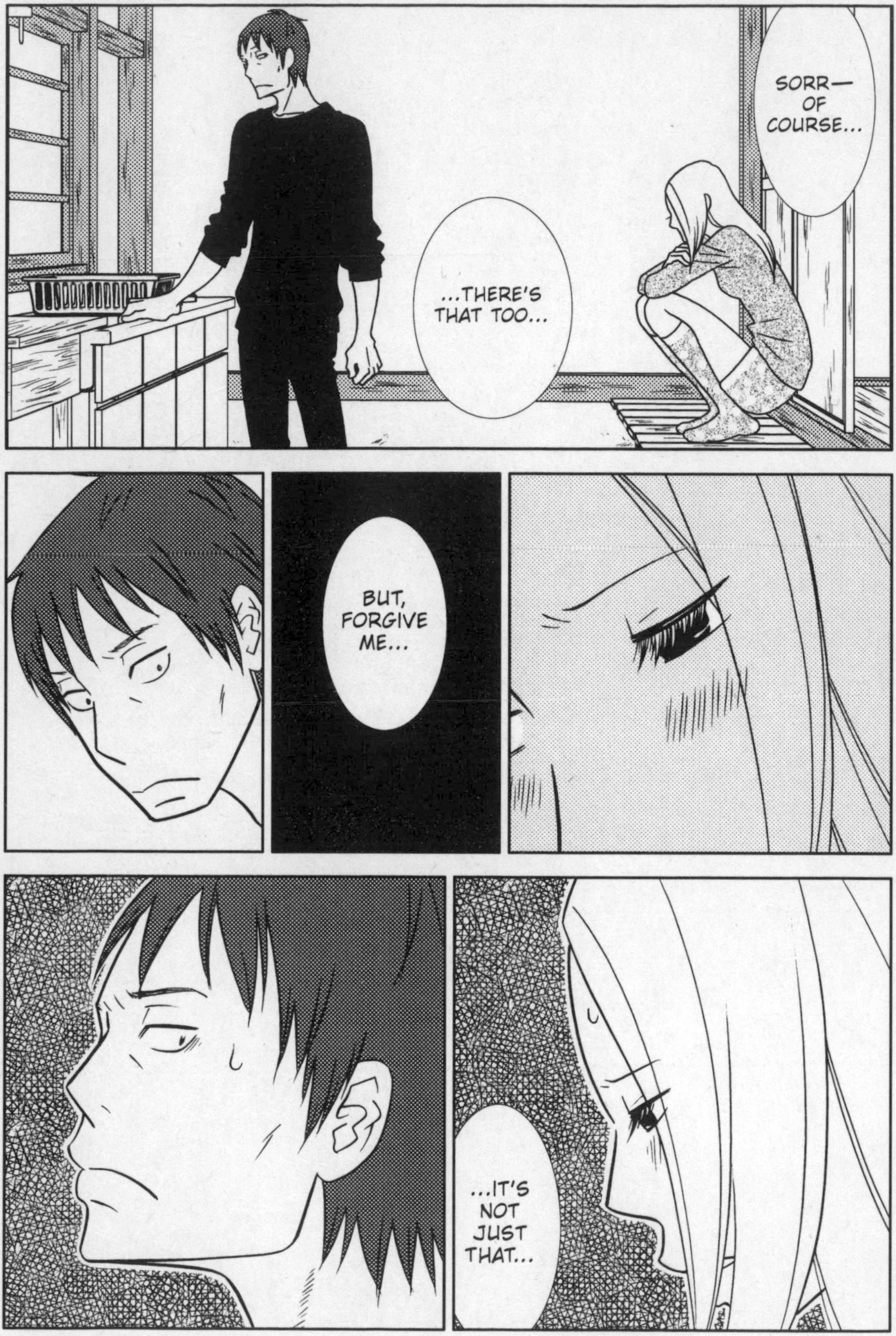
SORR— OF COURSE...
...THERE'S THAT TOO...
BUT, FORGIVE ME...
...IT'S NOT JUST THAT...

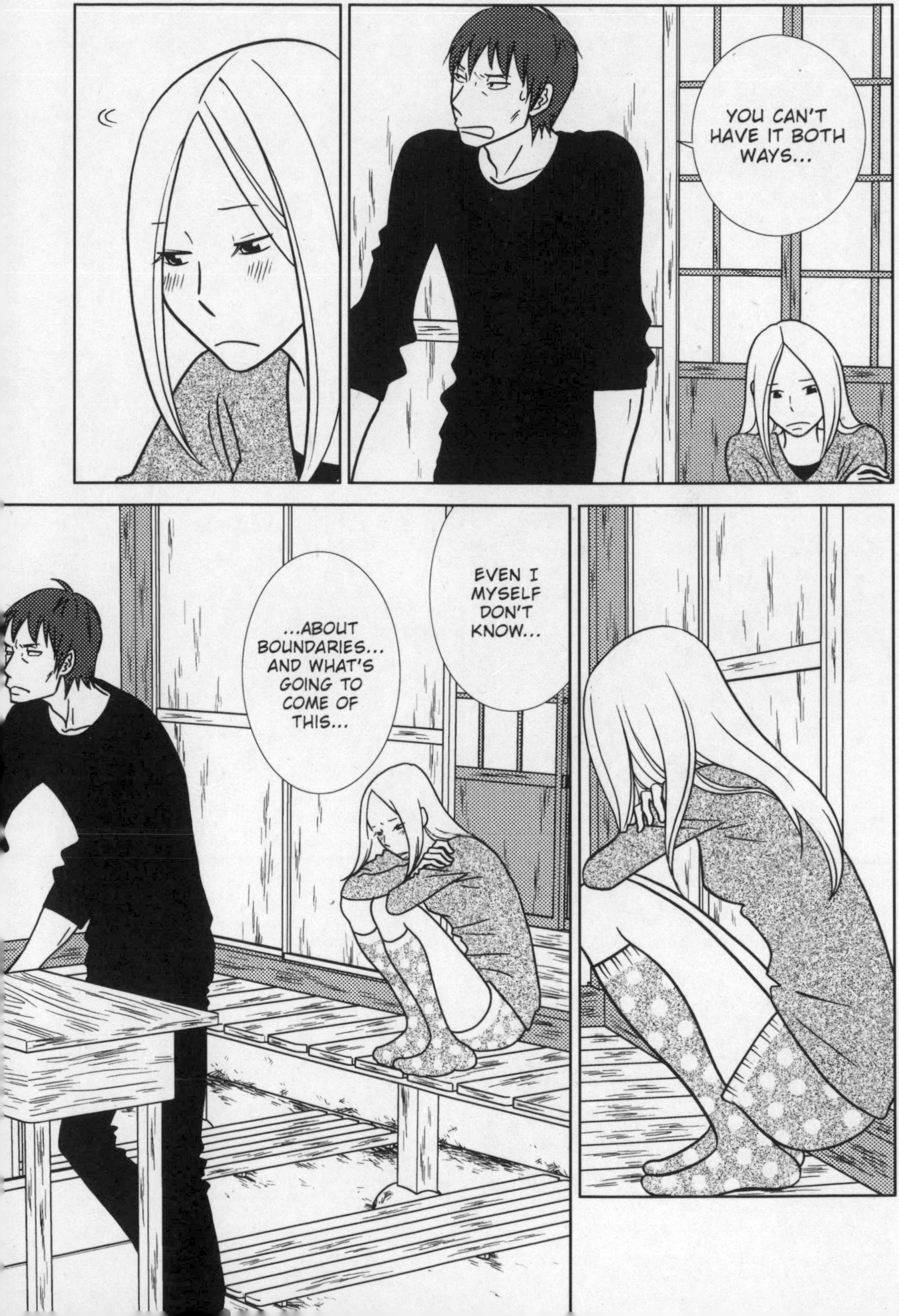
YOU CAN'T HAVE IT BOTH WAYS...
EVEN I MYSELF DON'T KNOW...
...ABOUT BOUNDARIES... AND WHAT'S GOING TO COME OF THIS...

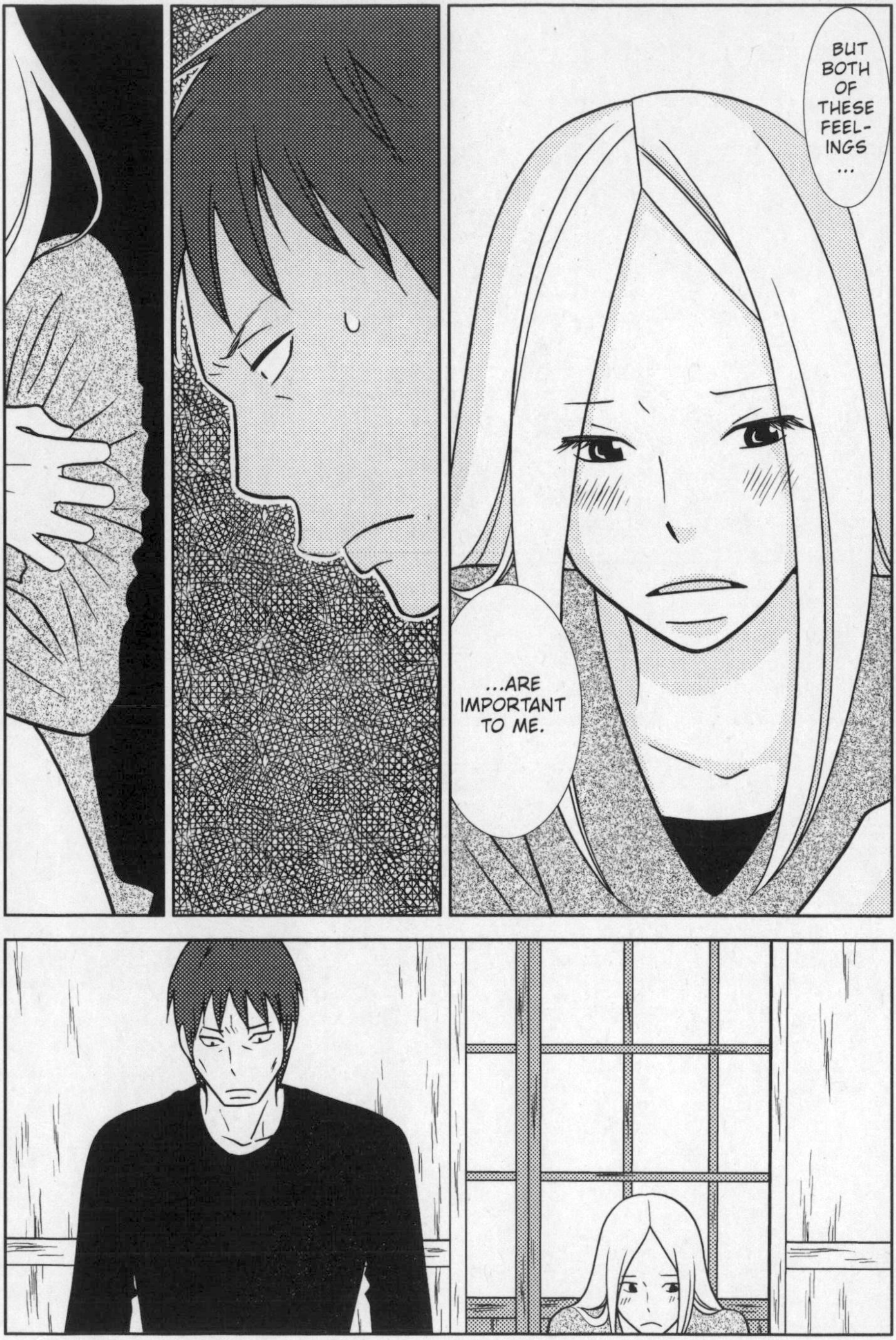
BUT BOTH OF THESE FEEL-INGS ...
...ARE IMPORTANT TO ME.

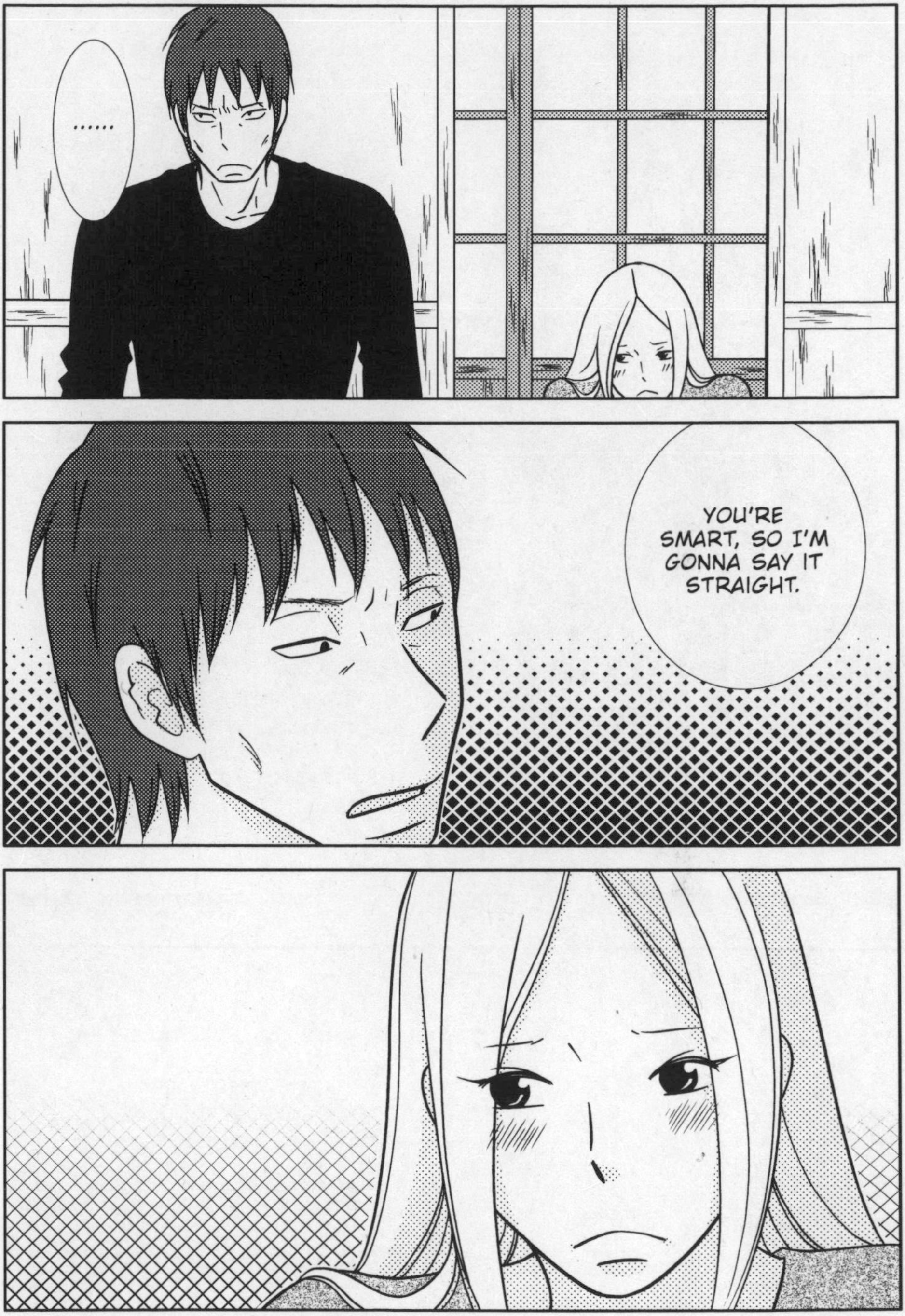
......
YOU'RE SMART, SO I'M GONNA SAY IT STRAIGHT.

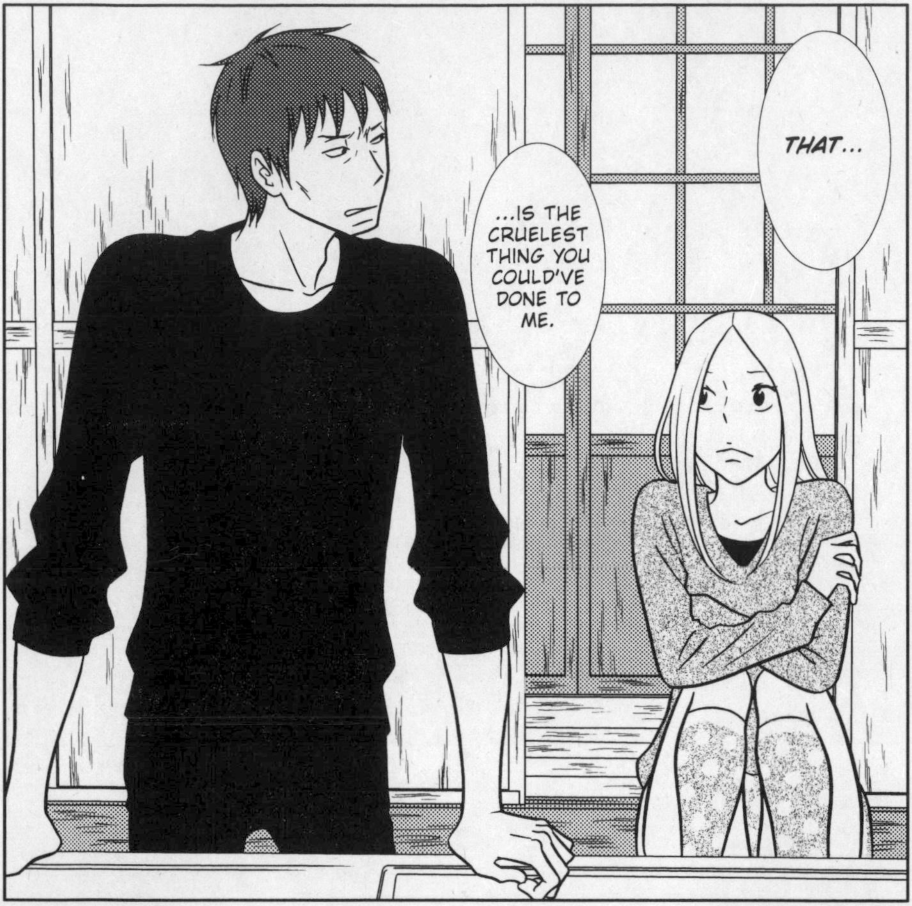
THAT...
...IS THE CRUELEST THING YOU COULD'VE DONE TO ME.
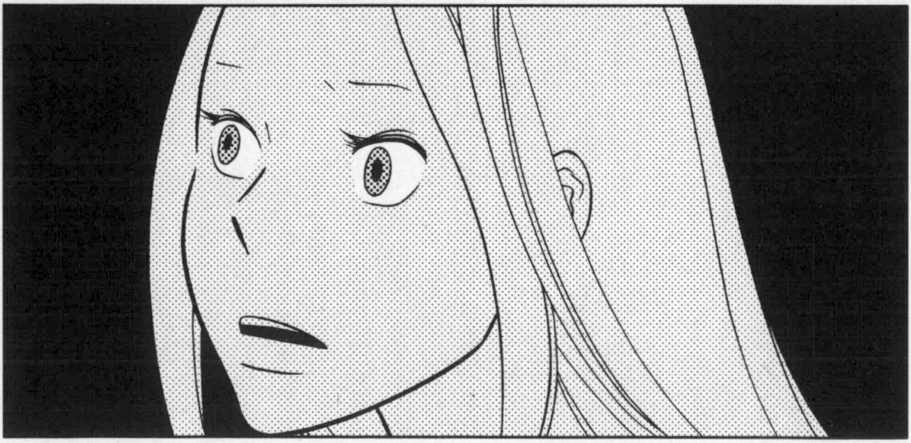

BUNNY**DROP**

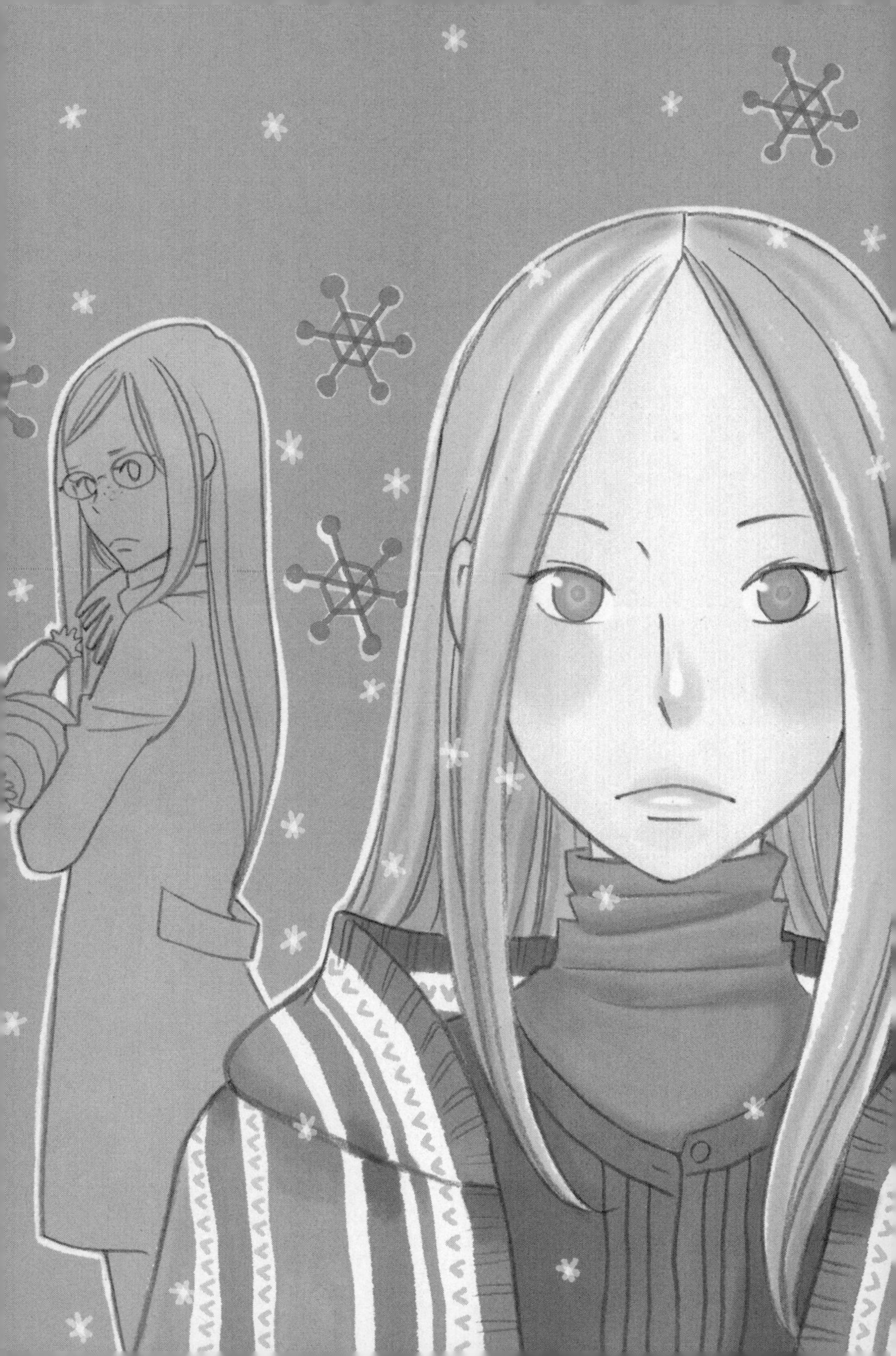

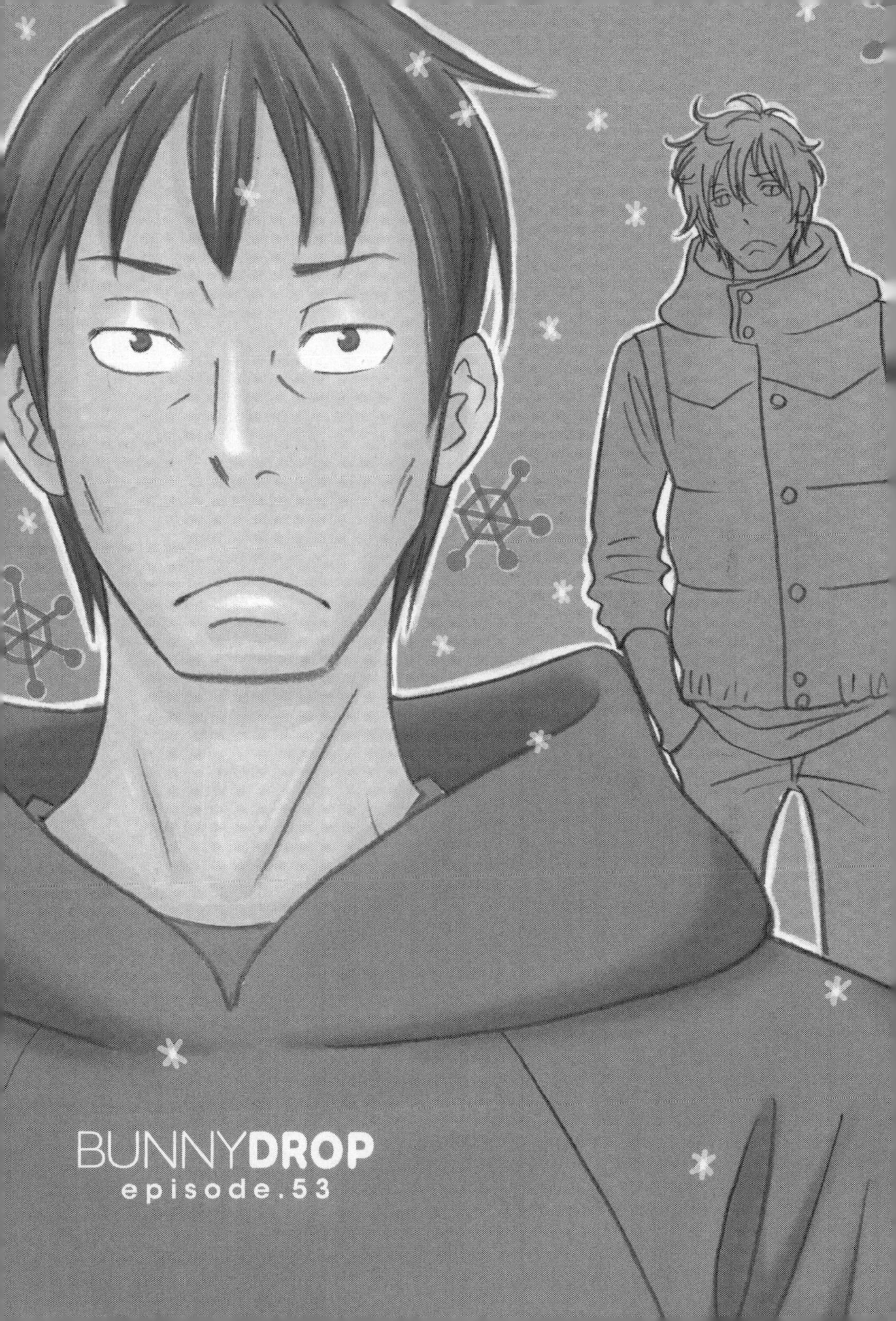
BUNNY DROP
episode.53

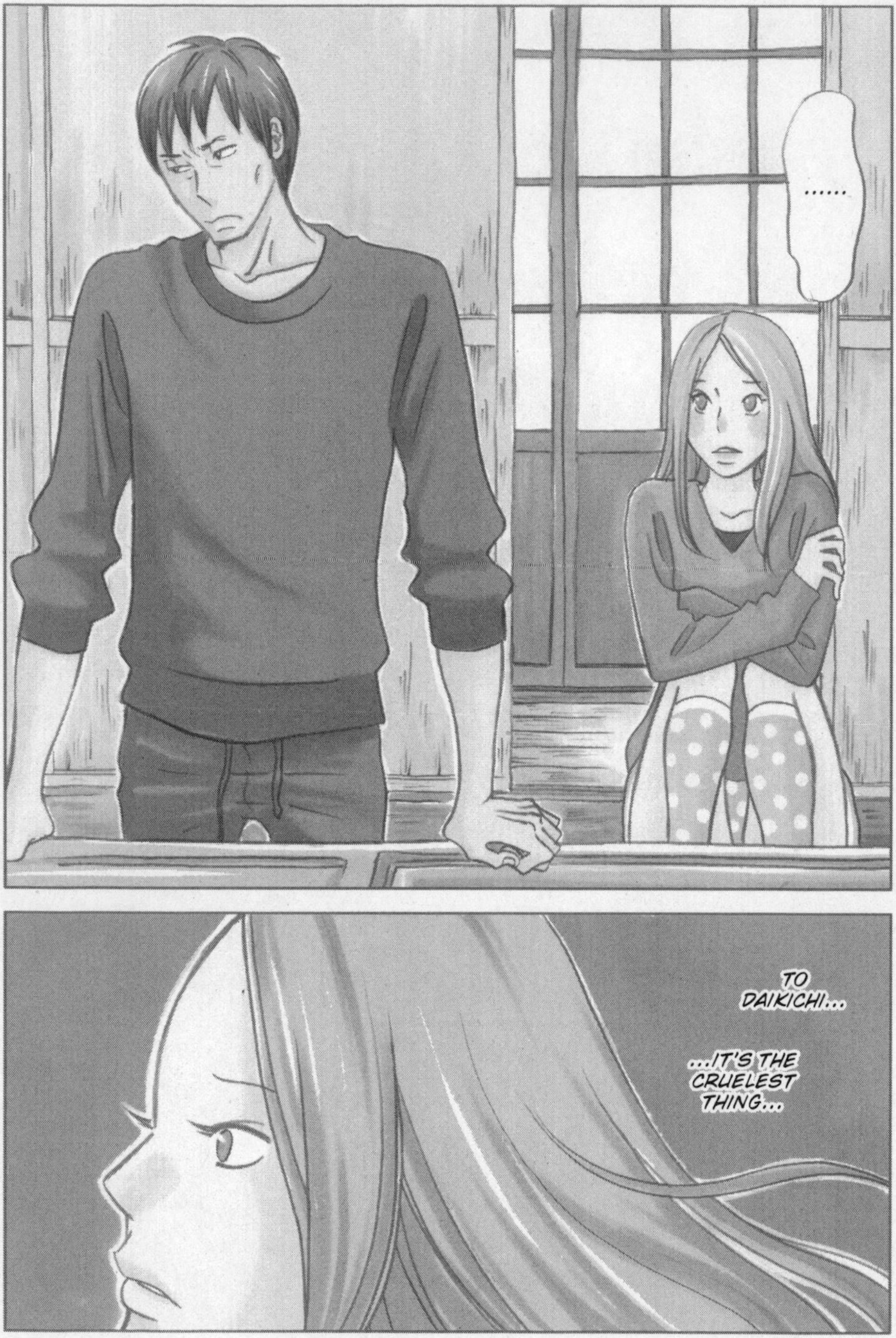
......
TO DAIKICHI...
...IT'S THE CRUELEST THING...

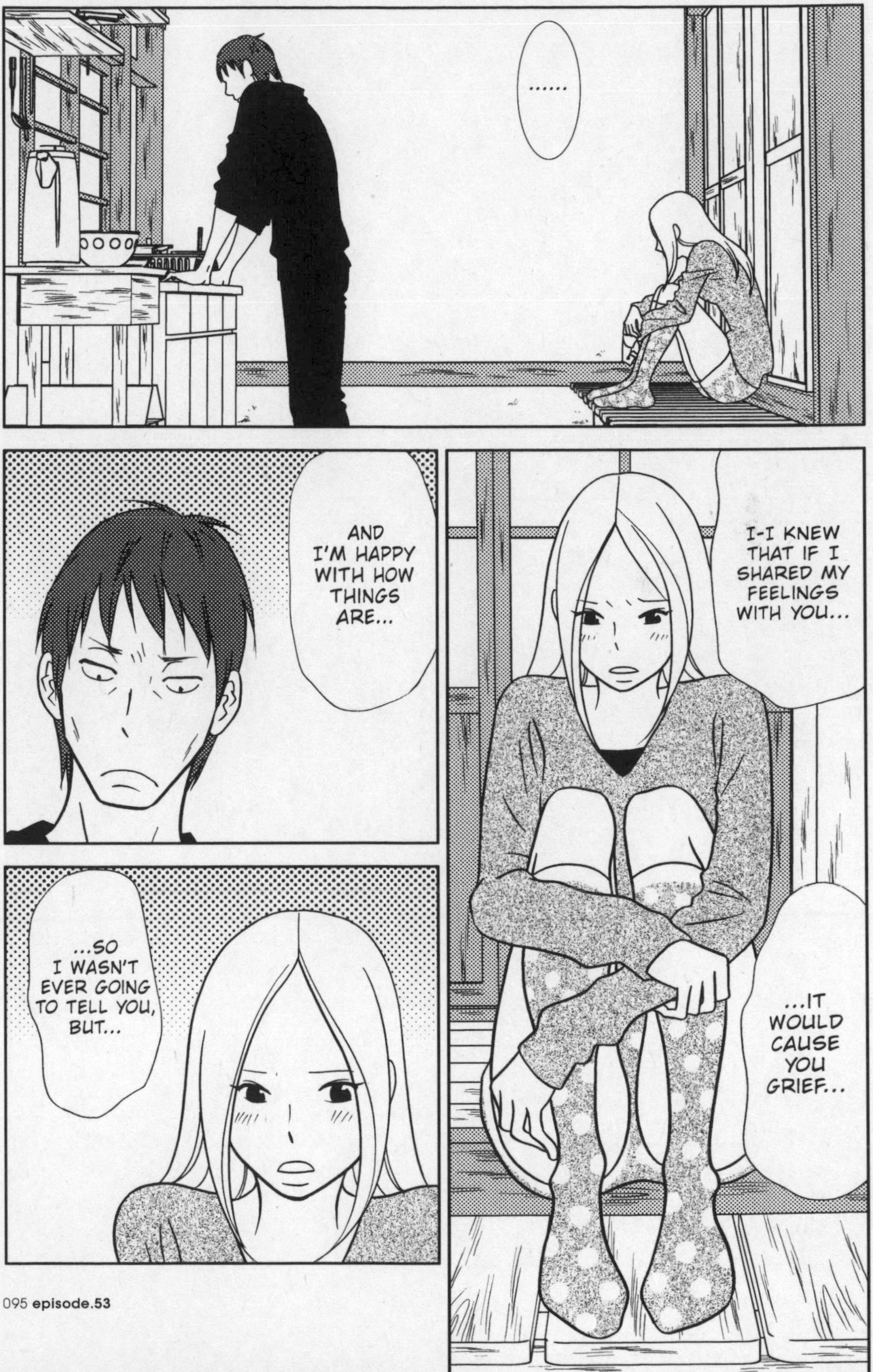
......
I-I KNEW THAT IF I SHARED MY FEELINGS WITH YOU...
...IT WOULD CAUSE YOU GRIEF...
AND I'M HAPPY WITH HOW THINGS ARE...
...SO I WASN'T EVER GOING TO TELL YOU, BUT...

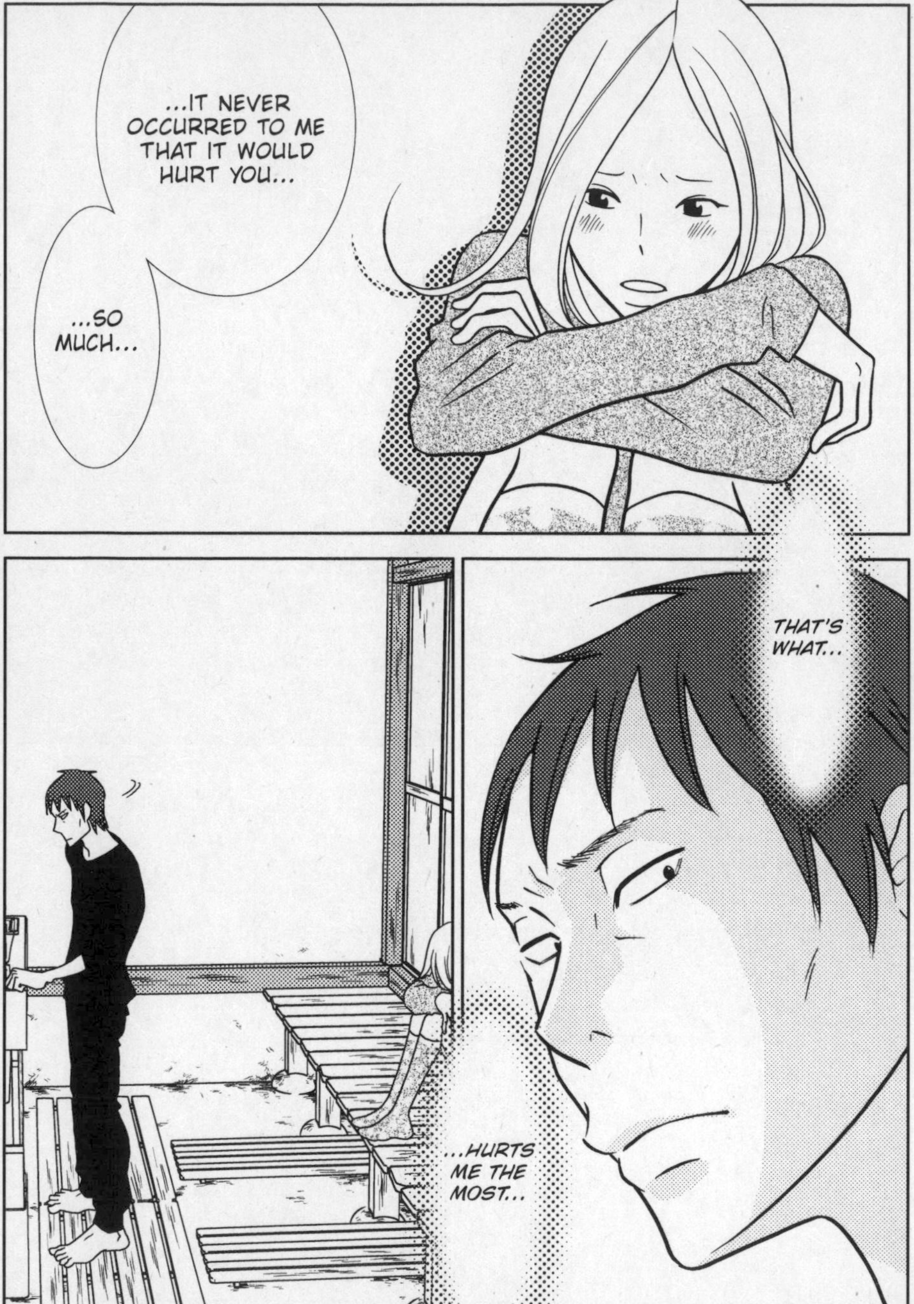
...IT NEVER OCCURRED TO ME THAT IT WOULD HURT YOU...
...SO MUCH...
THAT'S WHAT...
...HURTS ME THE MOST...

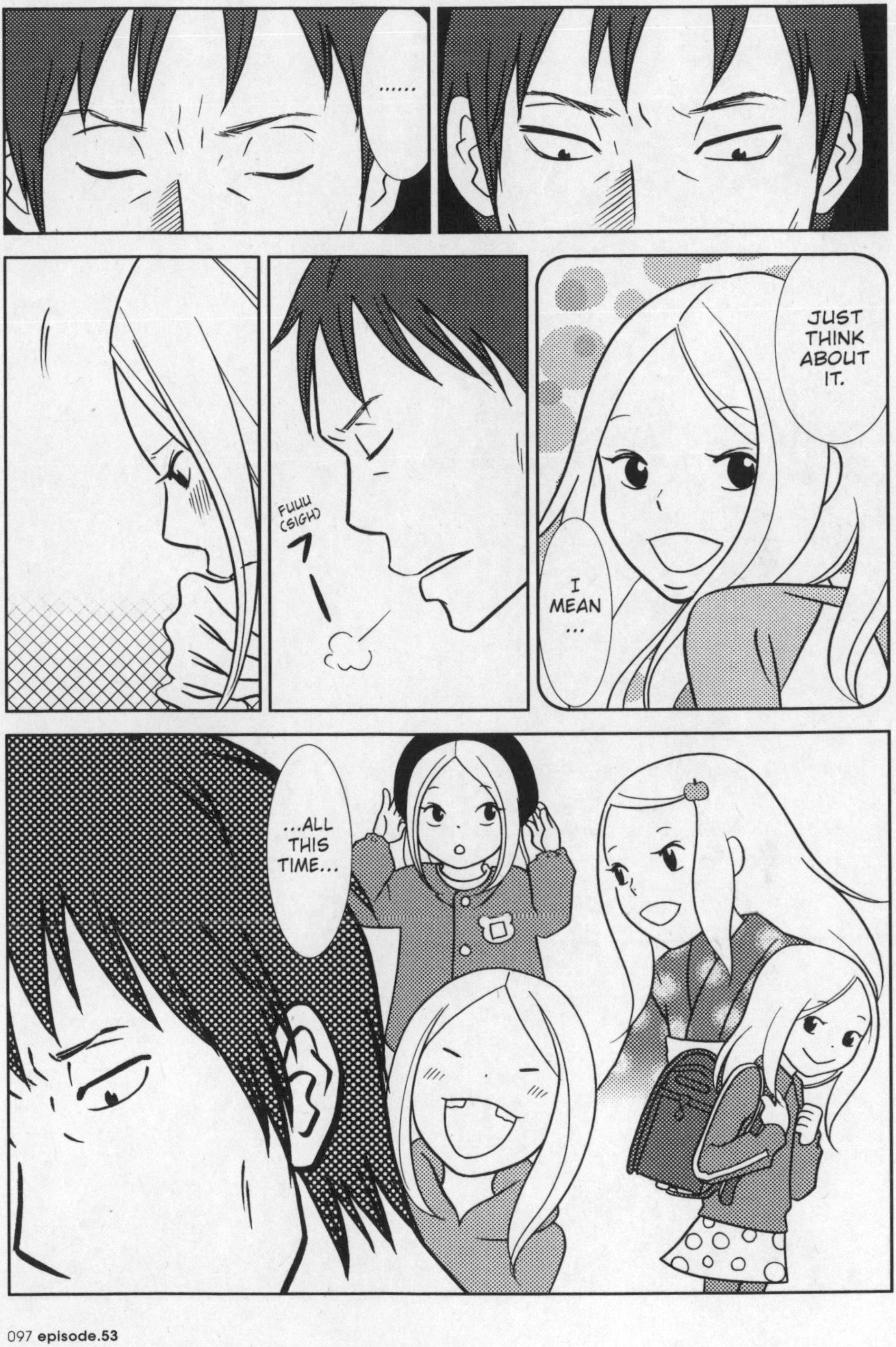
......
JUST THINK ABOUT IT.
I MEAN ...
FUUU (SIGH)
...ALL THIS TIME...

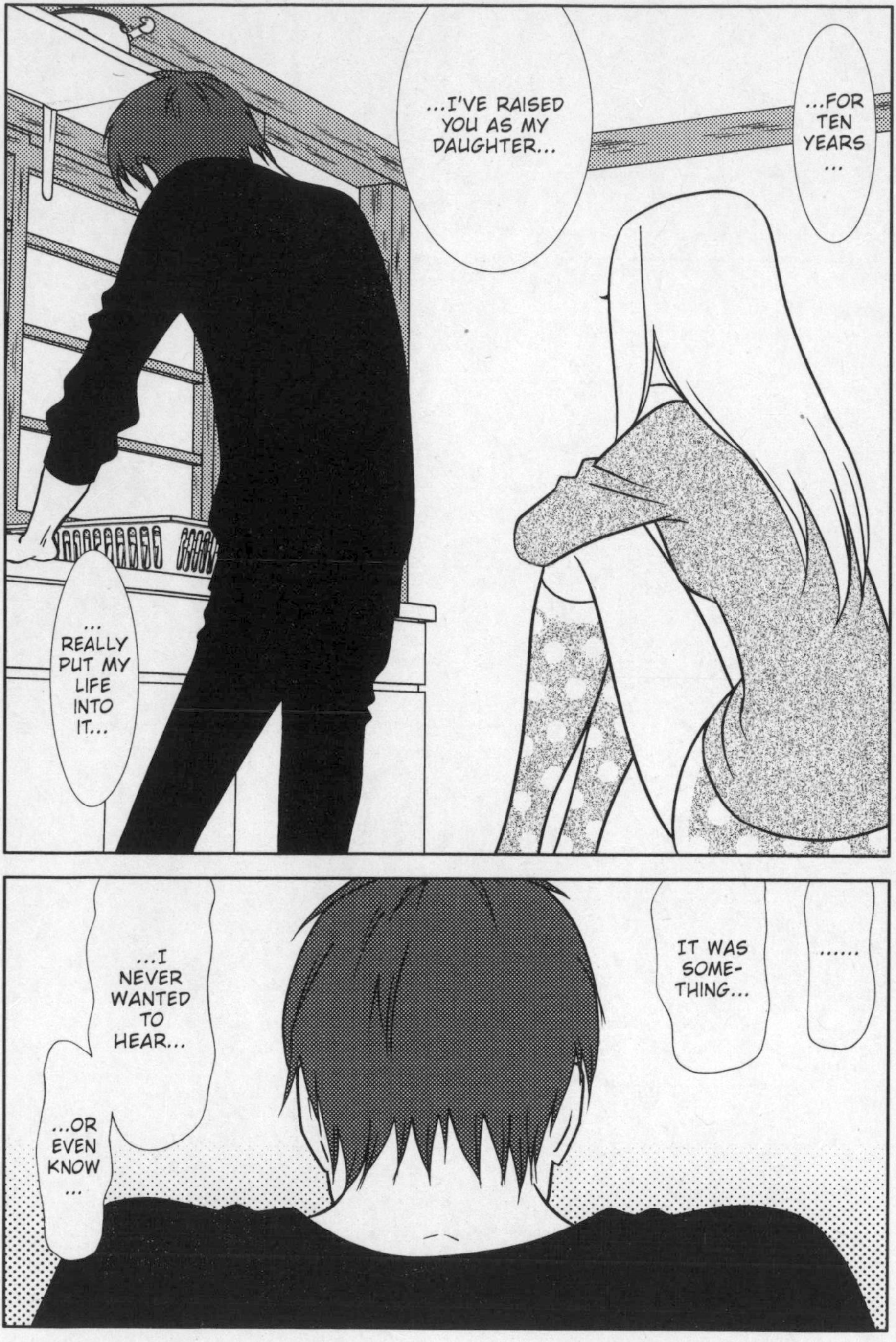
...FOR TEN YEARS...
...I'VE RAISED YOU AS MY DAUGHTER...
...REALLY PUT MY LIFE INTO IT...
......
IT WAS SOME-THING...
...I NEVER WANTED TO HEAR...
...OR EVEN KNOW...

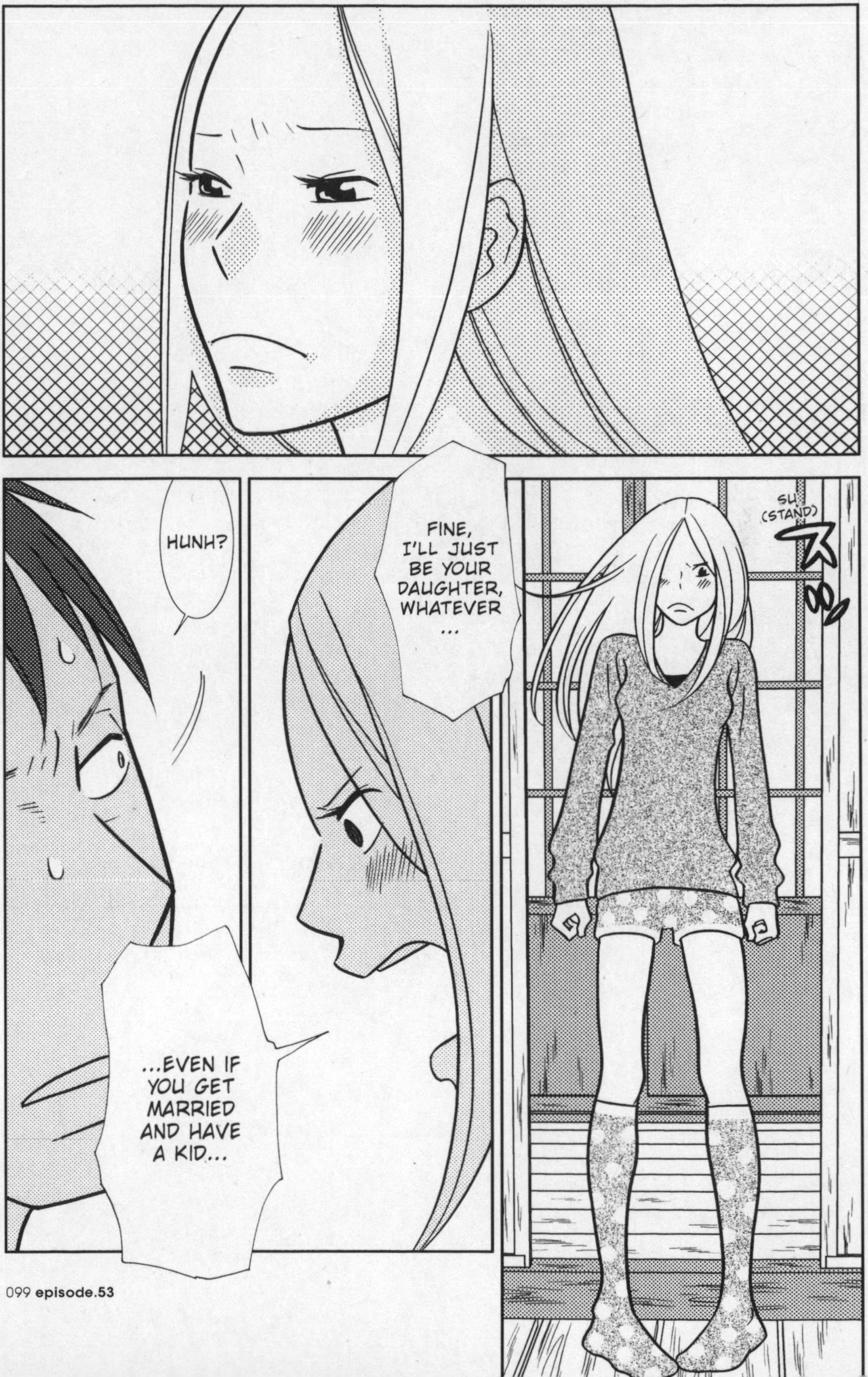
SU (STAND)
FINE, I'LL JUST BE YOUR DAUGHTER, WHATEVER ...
HUNH?
...EVEN IF YOU GET MARRIED AND HAVE A KID...

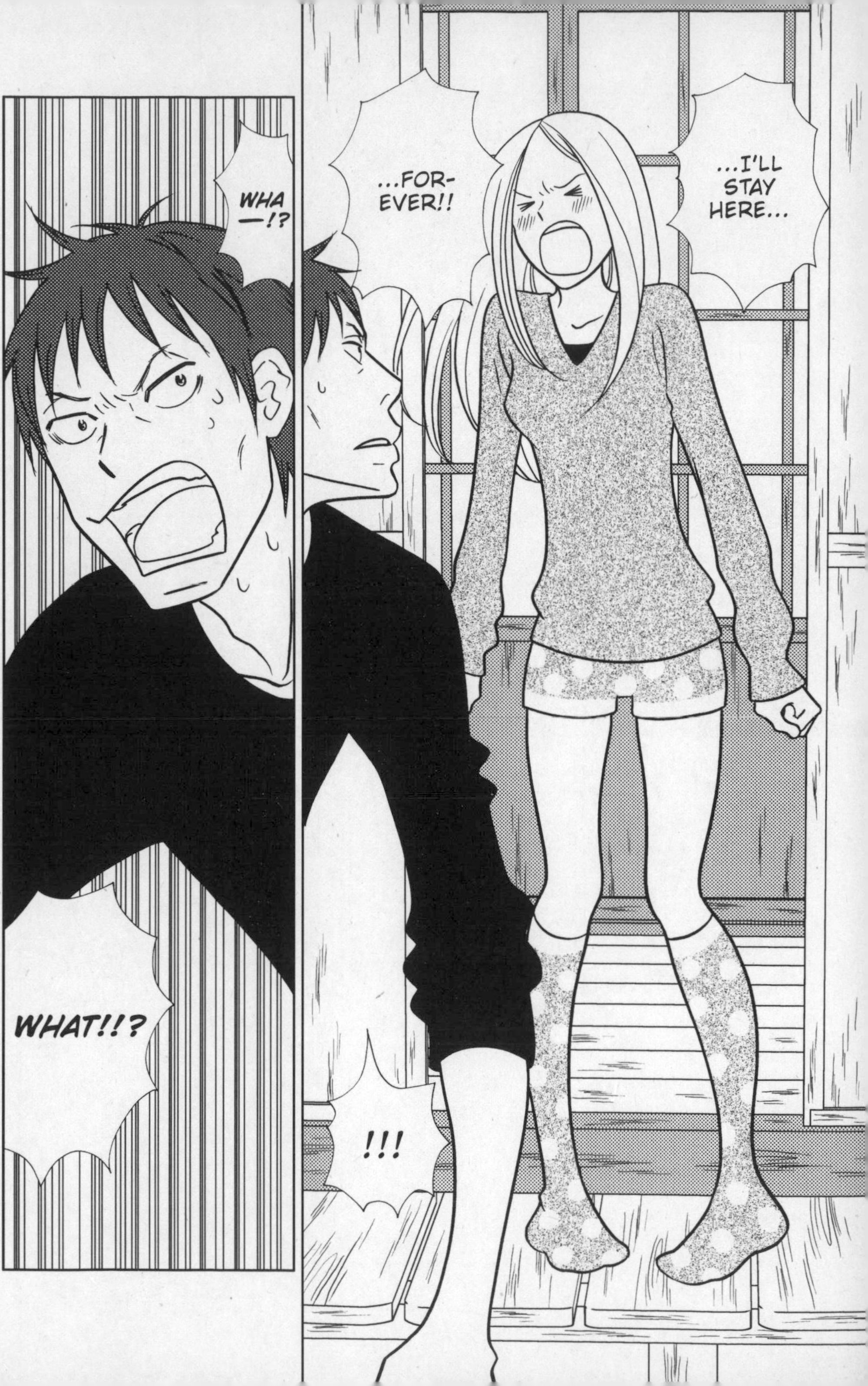
...I'LL STAY HERE...
...FOR-EVER!!
!!!
WHA—!?
WHAT!!?

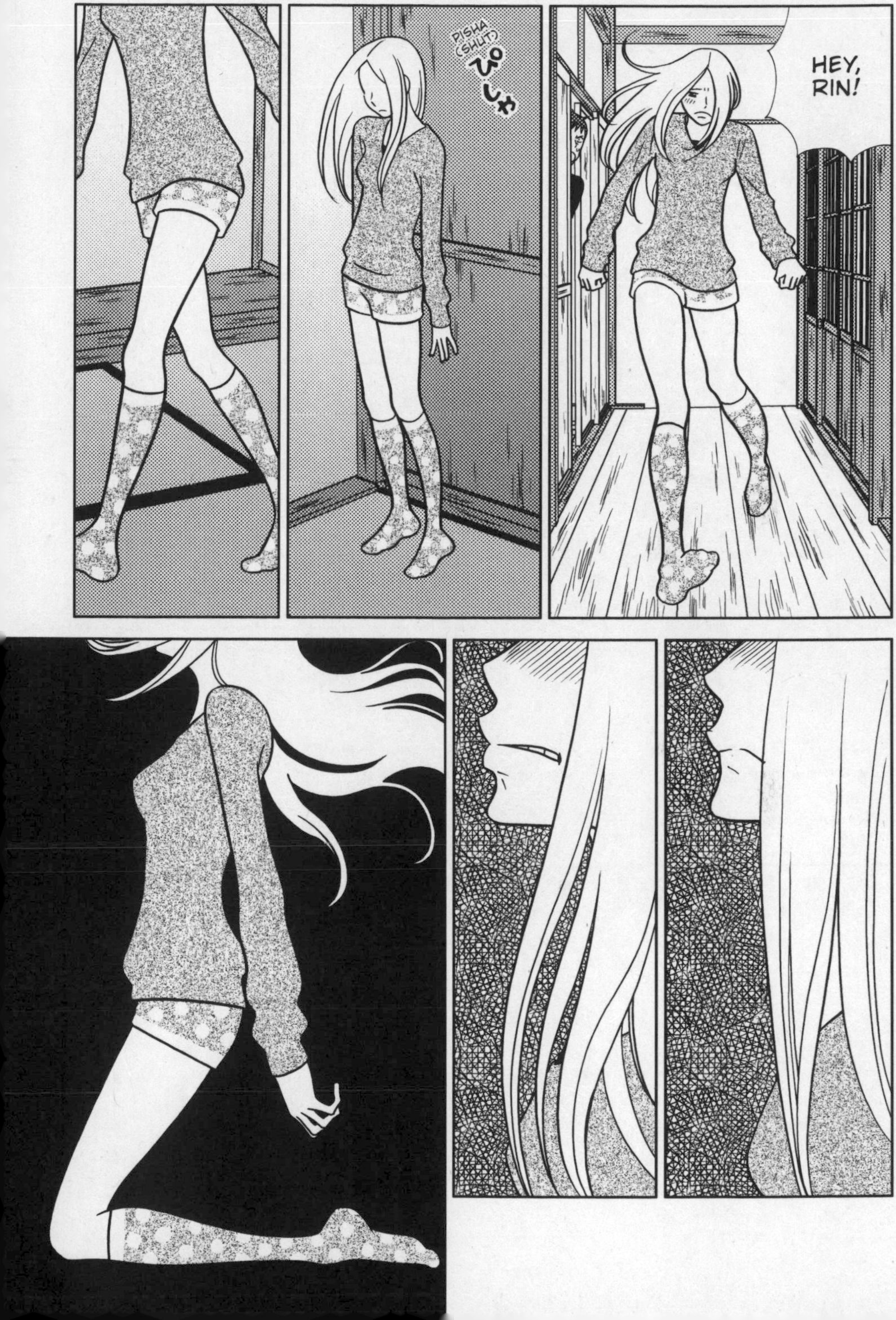
HEY, RIN!
PISHA (SHUT)
ぴしゃ

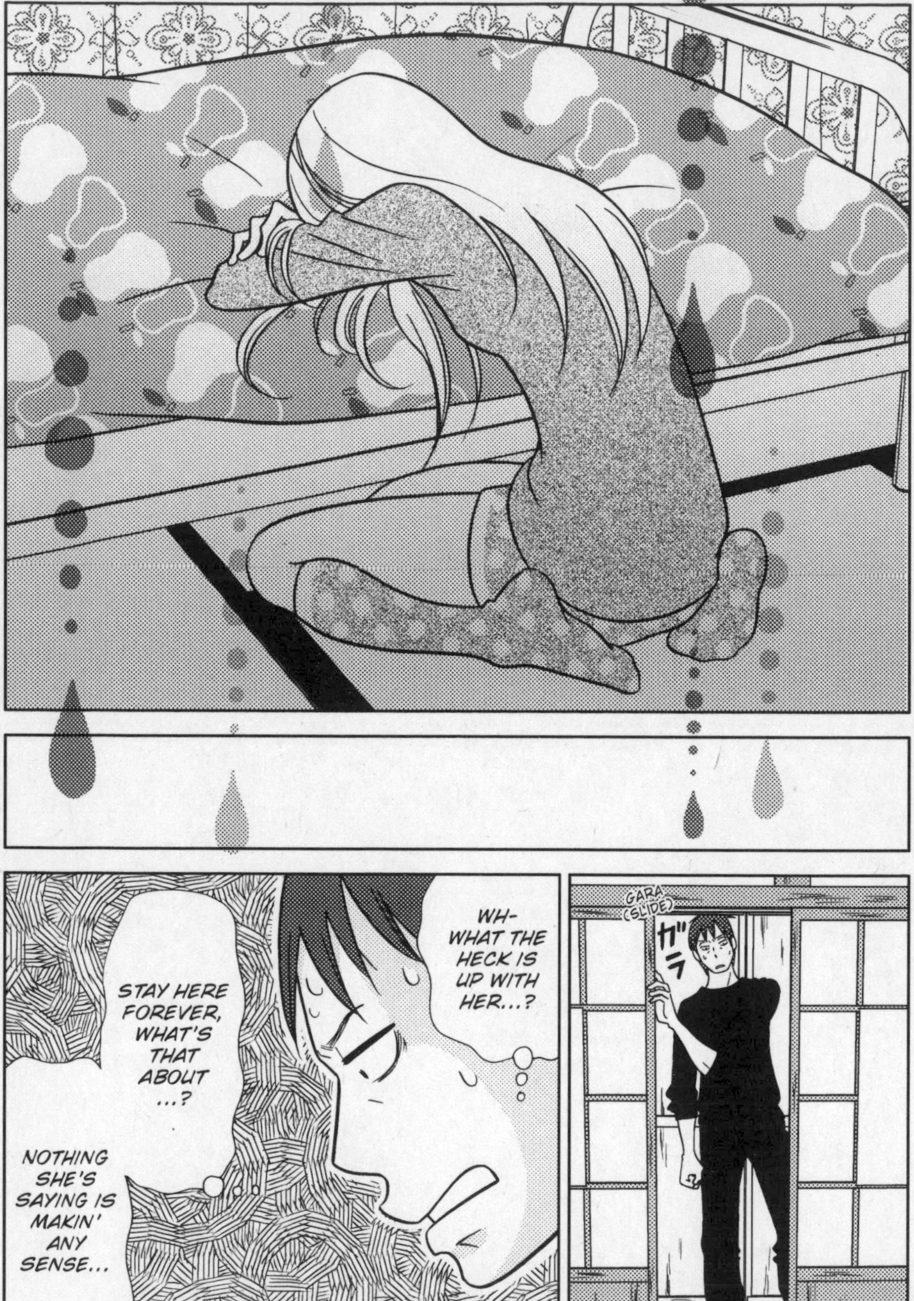
GARA (SLIDE)
ガラ
WH- WHAT THE HECK IS UP WITH HER...?
STAY HERE FOREVER, WHAT'S THAT ABOUT...?
NOTHING SHE'S SAYING IS MAKIN' ANY SENSE...

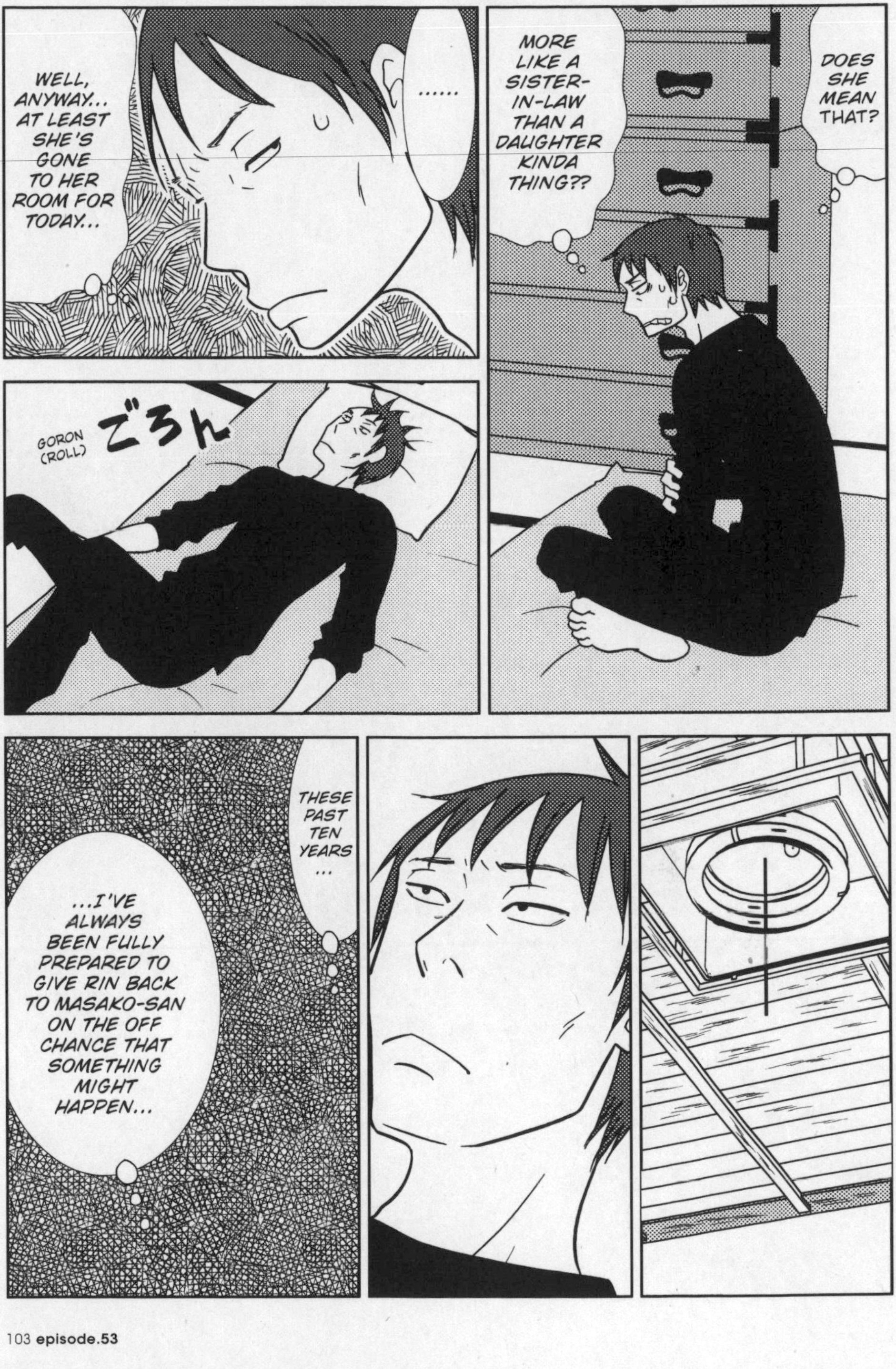
DOES SHE MEAN THAT?
MORE LIKE A SISTER-IN-LAW THAN A DAUGHTER KINDA THING??
......
WELL, ANYWAY... AT LEAST SHE'S GONE TO HER ROOM FOR TODAY...
ごろん
GORON (ROLL)
THESE PAST TEN YEARS...
...I'VE ALWAYS BEEN FULLY PREPARED TO GIVE RIN BACK TO MASAKO-SAN ON THE OFF CHANCE THAT SOMETHING MIGHT HAPPEN...

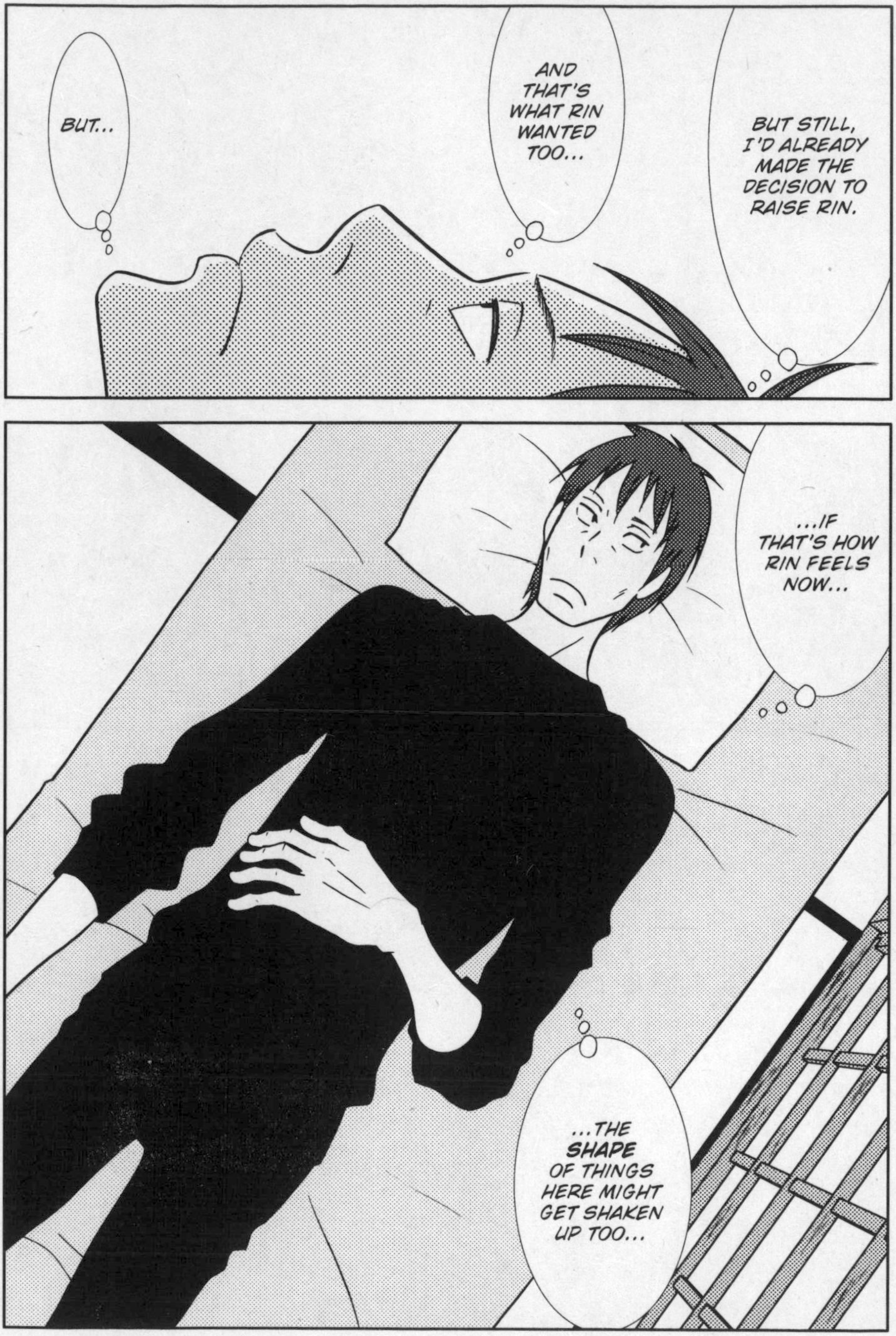
BUT STILL, I'D ALREADY MADE THE DECISION TO RAISE RIN.
AND THAT'S WHAT RIN WANTED TOO...
BUT...
...IF THAT'S HOW RIN FEELS NOW...
...THE **SHAPE** OF THINGS HERE MIGHT GET SHAKEN UP TOO...

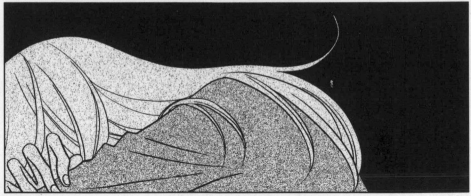

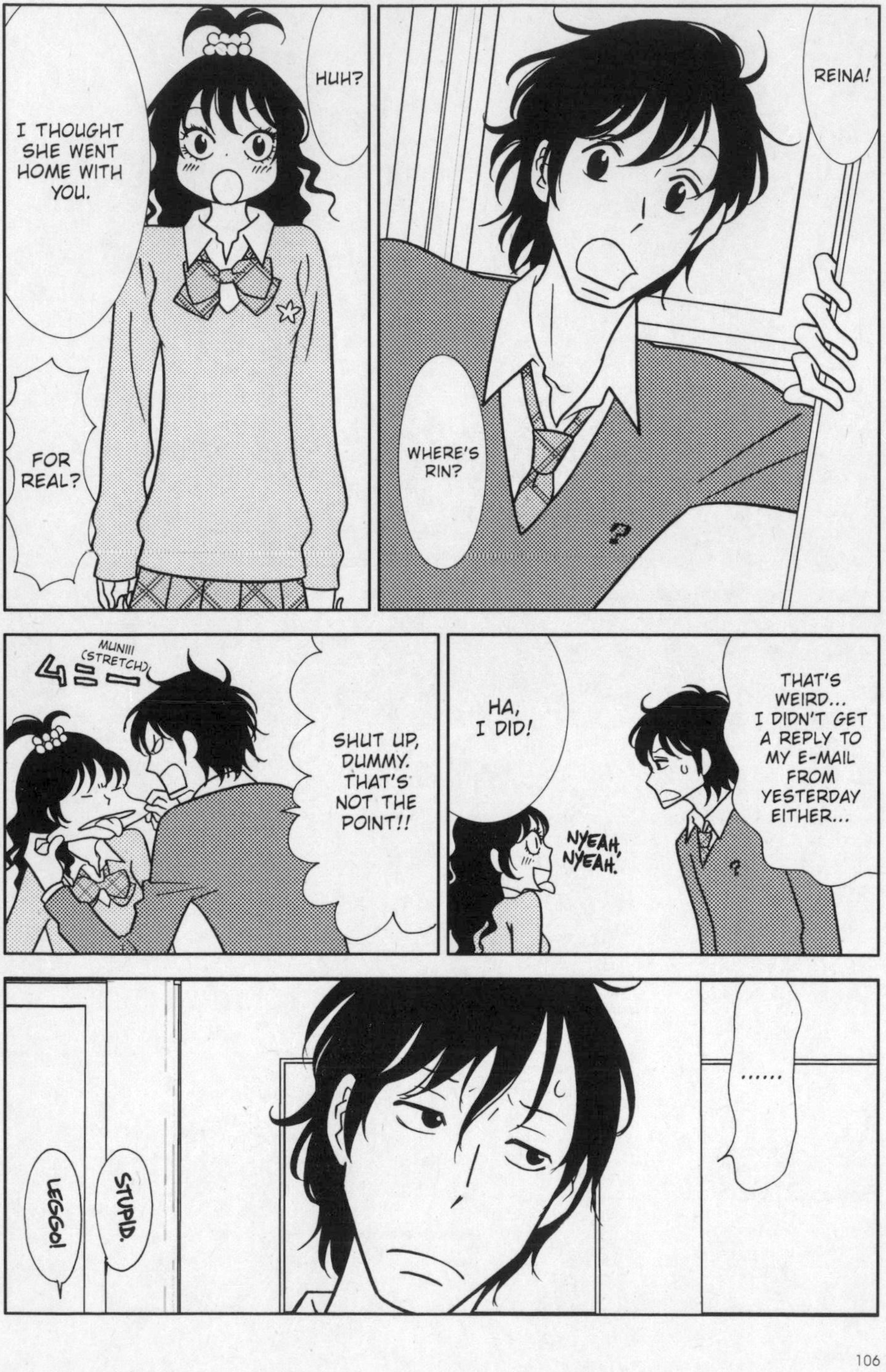
REINA!
WHERE'S RIN?
HUH?
I THOUGHT SHE WENT HOME WITH YOU.
FOR REAL?
THAT'S WEIRD... I DIDN'T GET A REPLY TO MY E-MAIL FROM YESTERDAY EITHER...
HA, I DID!
NYEAH, NYEAH.
SHUT UP, DUMMY. THAT'S NOT THE POINT!!
MUNIII (STRETCH)
......
STUPID.
LEGGO!

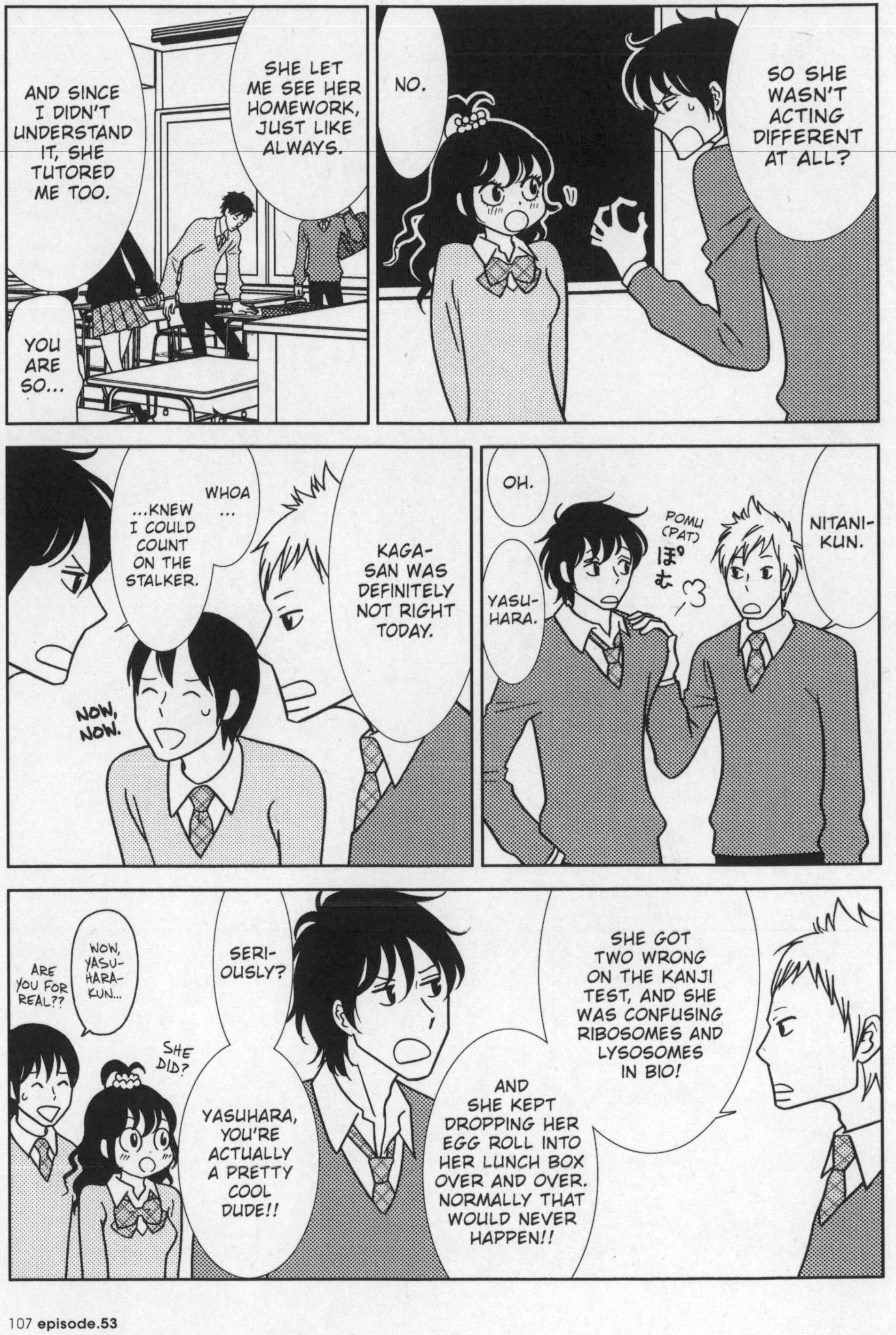
SO SHE WASN'T ACTING DIFFERENT AT ALL?
NO.
SHE LET ME SEE HER HOMEWORK, JUST LIKE ALWAYS.
AND SINCE I DIDN'T UNDERSTAND IT, SHE TUTORED ME TOO.
YOU ARE SO...
NITANI-KUN.
POMU (PAT)
ぽむ
OH.
YASU-HARA.
KAGA-SAN WAS DEFINITELY NOT RIGHT TODAY.
WHOA ...
...KNEW I COULD COUNT ON THE STALKER.
NOW, NOW.
SHE GOT TWO WRONG ON THE KANJI TEST, AND SHE WAS CONFUSING RIBOSOMES AND LYSOSOMES IN BIO!
AND SHE KEPT DROPPING HER EGG ROLL INTO HER LUNCH BOX OVER AND OVER. NORMALLY THAT WOULD NEVER HAPPEN!!
SERI-OUSLY?
YASUHARA, YOU'RE ACTUALLY A PRETTY COOL DUDE!!
WOW, YASU-HARA-KUN...
SHE DID?
ARE YOU FOR REAL??

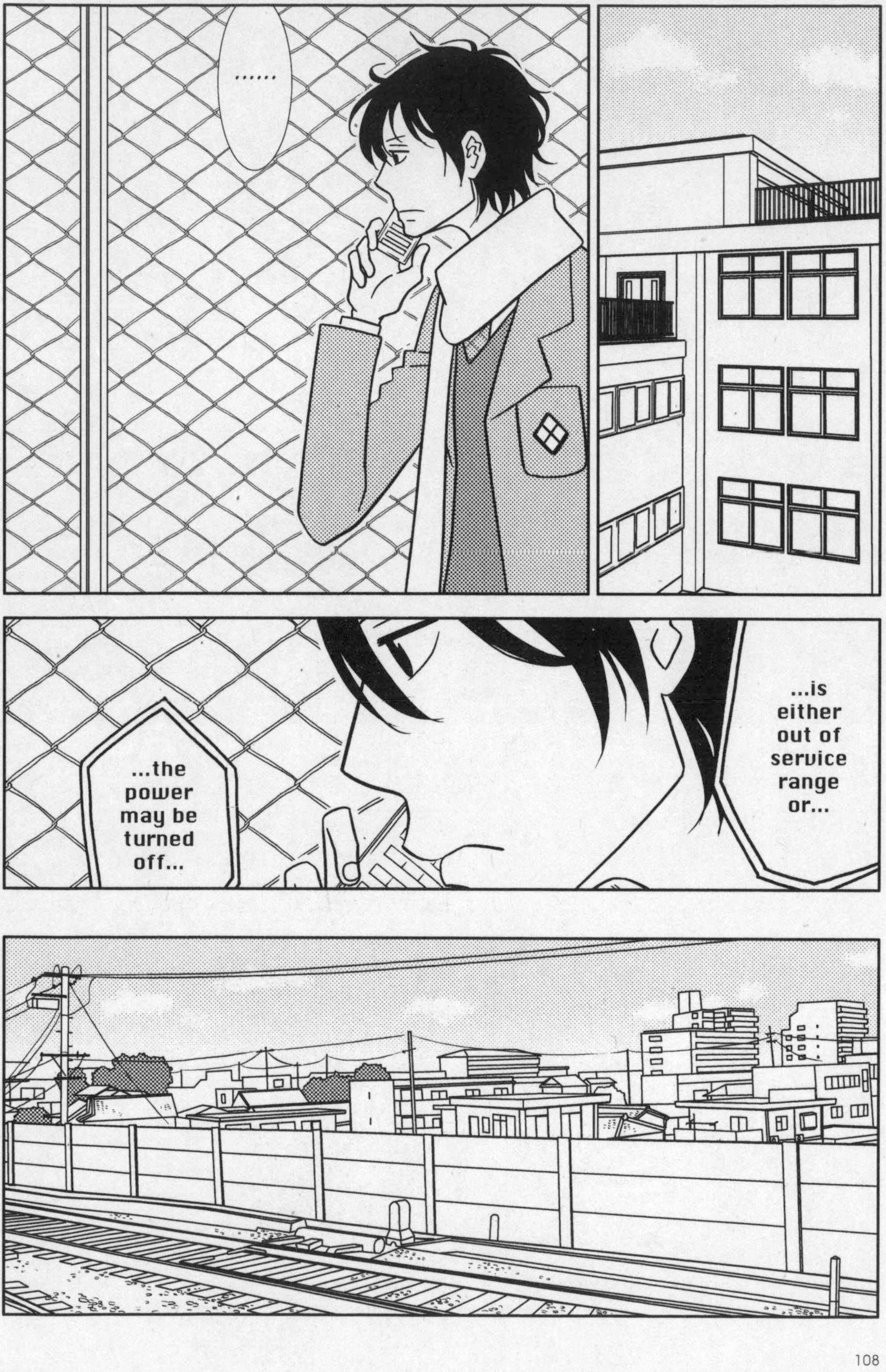
......
...is either out of service range or...
...the power may be turned off...

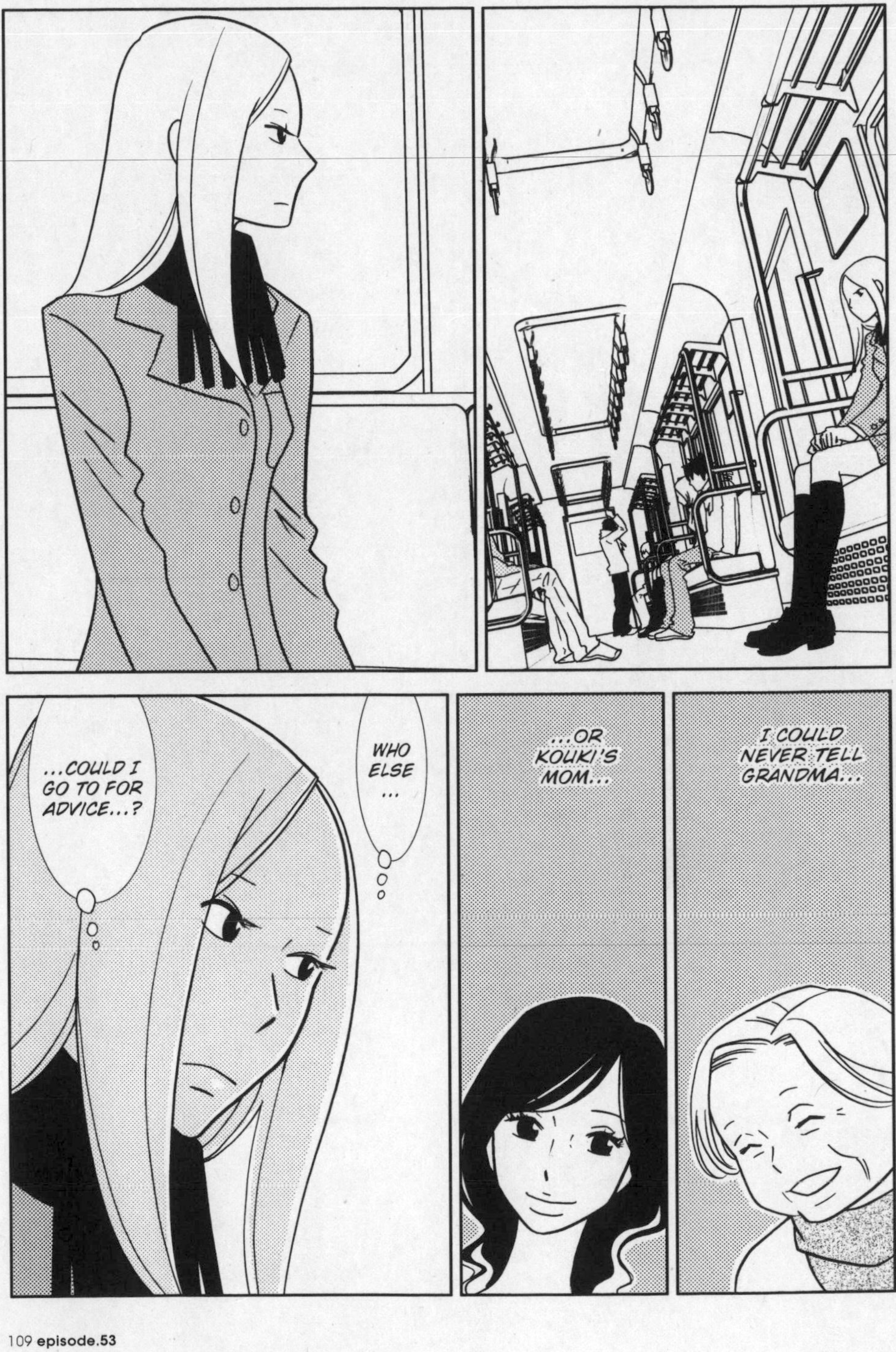
I COULD NEVER TELL GRANDMA...
...OR KOUKI'S MOM...
WHO ELSE ...
...COULD I GO TO FOR ADVICE...?

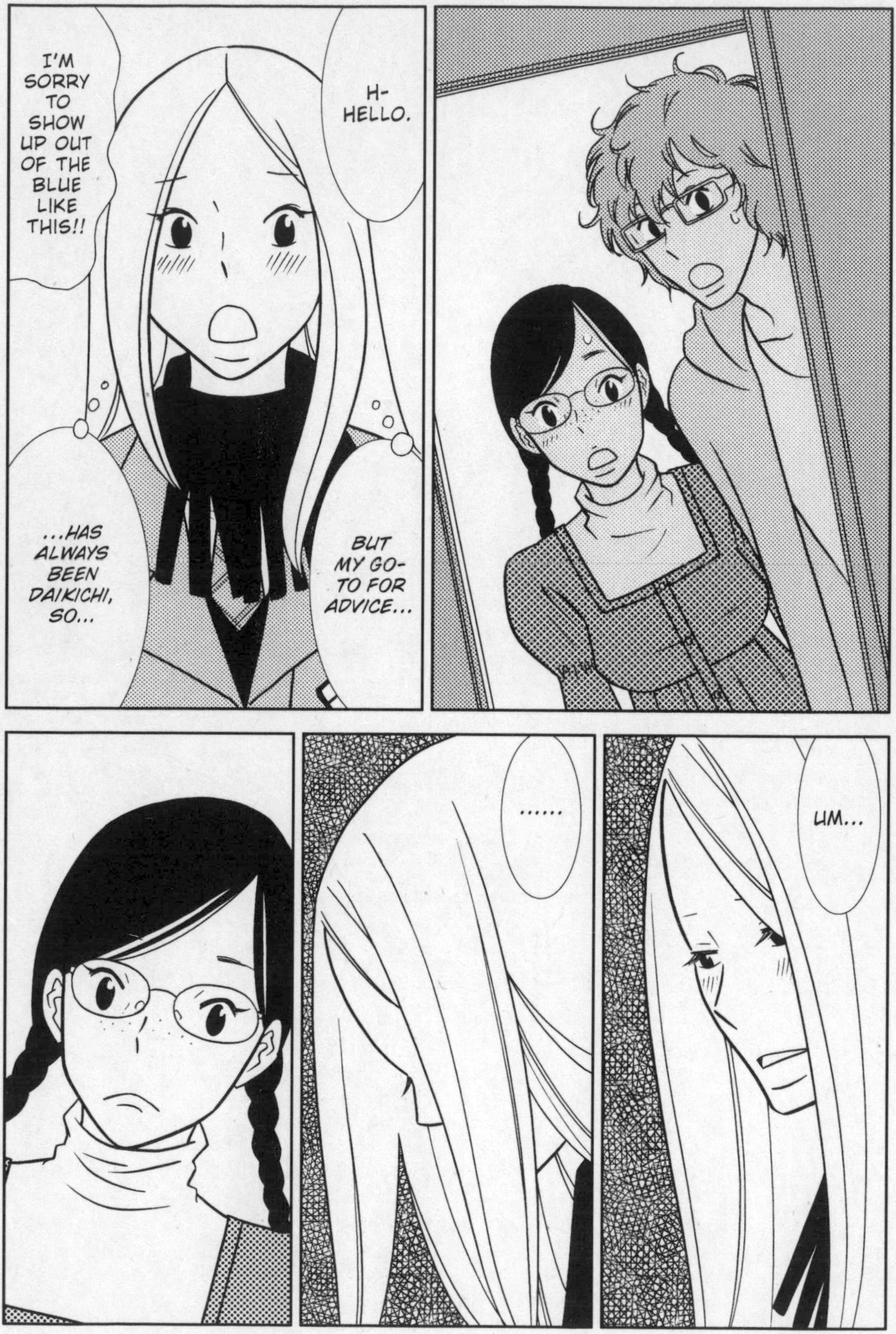
H-HELLO.
I'M SORRY TO SHOW UP OUT OF THE BLUE LIKE THIS!!
BUT MY GO-TO FOR ADVICE...
...HAS ALWAYS BEEN DAIKICHI, SO...
UM...
......

COME ON IN...
WOW...
SHE'S SO BIG NOW...
YOU THINK?
YOU CAN HOLD HER IF YOU WANT.

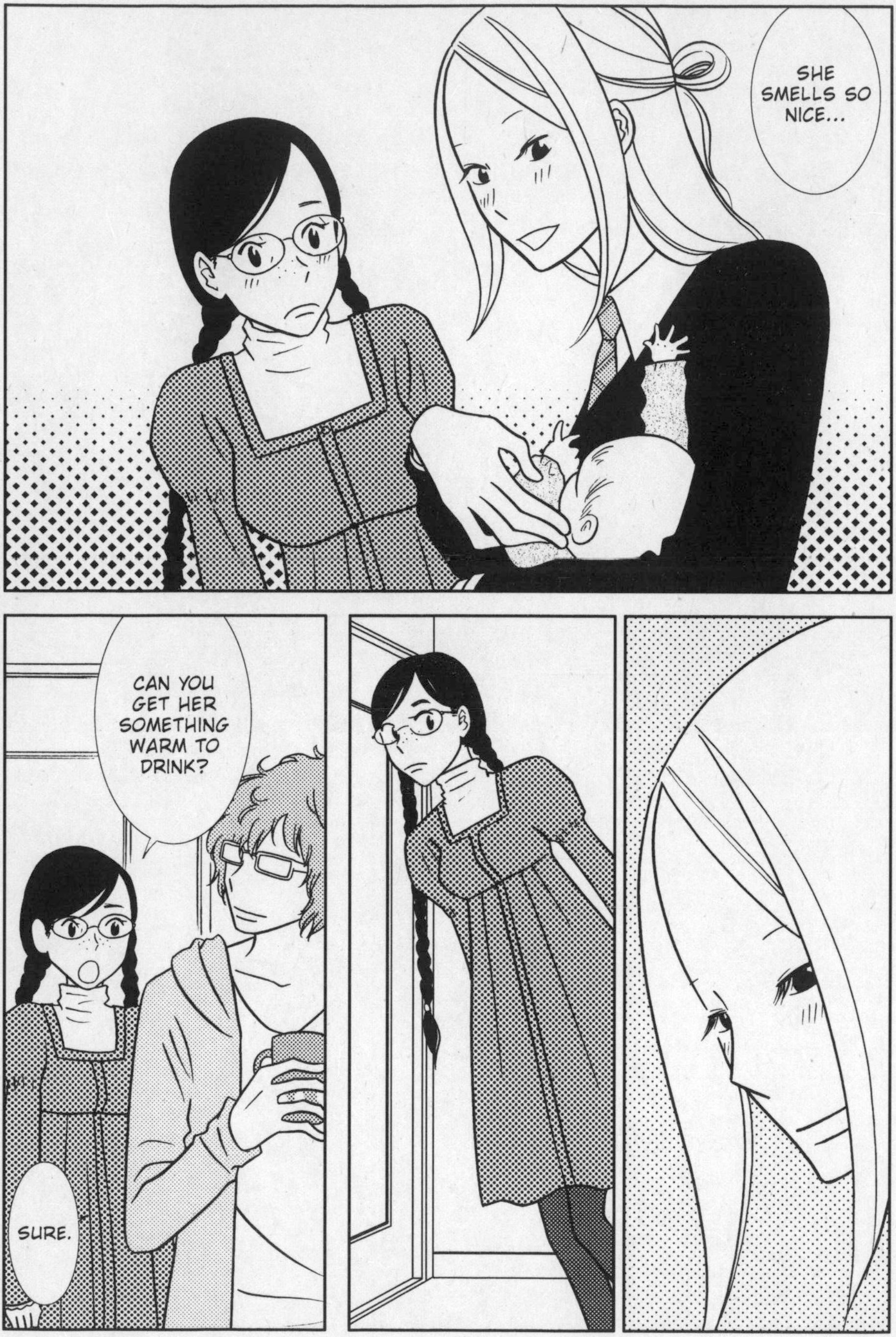
SHE SMELLS SO NICE...
CAN YOU GET HER SOMETHING WARM TO DRINK?
SURE.

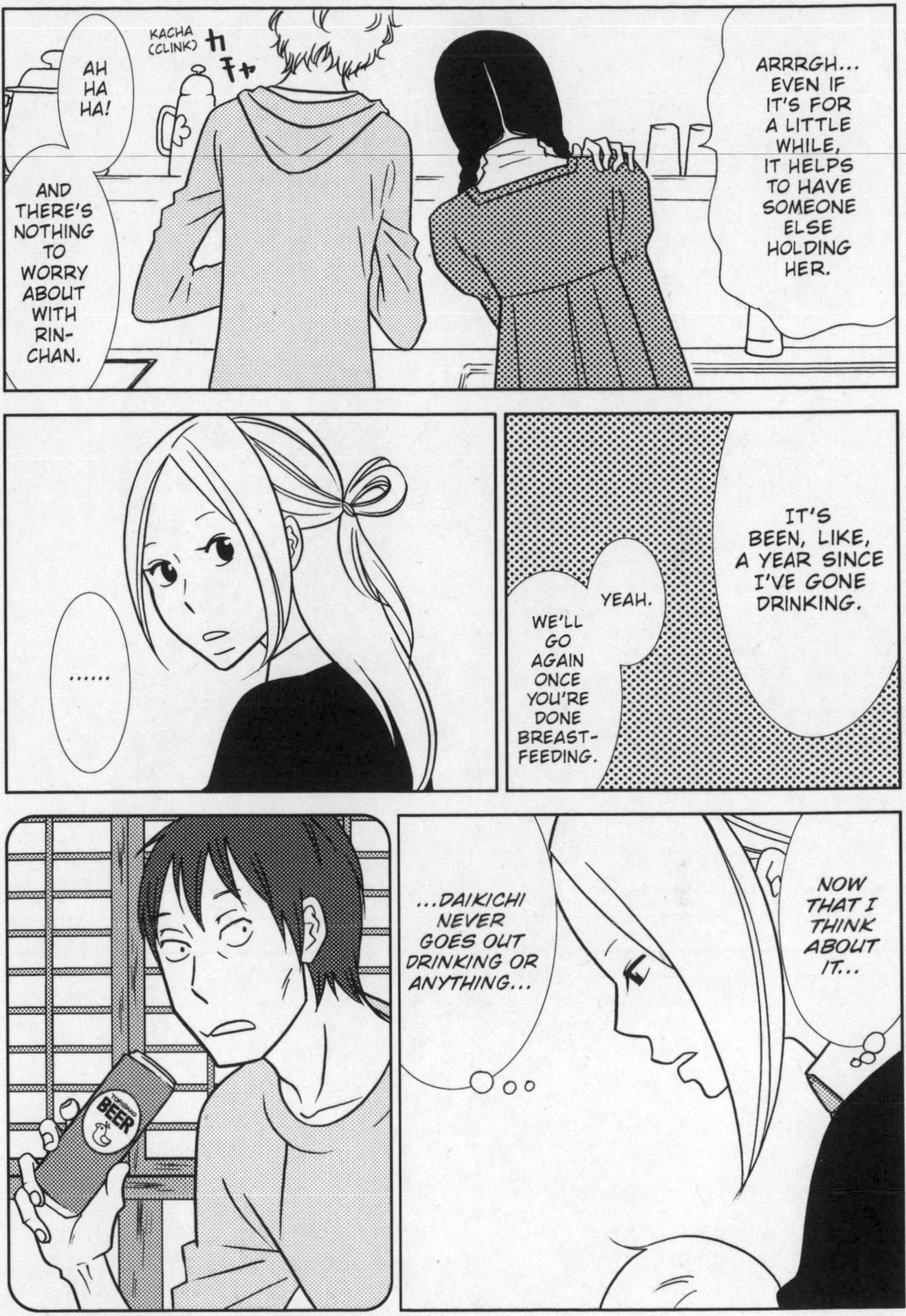
ARRRGH... EVEN IF IT'S FOR A LITTLE WHILE, IT HELPS TO HAVE SOMEONE ELSE HOLDING HER.
KACHA (CLINK) カチャ
AH HA HA!
AND THERE'S NOTHING TO WORRY ABOUT WITH RIN-CHAN.
IT'S BEEN, LIKE, A YEAR SINCE I'VE GONE DRINKING.
YEAH.
WE'LL GO AGAIN ONCE YOU'RE DONE BREAST-FEEDING.
......
NOW THAT I THINK ABOUT IT...
...DAIKICHI NEVER GOES OUT DRINKING OR ANYTHING...
BEER

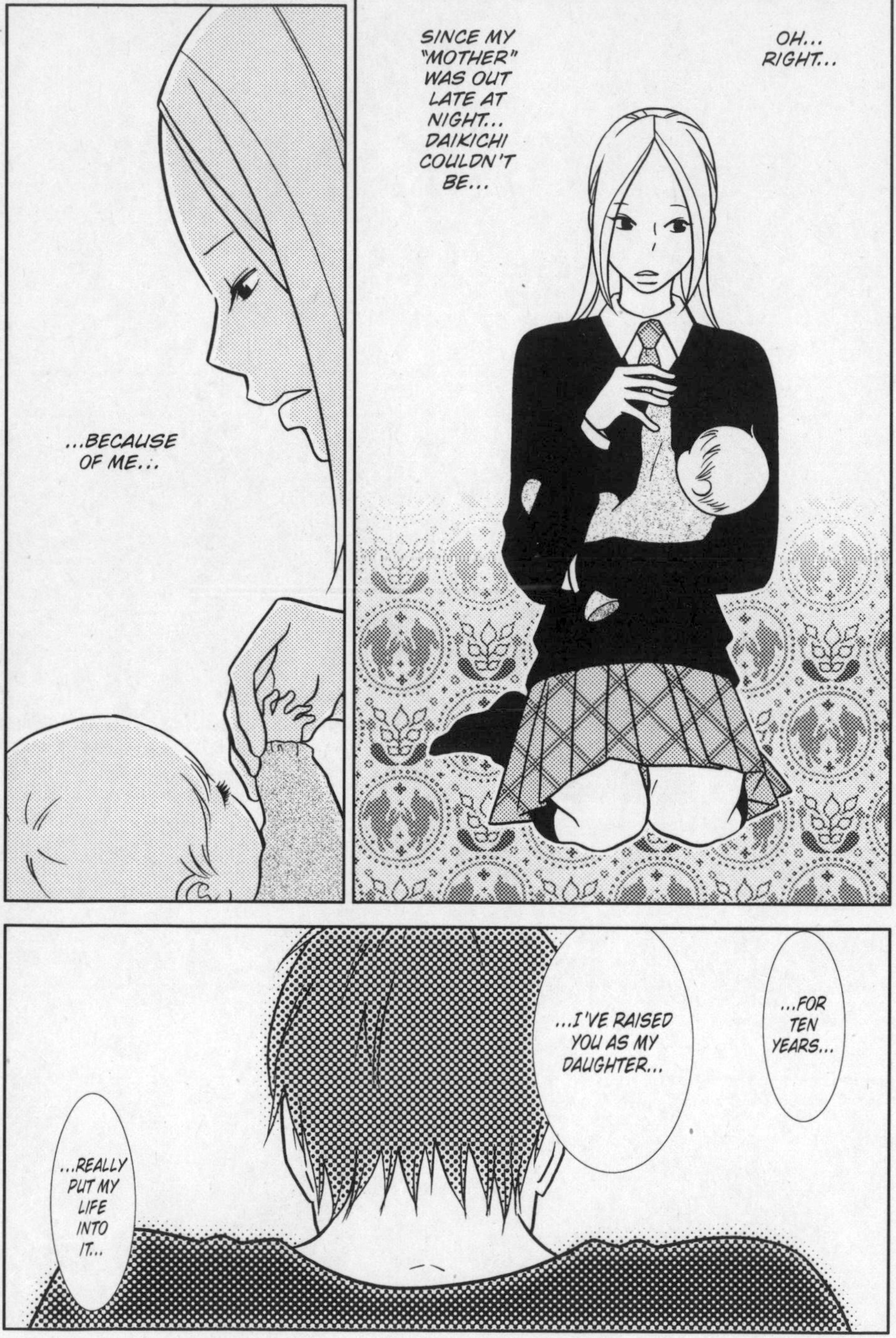
OH... RIGHT...
SINCE MY "MOTHER" WAS OUT LATE AT NIGHT... DAIKICHI COULDN'T BE...
...BECAUSE OF ME...
...FOR TEN YEARS...
...I'VE RAISED YOU AS MY DAUGHTER...
...REALLY PUT MY LIFE INTO IT...

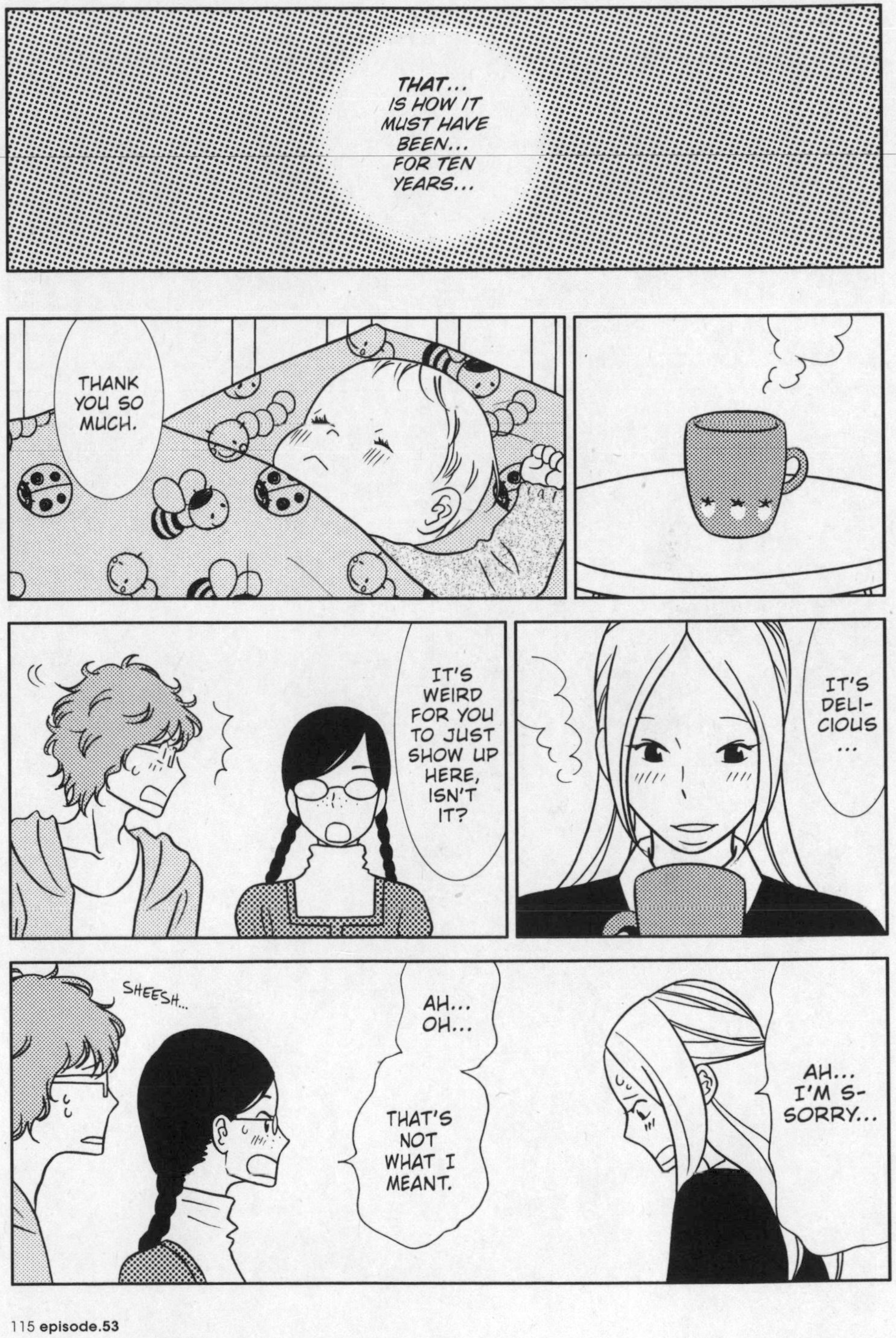
THAT... IS HOW IT MUST HAVE BEEN... FOR TEN YEARS...
THANK YOU SO MUCH.
IT'S DELI-CIOUS ...
IT'S WEIRD FOR YOU TO JUST SHOW UP HERE, ISN'T IT?
AH... I'M S-SORRY...
AH... OH...
THAT'S NOT WHAT I MEANT.
SHEESH...

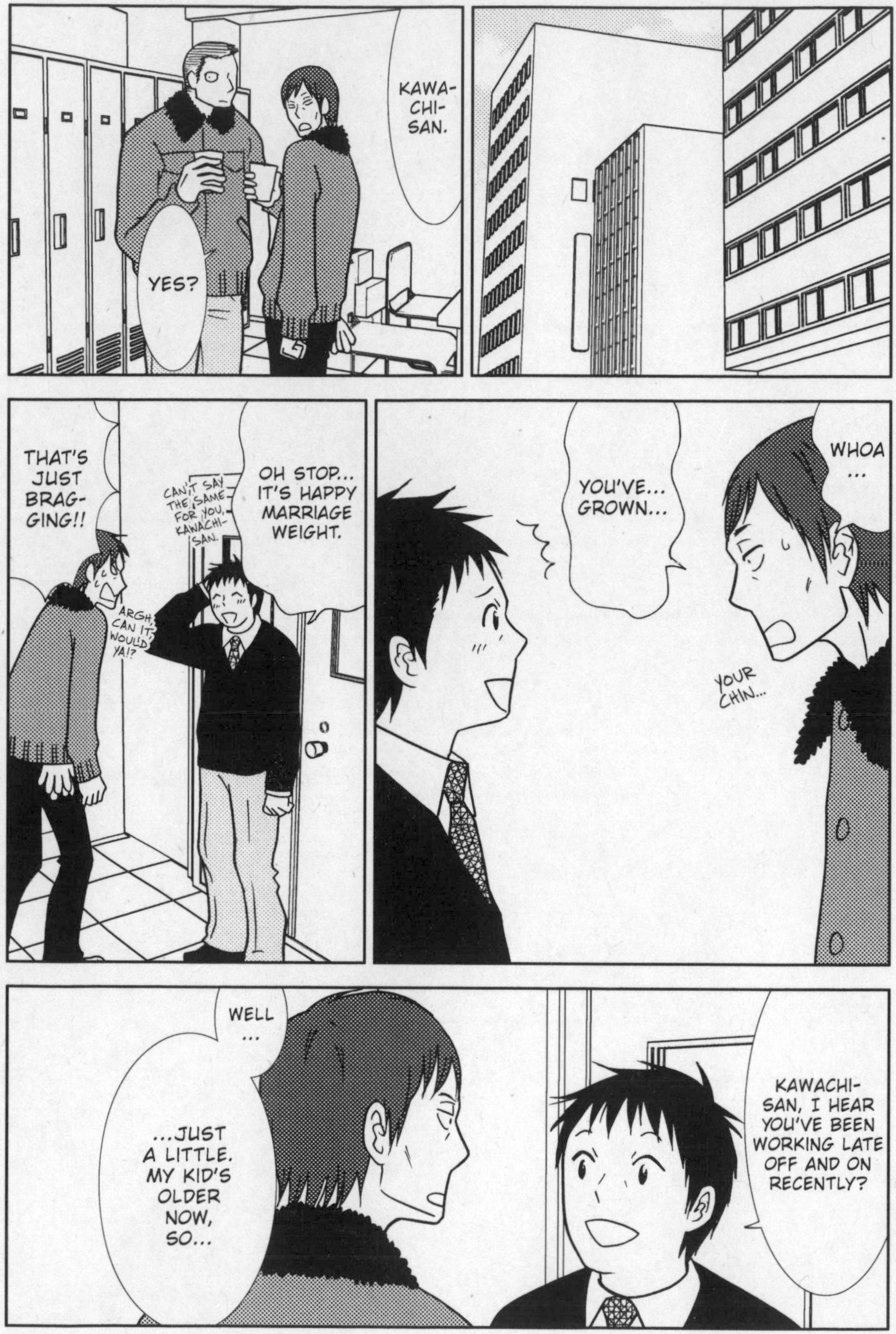
KAWA-CHI-SAN.
YES?
WHOA ...
YOUR CHIN...
YOU'VE... GROWN...
OH STOP... IT'S HAPPY MARRIAGE WEIGHT.
CAN'T SAY THE SAME FOR YOU, KAWACHI-SAN.
THAT'S JUST BRAG-GING!!
ARGH, CAN IT, WOULD YA!?
KAWACHI-SAN, I HEAR YOU'VE BEEN WORKING LATE OFF AND ON RECENTLY?
WELL ...
...JUST A LITTLE. MY KID'S OLDER NOW, SO...

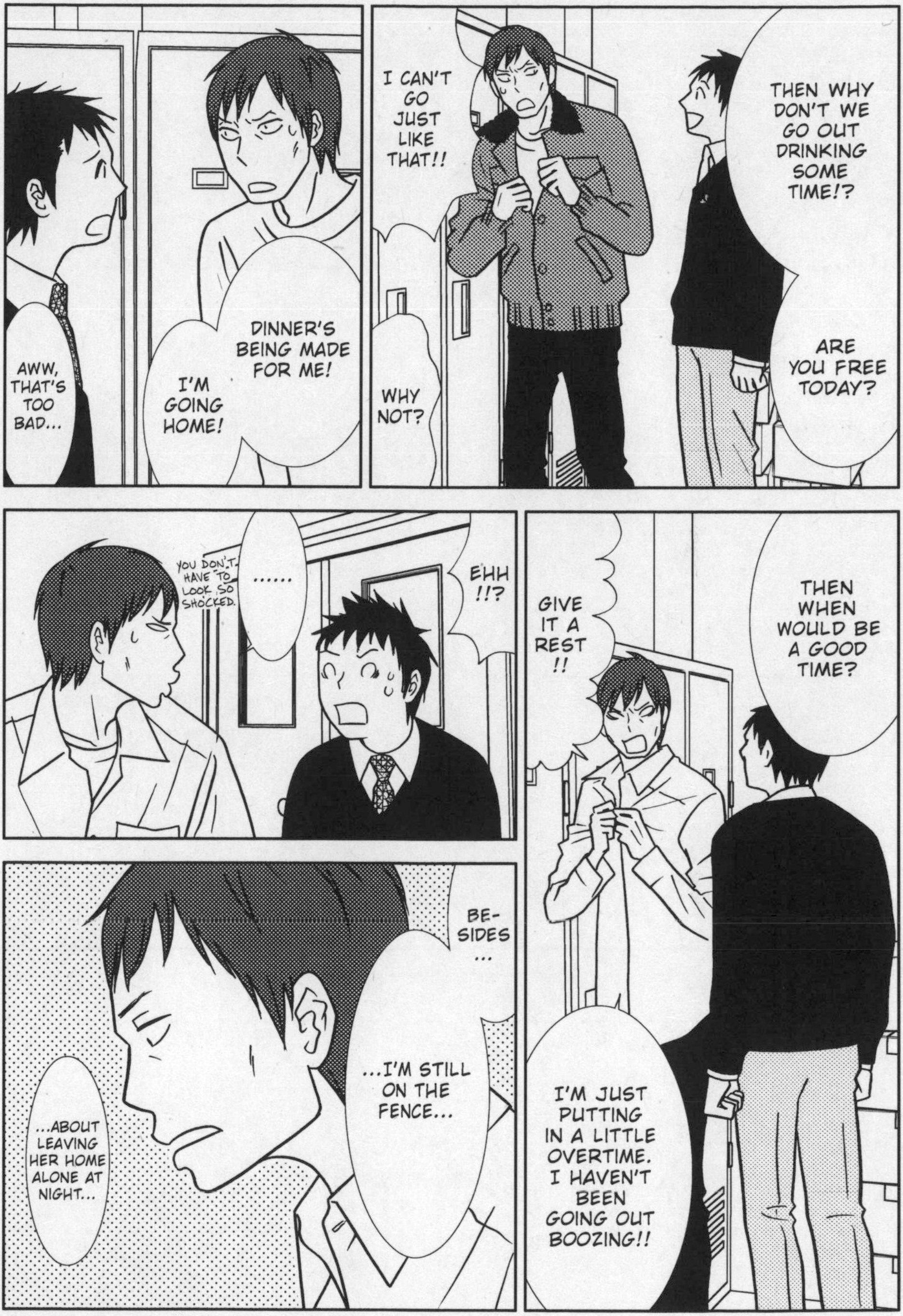
THEN WHY DON'T WE GO OUT DRINKING SOME TIME!?
ARE YOU FREE TODAY?
I CAN'T GO JUST LIKE THAT!!
WHY NOT?
DINNER'S BEING MADE FOR ME!
I'M GOING HOME!
AWW, THAT'S TOO BAD...
THEN WHEN WOULD BE A GOOD TIME?
GIVE IT A REST!!
I'M JUST PUTTING IN A LITTLE OVERTIME. I HAVEN'T BEEN GOING OUT BOOZING!!
EHH!!?
......
YOU DON'T HAVE TO LOOK SO SHOCKED.
BESIDES...
...I'M STILL ON THE FENCE...
...ABOUT LEAVING HER HOME ALONE AT NIGHT...

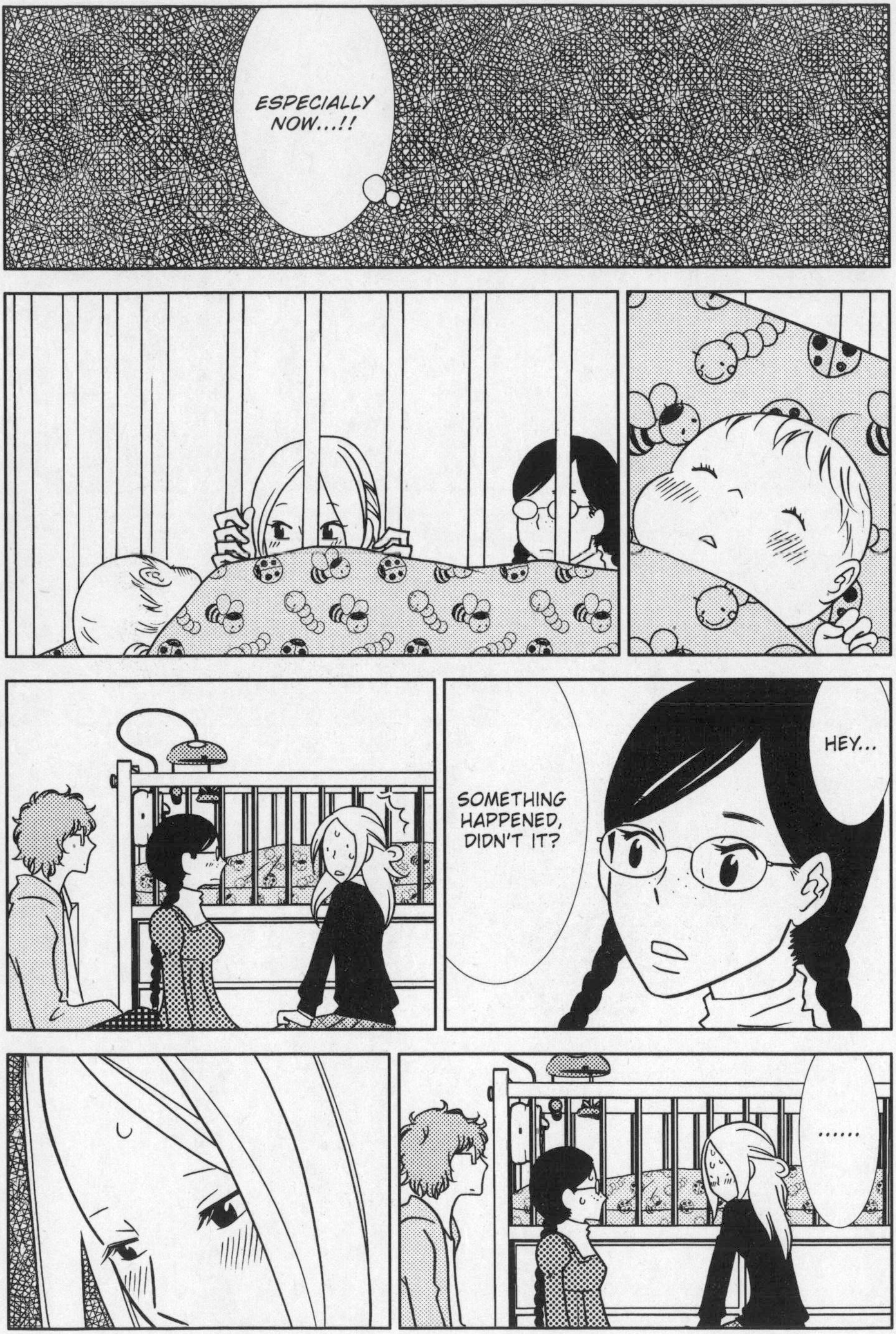
ESPECIALLY NOW...!!
HEY...
SOMETHING HAPPENED, DIDN'T IT?
......

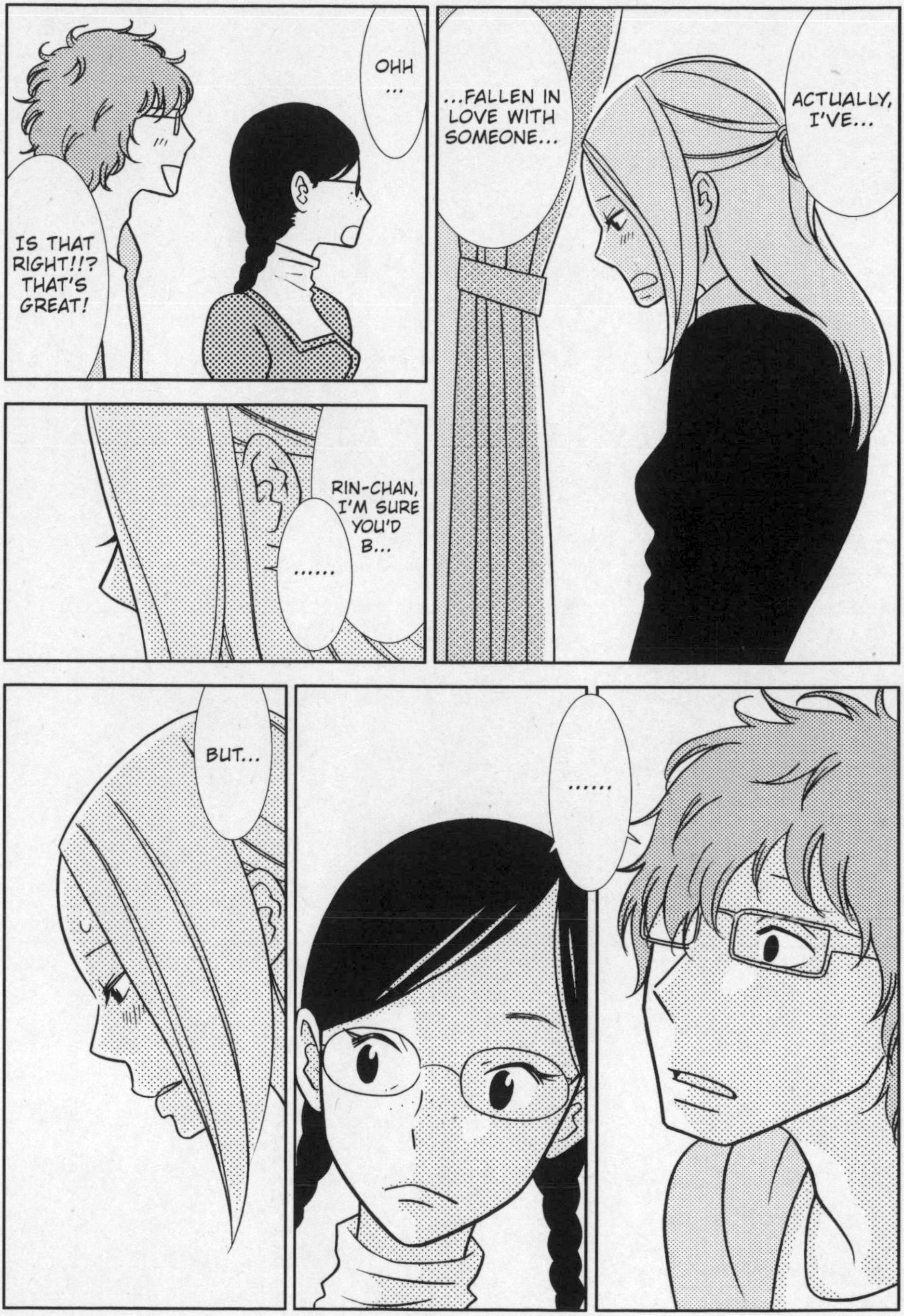
ACTUALLY, I'VE...
...FALLEN IN LOVE WITH SOMEONE...
OHH ...
IS THAT RIGHT!!? THAT'S GREAT!
RIN-CHAN, I'M SURE YOU'D B...
......
......
BUT...

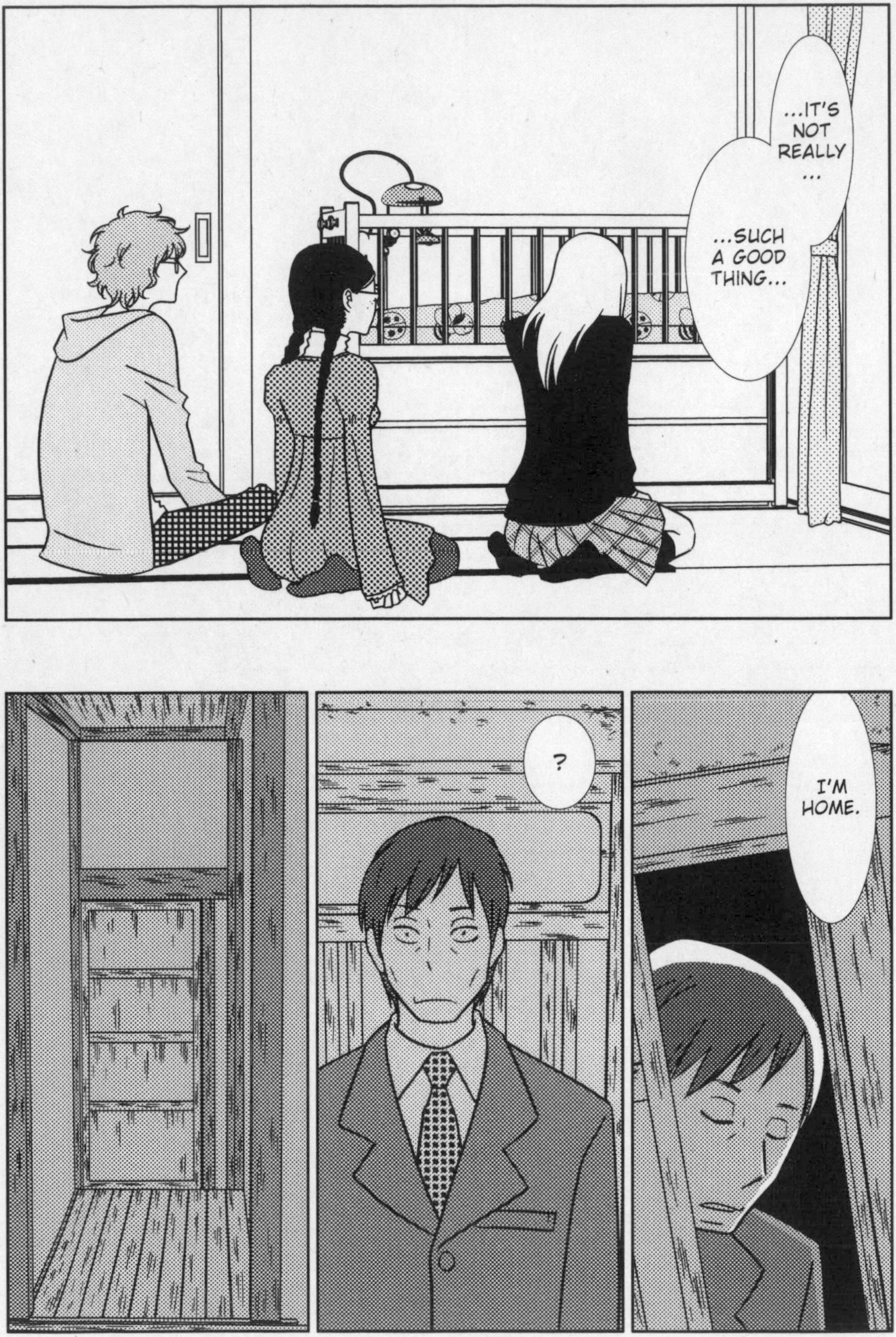
...IT'S NOT REALLY ...
...SUCH A GOOD THING...
I'M HOME.
?

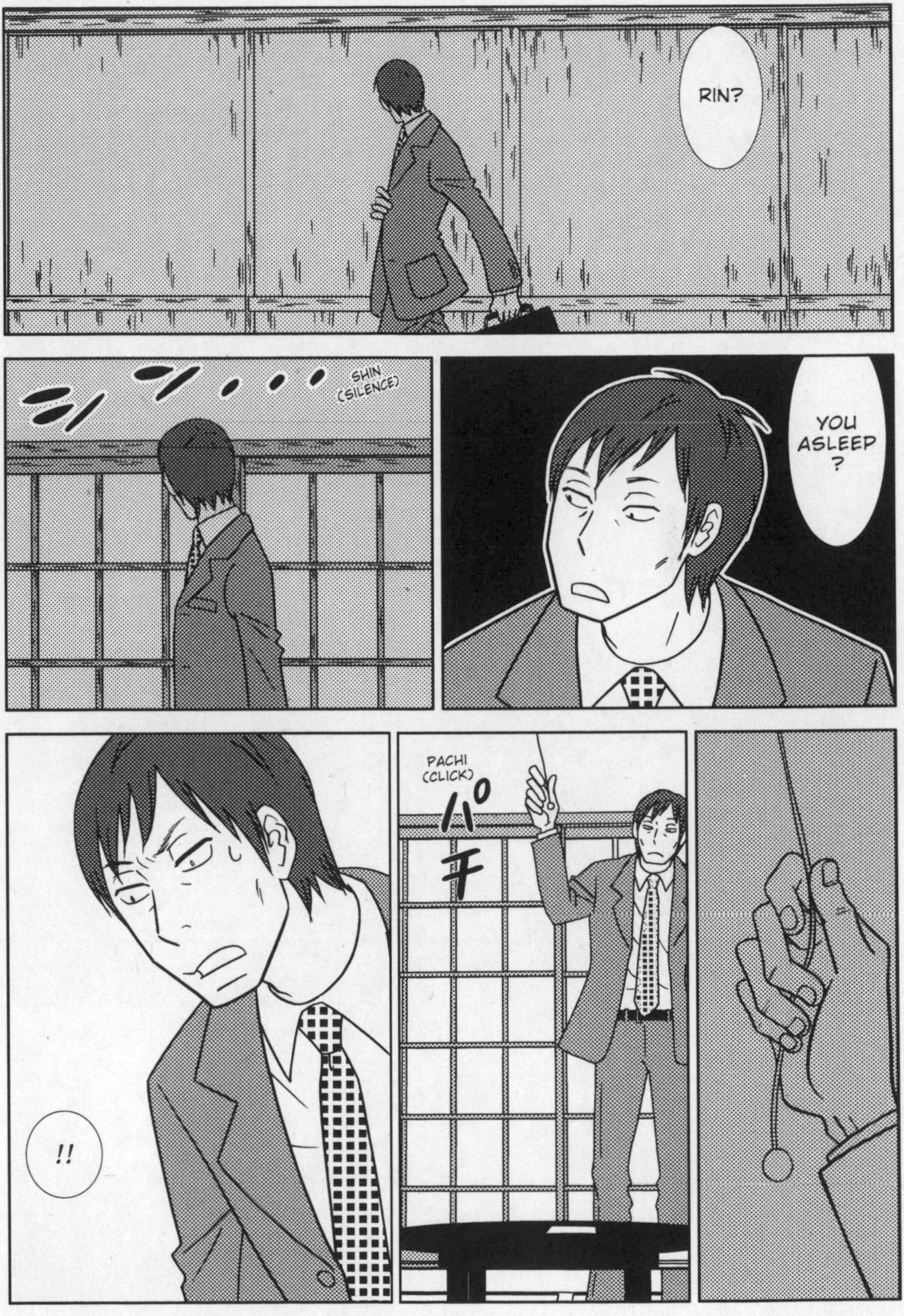
RIN?
YOU ASLEEP ?
SHIN (SILENCE)
PACHI (CLICK)
パチ
!!

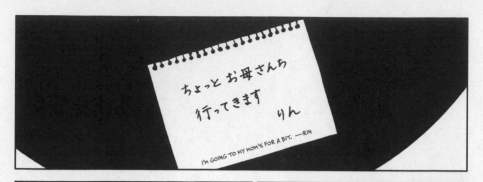

ちょっと お母さんち
行ってきます
りん

I'M GOING TO MY MOM'S FOR A BIT. —RIN

SHE HARDLY EVER SAID "MOM," TILL NOW...

AND WHAT'S "FOR A BIT" MEAN ...?

WH—

WHAAAT ...!?

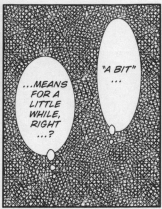
"A BIT" ...

...MEANS FOR A LITTLE WHILE, RIGHT ...?

ARGH, HOW LONG IS A "BIT"!?

THE REASON FOR THIS VISIT'S... GOTTA BE ME... ANY WAY YOU LOOK AT IT...

......

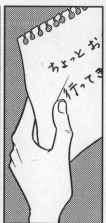

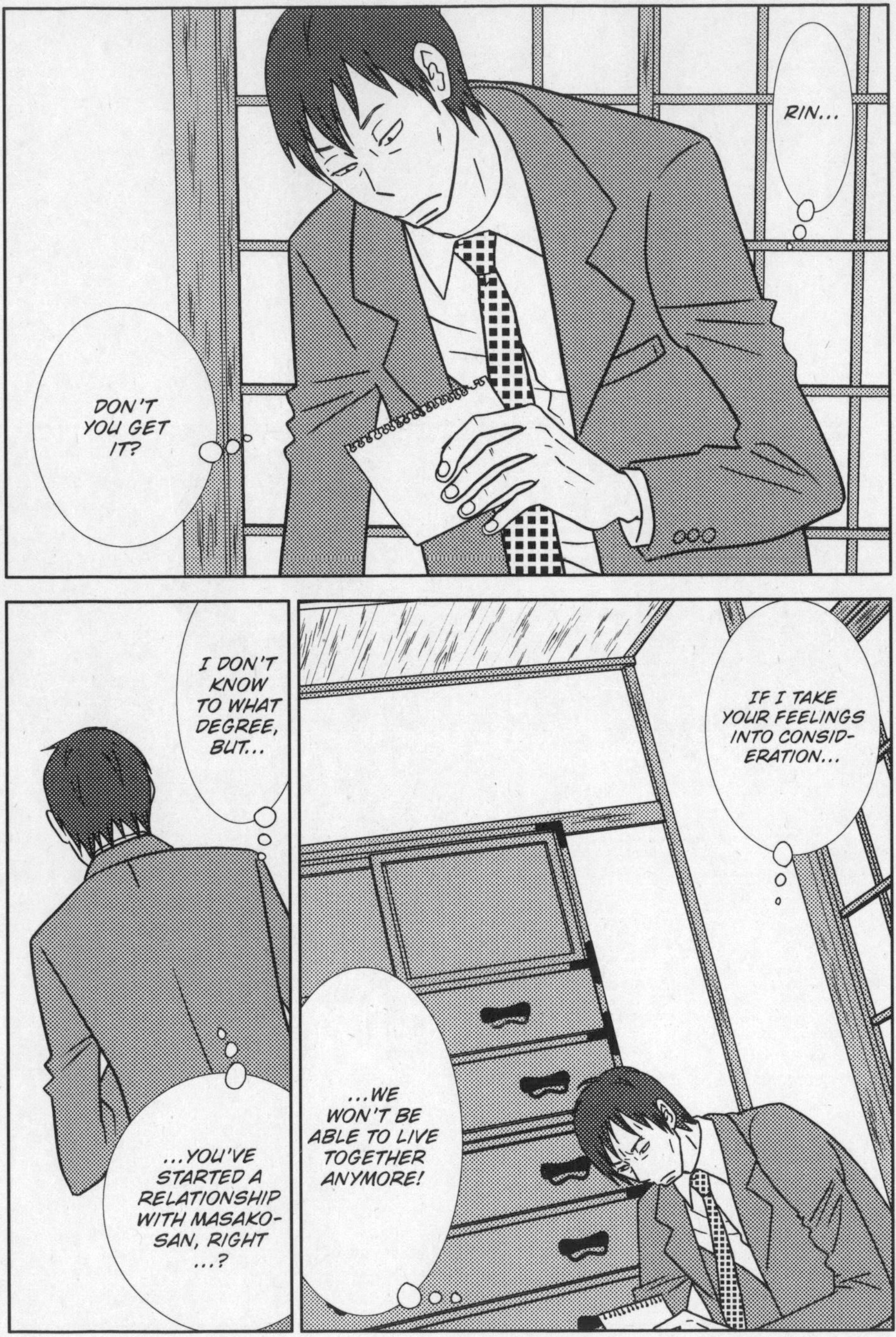
RIN...
DON'T YOU GET IT?
IF I TAKE YOUR FEELINGS INTO CONSID-ERATION...
...WE WON'T BE ABLE TO LIVE TOGETHER ANYMORE!
I DON'T KNOW TO WHAT DEGREE, BUT...
...YOU'VE STARTED A RELATIONSHIP WITH MASAKO-SAN, RIGHT ...?

...TO
MASAKO-
SAN...

...GIVING
YOU
BACK...

IT
WOULD
MEAN...

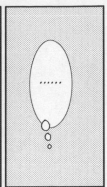

....

かがりん

ダイキチがつくる
にくじゃがはすごく
おいしいです
そしてダイキチは
はやくはしれるのと
なわとびがじょう
ずです

ダイキナ

DRAWING: RIN KAGA / DAIKICHI / THE MEAT-AND-POTATO STEW THAT DAIKICHI MAKES IS SO DELICIOUS. AND DAIKICHI CAN RUN REALLY FAST AND IS GOOD AT JUMP ROPE.

WAIT A
SEC...

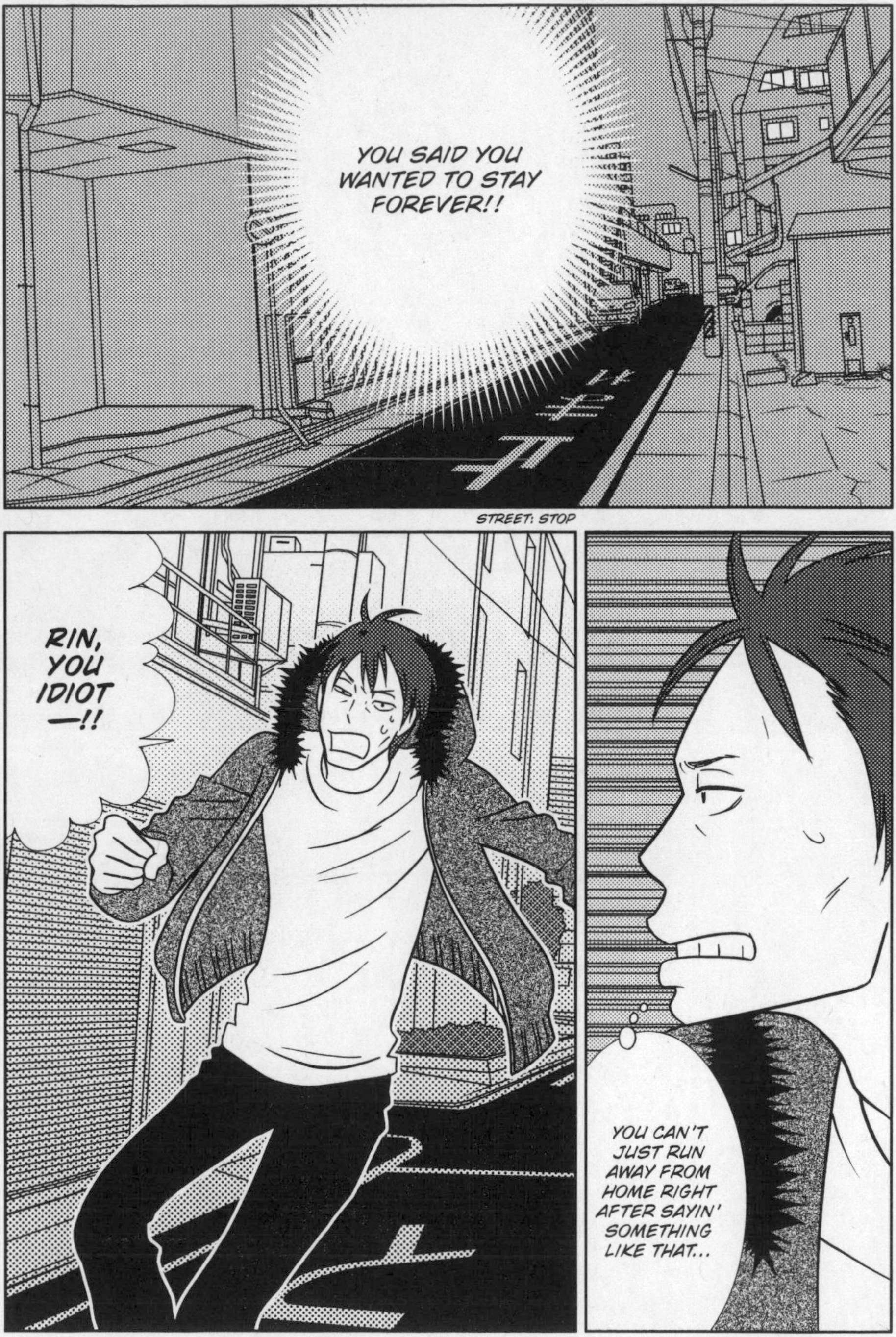
YOU SAID YOU WANTED TO STAY FOREVER!!
STREET: STOP
YOU CAN'T JUST RUN AWAY FROM HOME RIGHT AFTER SAYIN' SOMETHING LIKE THAT...
RIN, YOU IDIOT—!!

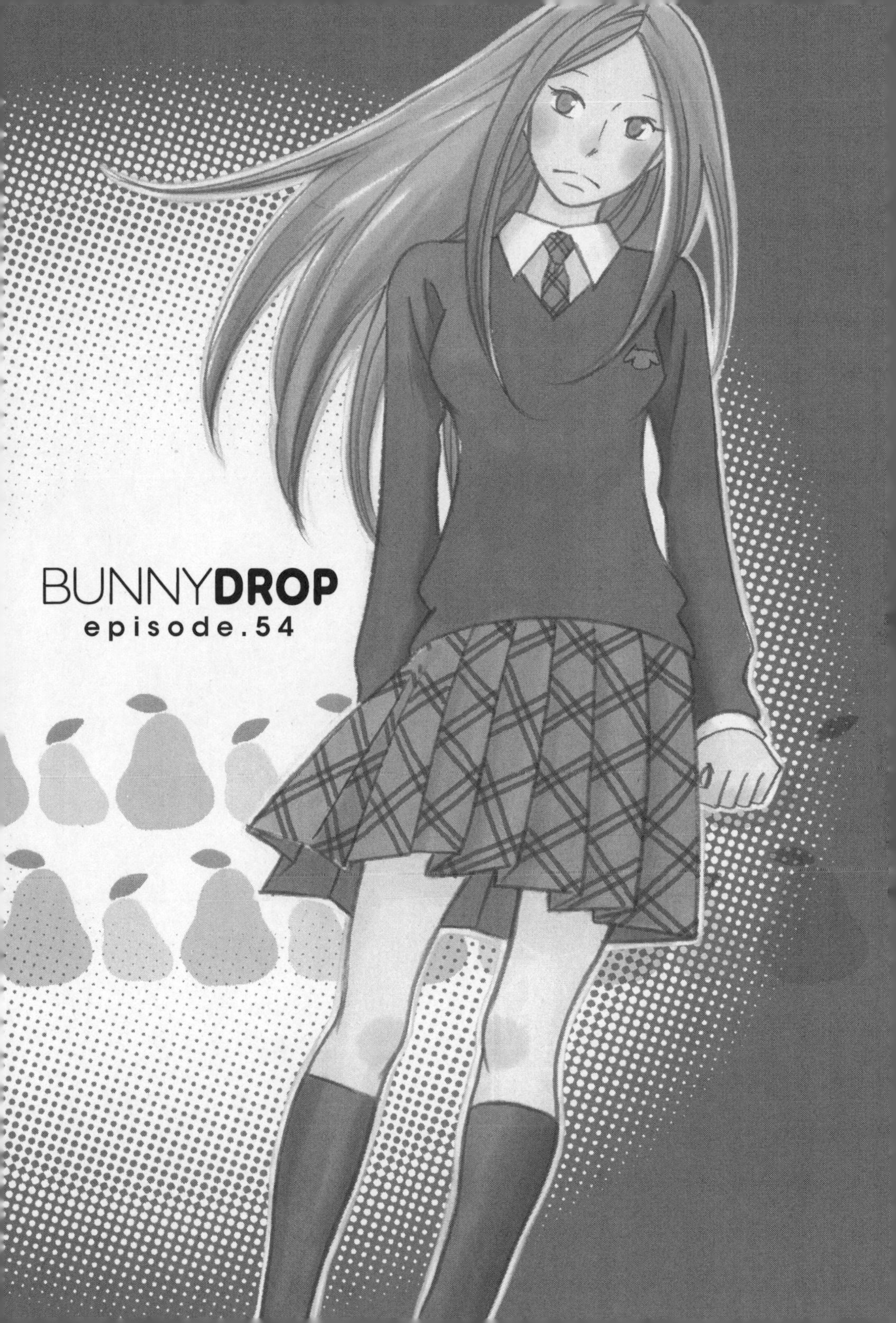
BUNNYDROP
episode.54

BUNNYDROP

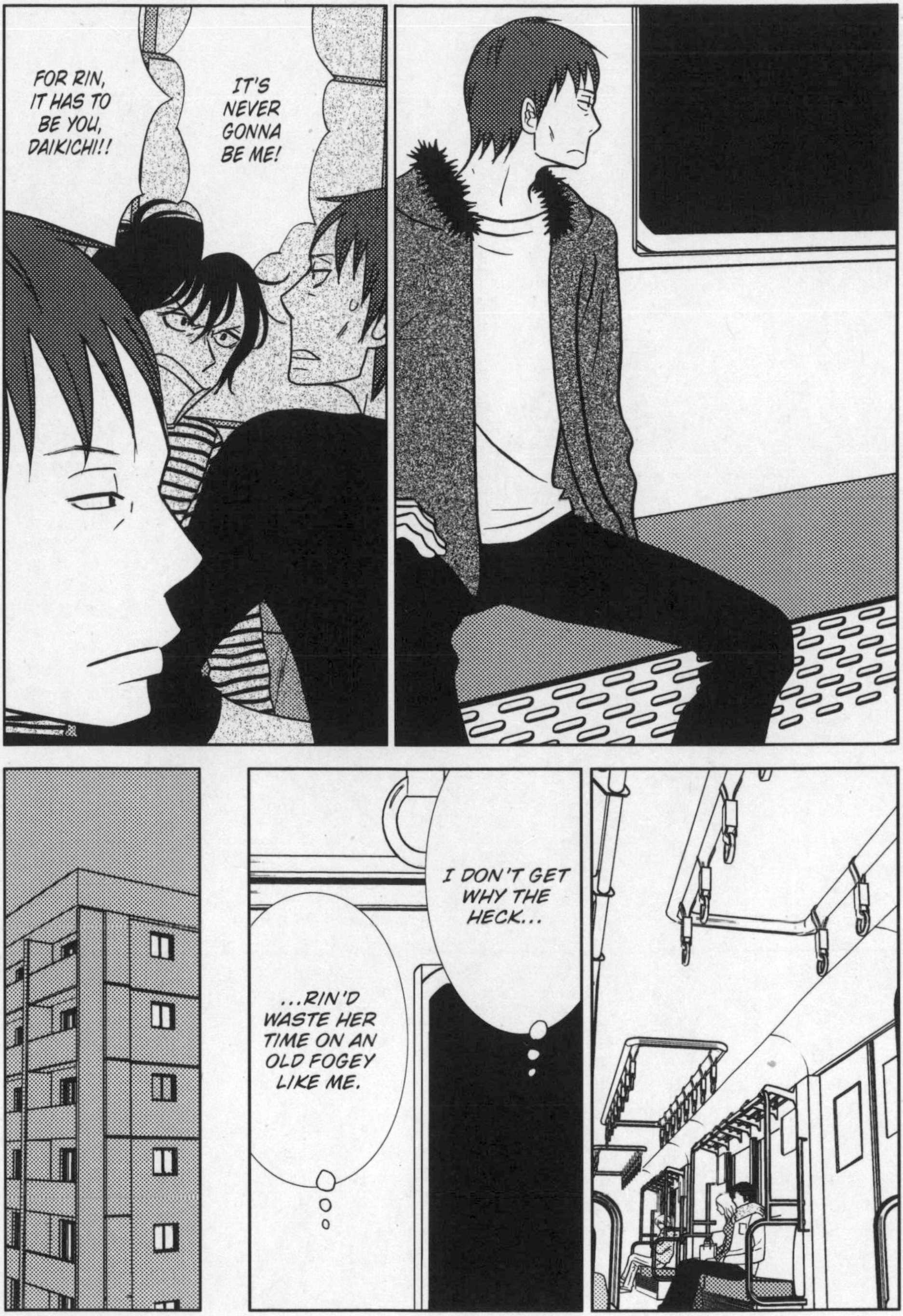
IT'S NEVER GONNA BE ME!
FOR RIN, IT HAS TO BE YOU, DAIKICHI!!
I DON'T GET WHY THE HECK...
...RIN'D WASTE HER TIME ON AN OLD FOGEY LIKE ME.

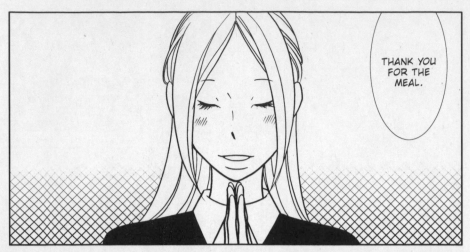

THANK YOU FOR THE MEAL.
I'M SORRY. YOU EVEN WENT AND GOT FOOD FOR US.
WE'RE SORRY TOO.
SINCE WE HAVE THE BABY, WE CAN'T GO OUT MUCH.
PIZZA
PLEASE, DON'T BE SORRY...
IT WAS REALLY TASTY...
MAY I HOLD HER FOR YOU?
OH... THANKS...
むぐ
MUGU (MUNCH)

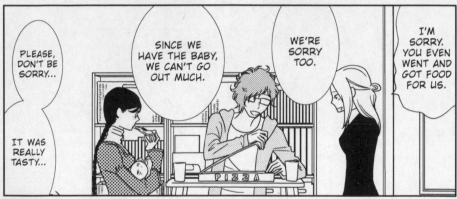

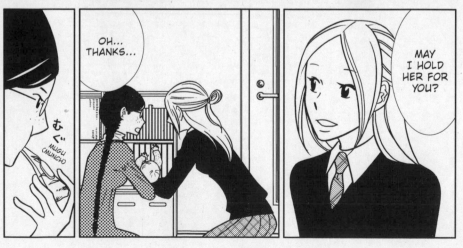

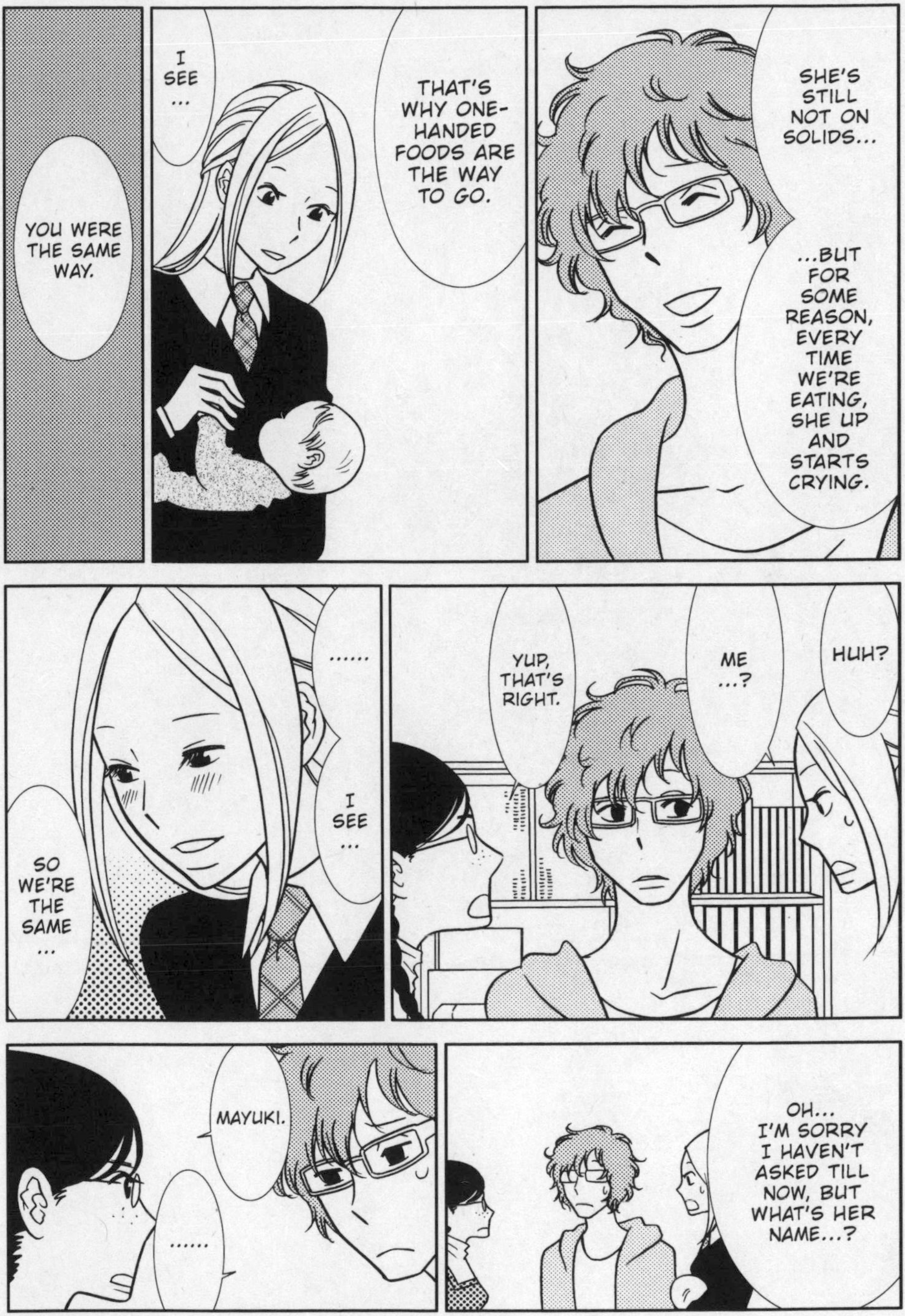
SHE'S STILL NOT ON SOLIDS...
...BUT FOR SOME REASON, EVERY TIME WE'RE EATING, SHE UP AND STARTS CRYING.
THAT'S WHY ONE-HANDED FOODS ARE THE WAY TO GO.
I SEE ...
YOU WERE THE SAME WAY.
HUH?
ME ...?
YUP, THAT'S RIGHT.
......
I SEE ...
SO WE'RE THE SAME ...
OH... I'M SORRY I HAVEN'T ASKED TILL NOW, BUT WHAT'S HER NAME...?
MAYUKI.
......

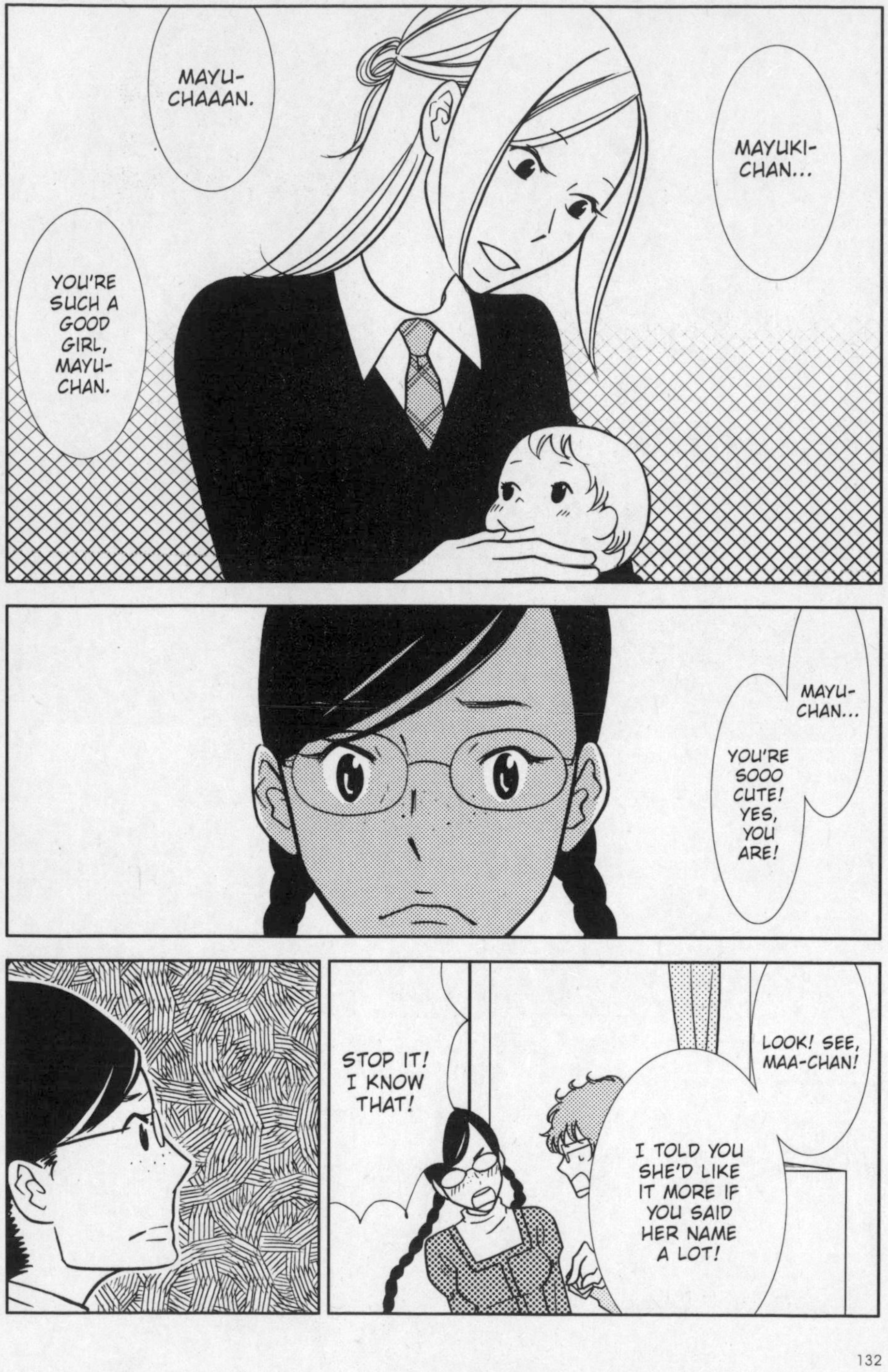
MAYUKI-CHAN...
MAYU-CHAAAN.
YOU'RE SUCH A GOOD GIRL, MAYU-CHAN.
MAYU-CHAN...
YOU'RE SOOO CUTE! YES, YOU ARE!
LOOK! SEE, MAA-CHAN!
I TOLD YOU SHE'D LIKE IT MORE IF YOU SAID HER NAME A LOT!
STOP IT! I KNOW THAT!

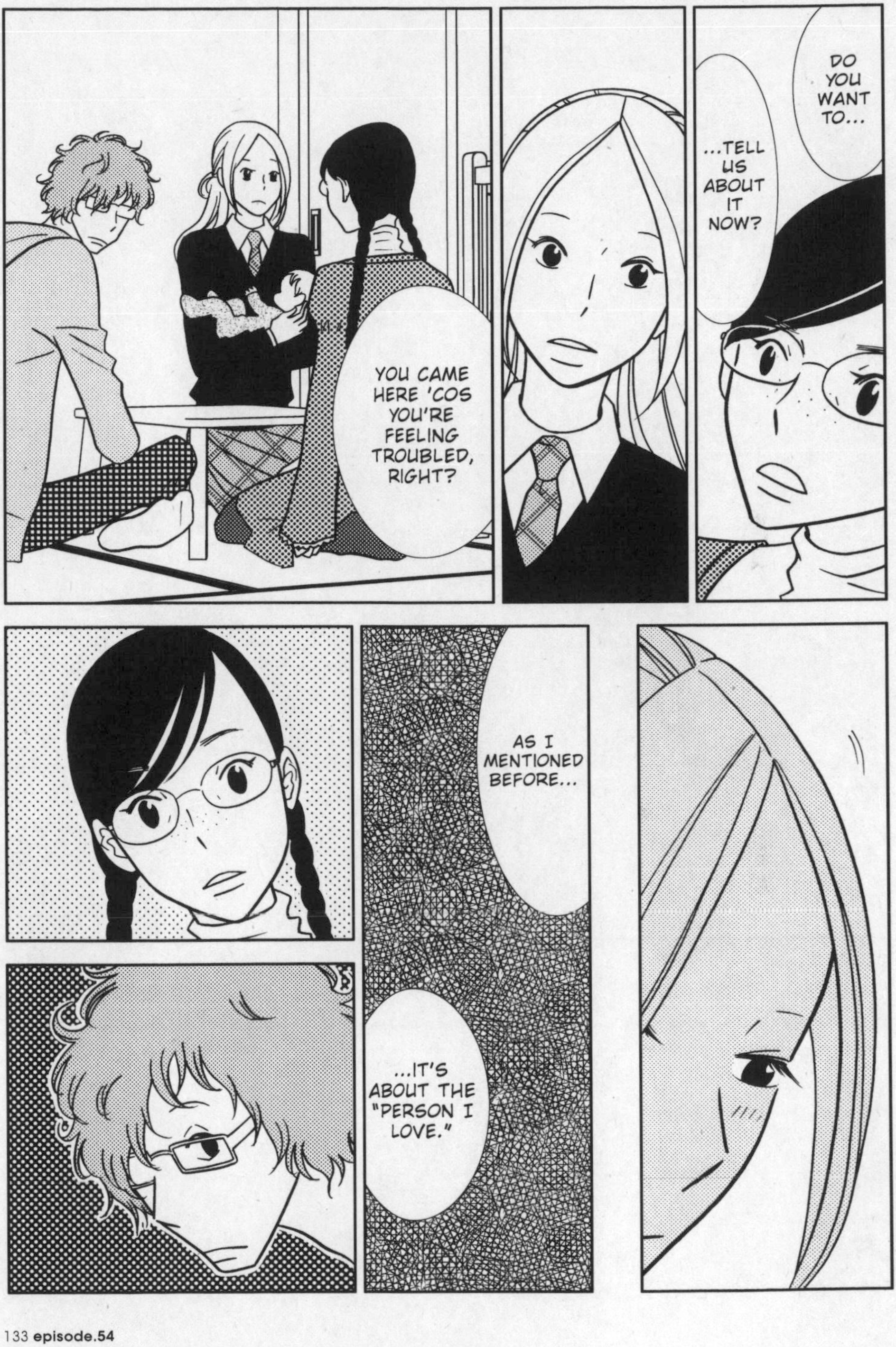
DO YOU WANT TO...
...TELL US ABOUT IT NOW?
YOU CAME HERE 'COS YOU'RE FEELING TROUBLED, RIGHT?
AS I MENTIONED BEFORE...
...IT'S ABOUT THE "PERSON I LOVE."

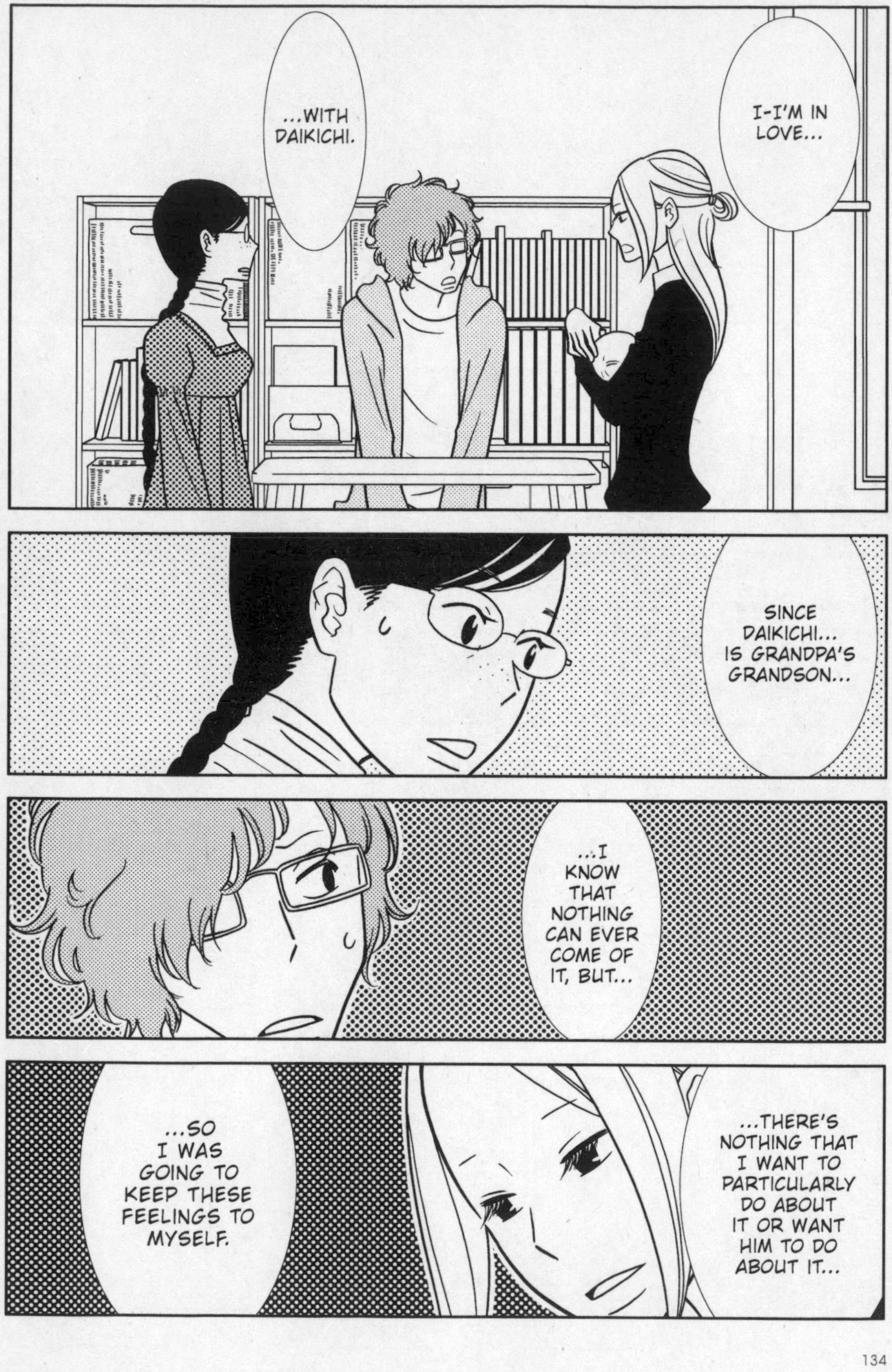
I-I'M IN LOVE...
...WITH DAIKICHI.
SINCE DAIKICHI... IS GRANDPA'S GRANDSON...
...I KNOW THAT NOTHING CAN EVER COME OF IT, BUT...
...THERE'S NOTHING THAT I WANT TO PARTICULARLY DO ABOUT IT OR WANT HIM TO DO ABOUT IT...
...SO I WAS GOING TO KEEP THESE FEELINGS TO MYSELF.

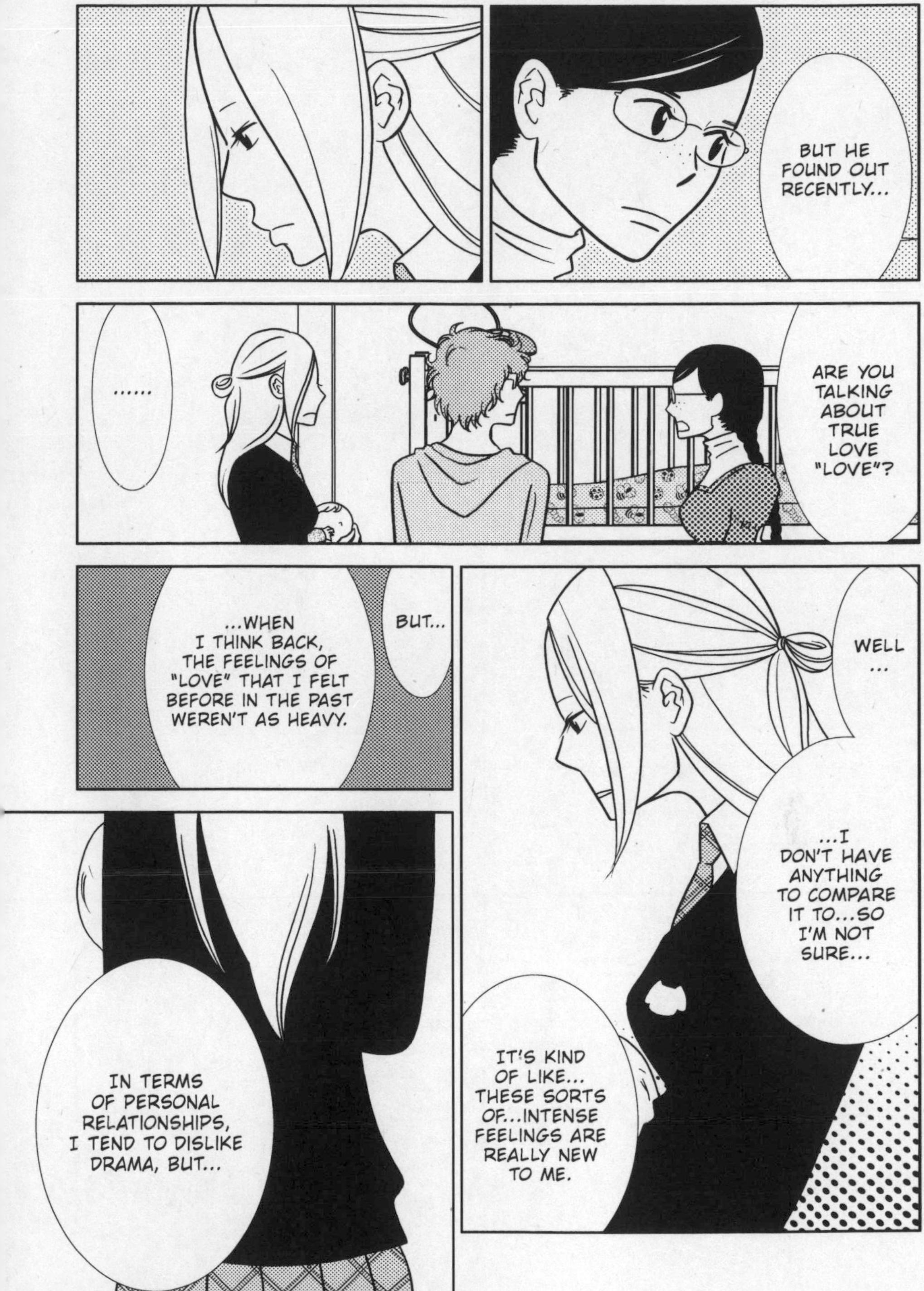
BUT HE FOUND OUT RECENTLY...
ARE YOU TALKING ABOUT TRUE LOVE "LOVE"?
......
WELL ...
...I DON'T HAVE ANYTHING TO COMPARE IT TO...SO I'M NOT SURE...
IT'S KIND OF LIKE... THESE SORTS OF...INTENSE FEELINGS ARE REALLY NEW TO ME.
BUT...
...WHEN I THINK BACK, THE FEELINGS OF "LOVE" THAT I FELT BEFORE IN THE PAST WEREN'T AS HEAVY.
IN TERMS OF PERSONAL RELATIONSHIPS, I TEND TO DISLIKE DRAMA, BUT...

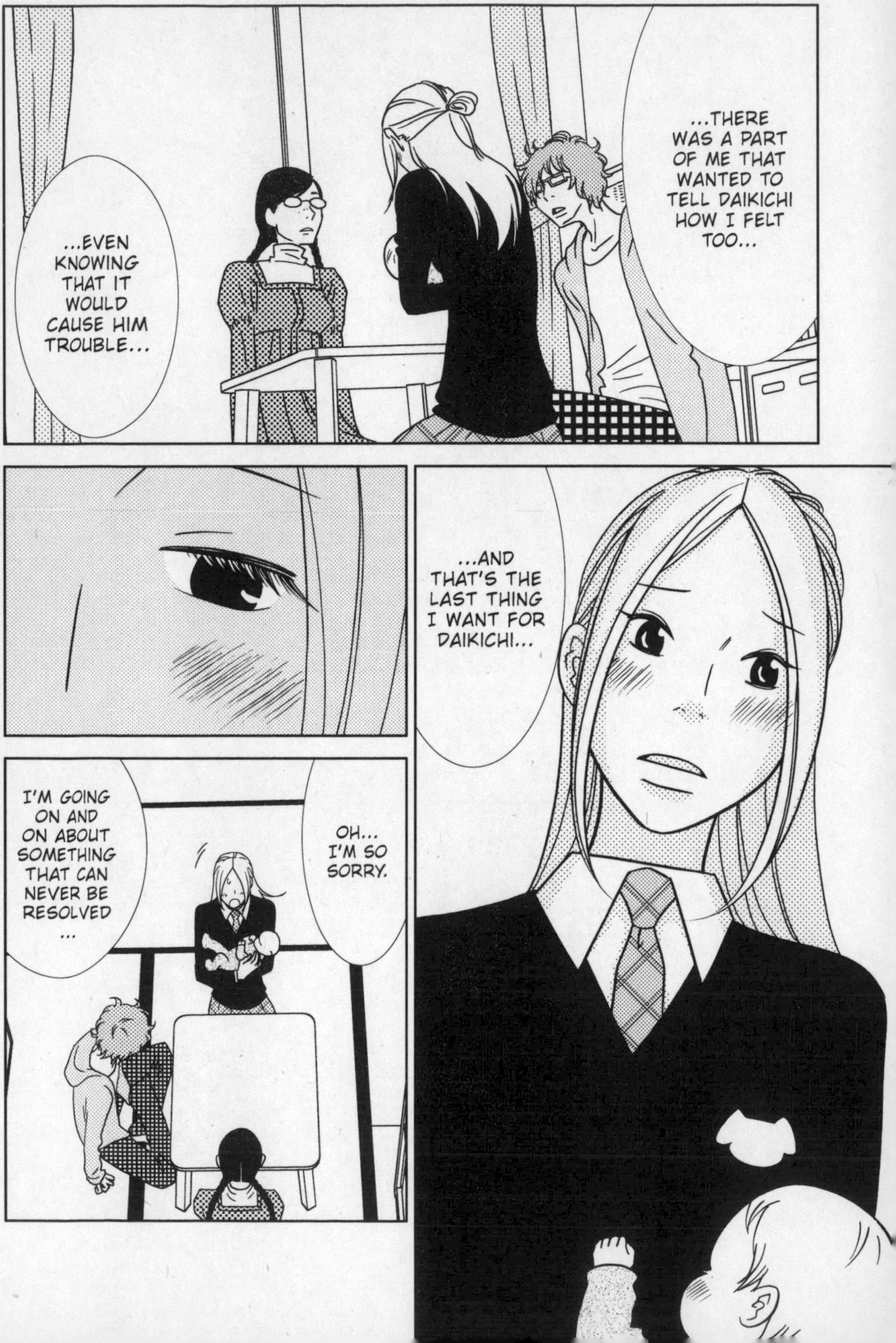
...THERE WAS A PART OF ME THAT WANTED TO TELL DAIKICHI HOW I FELT TOO...
...EVEN KNOWING THAT IT WOULD CAUSE HIM TROUBLE...
...AND THAT'S THE LAST THING I WANT FOR DAIKICHI...
OH... I'M SO SORRY.
I'M GOING ON AND ON ABOUT SOMETHING THAT CAN NEVER BE RESOLVED...

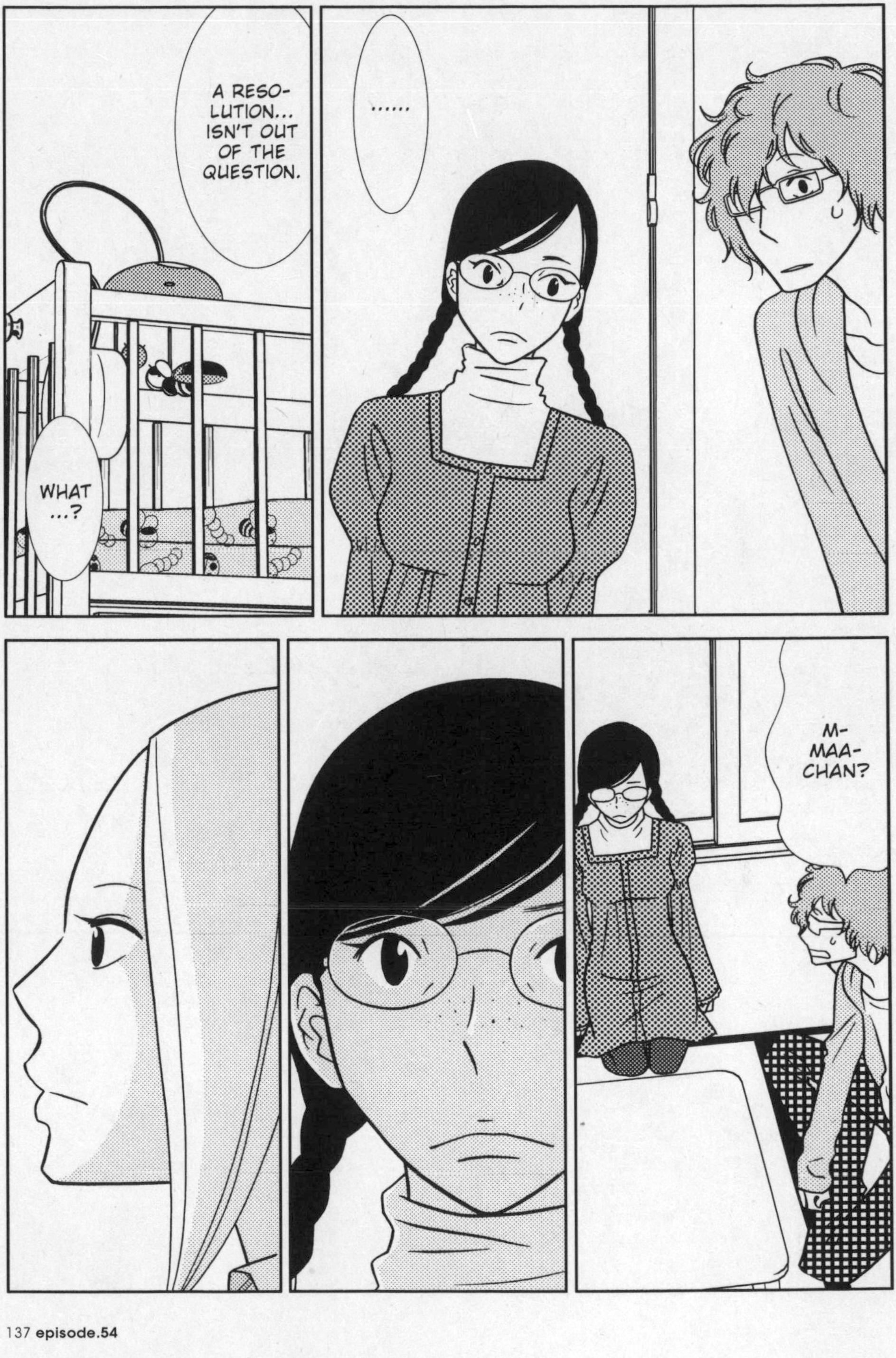
......
A RESO-LUTION... ISN'T OUT OF THE QUESTION.
WHAT ...?
M-MAA-CHAN?

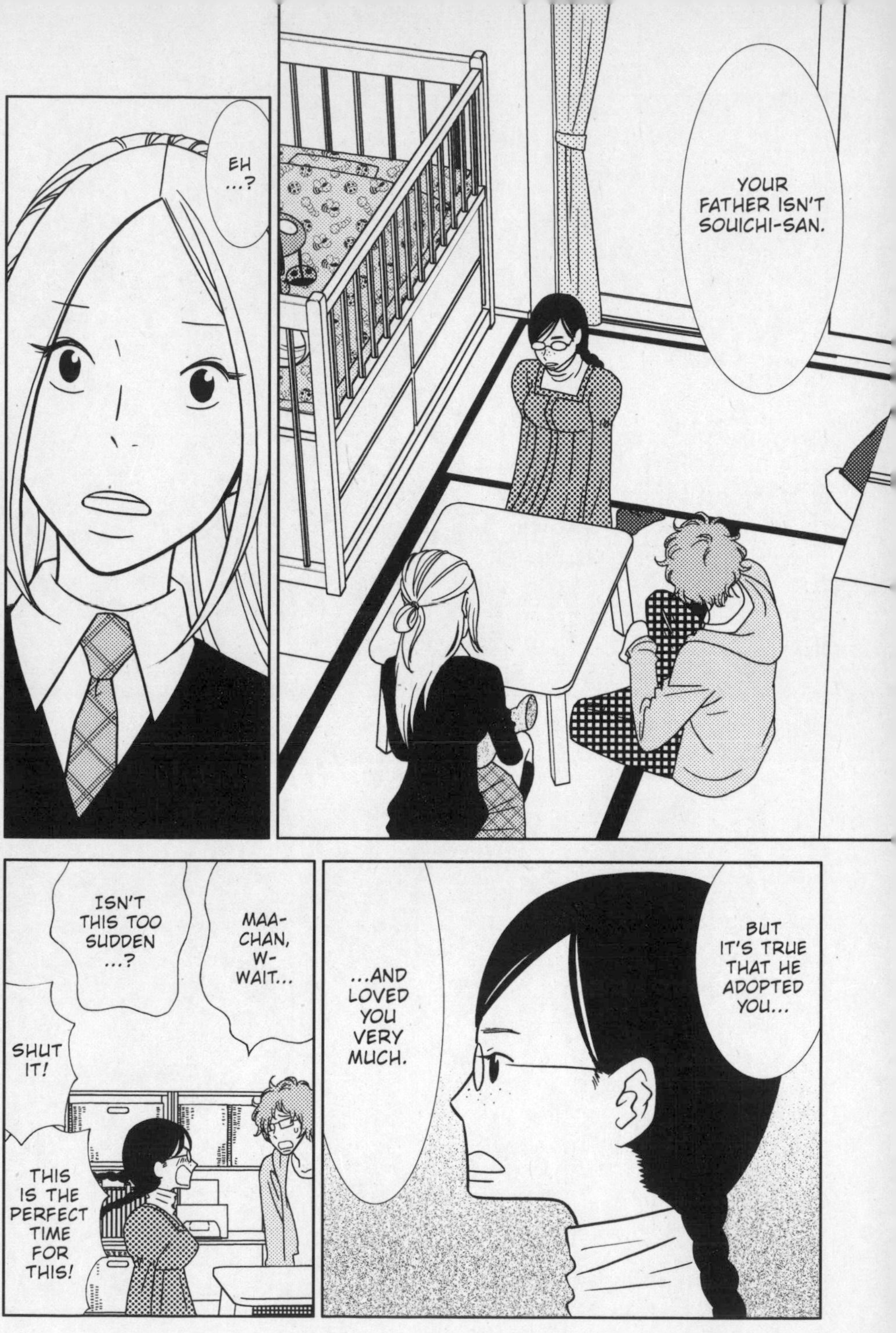
YOUR FATHER ISN'T SOUICHI-SAN.
EH ...?
BUT IT'S TRUE THAT HE ADOPTED YOU...
...AND LOVED YOU VERY MUCH.
MAA-CHAN, W-WAIT...
ISN'T THIS TOO SUDDEN ...?
SHUT IT!
THIS IS THE PERFECT TIME FOR THIS!

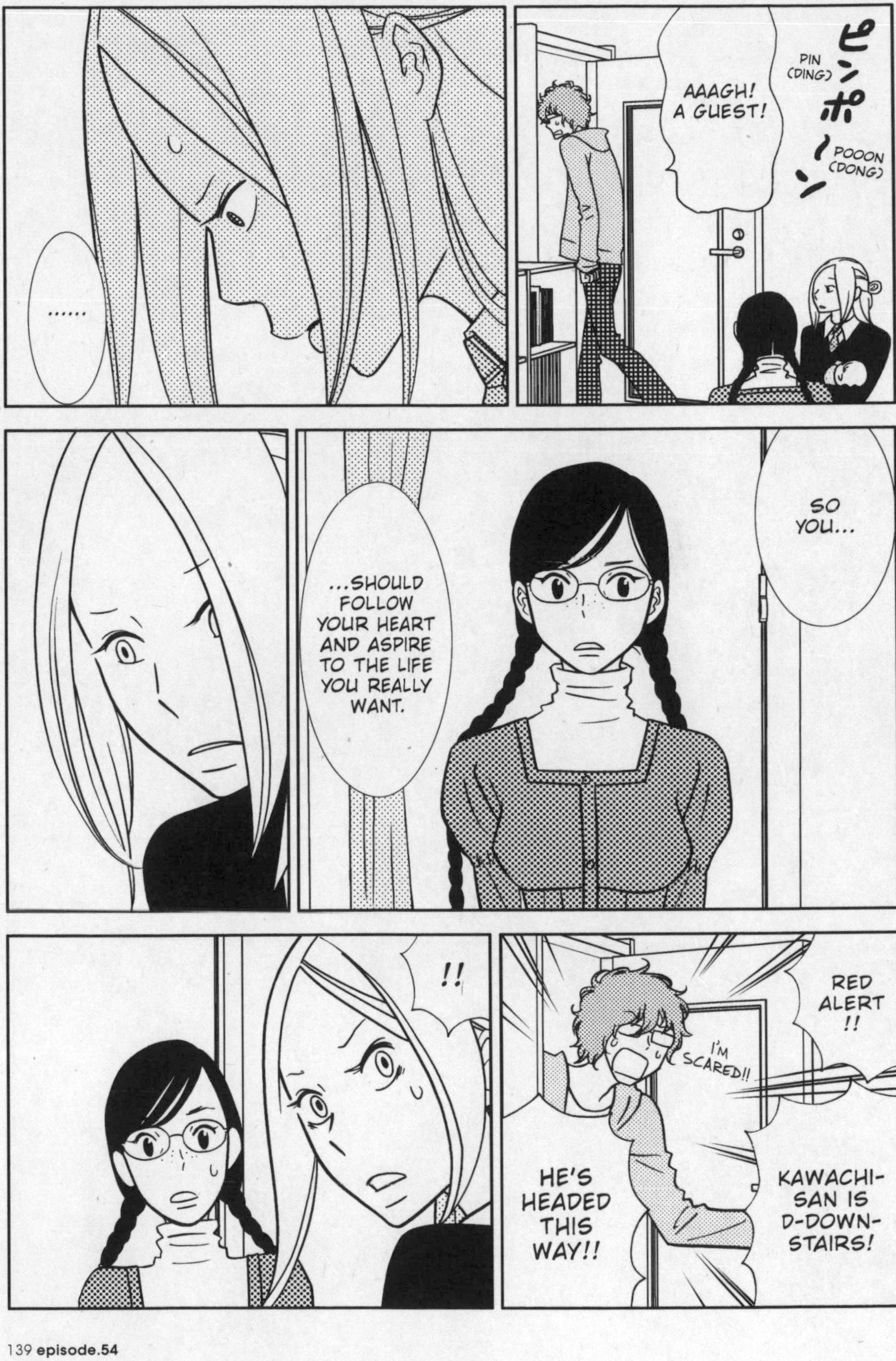
ピンポ～ン
PIN (DING)
POOON (DONG)
AAAGH! A GUEST!
......
SO YOU...
...SHOULD FOLLOW YOUR HEART AND ASPIRE TO THE LIFE YOU REALLY WANT.
RED ALERT!!
KAWACHI-SAN IS D-DOWN-STAIRS!
I'M SCARED!!
HE'S HEADED THIS WAY!!
!!

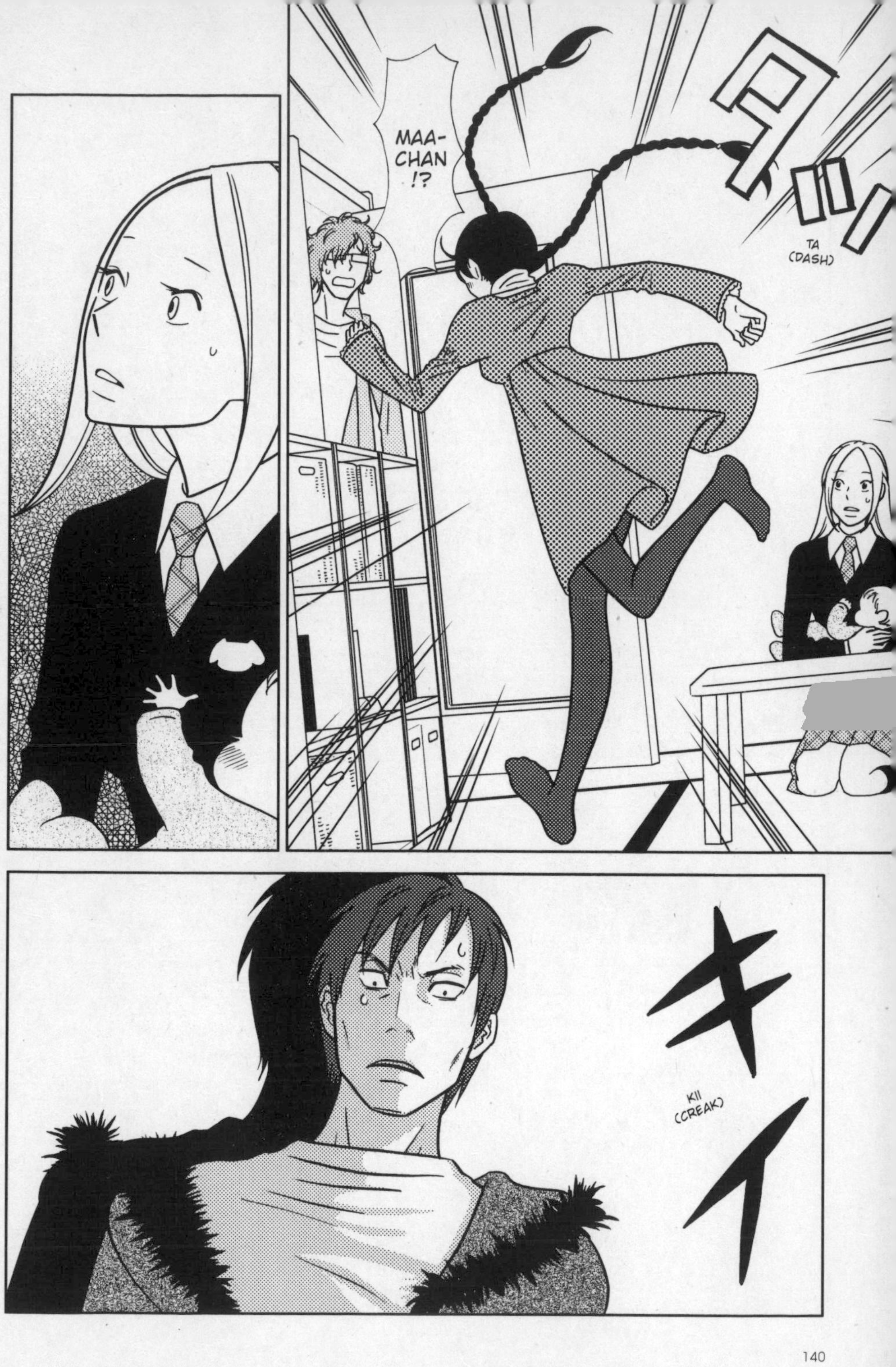
MAA-CHAN!?
TA (DASH)
KII (CREAK)

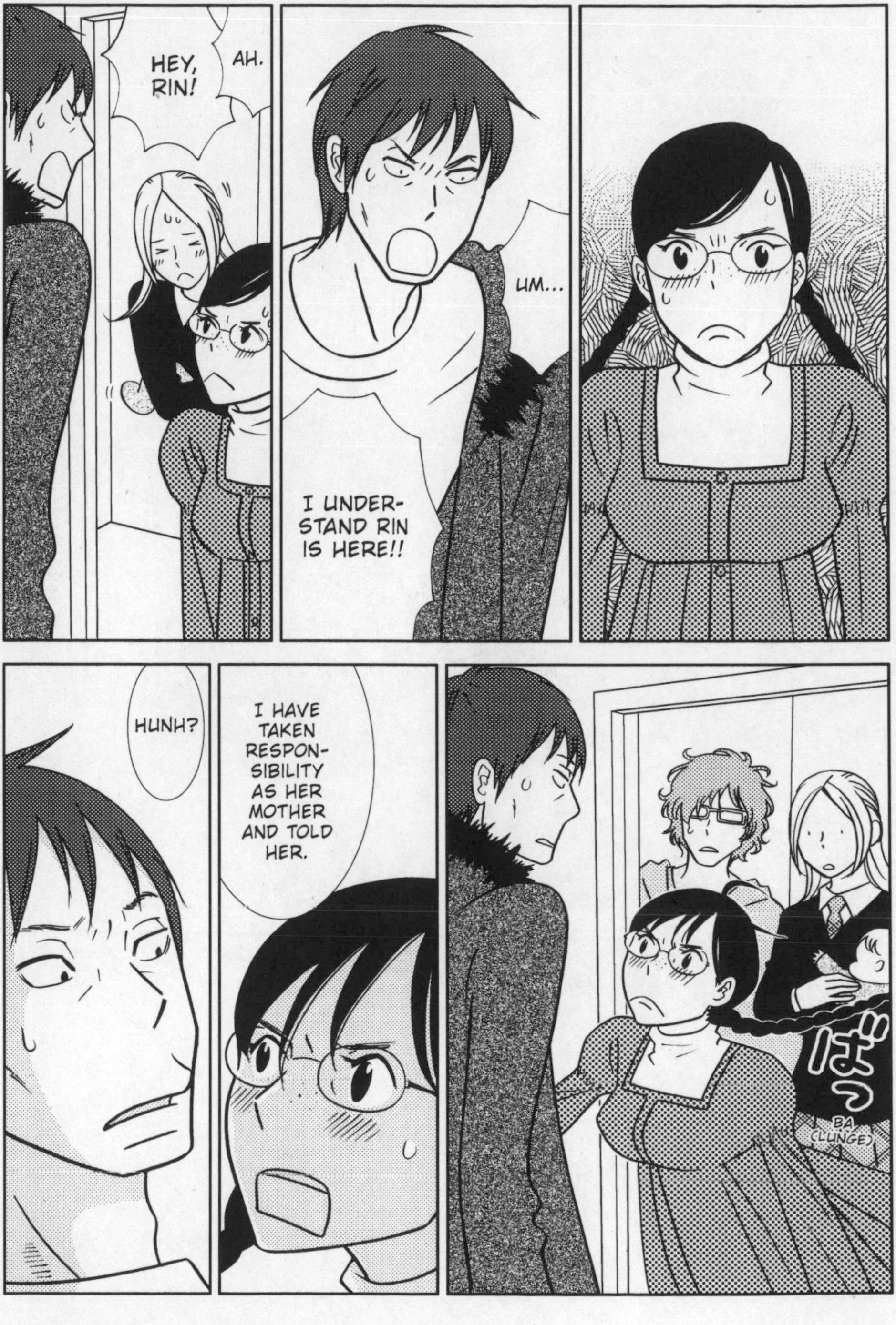
UM...
I UNDER-
STAND RIN
IS HERE!!
AH.
HEY,
RIN!
ぱっ
BA
(LUNGE)
I HAVE
TAKEN
RESPON-
SIBILITY
AS HER
MOTHER
AND TOLD
HER.
HUNH?

I JUST INFORMED HER...
...THAT SOUICHI-SAN IS NOT HER FATHER.
!!!
WH...
WH...
AWA (PANIC)
アワ...
AWA
アワ...
WHAT THE HECK HAVE YOU DONE!!?

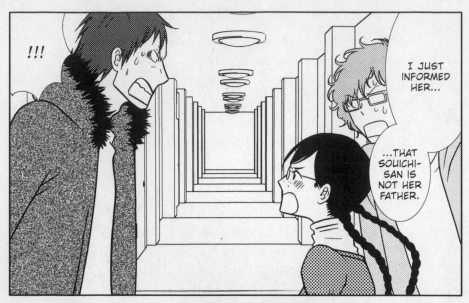

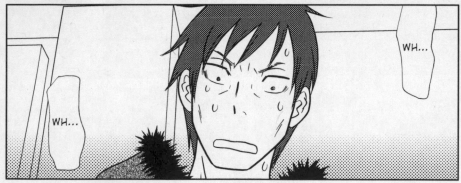

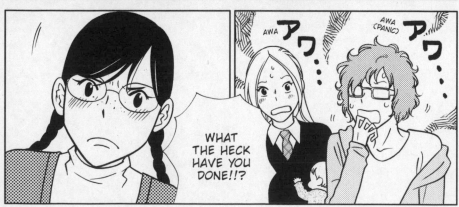

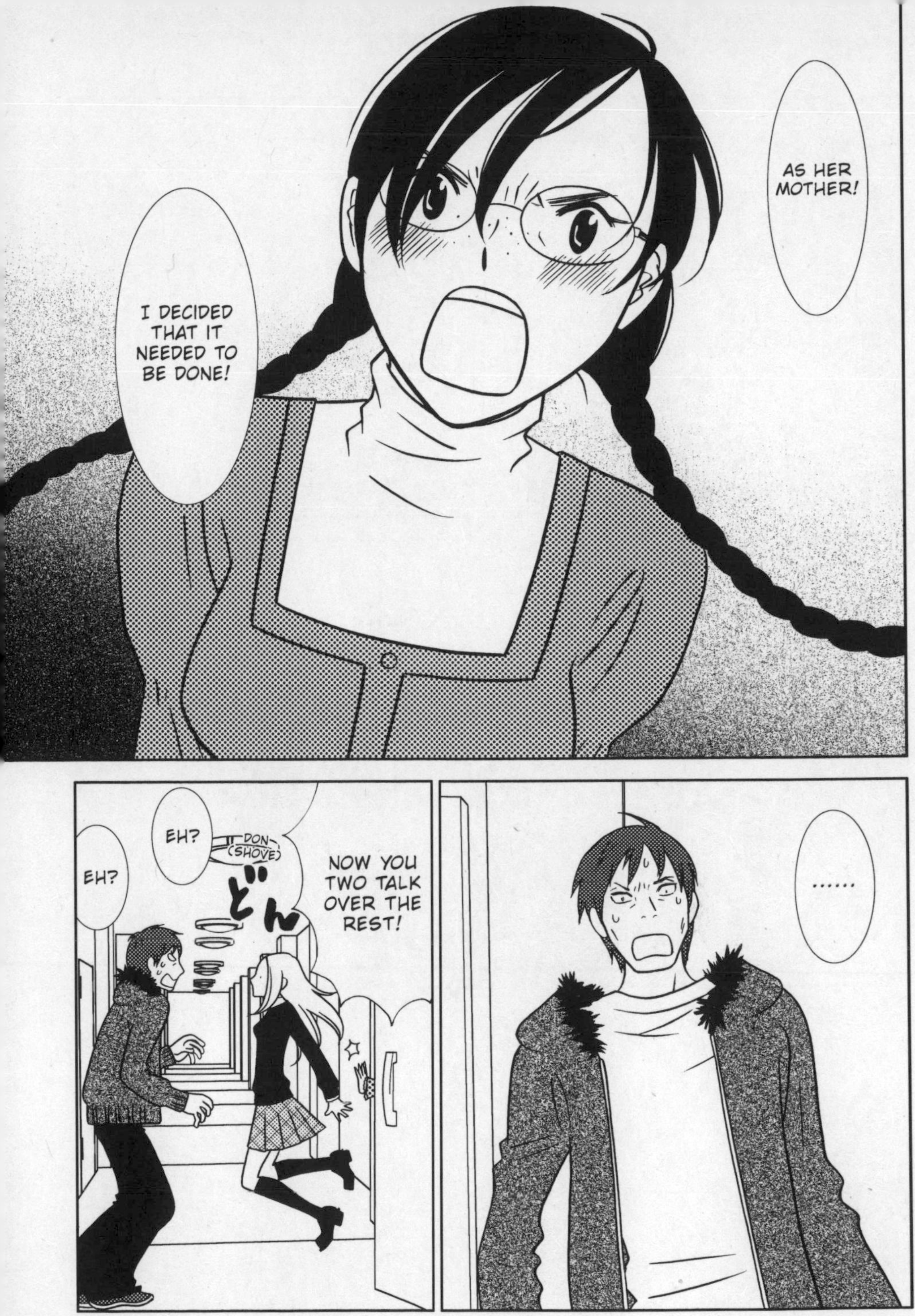
AS HER MOTHER!
I DECIDED THAT IT NEEDED TO BE DONE!
......
NOW YOU TWO TALK OVER THE REST!
DON (SHOVE)
どん
EH?
EH?

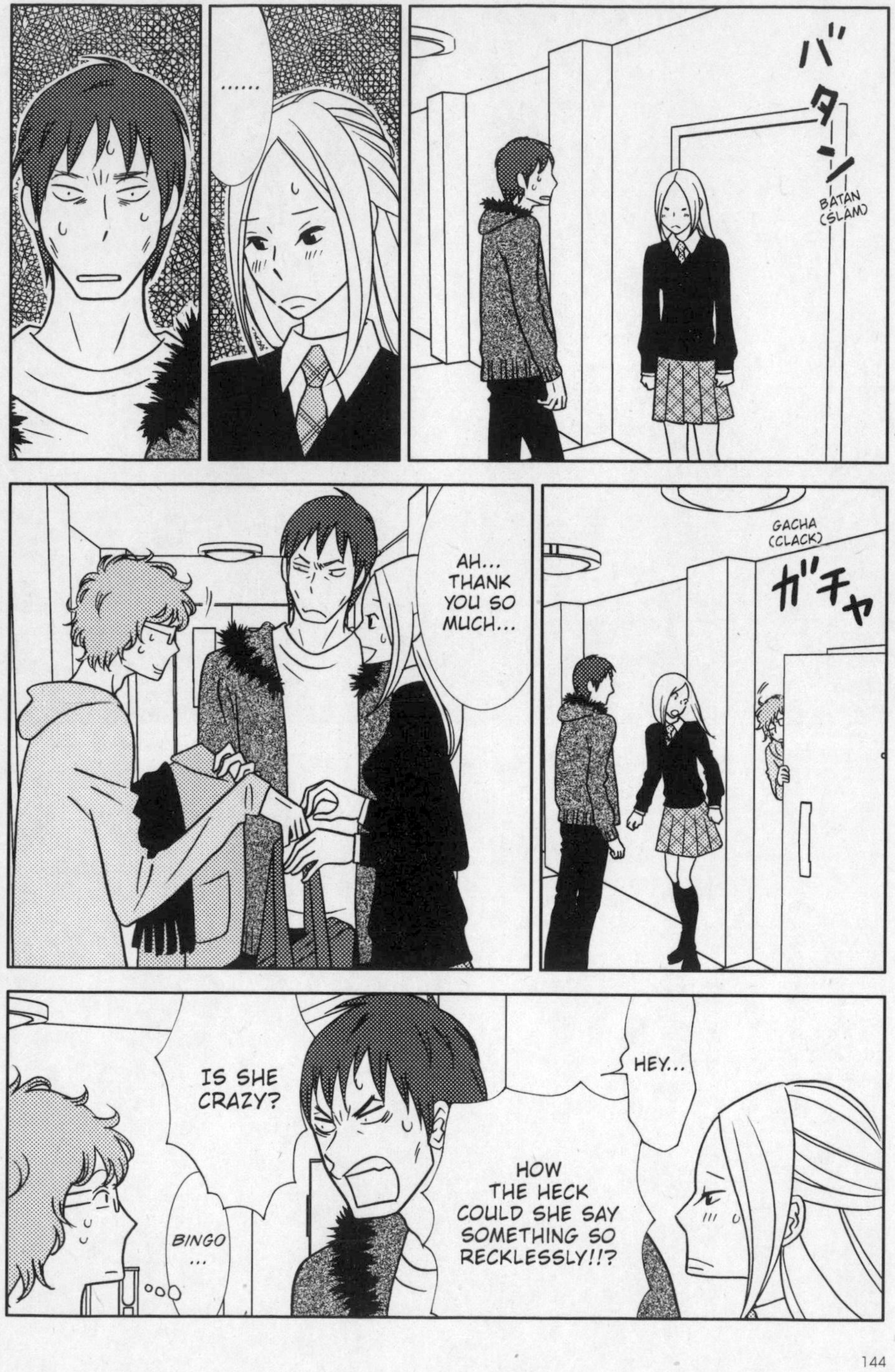
バターン
BATAN (SLAM)
......
GACHA (CLACK)
ガチャ
AH... THANK YOU SO MUCH...
HEY...
HOW THE HECK COULD SHE SAY SOMETHING SO RECKLESSLY!!?
IS SHE CRAZY?
BINGO ...

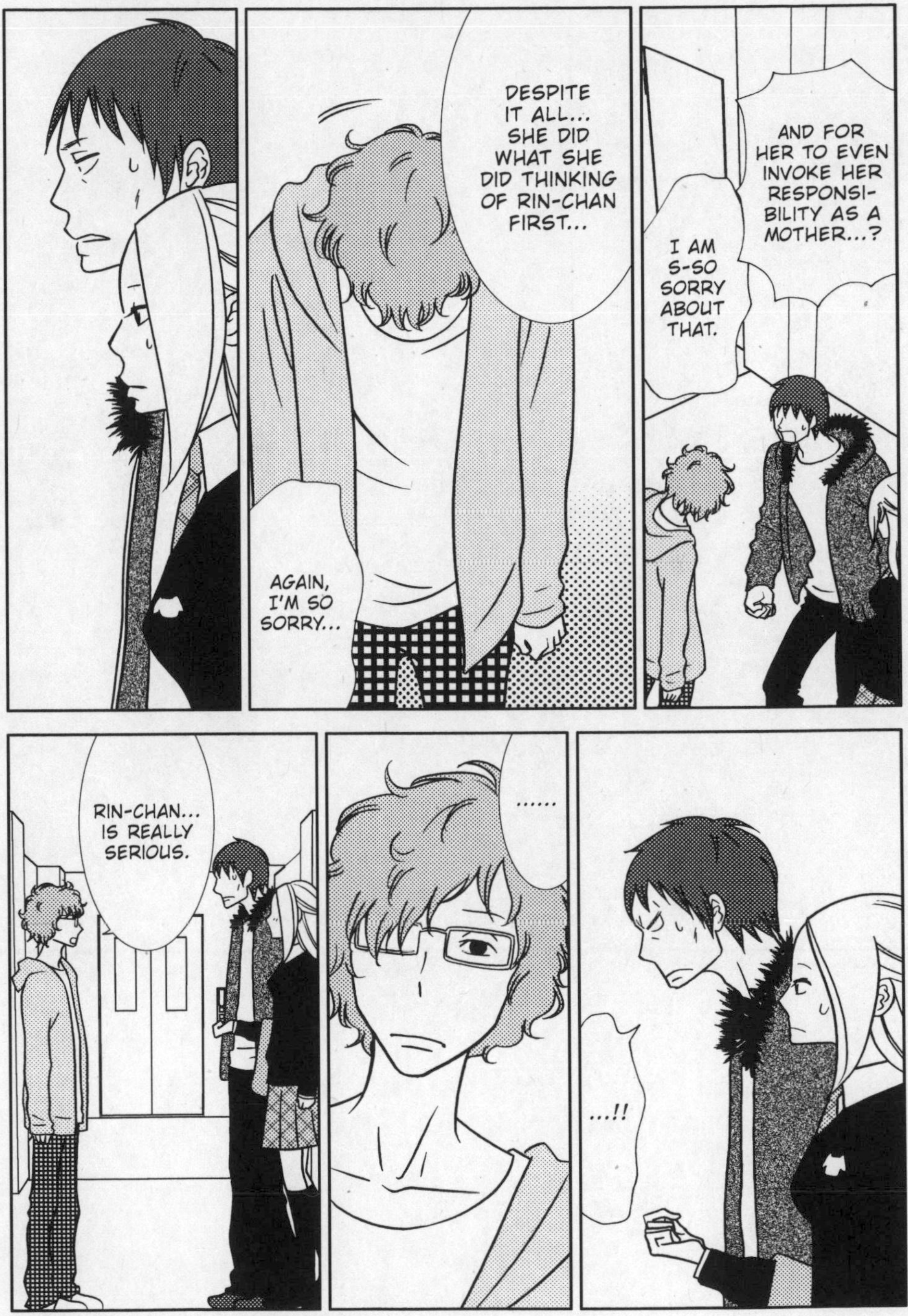
AND FOR HER TO EVEN INVOKE HER RESPONSI-BILITY AS A MOTHER...?
I AM S-SO SORRY ABOUT THAT.
DESPITE IT ALL... SHE DID WHAT SHE DID THINKING OF RIN-CHAN FIRST...
AGAIN, I'M SO SORRY...
...!!
......
RIN-CHAN... IS REALLY SERIOUS.

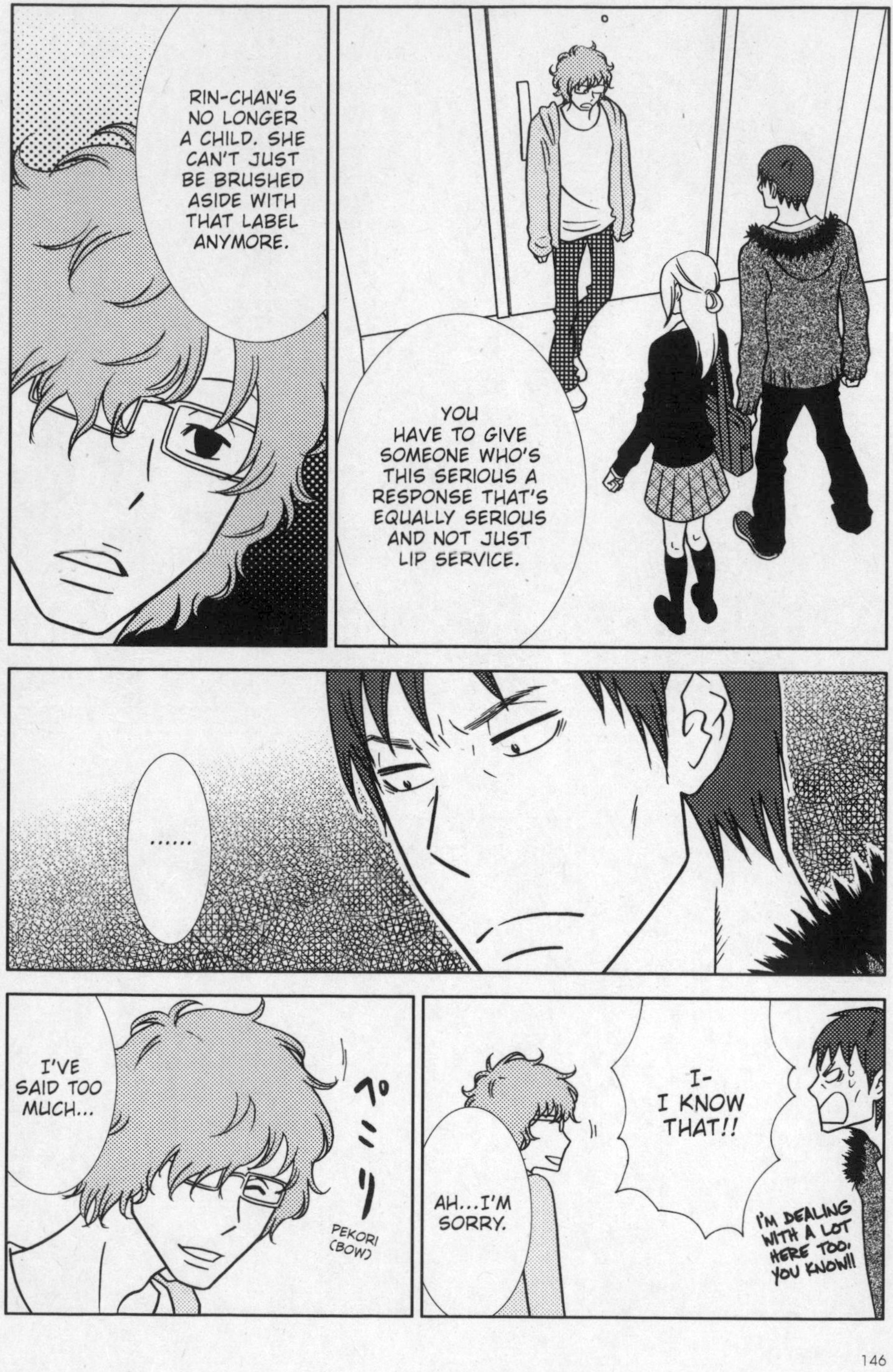
YOU HAVE TO GIVE SOMEONE WHO'S THIS SERIOUS A RESPONSE THAT'S EQUALLY SERIOUS AND NOT JUST LIP SERVICE.
RIN-CHAN'S NO LONGER A CHILD. SHE CAN'T JUST BE BRUSHED ASIDE WITH THAT LABEL ANYMORE.
......
I- I KNOW THAT!!
I'M DEALING WITH A LOT HERE TOO, YOU KNOW!!
AH...I'M SORRY.
I'VE SAID TOO MUCH...
ぺこり
PEKORI (BOW)

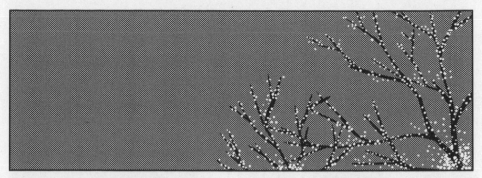

WERE YOU SHOCKED?

...... YEAH...

I... KNEW, OF COURSE.

THAT GRAMPS WASN'T YOUR ACTUAL DAD.

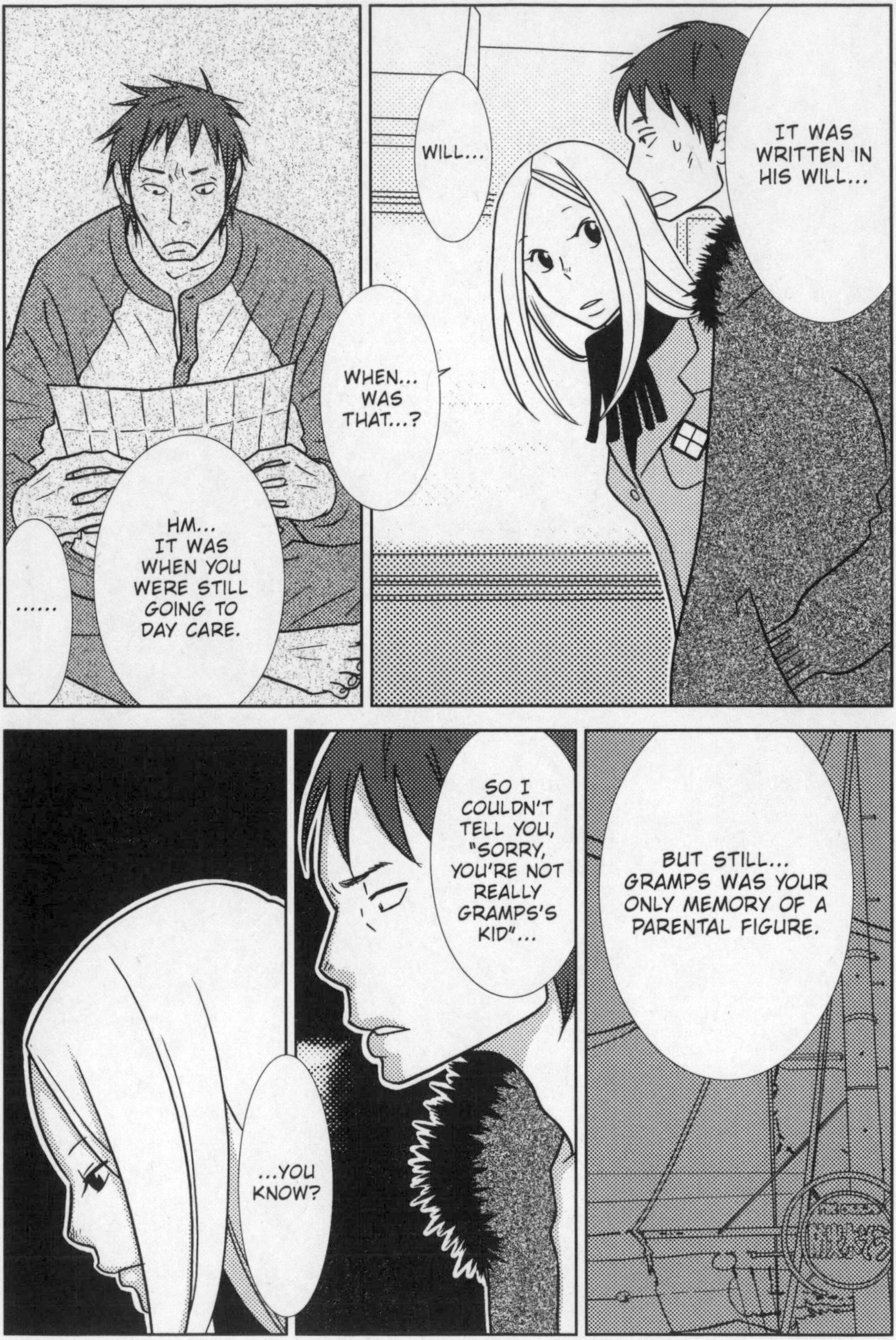
IT WAS WRITTEN IN HIS WILL...
WILL...
WHEN... WAS THAT...?
HM... IT WAS WHEN YOU WERE STILL GOING TO DAY CARE.
......
BUT STILL... GRAMPS WAS YOUR ONLY MEMORY OF A PARENTAL FIGURE.
SO I COULDN'T TELL YOU, "SORRY, YOU'RE NOT REALLY GRAMPS'S KID"...
...YOU KNOW?

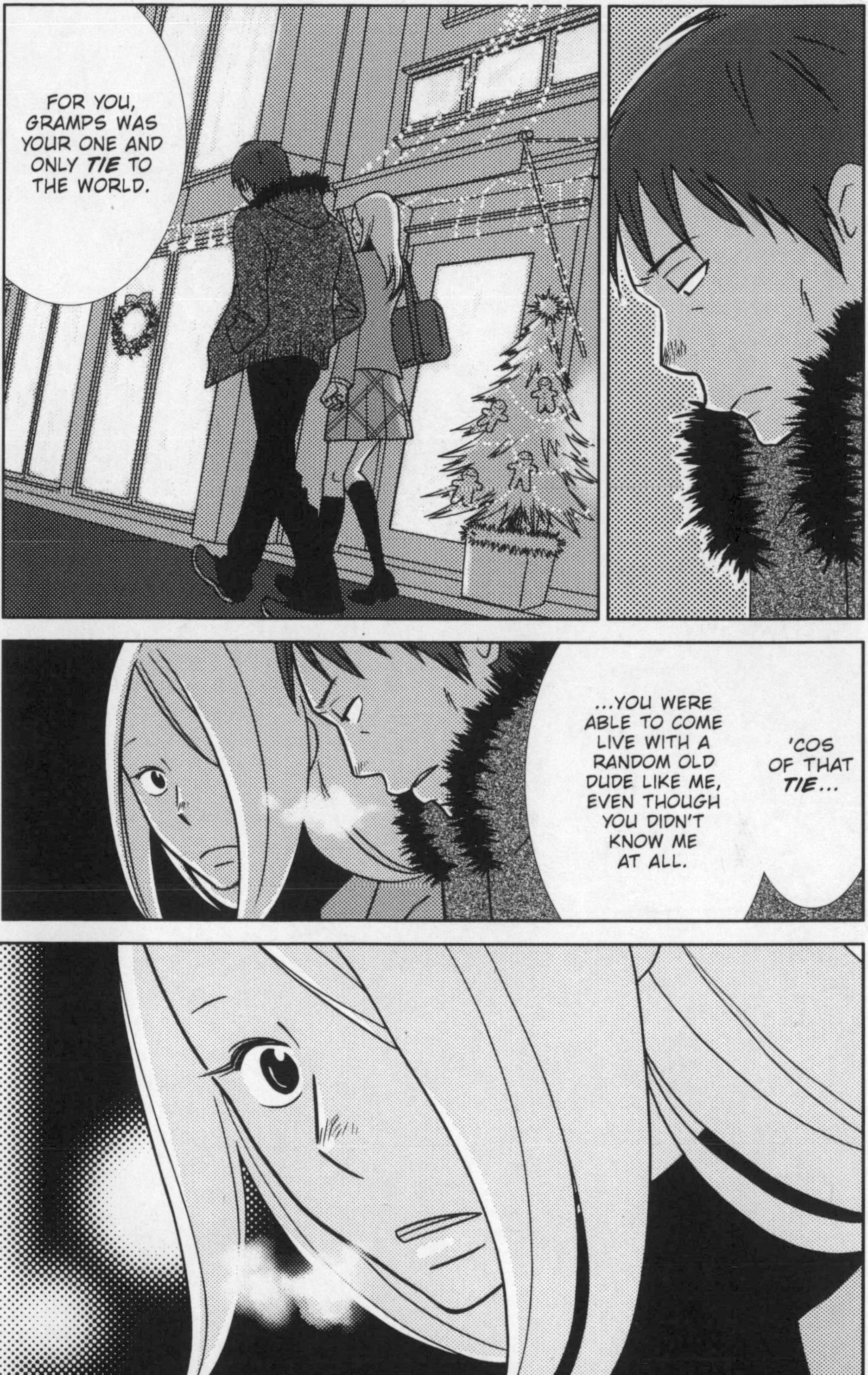
FOR YOU, GRAMPS WAS YOUR ONE AND ONLY *TIE* TO THE WORLD.
'COS OF THAT *TIE*...
...YOU WERE ABLE TO COME LIVE WITH A RANDOM OLD DUDE LIKE ME, EVEN THOUGH YOU DIDN'T KNOW ME AT ALL.

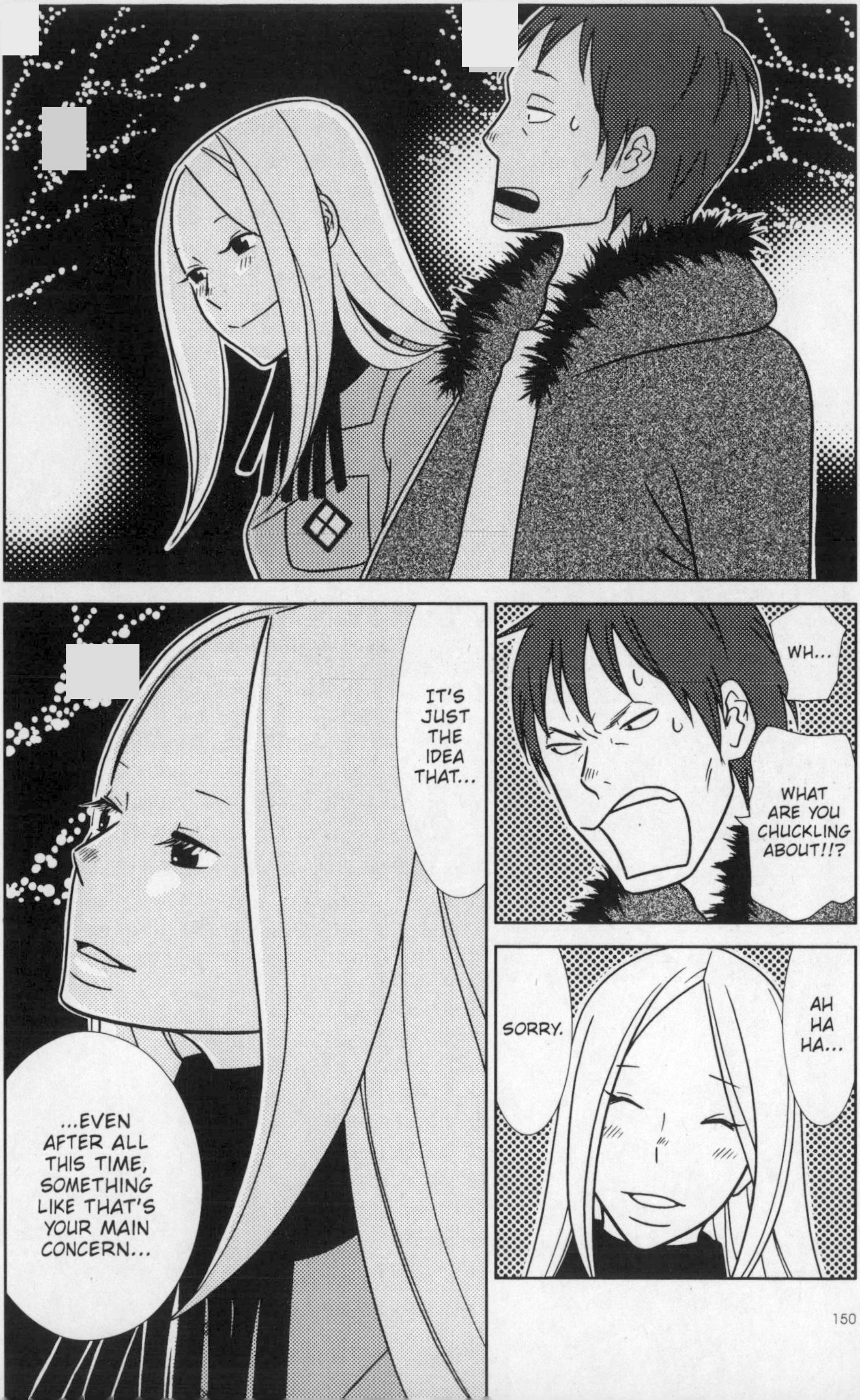
WH...
WHAT ARE YOU CHUCKLING ABOUT!!?
AH HA HA...
SORRY.
IT'S JUST THE IDEA THAT...
...EVEN AFTER ALL THIS TIME, SOMETHING LIKE THAT'S YOUR MAIN CONCERN...

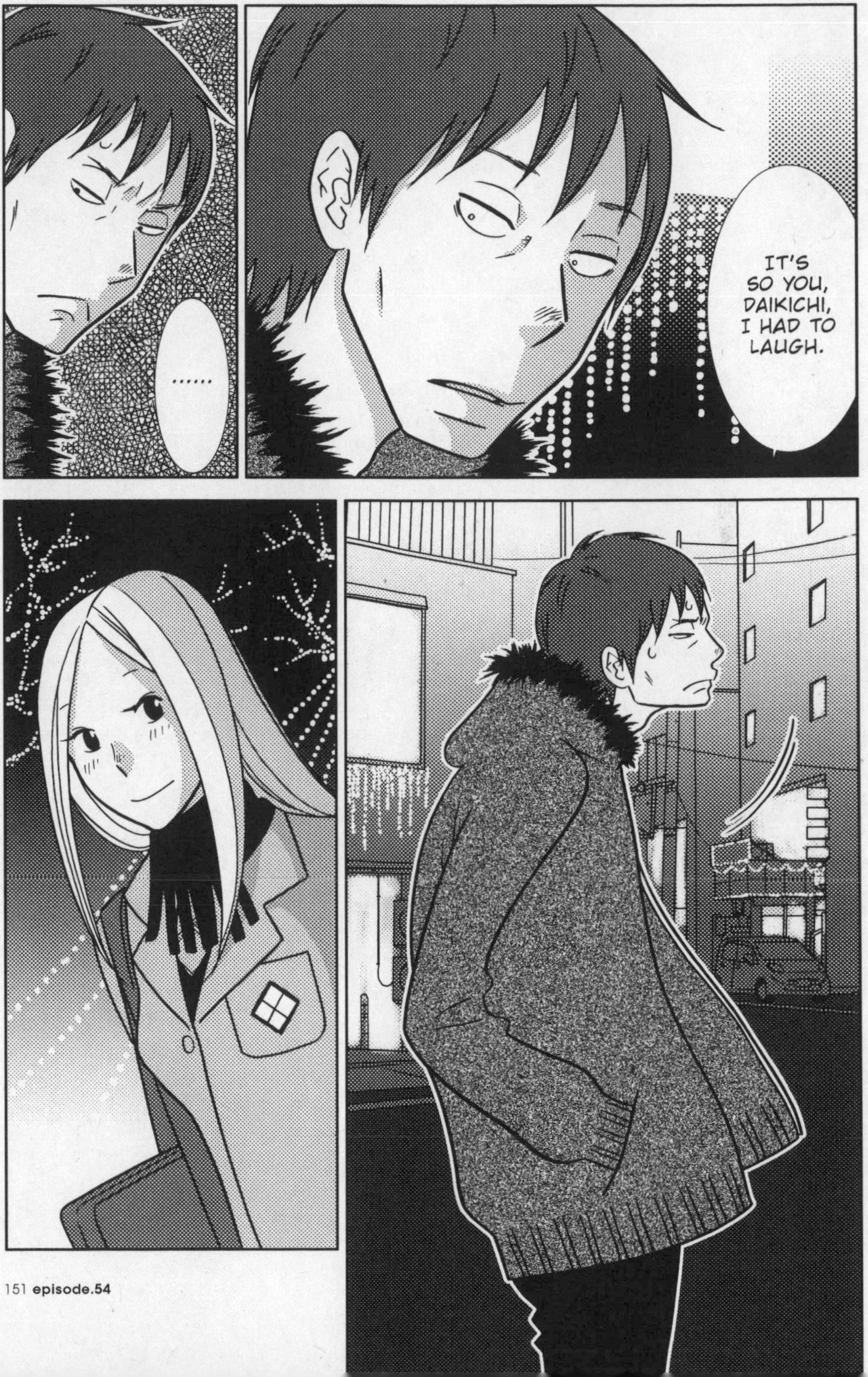
IT'S SO YOU, DAIKICHI, I HAD TO LAUGH.
……

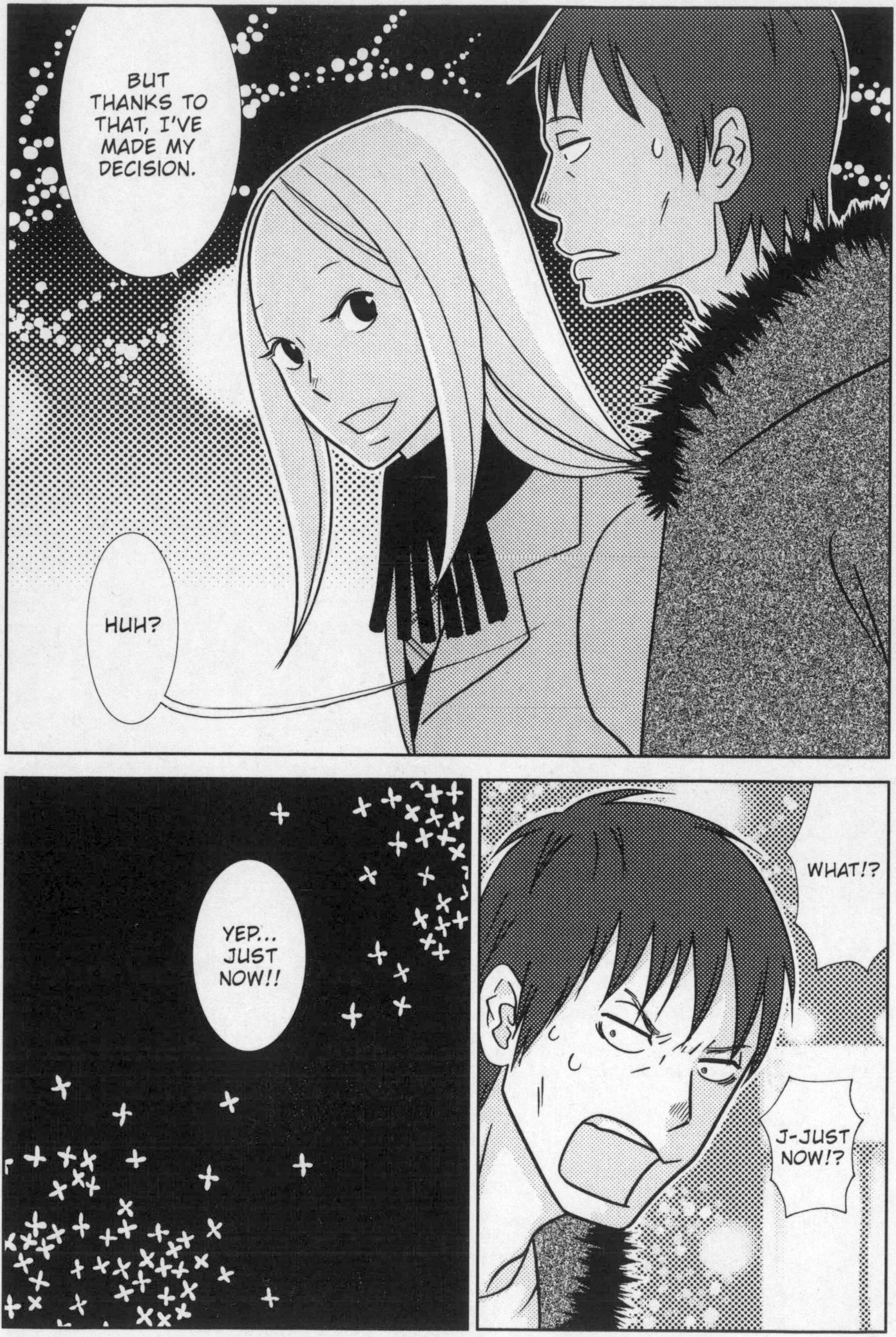
BUT THANKS TO THAT, I'VE MADE MY DECISION.
HUH?
YEP... JUST NOW!!
WHAT!?
J-JUST NOW!?

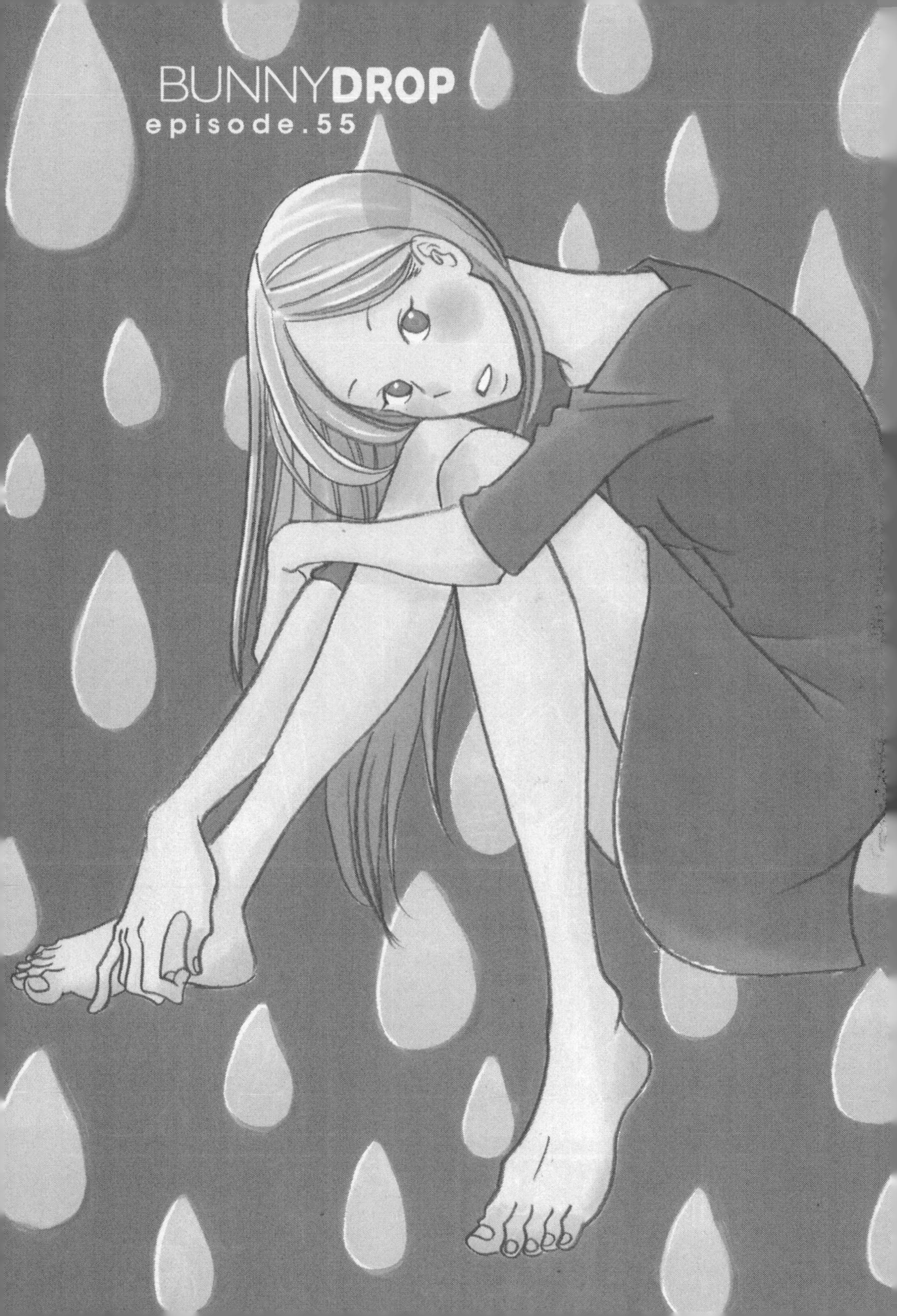
BUNNYDROP
episode.55

BUNNY**DROP**

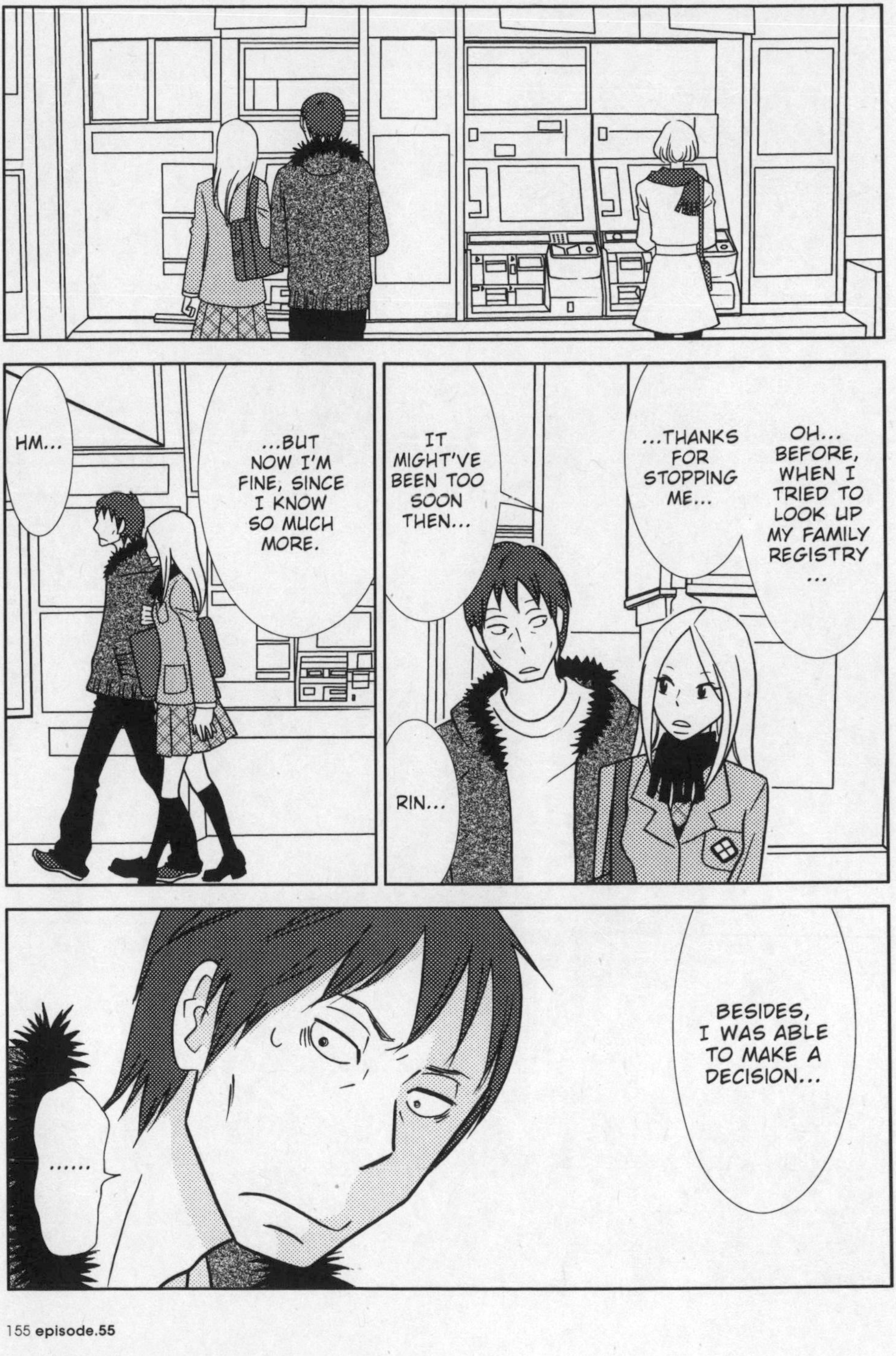
OH... BEFORE, WHEN I TRIED TO LOOK UP MY FAMILY REGISTRY ...
...THANKS FOR STOPPING ME...
IT MIGHT'VE BEEN TOO SOON THEN...
RIN...
...BUT NOW I'M FINE, SINCE I KNOW SO MUCH MORE.
HM...
BESIDES, I WAS ABLE TO MAKE A DECISION...
......

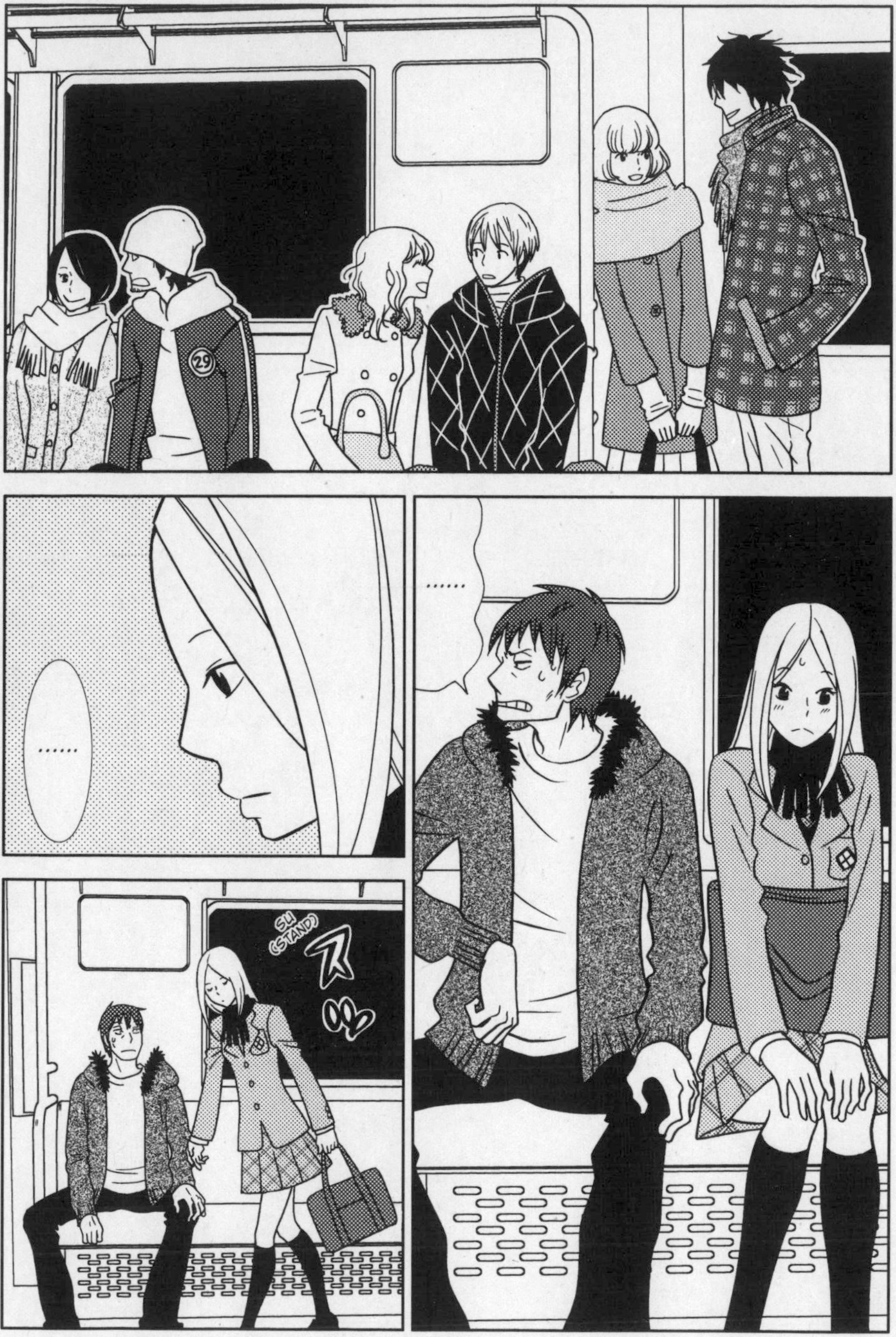
……
……
SU (STAND)
スッ

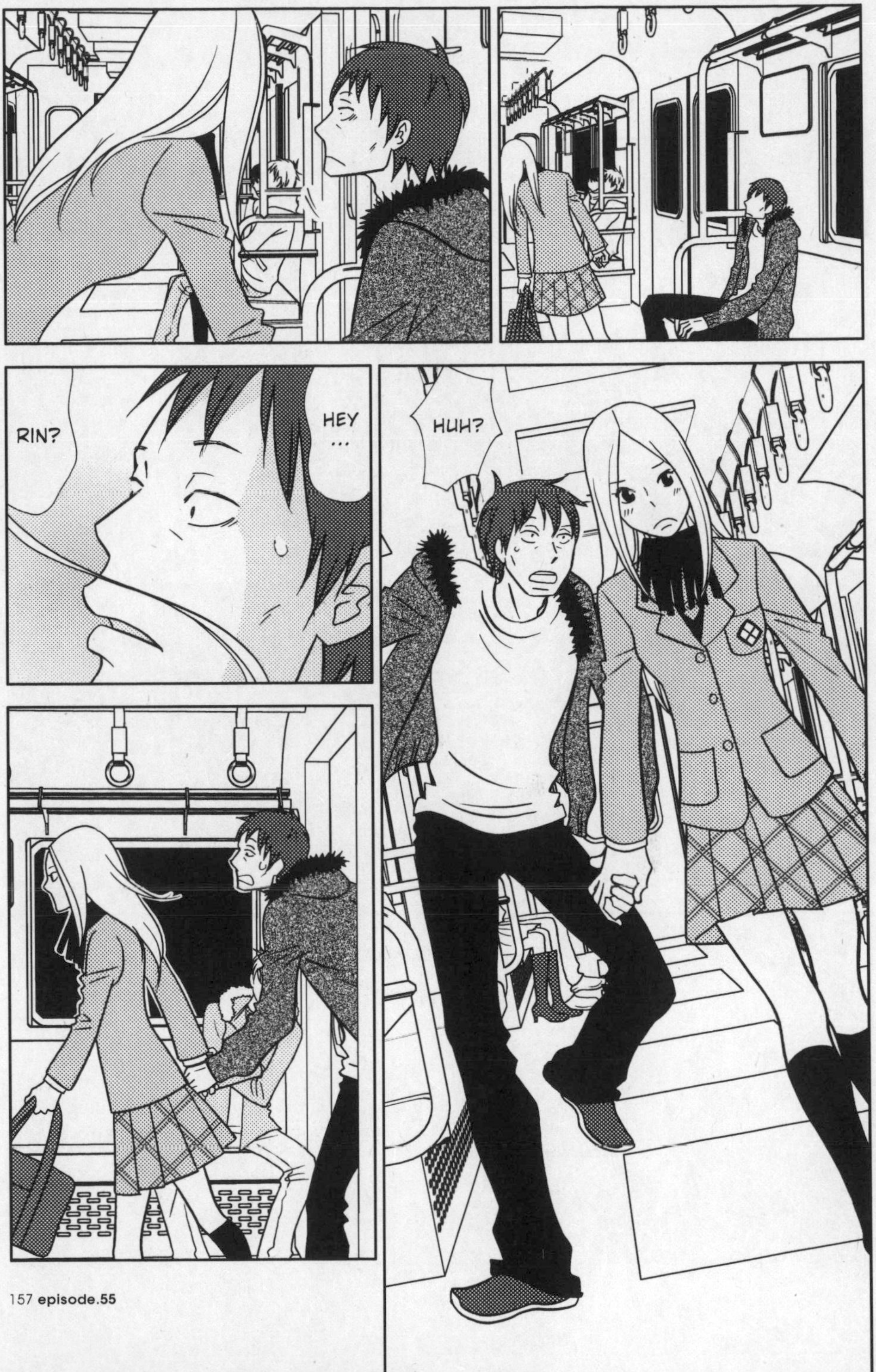
HUH?
HEY ...
RIN?

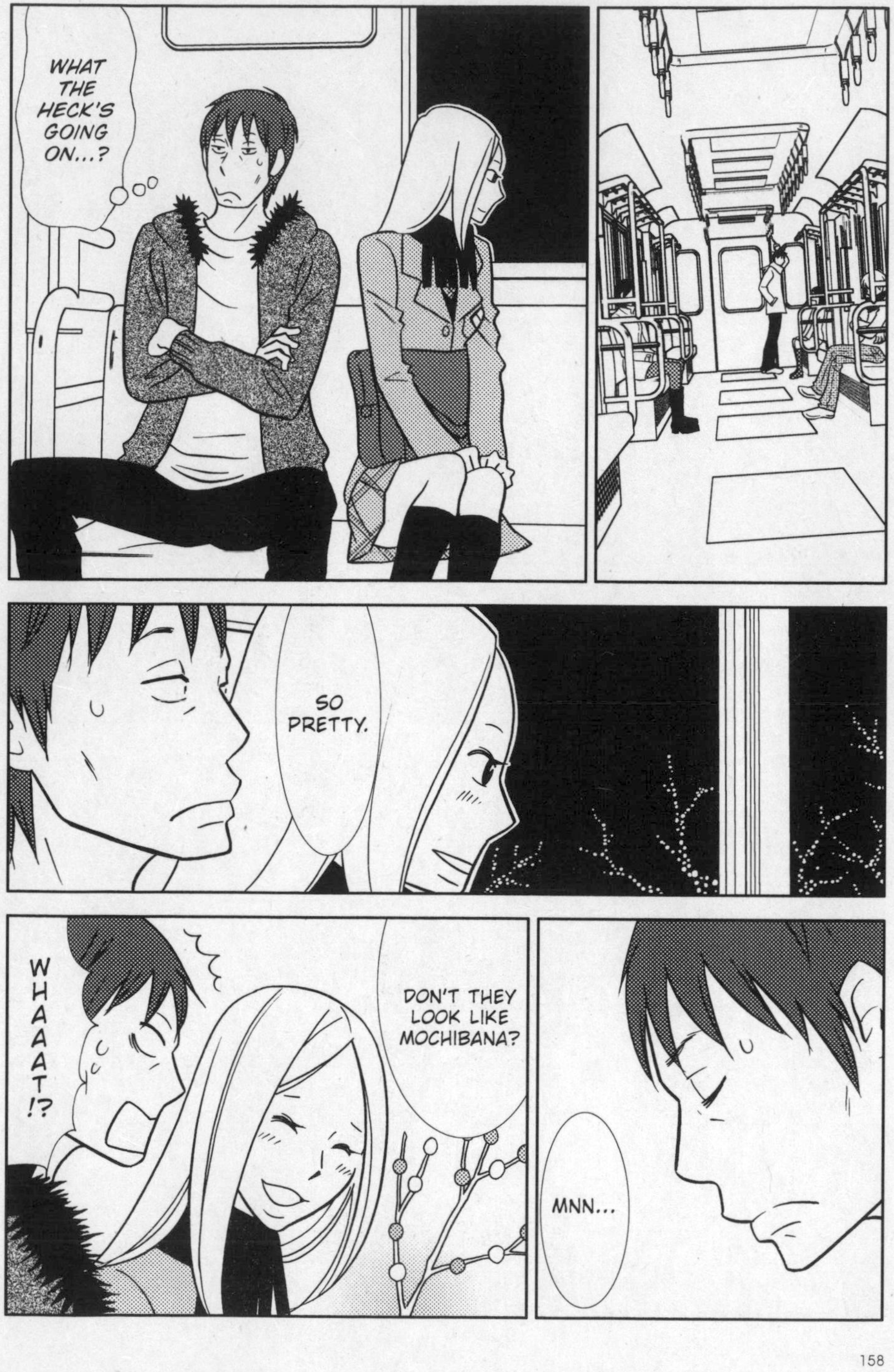
WHAT THE HECK'S GOING ON...?
SO PRETTY.
MNN...
DON'T THEY LOOK LIKE MOCHIBANA?
WHAAAT!?

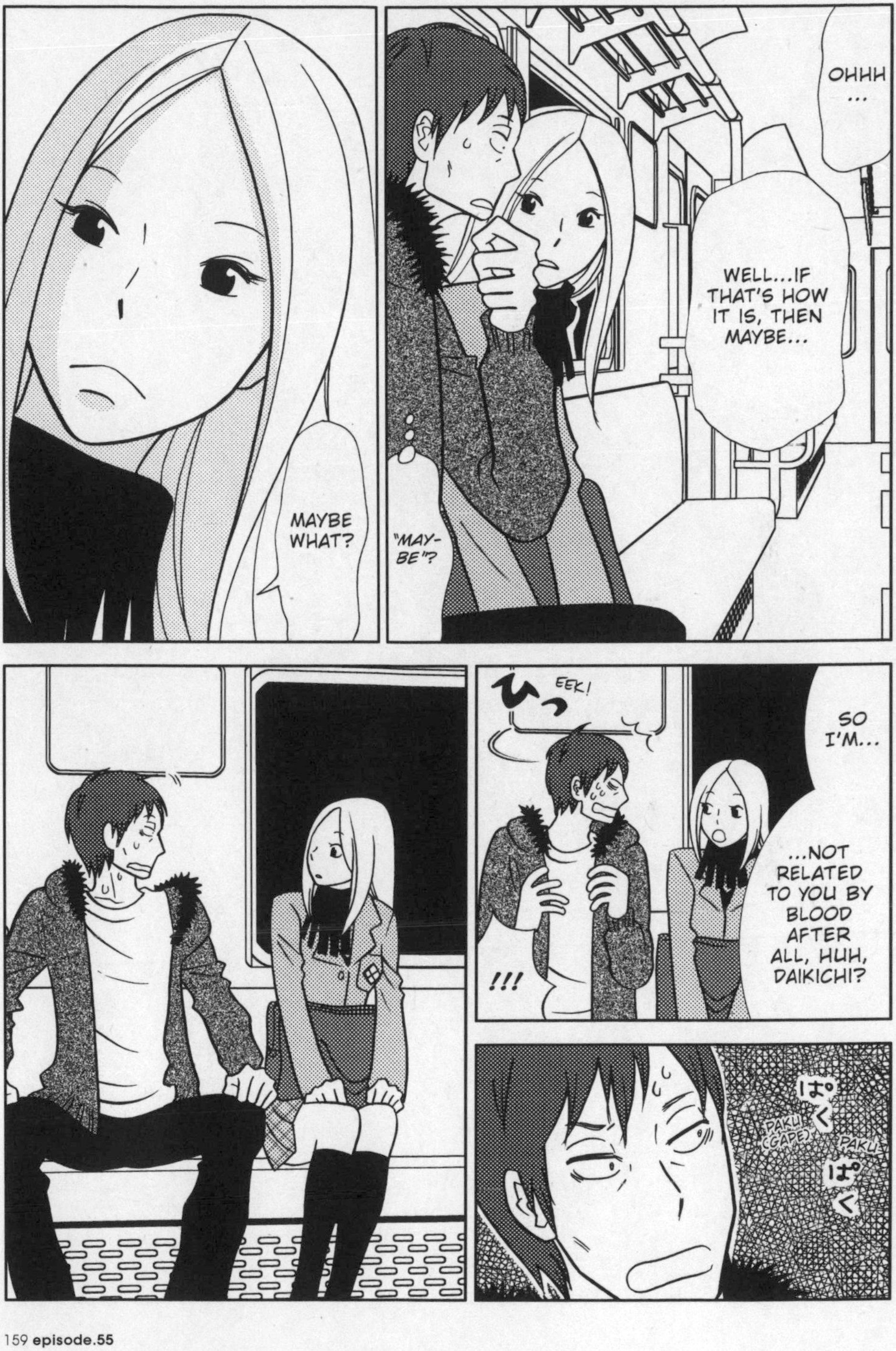
OHHH...
WELL...IF THAT'S HOW IT IS, THEN MAYBE...
"MAY-BE"?
MAYBE WHAT?
SO I'M...
...NOT RELATED TO YOU BY BLOOD AFTER ALL, HUH, DAIKICHI?
ひっ
EEK!
!!!
ぱく ぱく
PAKU (GAPE) PAKU

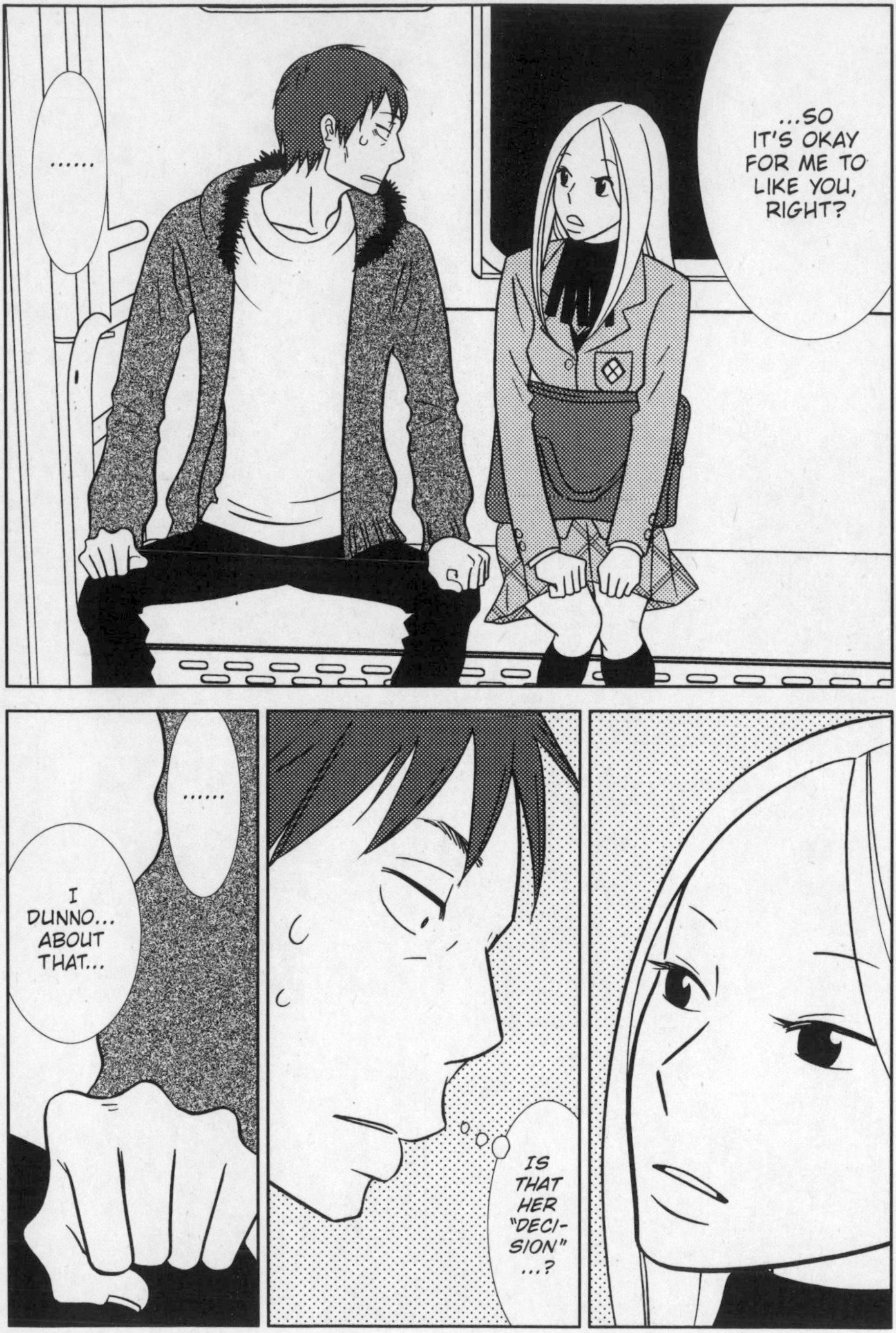
...SO IT'S OKAY FOR ME TO LIKE YOU, RIGHT?
......
IS THAT HER "DECISION" ...?
......
I DUNNO... ABOUT THAT...

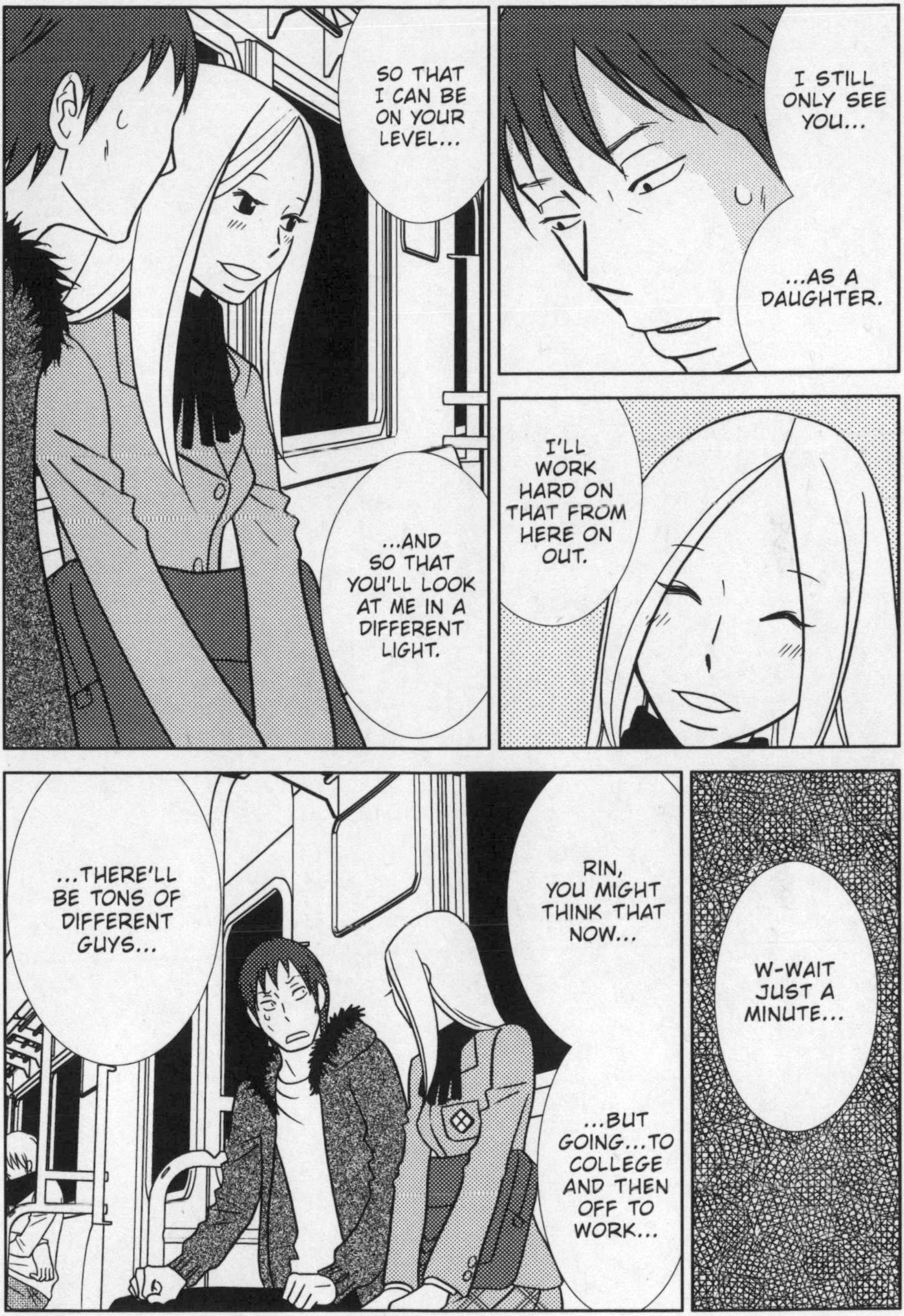
I STILL ONLY SEE YOU...
...AS A DAUGHTER.
I'LL WORK HARD ON THAT FROM HERE ON OUT.
SO THAT I CAN BE ON YOUR LEVEL...
...AND SO THAT YOU'LL LOOK AT ME IN A DIFFERENT LIGHT.
W-WAIT JUST A MINUTE...
RIN, YOU MIGHT THINK THAT NOW...
...BUT GOING...TO COLLEGE AND THEN OFF TO WORK...
...THERE'LL BE TONS OF DIFFERENT GUYS...

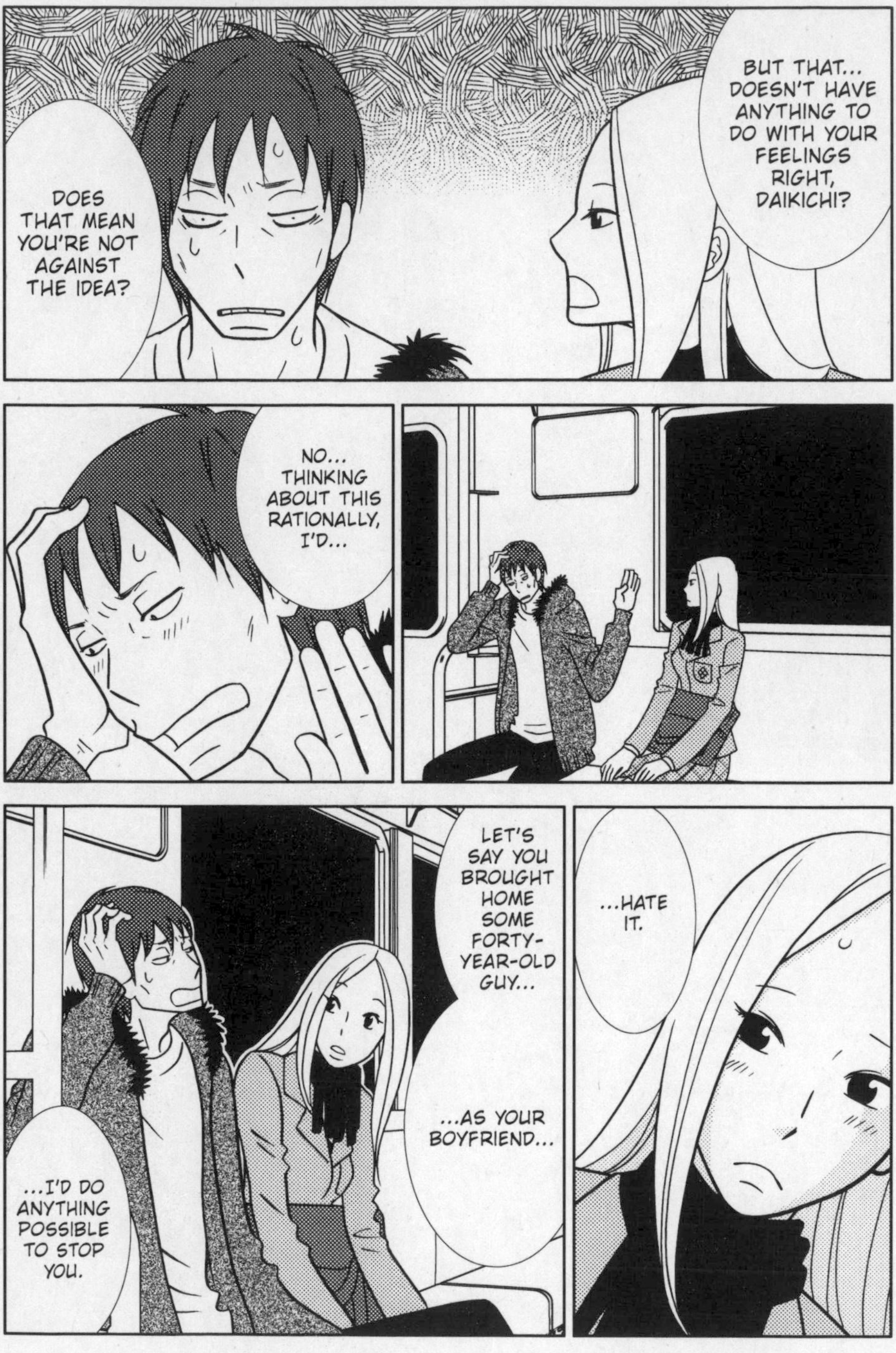
BUT THAT... DOESN'T HAVE ANYTHING TO DO WITH YOUR FEELINGS RIGHT, DAIKICHI?
DOES THAT MEAN YOU'RE NOT AGAINST THE IDEA?
NO... THINKING ABOUT THIS RATIONALLY, I'D...
...HATE IT.
LET'S SAY YOU BROUGHT HOME SOME FORTY-YEAR-OLD GUY...
...AS YOUR BOYFRIEND...
...I'D DO ANYTHING POSSIBLE TO STOP YOU.

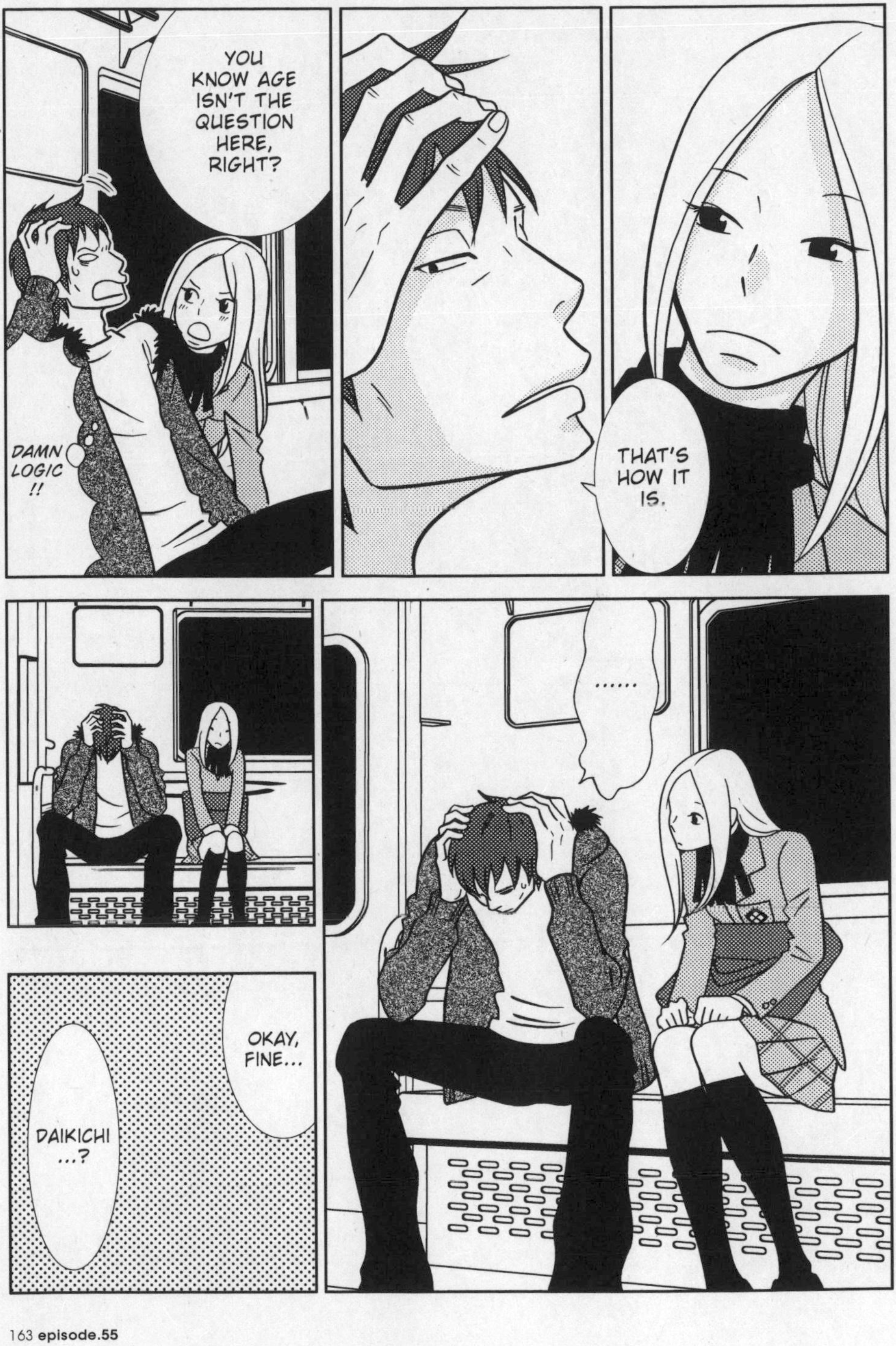
THAT'S HOW IT IS.
YOU KNOW AGE ISN'T THE QUESTION HERE, RIGHT?
DAMN LOGIC !!
......
OKAY, FINE...
DAIKICHI ...?

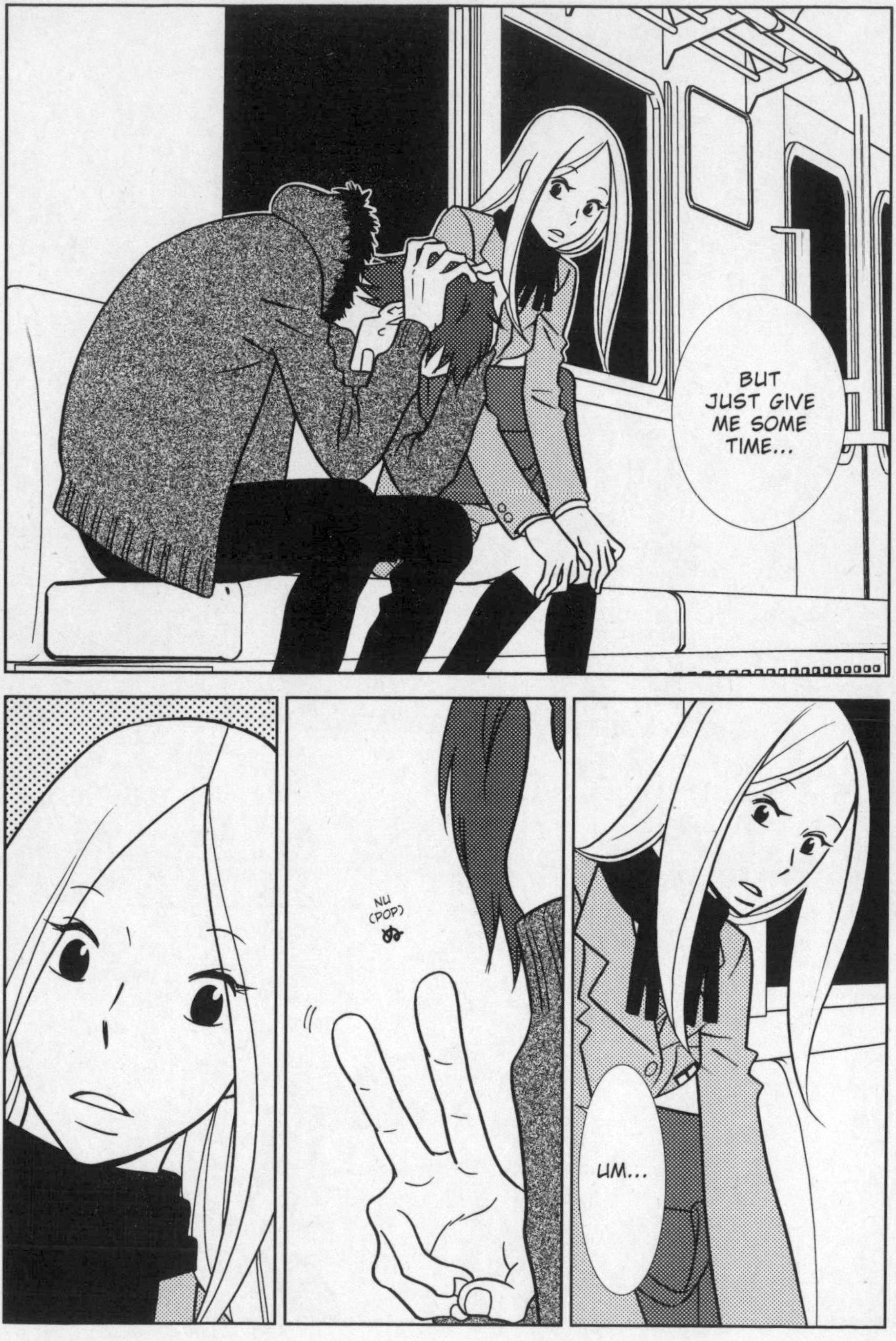
BUT JUST GIVE ME SOME TIME...
UM...
NU (POP)

TWO DAYS ...?
NO WAY!!
TWO MONTHS ...?
NO!!
WHAT IS IT WITH YOU KIDS !!?
AT LEAST TWO YEARS...
GIVE ME UNTIL YOU GRADUATE.
TWO YEARS ...
RIGHT NOW, IT'S TOO MUCH TO WRAP MY HEAD AROUND...
HUH... SO I JUST HAVE TO GRADUATE, THEN IT'S OKAY...?
......
I'VE NEVER THOUGHT OF YOU IN THAT WAY, RIN...
...SO LET ME THINK IT OVER FOR AWHILE...
AND...
...DURING THAT TIME, YOU'LL GO ABOUT LIKE NORMAL...
...AND SO WILL I.

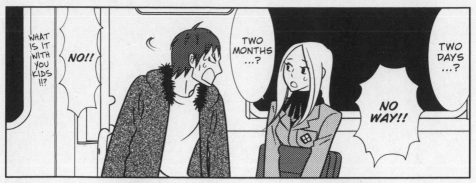

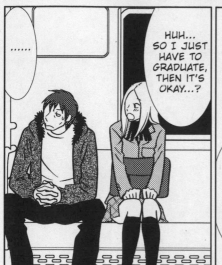

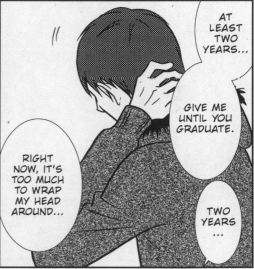

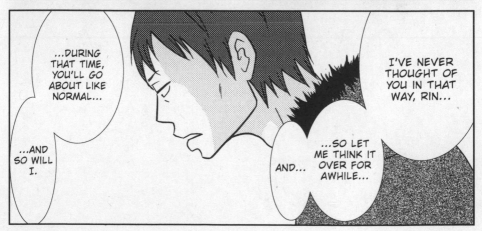

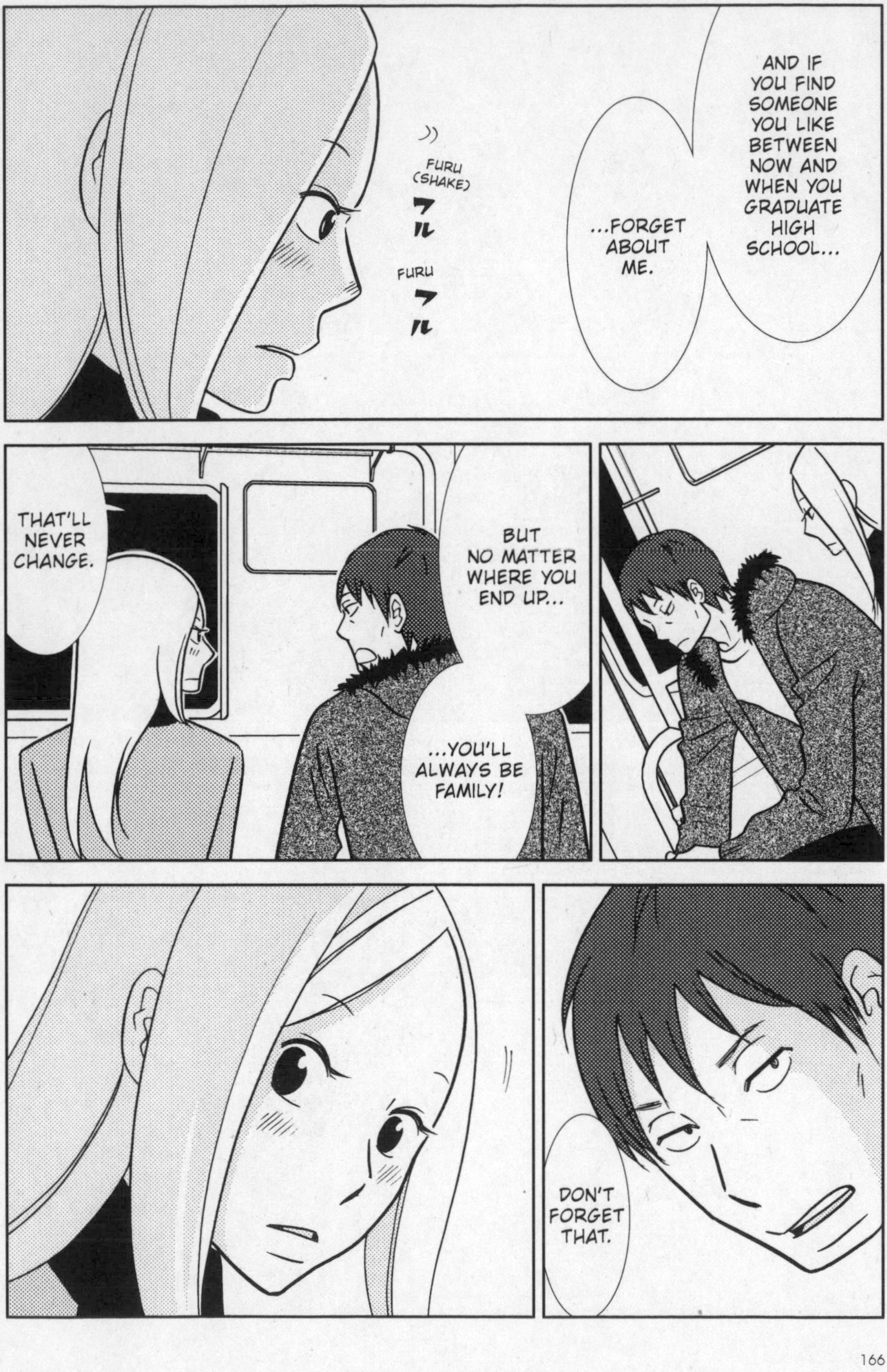
AND IF YOU FIND SOMEONE YOU LIKE BETWEEN NOW AND WHEN YOU GRADUATE HIGH SCHOOL...
...FORGET ABOUT ME.
FURU (SHAKE) フル
FURU フル
BUT NO MATTER WHERE YOU END UP...
...YOU'LL ALWAYS BE FAMILY!
THAT'LL NEVER CHANGE.
DON'T FORGET THAT.

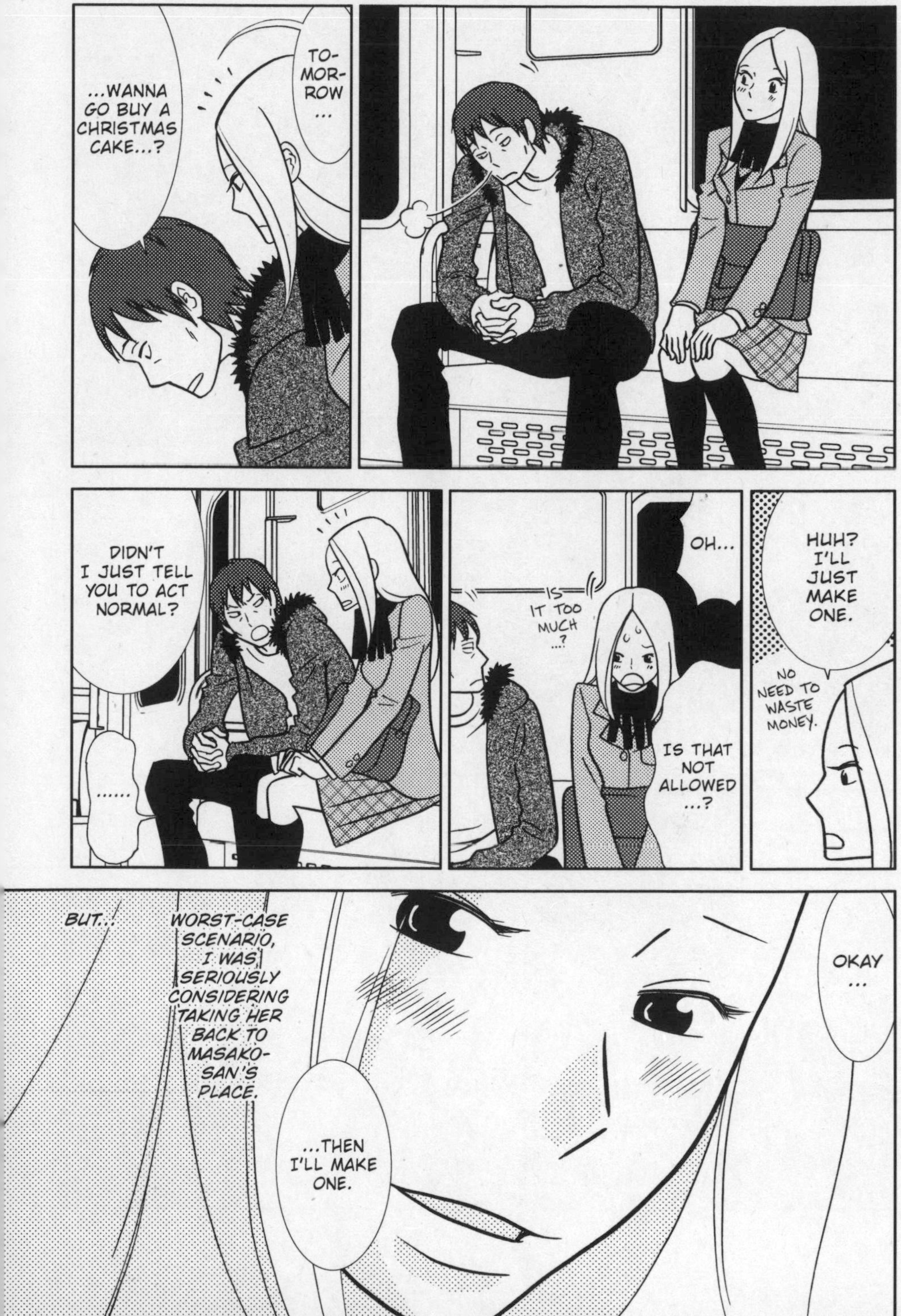
TO-MORROW...
...WANNA GO BUY A CHRISTMAS CAKE...?
HUH? I'LL JUST MAKE ONE.
NO NEED TO WASTE MONEY.
OH...
IS IT TOO MUCH...?
IS THAT NOT ALLOWED...?
DIDN'T I JUST TELL YOU TO ACT NORMAL?
......
OKAY...
...THEN I'LL MAKE ONE.
BUT...
WORST-CASE SCENARIO, I WAS SERIOUSLY CONSIDERING TAKING HER BACK TO MASAKO-SAN'S PLACE.

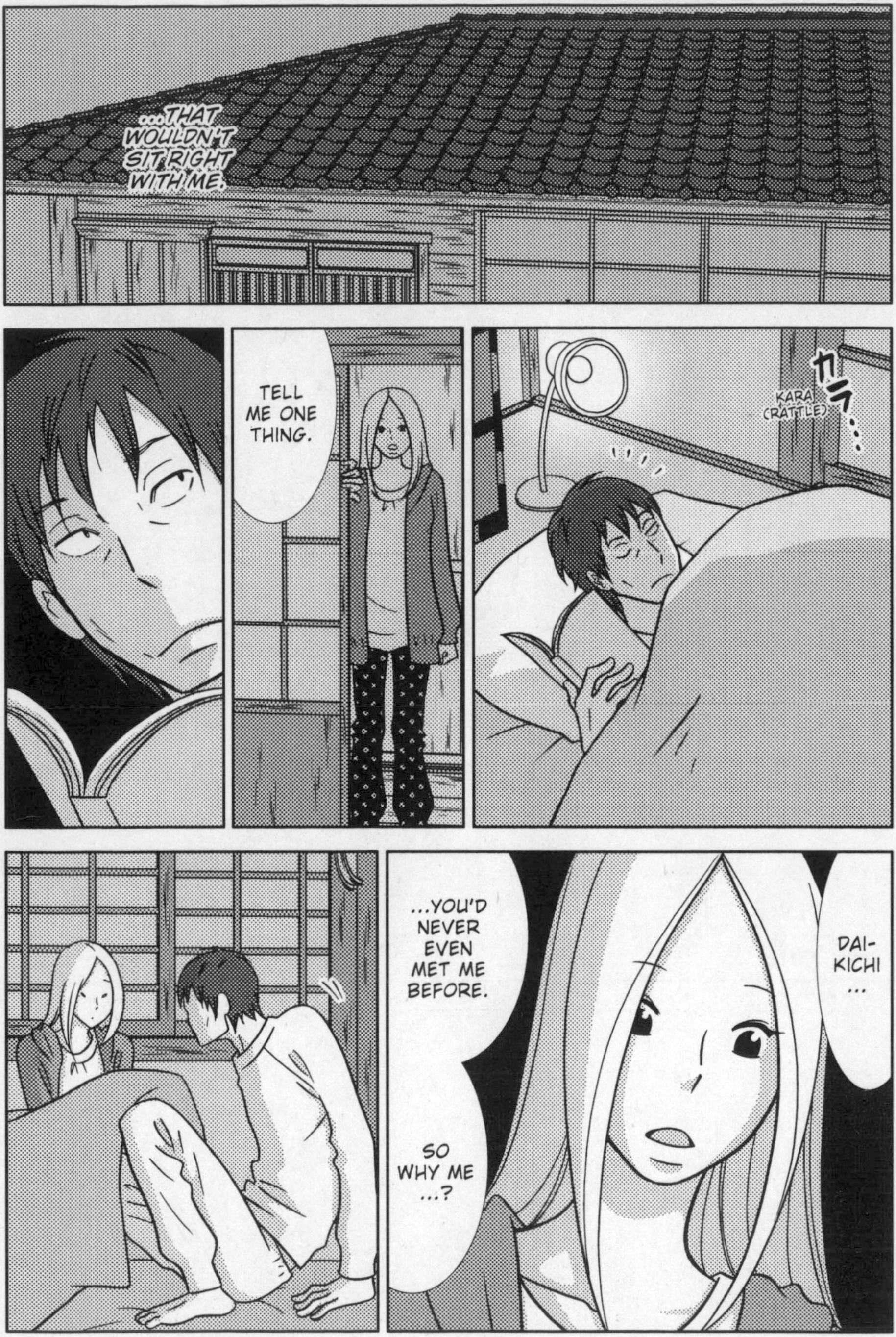
...THAT WOULDN'T SIT RIGHT WITH ME.
カラ...
KARA (RATTLE)
TELL ME ONE THING.
DAI-KICHI ...
...YOU'D NEVER EVEN MET ME BEFORE.
SO WHY ME ...?

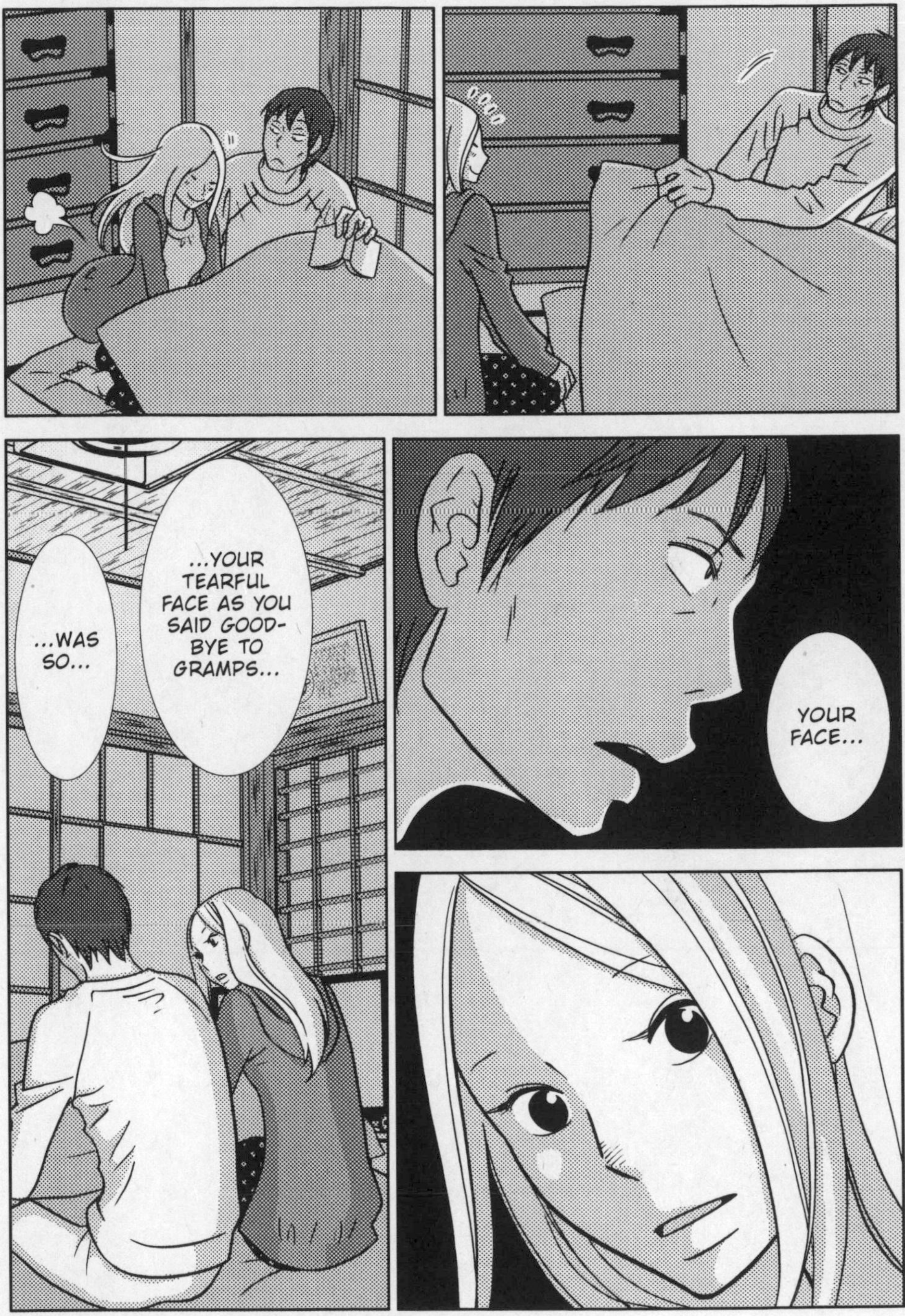
YOUR FACE...
...YOUR TEARFUL FACE AS YOU SAID GOOD-BYE TO GRAMPS...
...WAS SO...

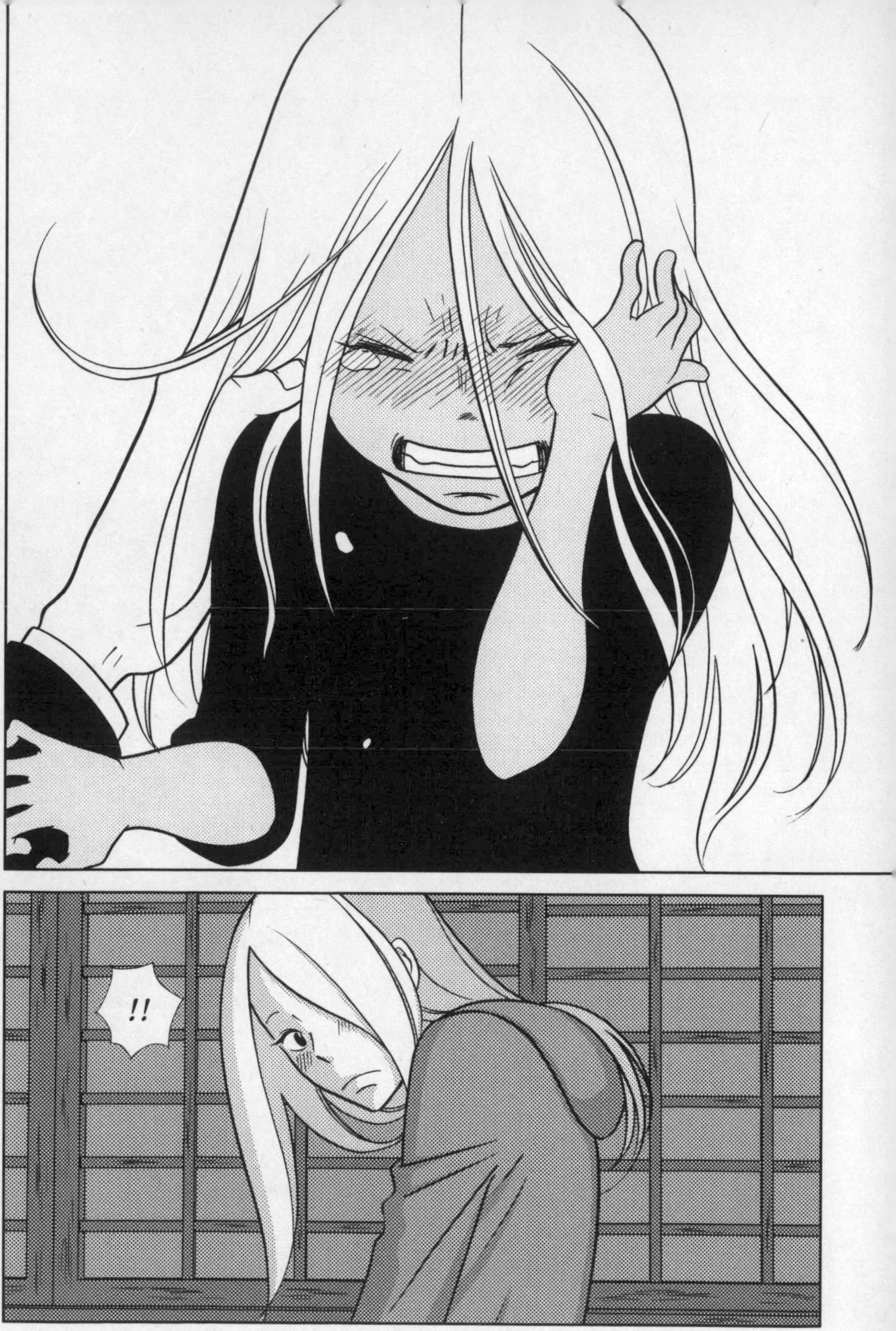
!!

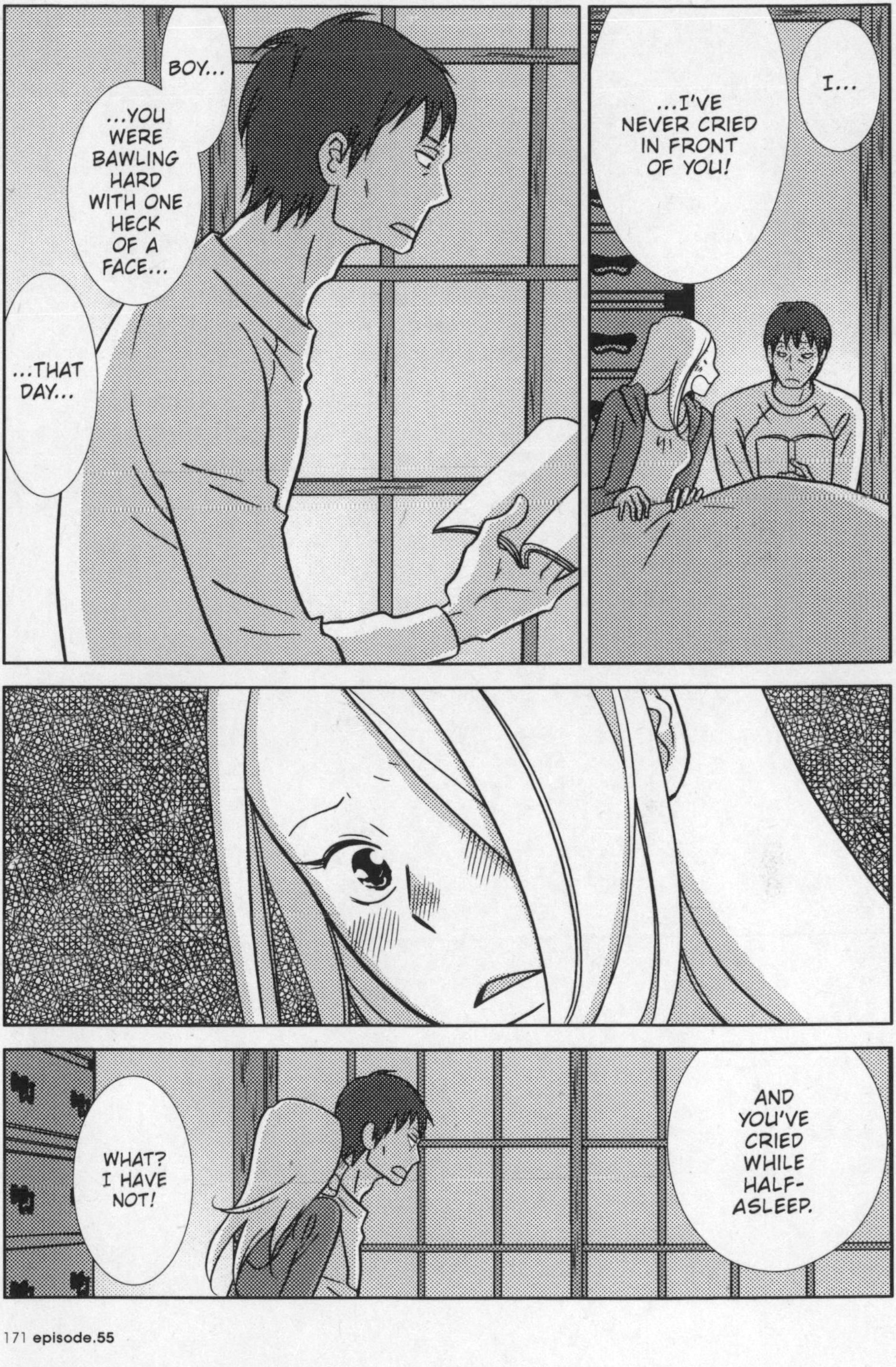
I...
...I'VE NEVER CRIED IN FRONT OF YOU!
BOY...
...YOU WERE BAWLING HARD WITH ONE HECK OF A FACE...
...THAT DAY...
AND YOU'VE CRIED WHILE HALF-ASLEEP.
WHAT? I HAVE NOT!

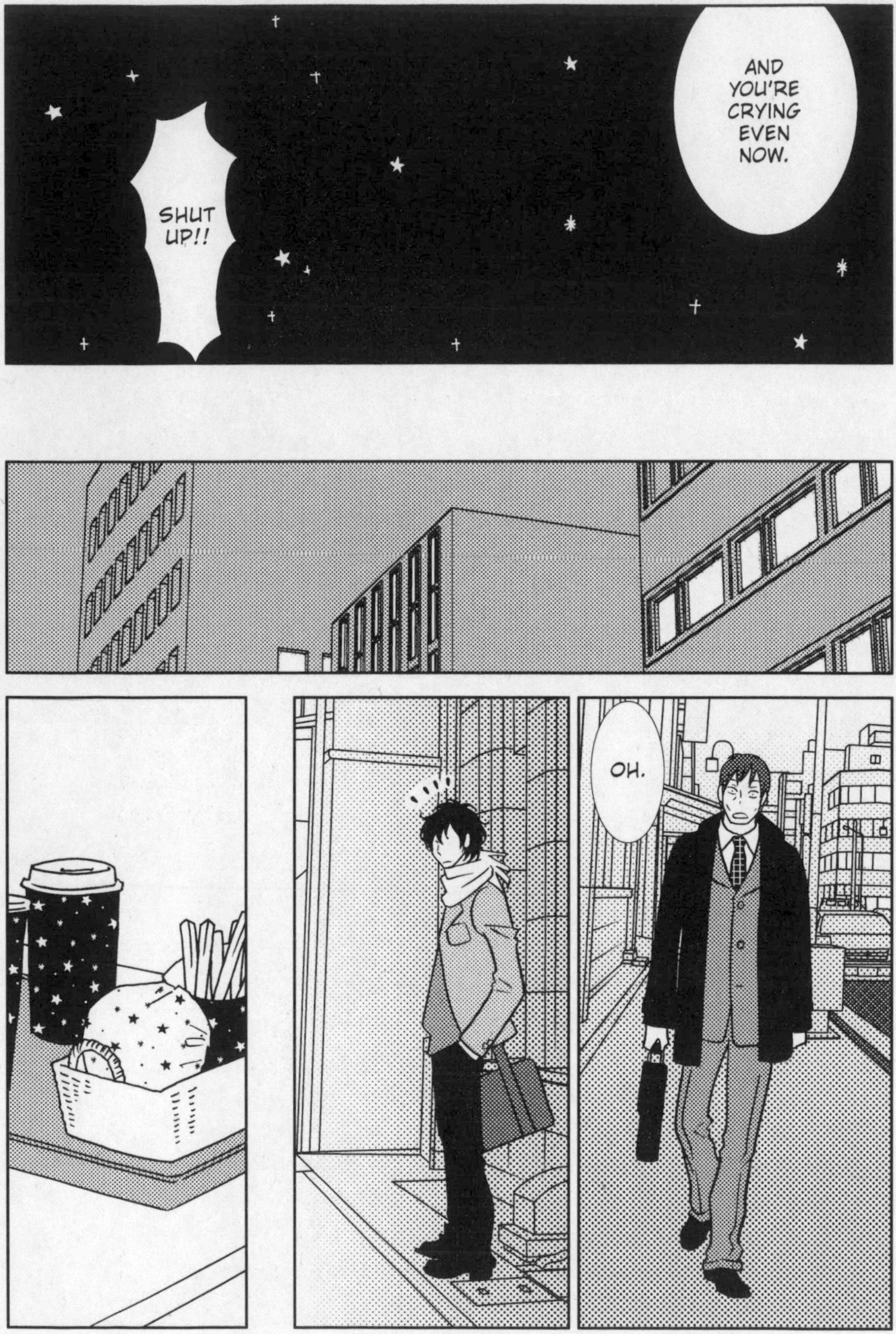
AND YOU'RE CRYING EVEN NOW.
SHUT UP!!
OH.

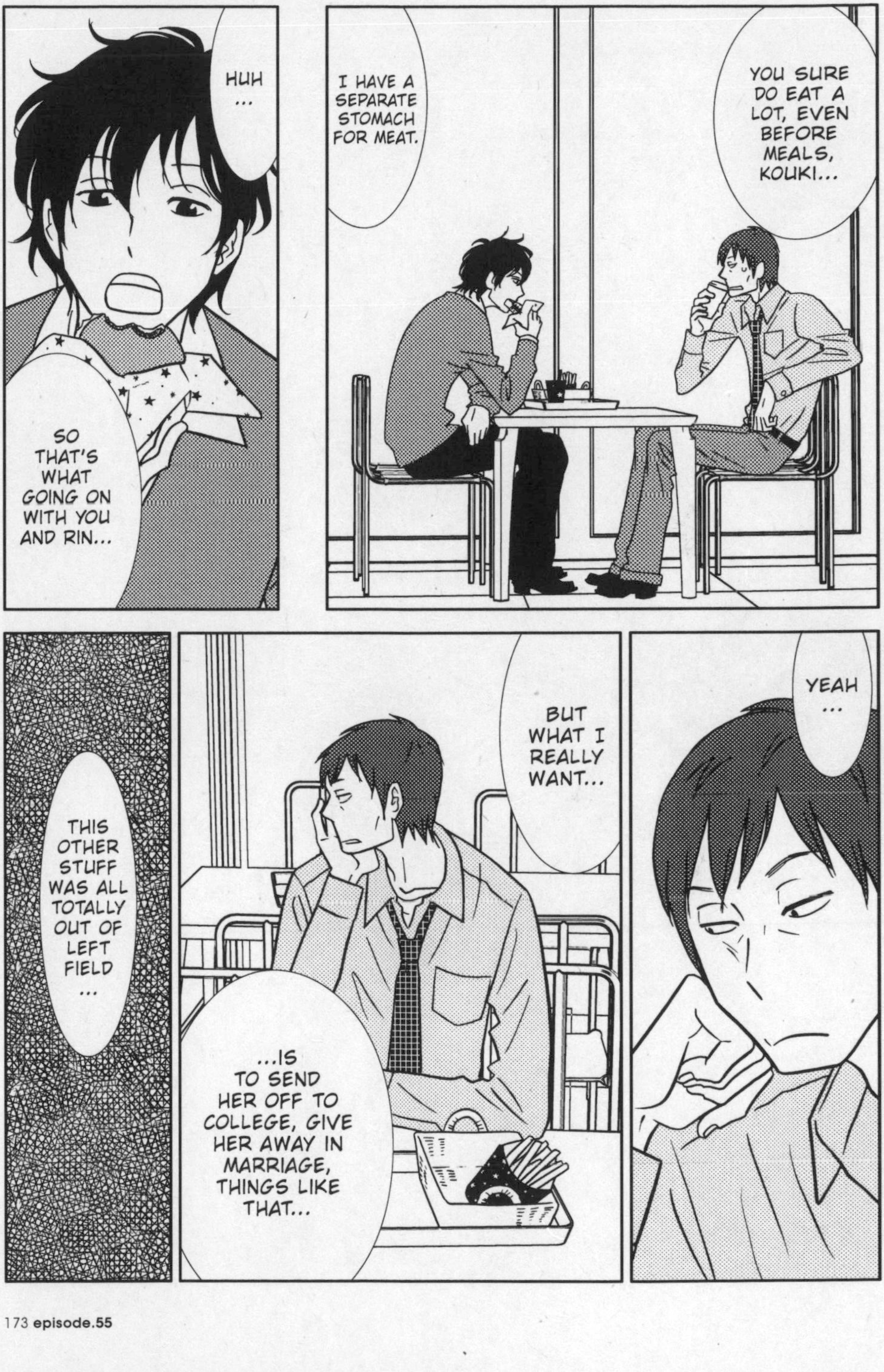
YOU SURE DO EAT A LOT, EVEN BEFORE MEALS, KOUKI...
I HAVE A SEPARATE STOMACH FOR MEAT.
HUH ...
SO THAT'S WHAT GOING ON WITH YOU AND RIN...
YEAH ...
BUT WHAT I REALLY WANT...
...IS TO SEND HER OFF TO COLLEGE, GIVE HER AWAY IN MARRIAGE, THINGS LIKE THAT...
THIS OTHER STUFF WAS ALL TOTALLY OUT OF LEFT FIELD ...

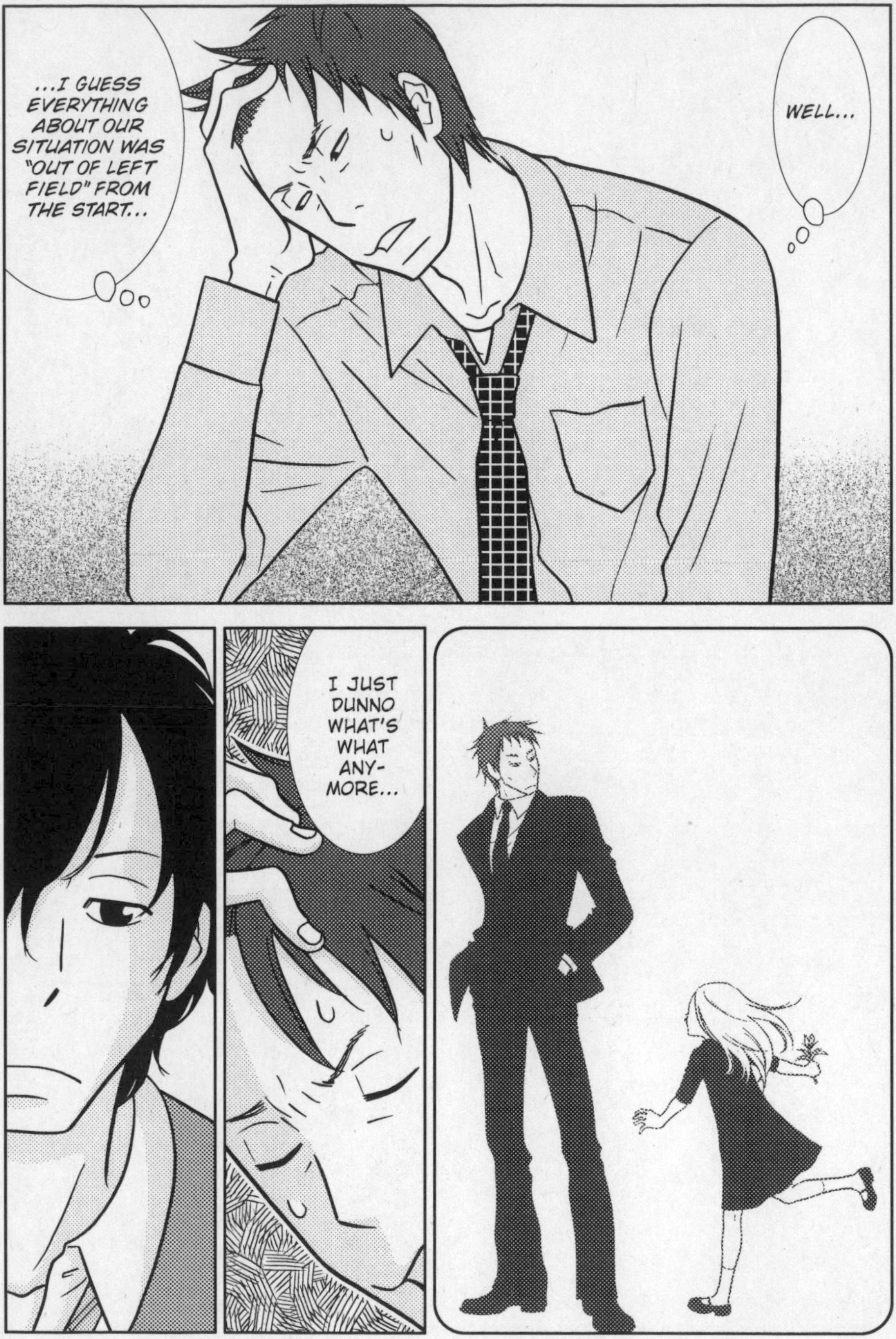
WELL...
...I GUESS EVERYTHING ABOUT OUR SITUATION WAS "OUT OF LEFT FIELD" FROM THE START...
I JUST DUNNO WHAT'S WHAT ANY-MORE...

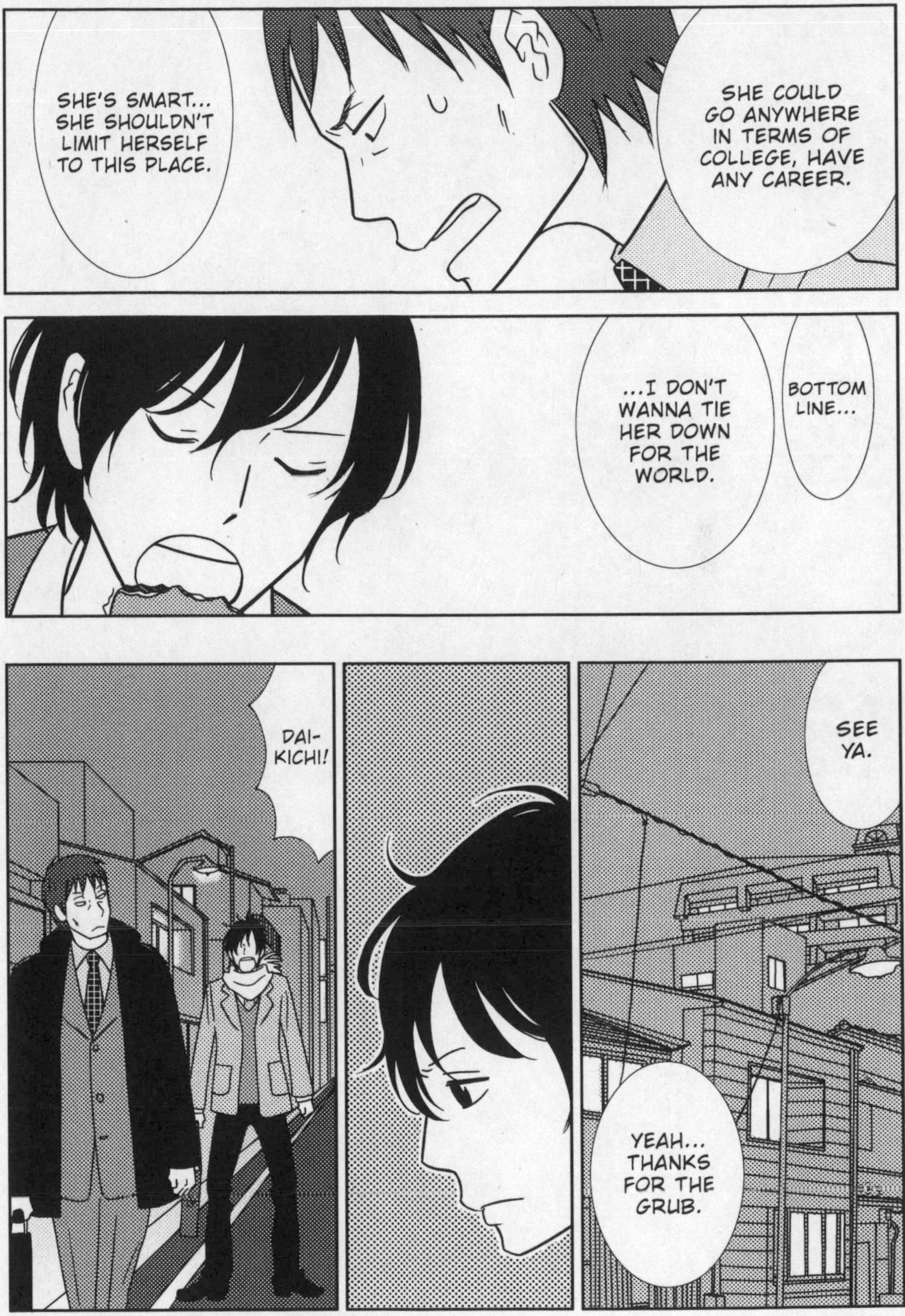
SHE COULD GO ANYWHERE IN TERMS OF COLLEGE, HAVE ANY CAREER.
SHE'S SMART... SHE SHOULDN'T LIMIT HERSELF TO THIS PLACE.
BOTTOM LINE...
...I DON'T WANNA TIE HER DOWN FOR THE WORLD.
SEE YA.
YEAH... THANKS FOR THE GRUB.
DAI-KICHI!

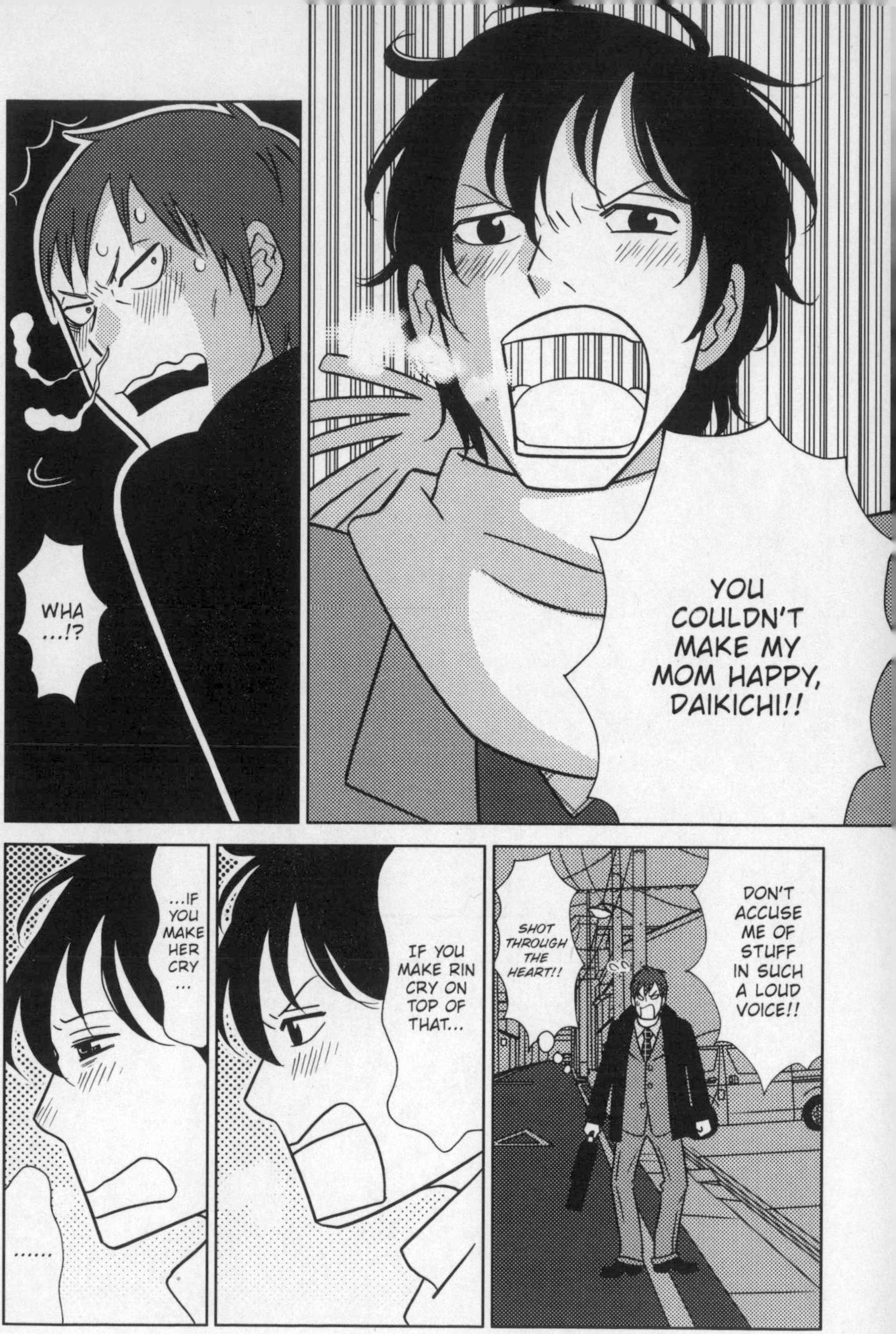
YOU COULDN'T MAKE MY MOM HAPPY, DAIKICHI!!
WHA ...!?
DON'T ACCUSE ME OF STUFF IN SUCH A LOUD VOICE!!
SHOT THROUGH THE HEART!!
IF YOU MAKE RIN CRY ON TOP OF THAT...
...IF YOU MAKE HER CRY ...
......

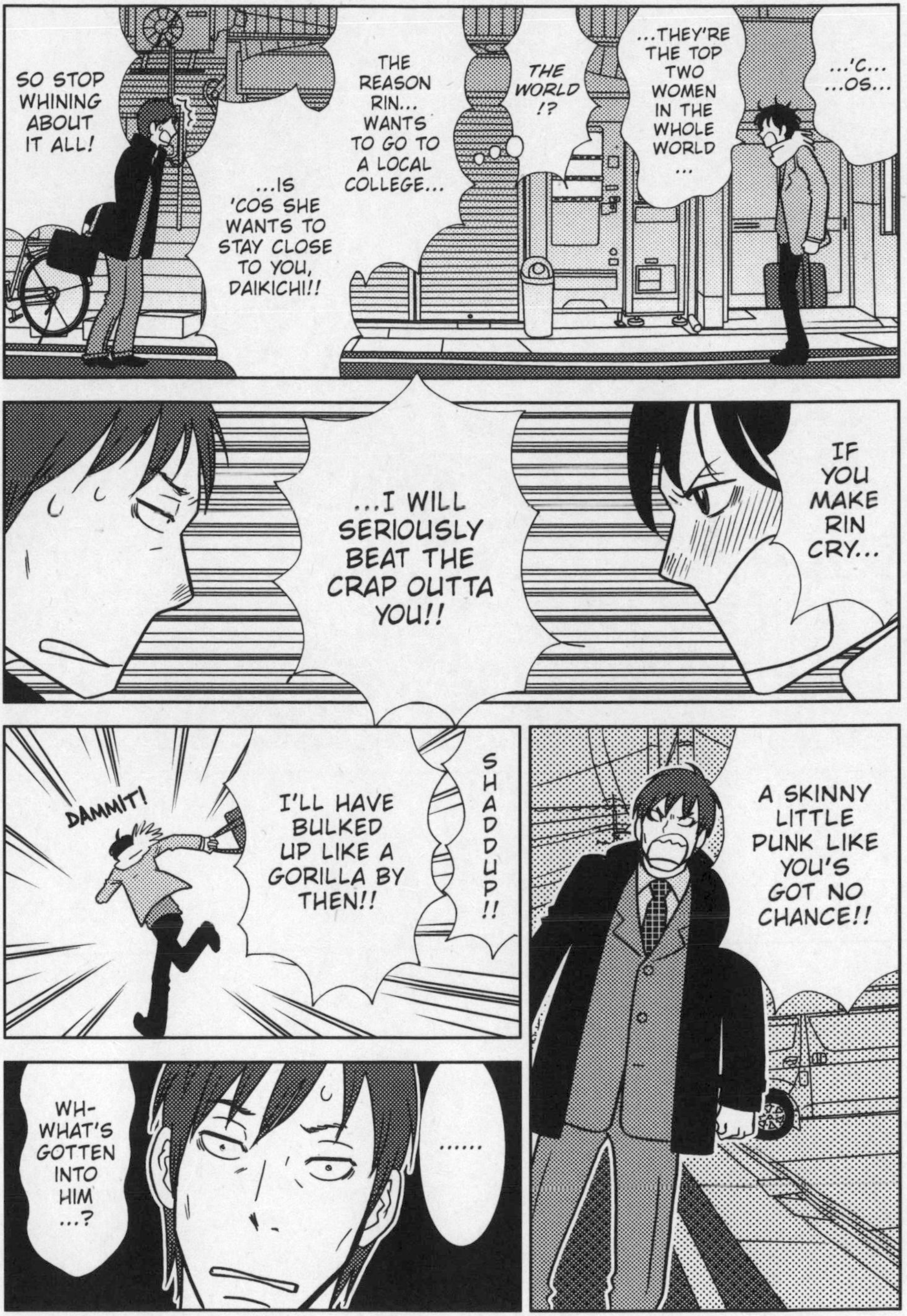
...'C... ...OS...
...THEY'RE THE TOP TWO WOMEN IN THE WHOLE WORLD...
THE WORLD!?
THE REASON RIN... WANTS TO GO TO A LOCAL COLLEGE...
...IS 'COS SHE WANTS TO STAY CLOSE TO YOU, DAIKICHI!!
SO STOP WHINING ABOUT IT ALL!
IF YOU MAKE RIN CRY...
...I WILL SERIOUSLY BEAT THE CRAP OUTTA YOU!!
A SKINNY LITTLE PUNK LIKE YOU'S GOT NO CHANCE!!
SHADDUP!!
I'LL HAVE BULKED UP LIKE A GORILLA BY THEN!!
DAMMIT!
......
WH-WHAT'S GOTTEN INTO HIM...?

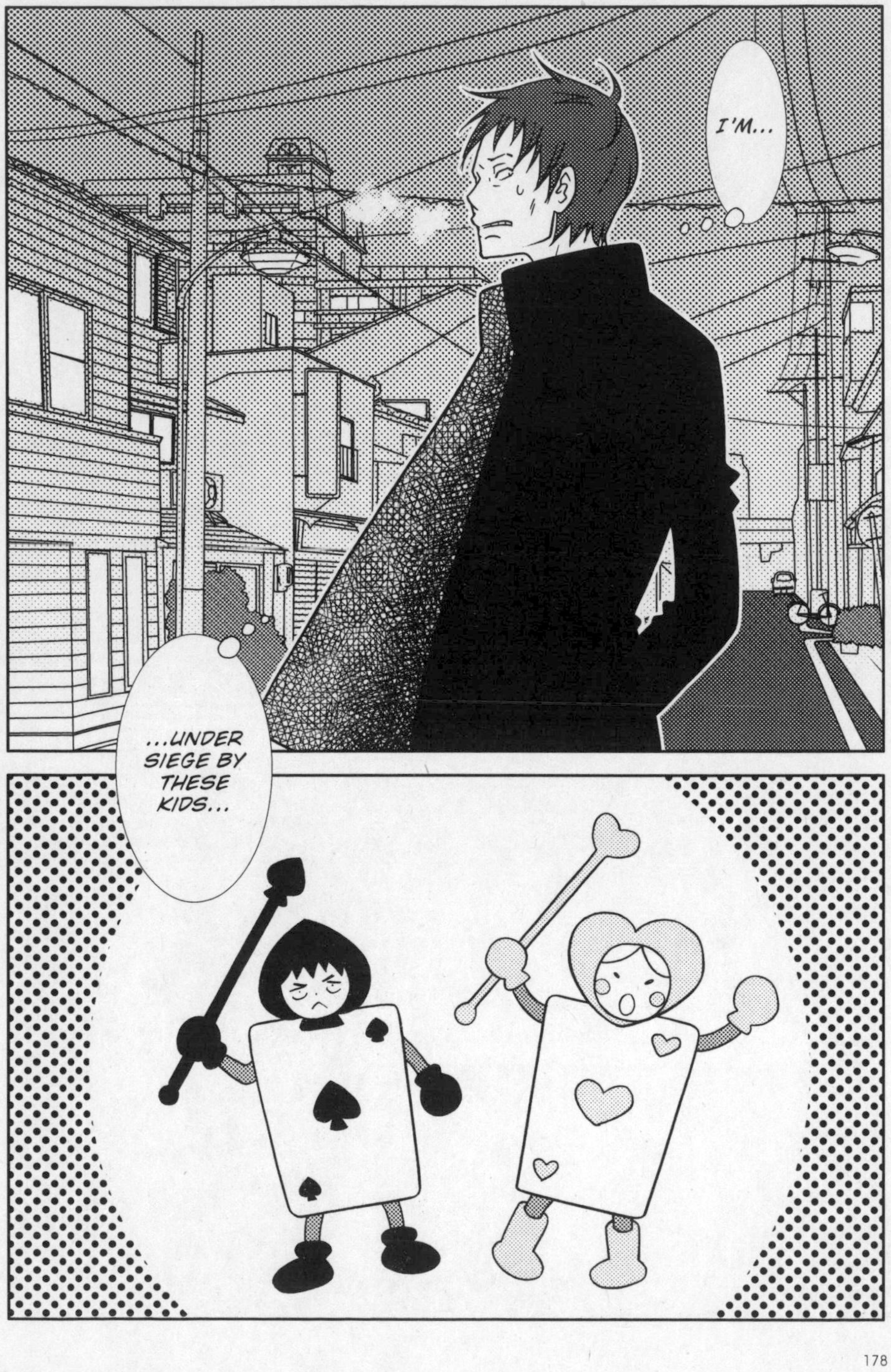
I'M...
...UNDER SIEGE BY THESE KIDS...

BUNNY**DROP**

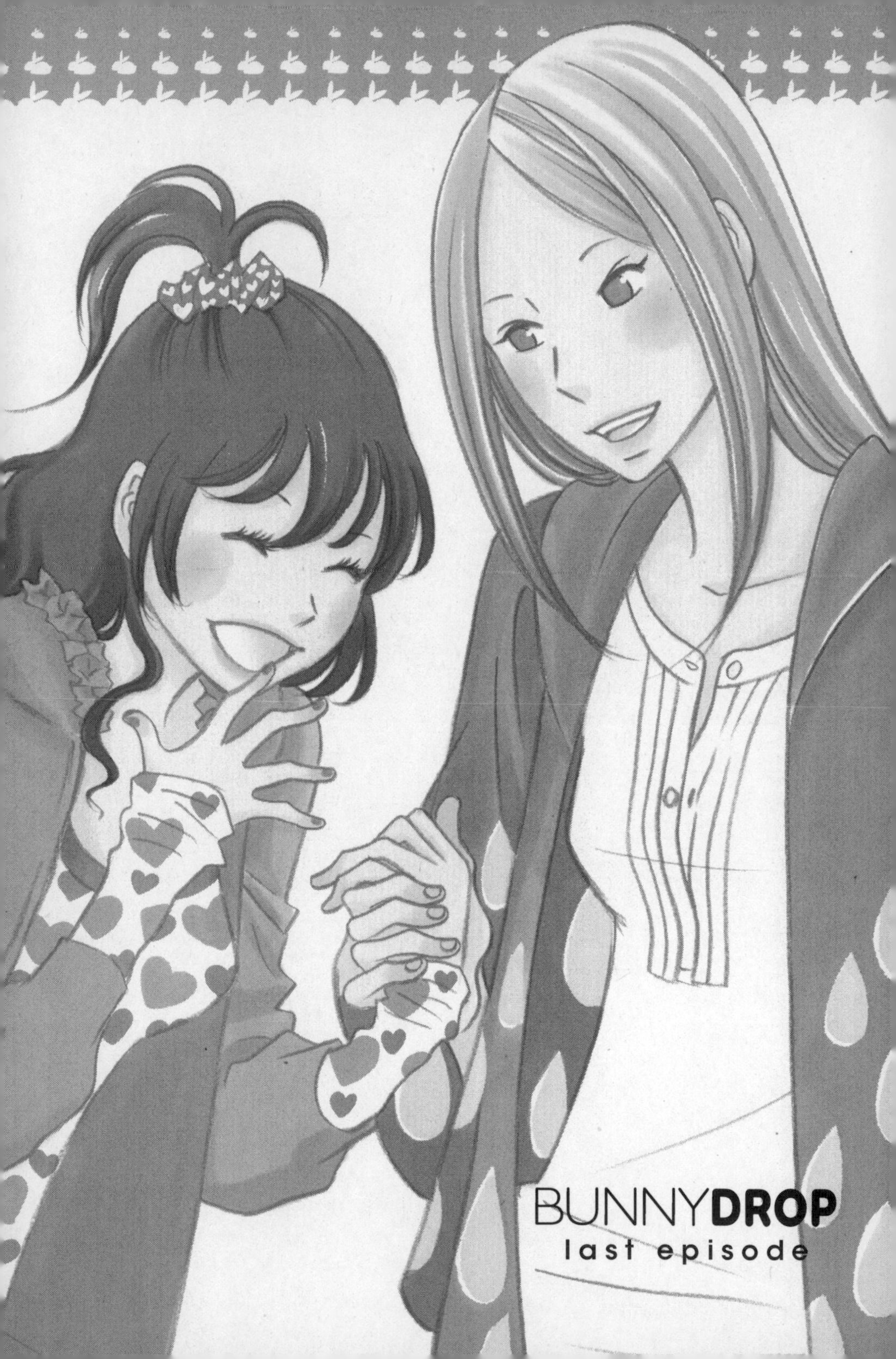
BUNNYDROP
last episode

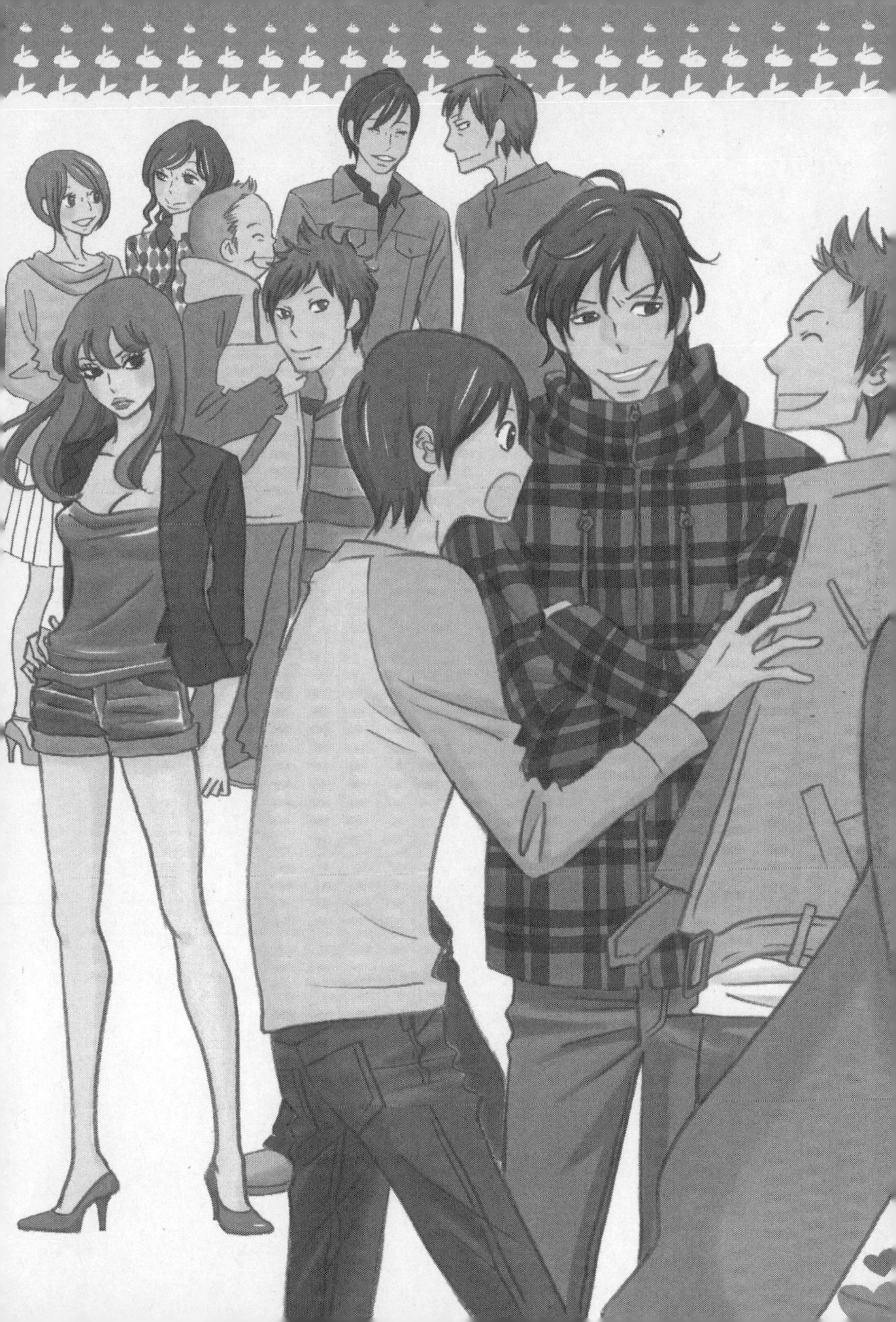

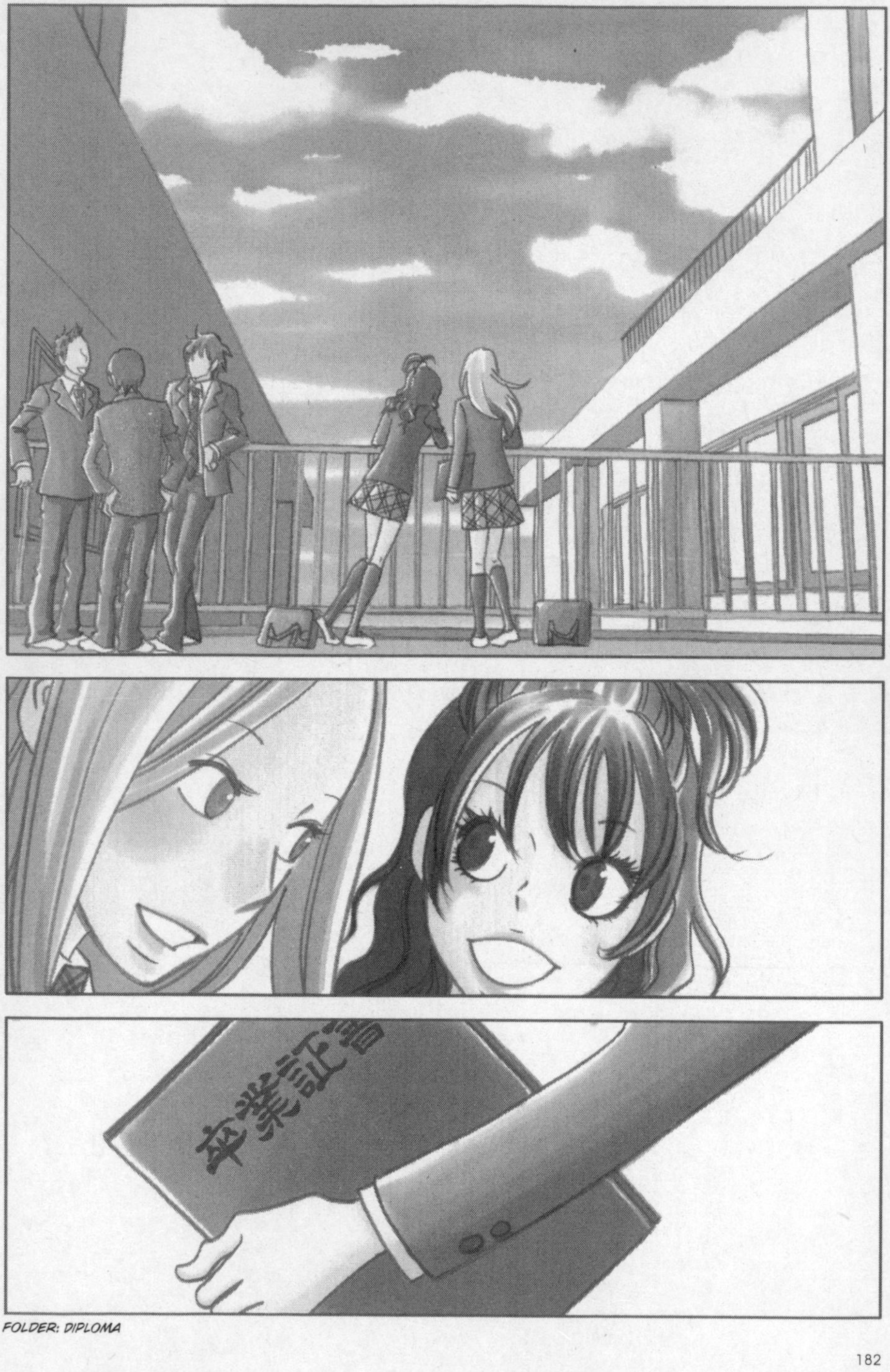
卒業証書

FOLDER: DIPLOMA

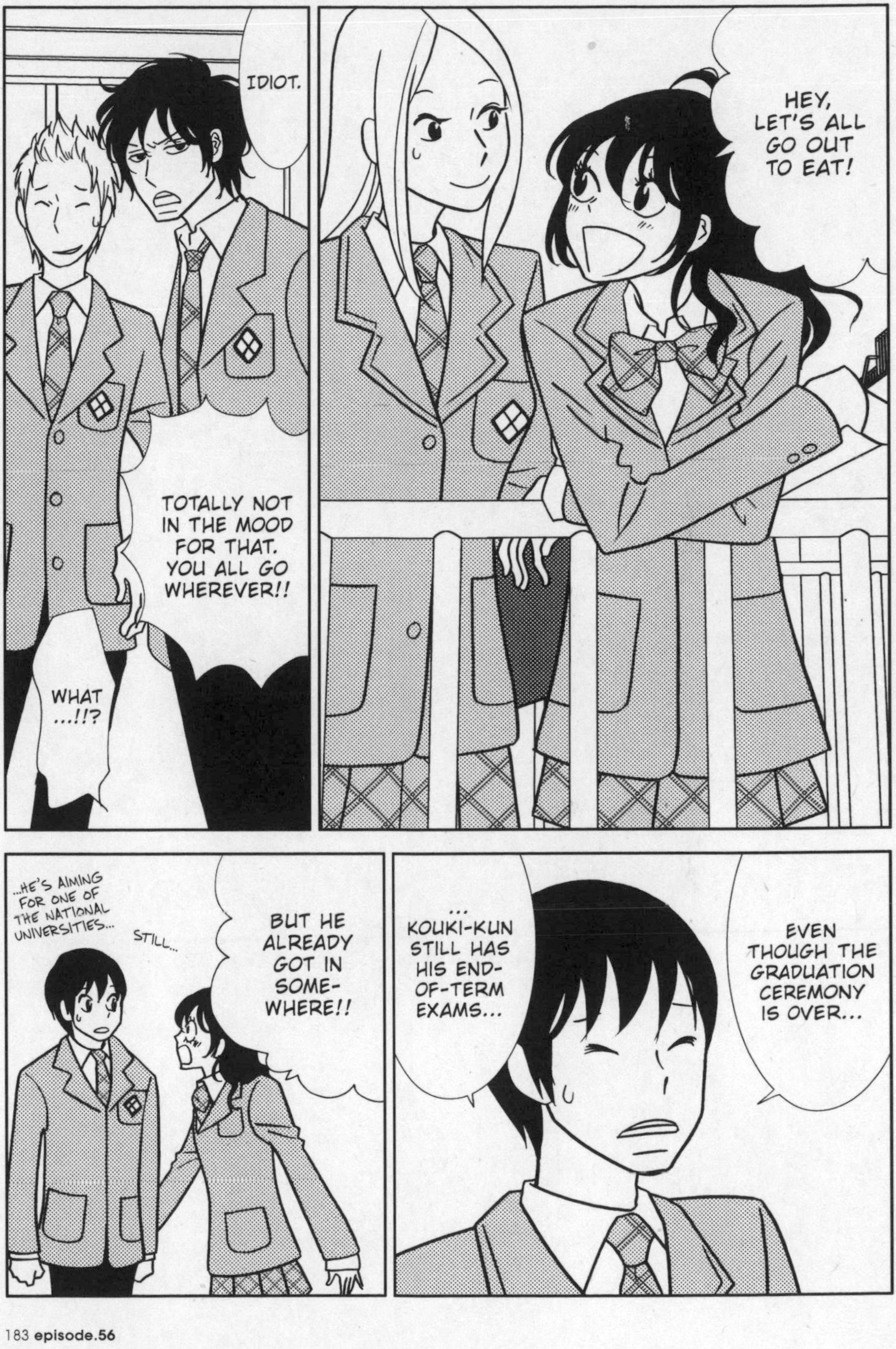
HEY, LET'S ALL GO OUT TO EAT!
IDIOT.
TOTALLY NOT IN THE MOOD FOR THAT. YOU ALL GO WHEREVER!!
WHAT ...!!?
EVEN THOUGH THE GRADUATION CEREMONY IS OVER...
... KOUKI-KUN STILL HAS HIS END-OF-TERM EXAMS...
BUT HE ALREADY GOT IN SOME-WHERE!!
STILL...
...HE'S AIMING FOR ONE OF THE NATIONAL UNIVERSITIES...

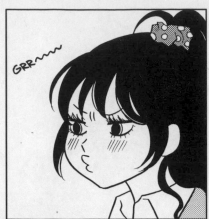

YOU ARE SUCH A LITTLE PRINCESS!!
ALTHOUGH RIN ALREADY GOT ACCEPTED!
WE HAVE FINANCIAL AID ISSUES TO DEAL WITH!!
GRR~~~
BUT YOU HAVE A DAD NOW, SO IT'LL BE FINE!!
MUNIII (STRETCH)
SO OTHER THAN ME AND KOUKI, EVERYONE'S GOING LOCAL, HUH?
LET'S GET TOGETHER IN THE SUMMER.
GOLDEN WEEK!
GOLDEN WEEK!!
RIGHT, THAT'LL BE COMING UP SOON...

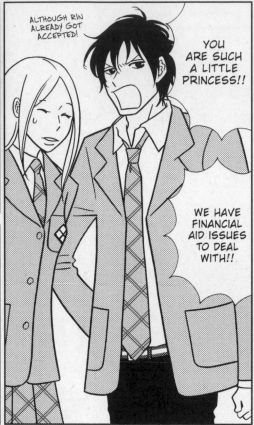

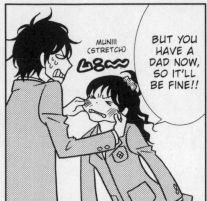

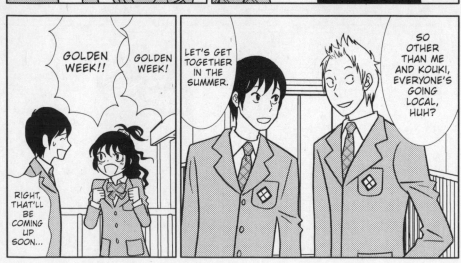

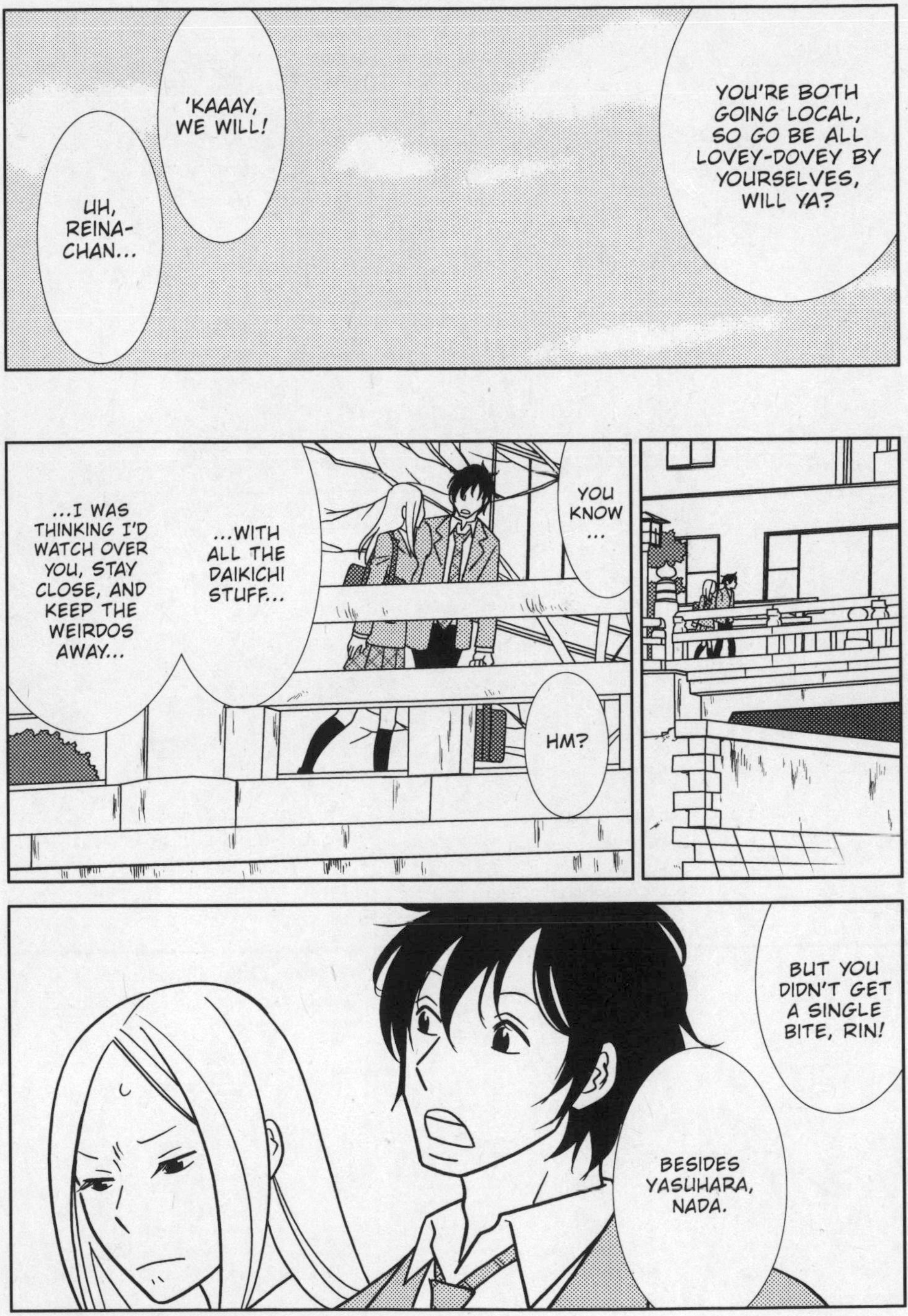
YOU'RE BOTH GOING LOCAL, SO GO BE ALL LOVEY-DOVEY BY YOURSELVES, WILL YA?
'KAAAY, WE WILL!
UH, REINA-CHAN...
YOU KNOW...
HM?
...WITH ALL THE DAIKICHI STUFF...
...I WAS THINKING I'D WATCH OVER YOU, STAY CLOSE, AND KEEP THE WEIRDOS AWAY...
BUT YOU DIDN'T GET A SINGLE BITE, RIN!
BESIDES YASUHARA, NADA.

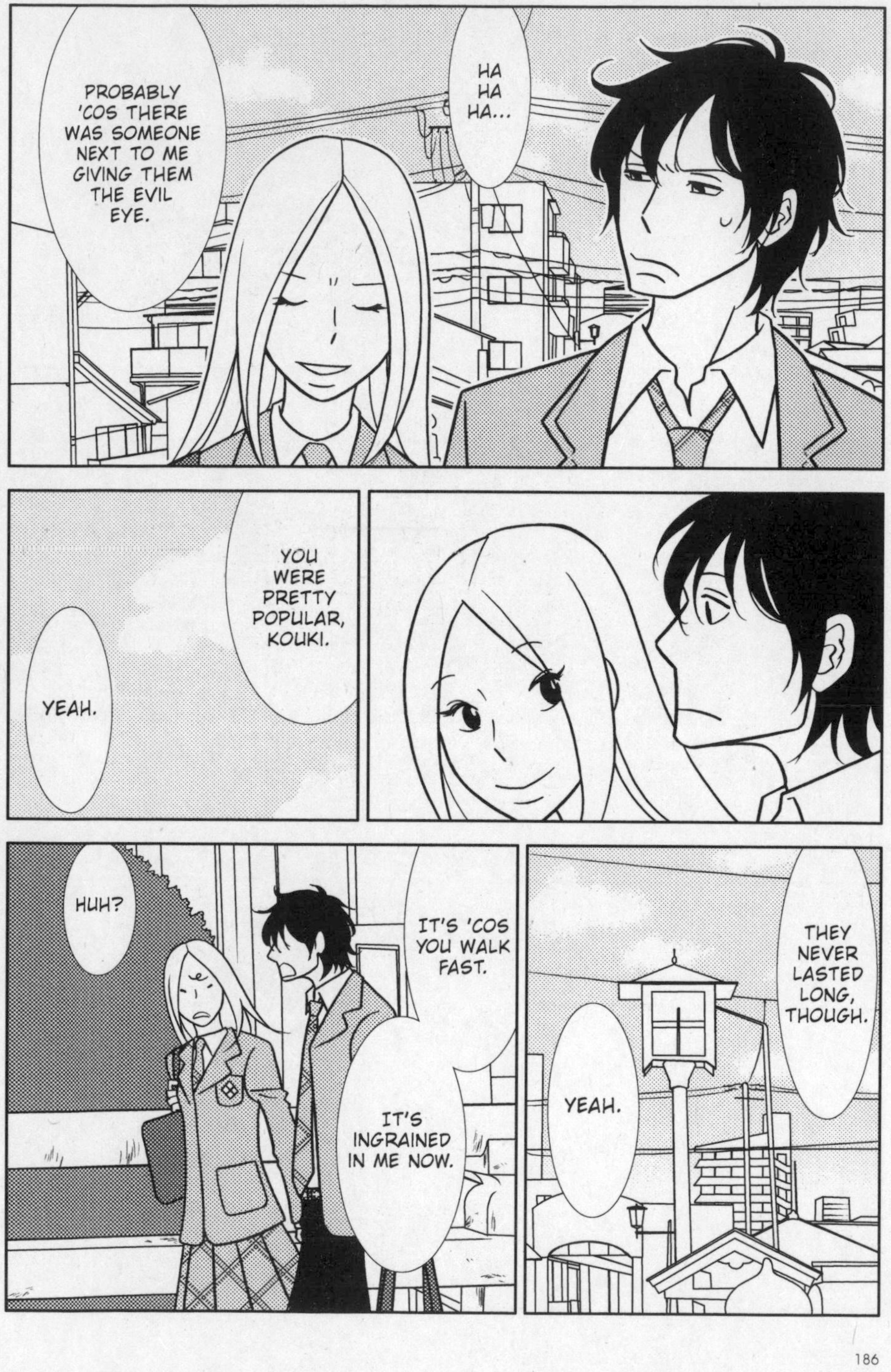
HA HA HA...
PROBABLY 'COS THERE WAS SOMEONE NEXT TO ME GIVING THEM THE EVIL EYE.
YOU WERE PRETTY POPULAR, KOUKI.
YEAH.
THEY NEVER LASTED LONG, THOUGH.
YEAH.
IT'S 'COS YOU WALK FAST.
HUH?
IT'S INGRAINED IN ME NOW.

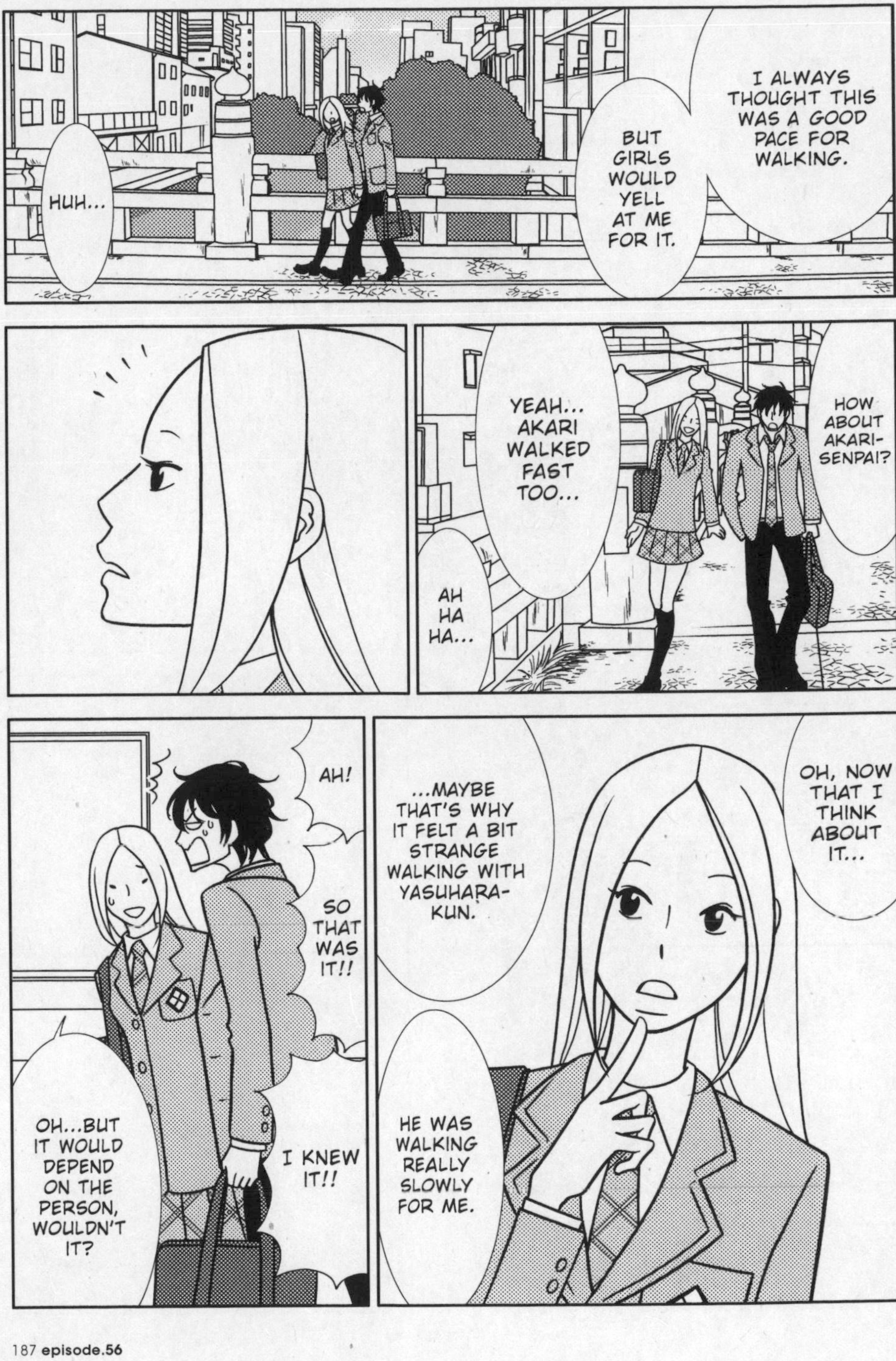
I ALWAYS THOUGHT THIS WAS A GOOD PACE FOR WALKING.
BUT GIRLS WOULD YELL AT ME FOR IT.
HUH...
HOW ABOUT AKARI-SENPAI?
YEAH... AKARI WALKED FAST TOO...
AH HA HA...
OH, NOW THAT I THINK ABOUT IT...
...MAYBE THAT'S WHY IT FELT A BIT STRANGE WALKING WITH YASUHARA-KUN.
HE WAS WALKING REALLY SLOWLY FOR ME.
AH!
SO THAT WAS IT!!
I KNEW IT!!
OH...BUT IT WOULD DEPEND ON THE PERSON, WOULDN'T IT?

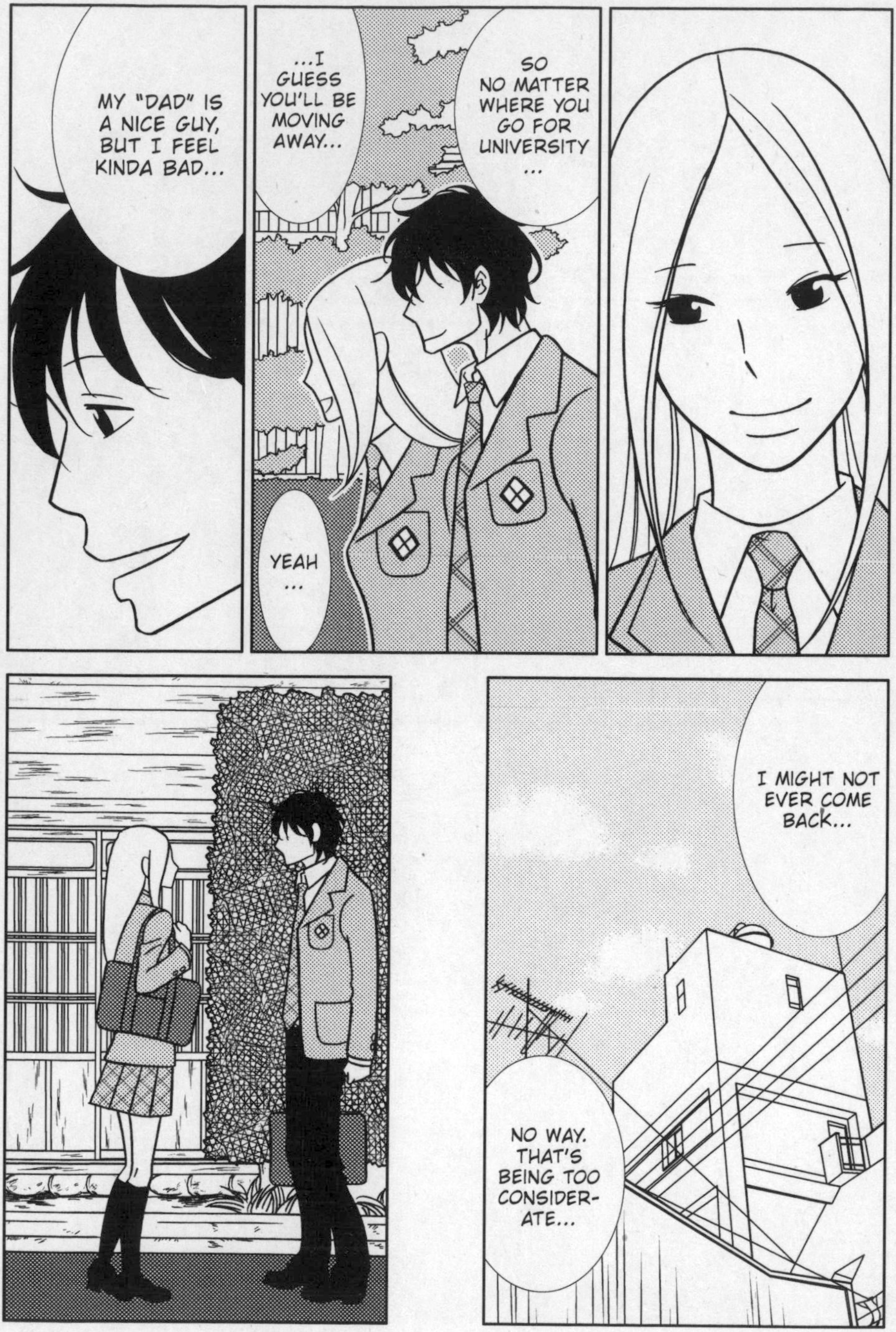
SO NO MATTER WHERE YOU GO FOR UNIVERSITY ...
...I GUESS YOU'LL BE MOVING AWAY...
YEAH ...
MY "DAD" IS A NICE GUY, BUT I FEEL KINDA BAD...
I MIGHT NOT EVER COME BACK...
NO WAY. THAT'S BEING TOO CONSIDER-ATE...

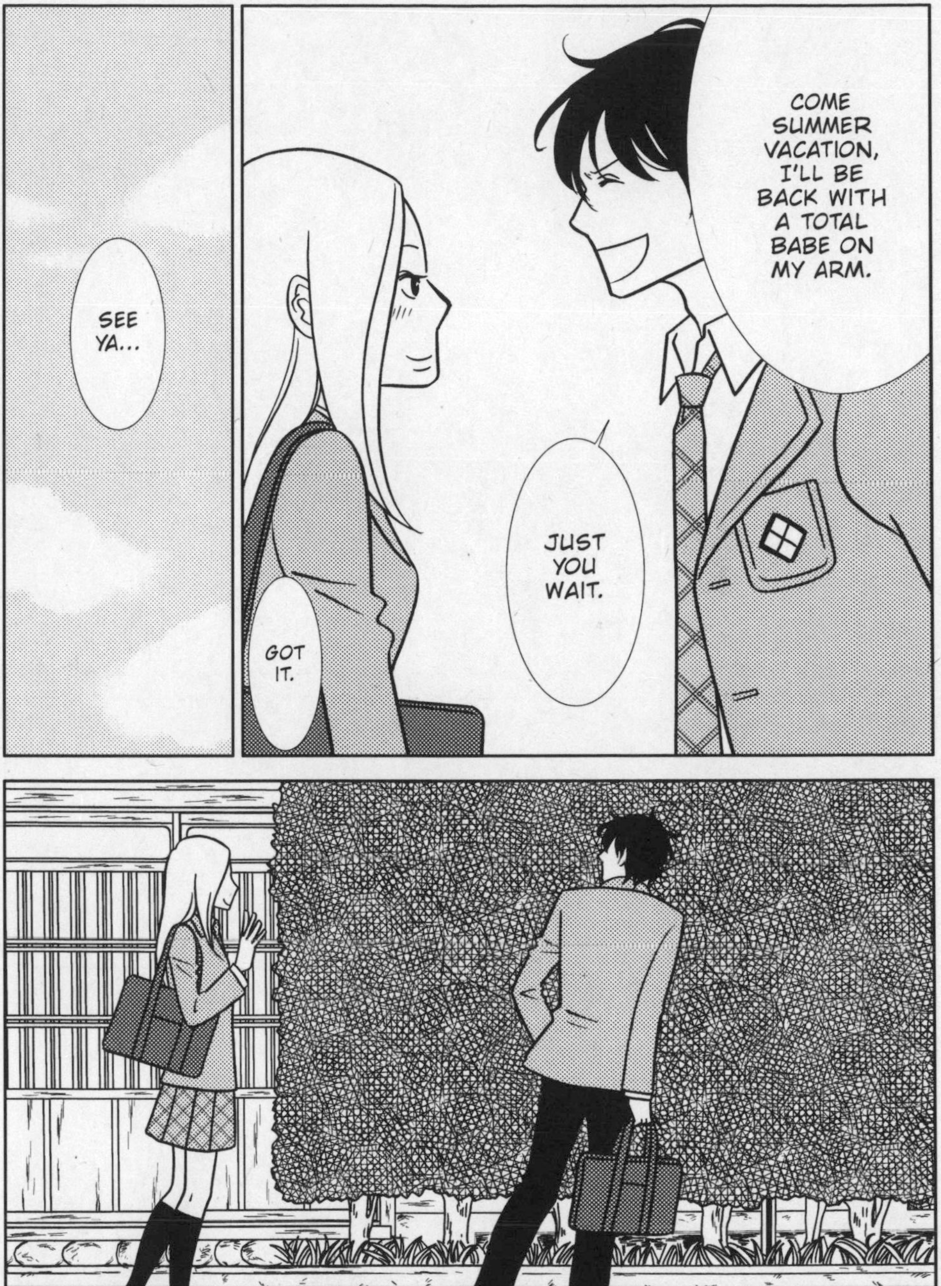
COME SUMMER VACATION, I'LL BE BACK WITH A TOTAL BABE ON MY ARM.
JUST YOU WAIT.
GOT IT.
SEE YA...

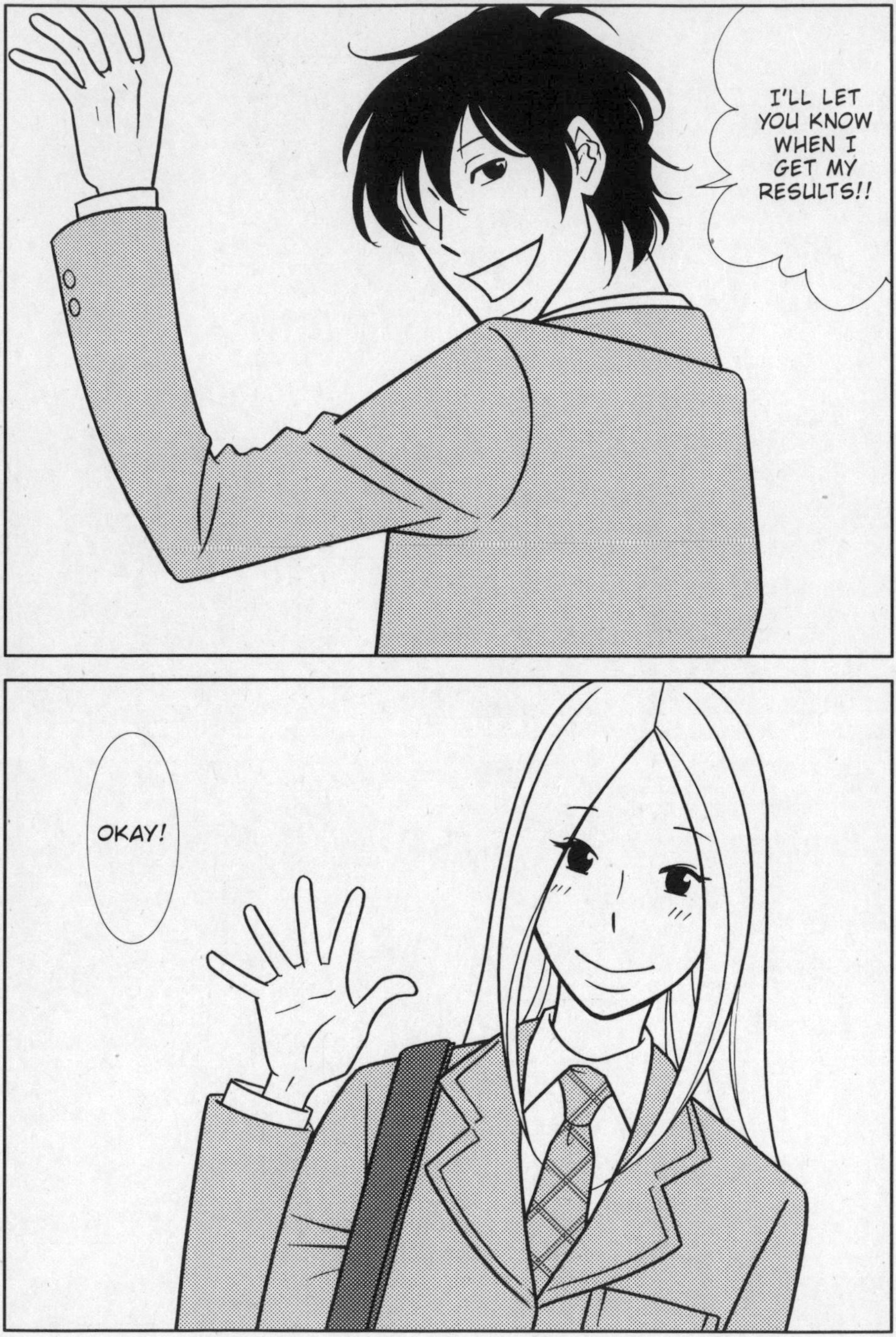
I'LL LET YOU KNOW WHEN I GET MY RESULTS!!
OKAY!

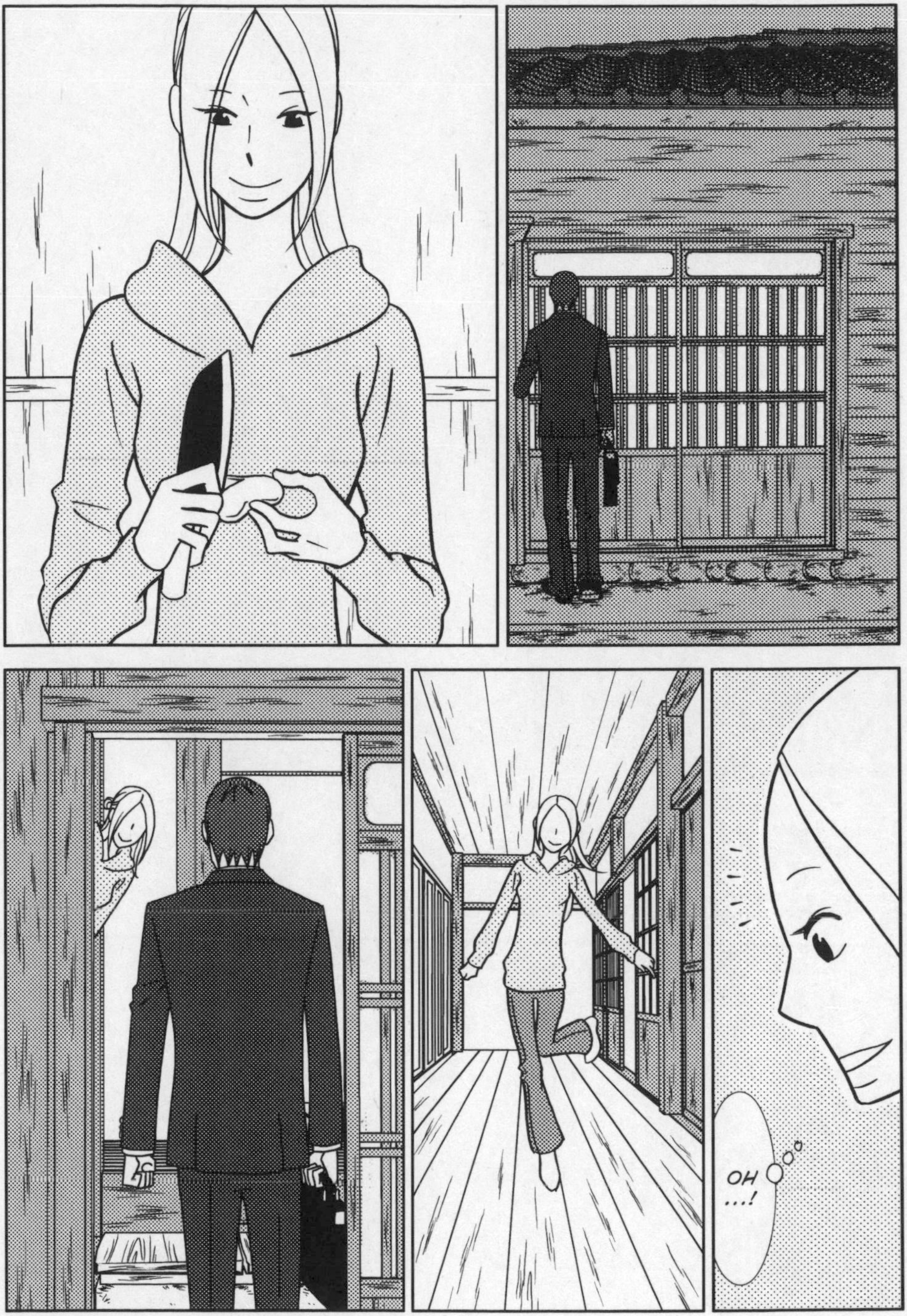
OH ...!

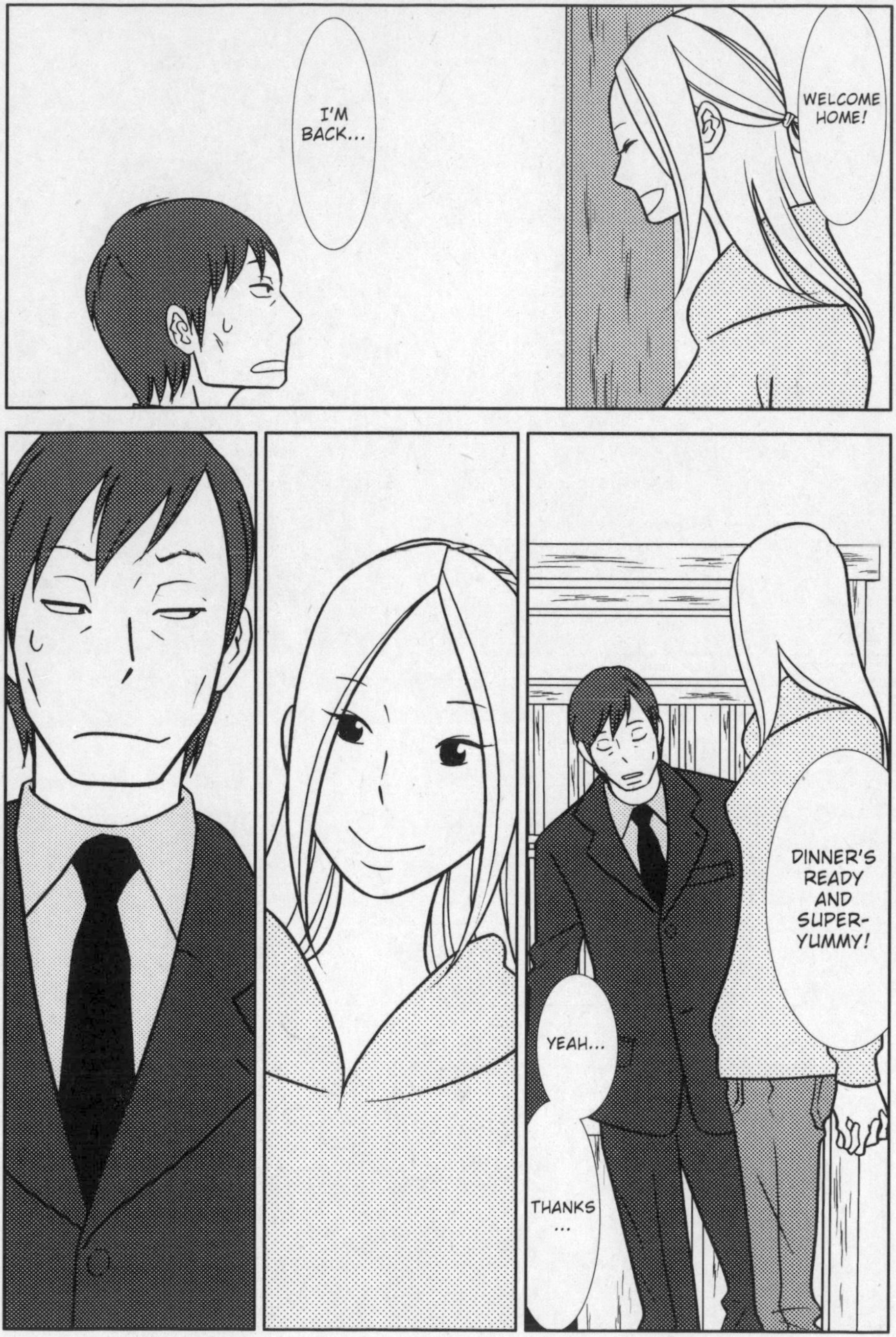
WELCOME HOME!
I'M BACK...
DINNER'S READY AND SUPER-YUMMY!
YEAH...
THANKS...

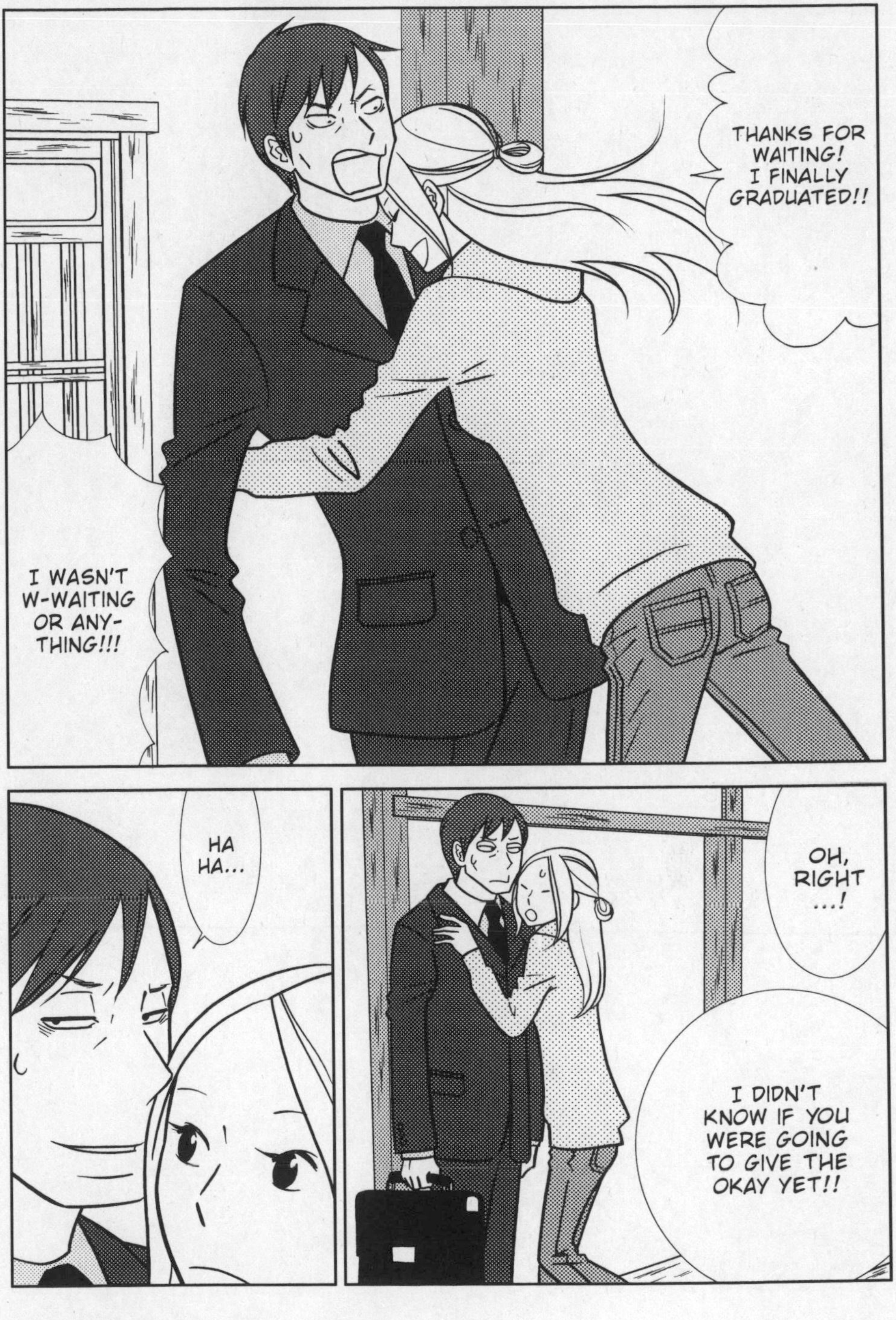
THANKS FOR WAITING! I FINALLY GRADUATED!!
I WASN'T W-WAITING OR ANY-THING!!!
OH, RIGHT ...!
I DIDN'T KNOW IF YOU WERE GOING TO GIVE THE OKAY YET!!
HA HA...

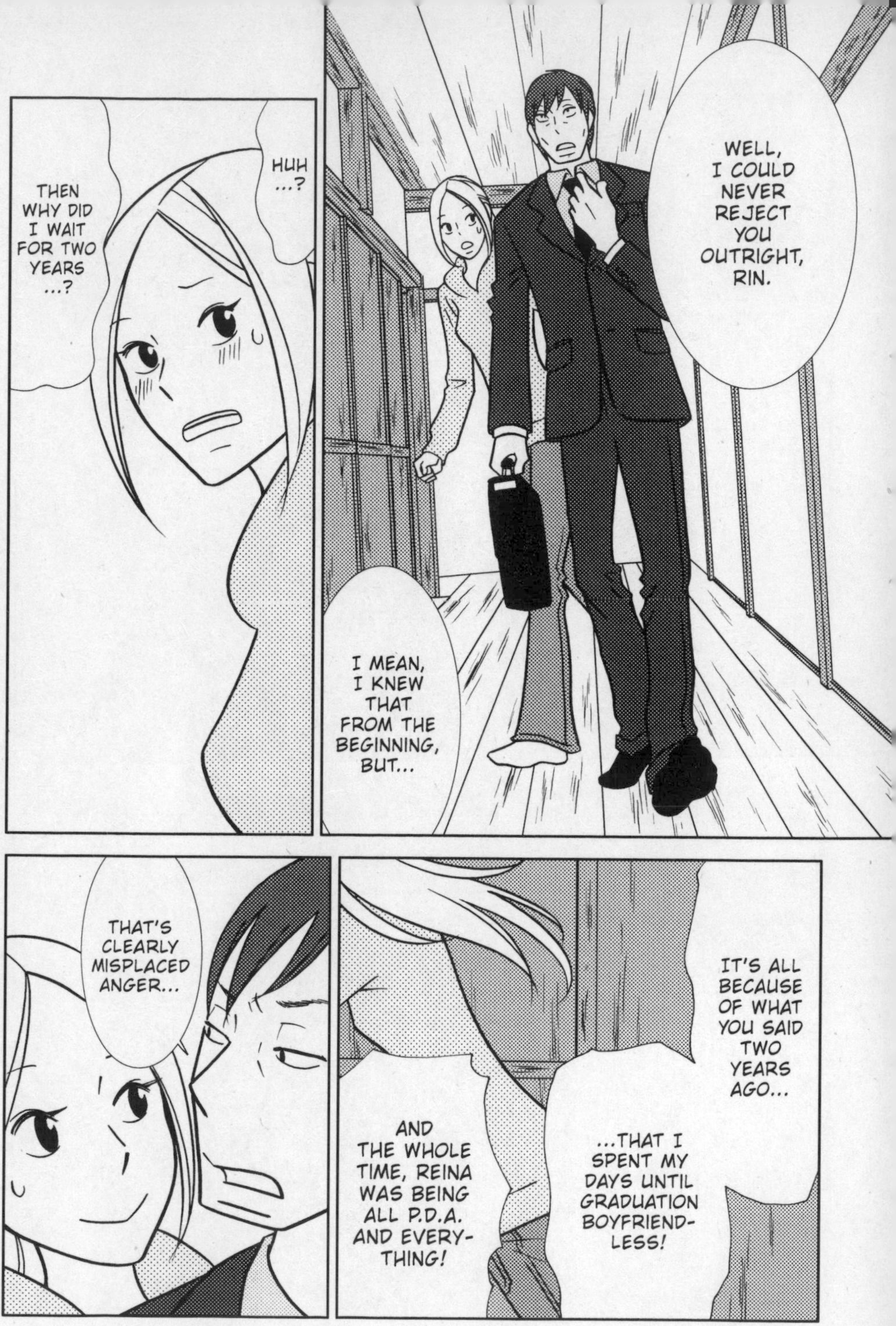
WELL, I COULD NEVER REJECT YOU OUTRIGHT, RIN.
I MEAN, I KNEW THAT FROM THE BEGINNING, BUT...
HUH ...?
THEN WHY DID I WAIT FOR TWO YEARS ...?
IT'S ALL BECAUSE OF WHAT YOU SAID TWO YEARS AGO...
...THAT I SPENT MY DAYS UNTIL GRADUATION BOYFRIEND-LESS!
AND THE WHOLE TIME, REINA WAS BEING ALL P.D.A. AND EVERY-THING!
THAT'S CLEARLY MISPLACED ANGER...

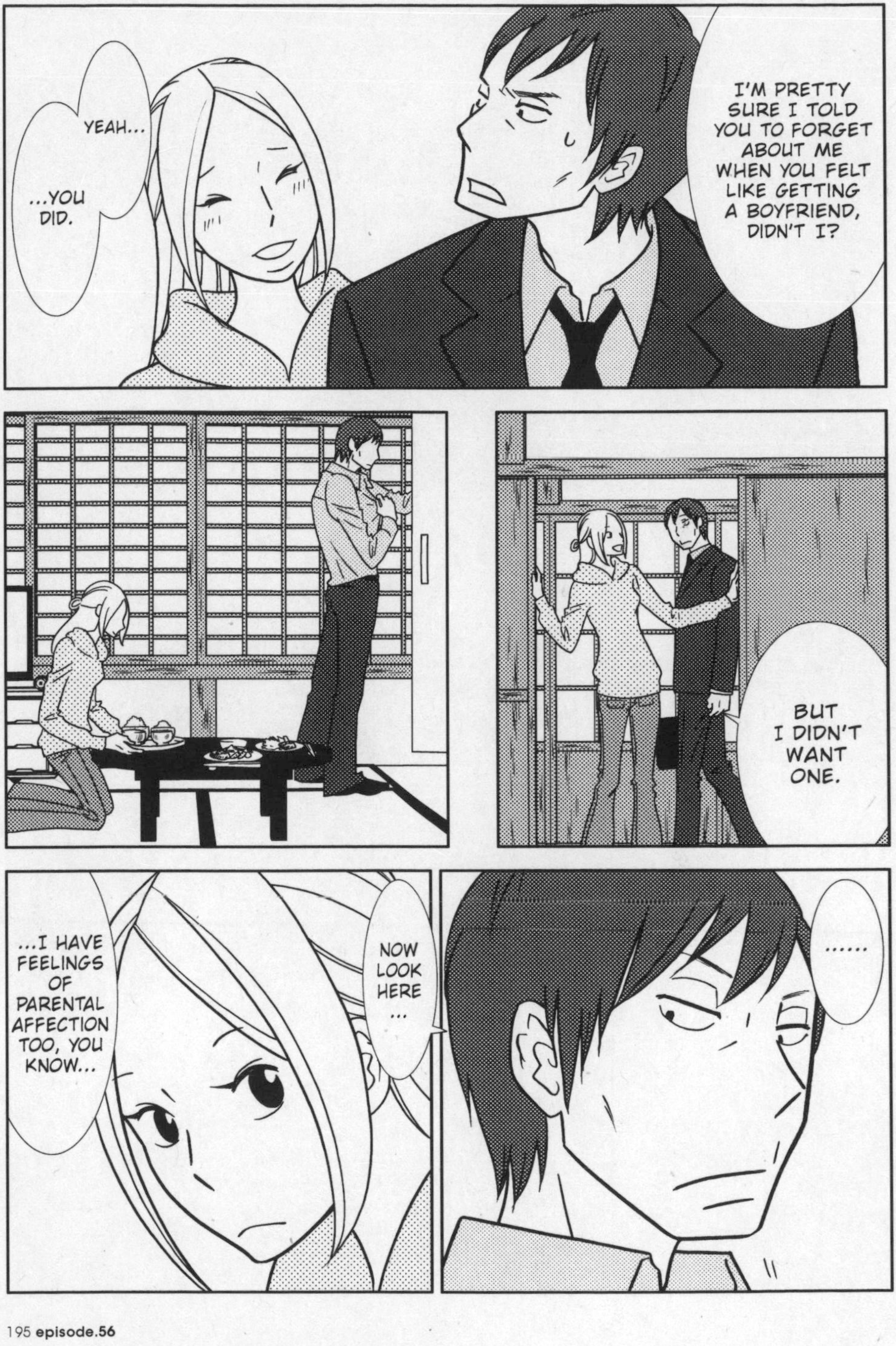
I'M PRETTY SURE I TOLD YOU TO FORGET ABOUT ME WHEN YOU FELT LIKE GETTING A BOYFRIEND, DIDN'T I?
YEAH...
...YOU DID.
BUT I DIDN'T WANT ONE.
......
NOW LOOK HERE ...
...I HAVE FEELINGS OF PARENTAL AFFECTION TOO, YOU KNOW...

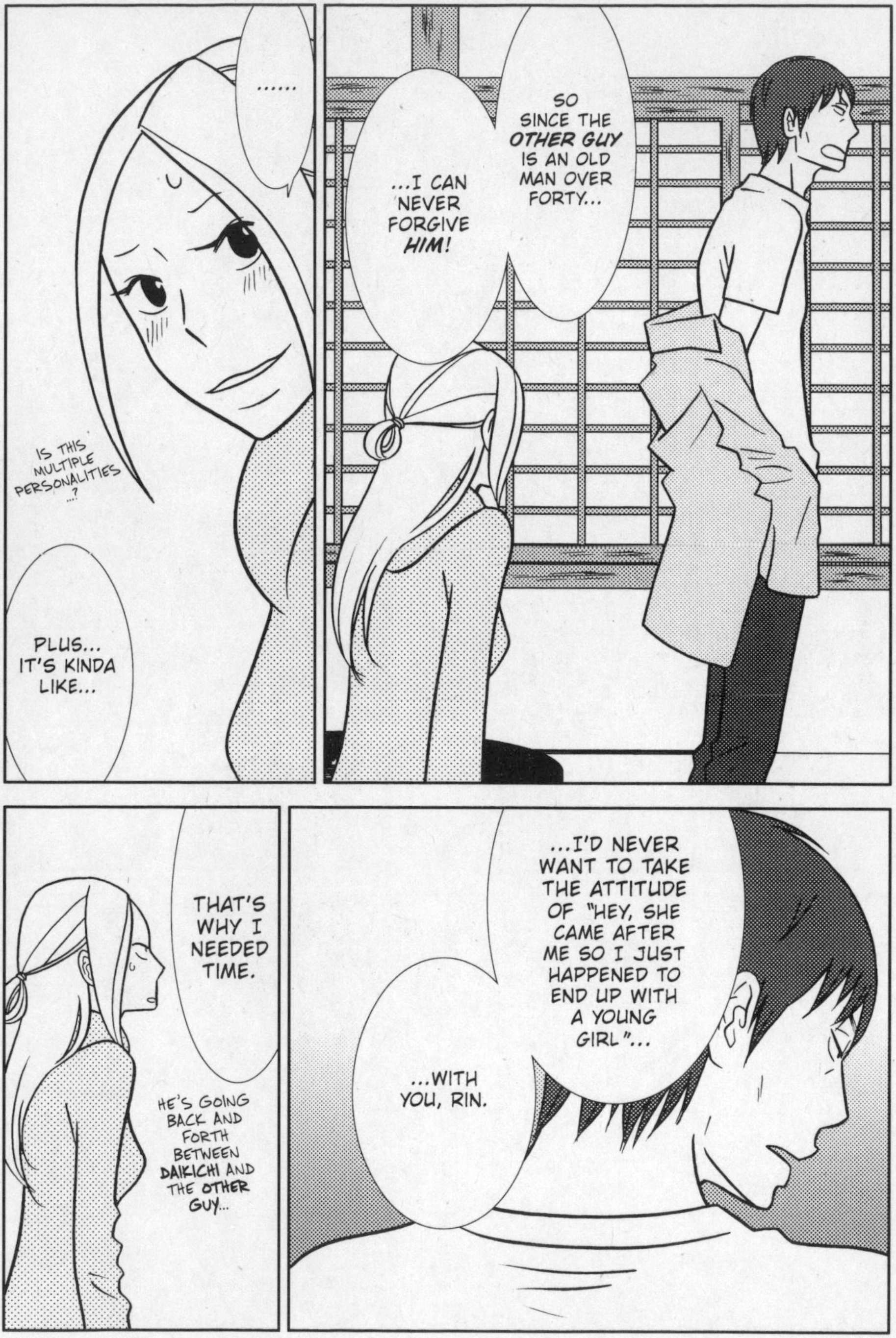
SO SINCE THE OTHER GUY IS AN OLD MAN OVER FORTY...
...I CAN NEVER FORGIVE HIM!
......
IS THIS MULTIPLE PERSONALITIES ...?
PLUS... IT'S KINDA LIKE...
...I'D NEVER WANT TO TAKE THE ATTITUDE OF "HEY, SHE CAME AFTER ME SO I JUST HAPPENED TO END UP WITH A YOUNG GIRL"...
...WITH YOU, RIN.
THAT'S WHY I NEEDED TIME.
HE'S GOING BACK AND FORTH BETWEEN DAIKICHI AND THE OTHER GUY...

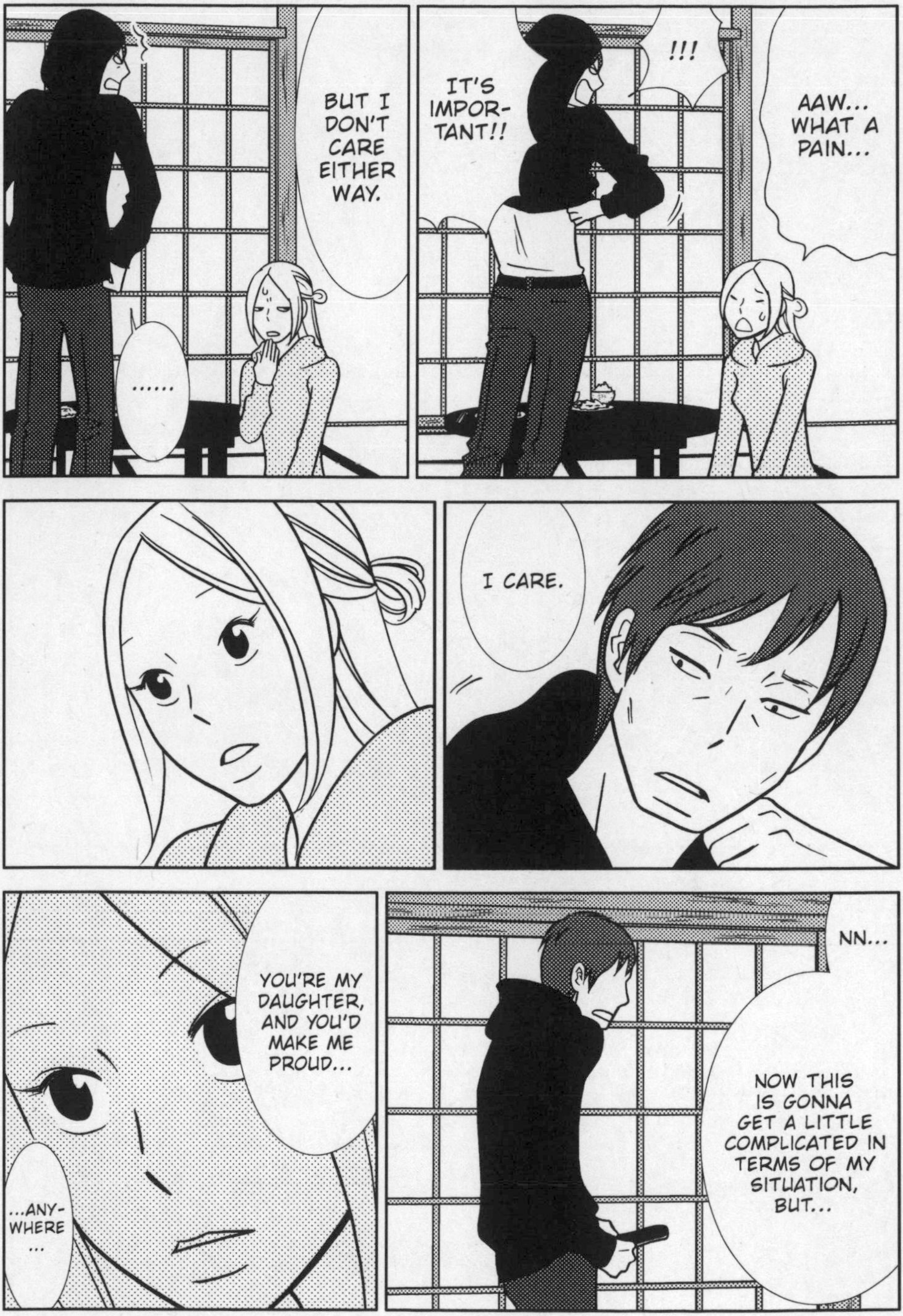
AAW... WHAT A PAIN...
!!!
IT'S IMPORTANT!!
BUT I DON'T CARE EITHER WAY.
......
I CARE.
NN...
NOW THIS IS GONNA GET A LITTLE COMPLICATED IN TERMS OF MY SITUATION, BUT...
YOU'RE MY DAUGHTER, AND YOU'D MAKE ME PROUD...
...ANY-WHERE...

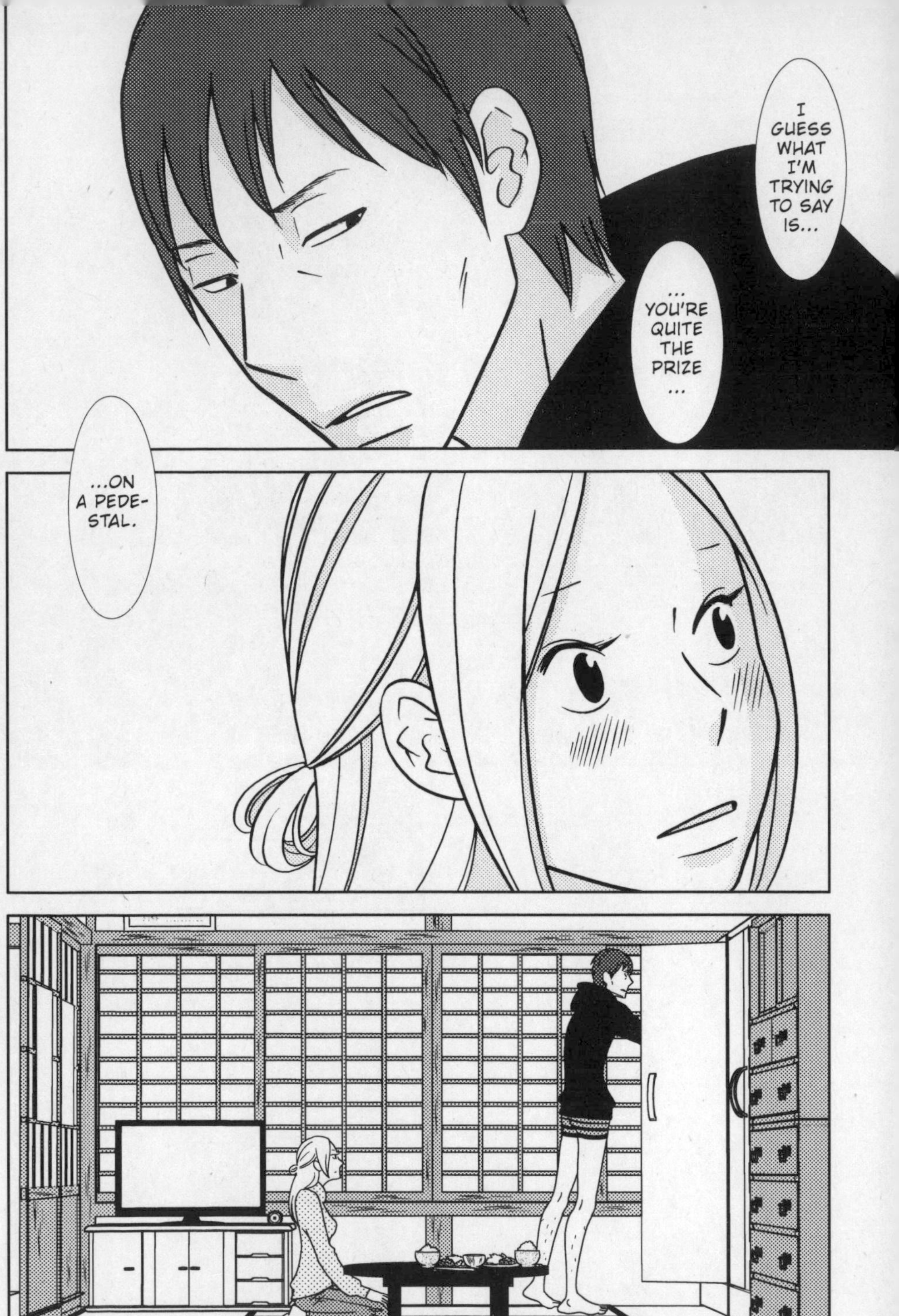
I GUESS WHAT I'M TRYING TO SAY IS...
...YOU'RE QUITE THE PRIZE...
...ON A PEDESTAL.

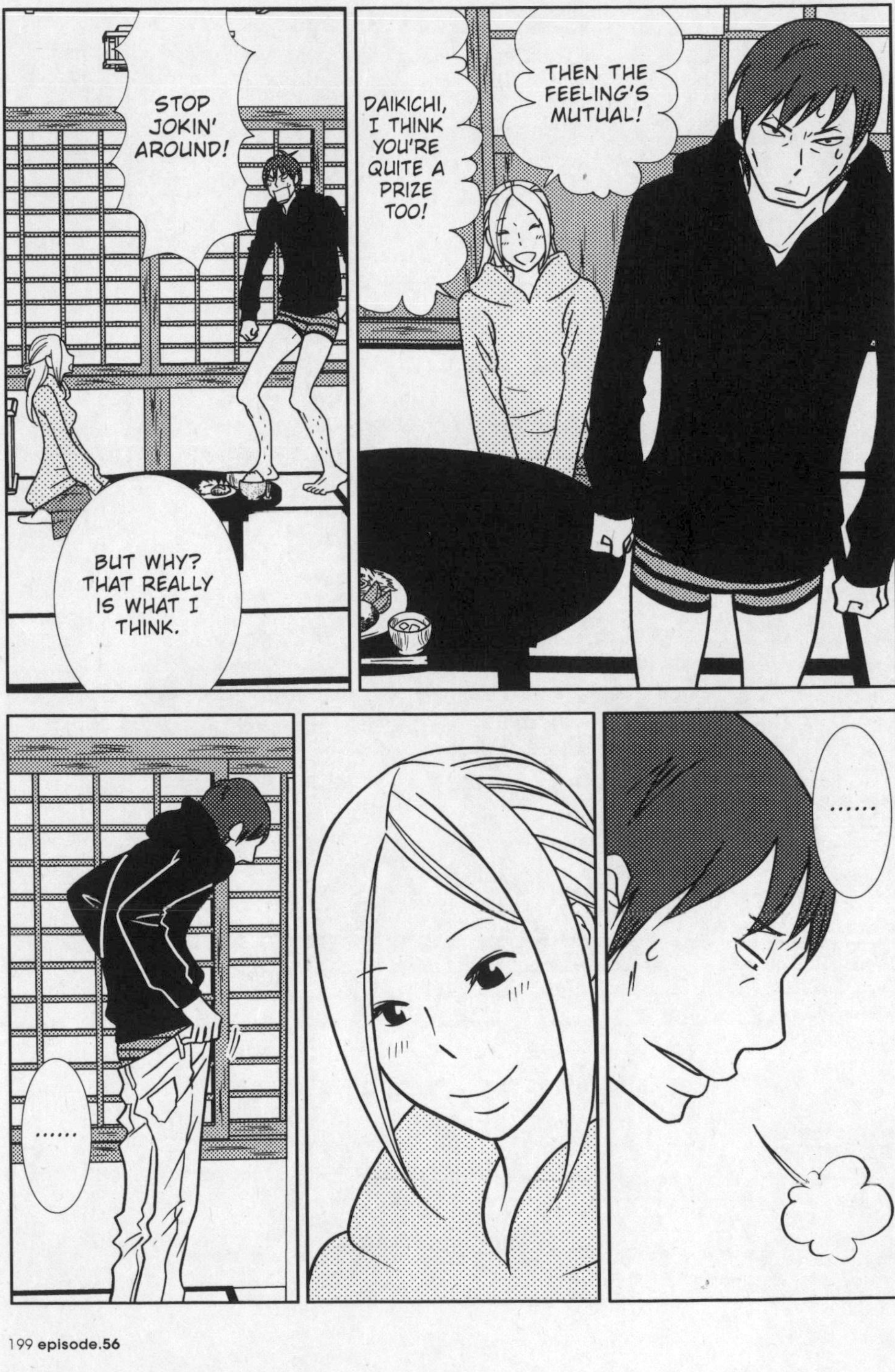
THEN THE FEELING'S MUTUAL!
DAIKICHI, I THINK YOU'RE QUITE A PRIZE TOO!
STOP JOKIN' AROUND!
BUT WHY? THAT REALLY IS WHAT I THINK.
......
......

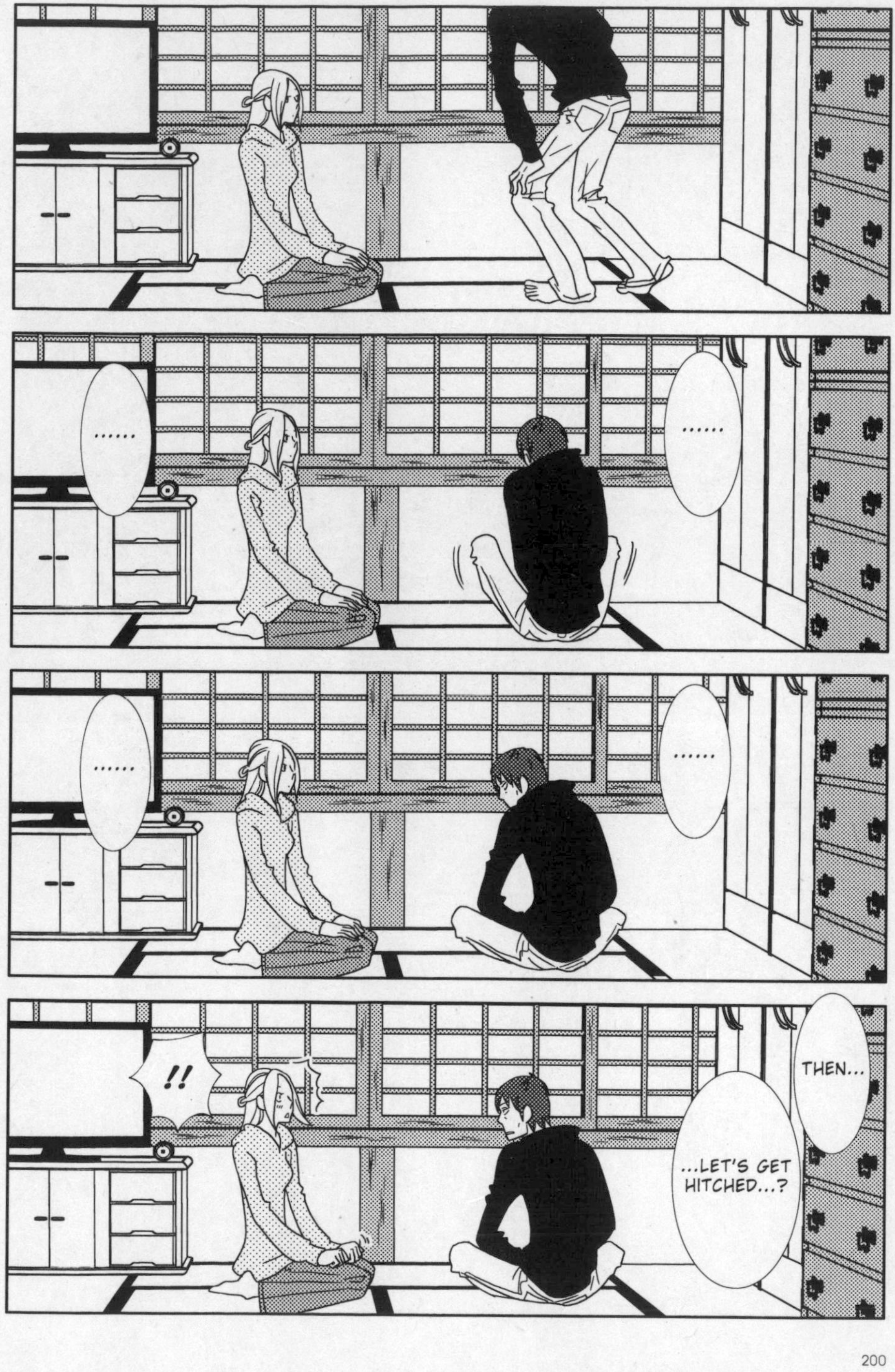
......
......
......
......
THEN...
...LET'S GET HITCHED...?
!!

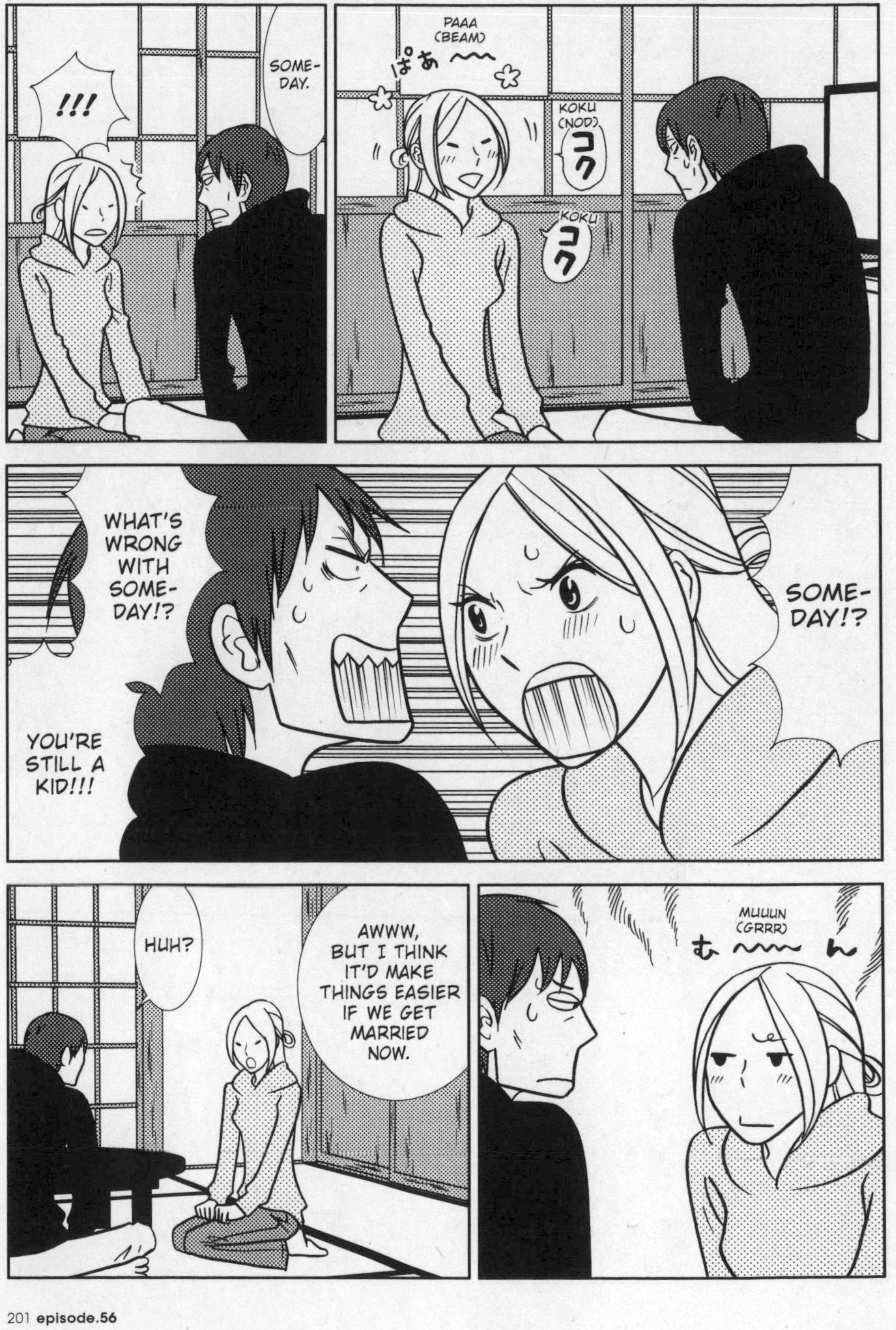
PAAA (BEAM)
ぱあ～～
KOKU (NOD)
コク
KOKU
コク
SOME-DAY.
!!!
SOME-DAY!?
WHAT'S WRONG WITH SOME-DAY!?
YOU'RE STILL A KID!!!
MUUUN (GRRR)
む～～ん
AWWW, BUT I THINK IT'D MAKE THINGS EASIER IF WE GET MARRIED NOW.
HUH?

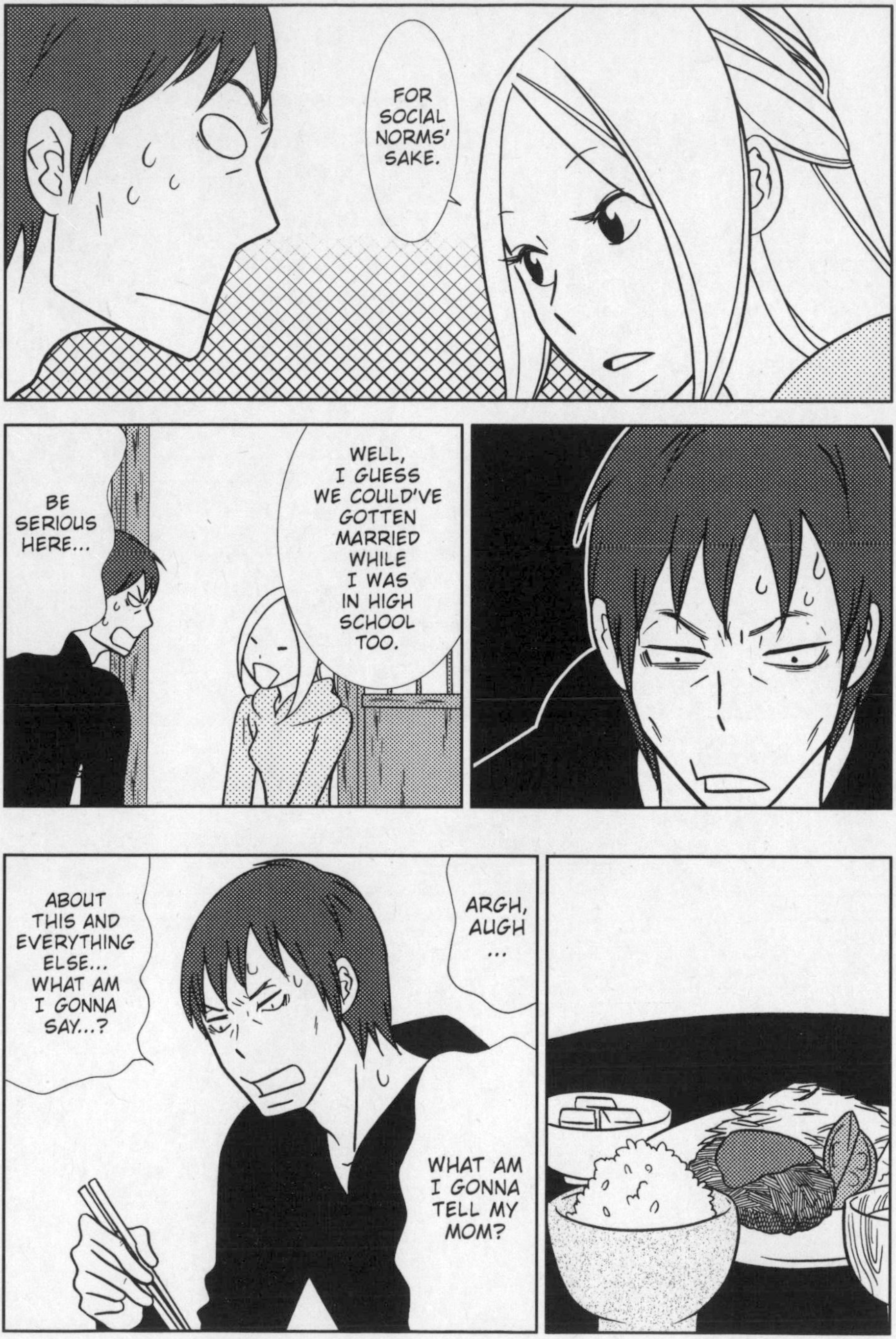
FOR SOCIAL NORMS' SAKE.
WELL, I GUESS WE COULD'VE GOTTEN MARRIED WHILE I WAS IN HIGH SCHOOL TOO.
BE SERIOUS HERE...
ARGH, AUGH ...
ABOUT THIS AND EVERYTHING ELSE... WHAT AM I GONNA SAY...?
WHAT AM I GONNA TELL MY MOM?

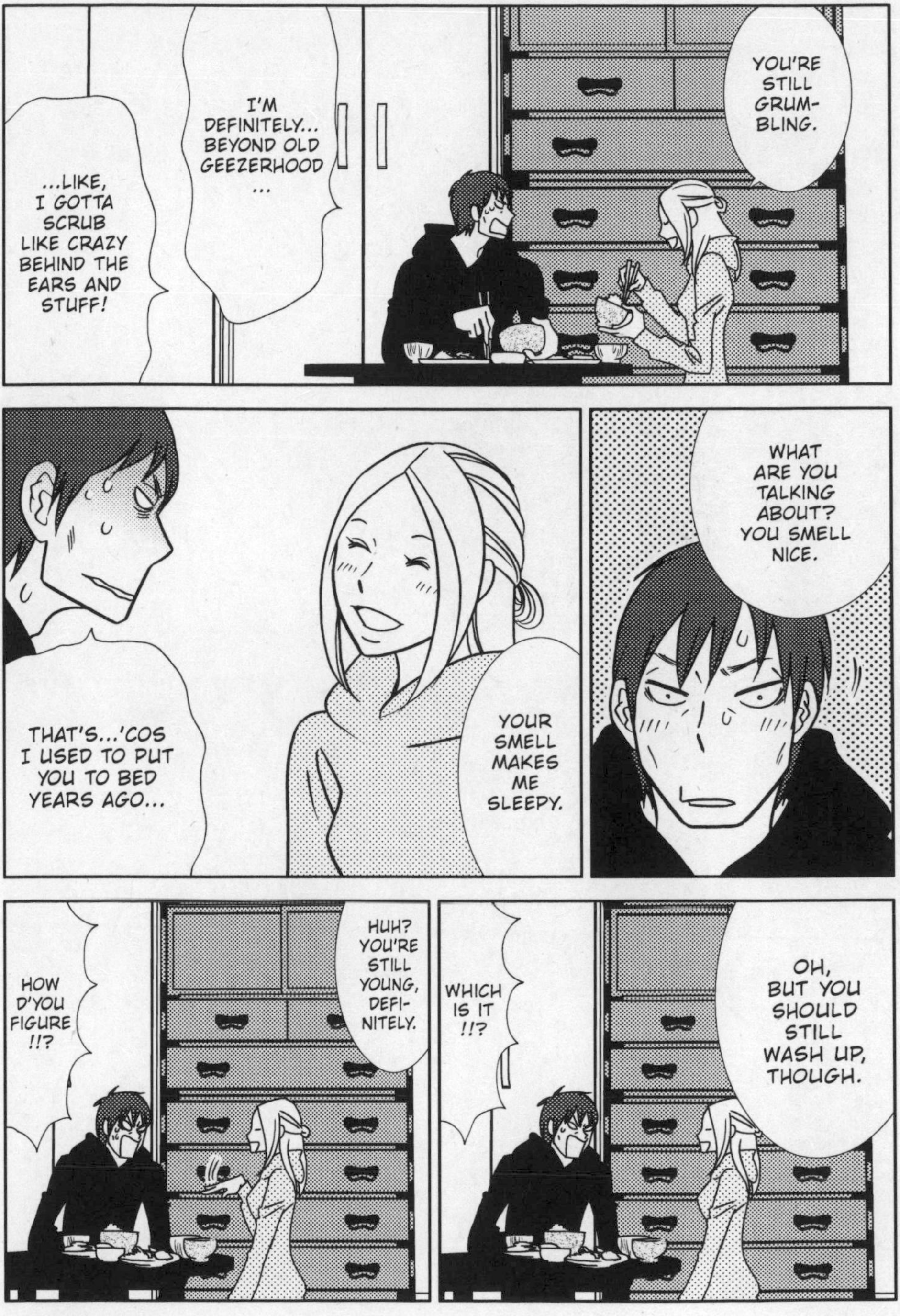
YOU'RE STILL GRUMBLING.
I'M DEFINITELY... BEYOND OLD GEEZERHOOD ...
...LIKE, I GOTTA SCRUB LIKE CRAZY BEHIND THE EARS AND STUFF!
WHAT ARE YOU TALKING ABOUT? YOU SMELL NICE.
YOUR SMELL MAKES ME SLEEPY.
THAT'S...'COS I USED TO PUT YOU TO BED YEARS AGO...
OH, BUT YOU SHOULD STILL WASH UP, THOUGH.
WHICH IS IT !!?
HUH? YOU'RE STILL YOUNG, DEFINITELY.
HOW D'YOU FIGURE !!?

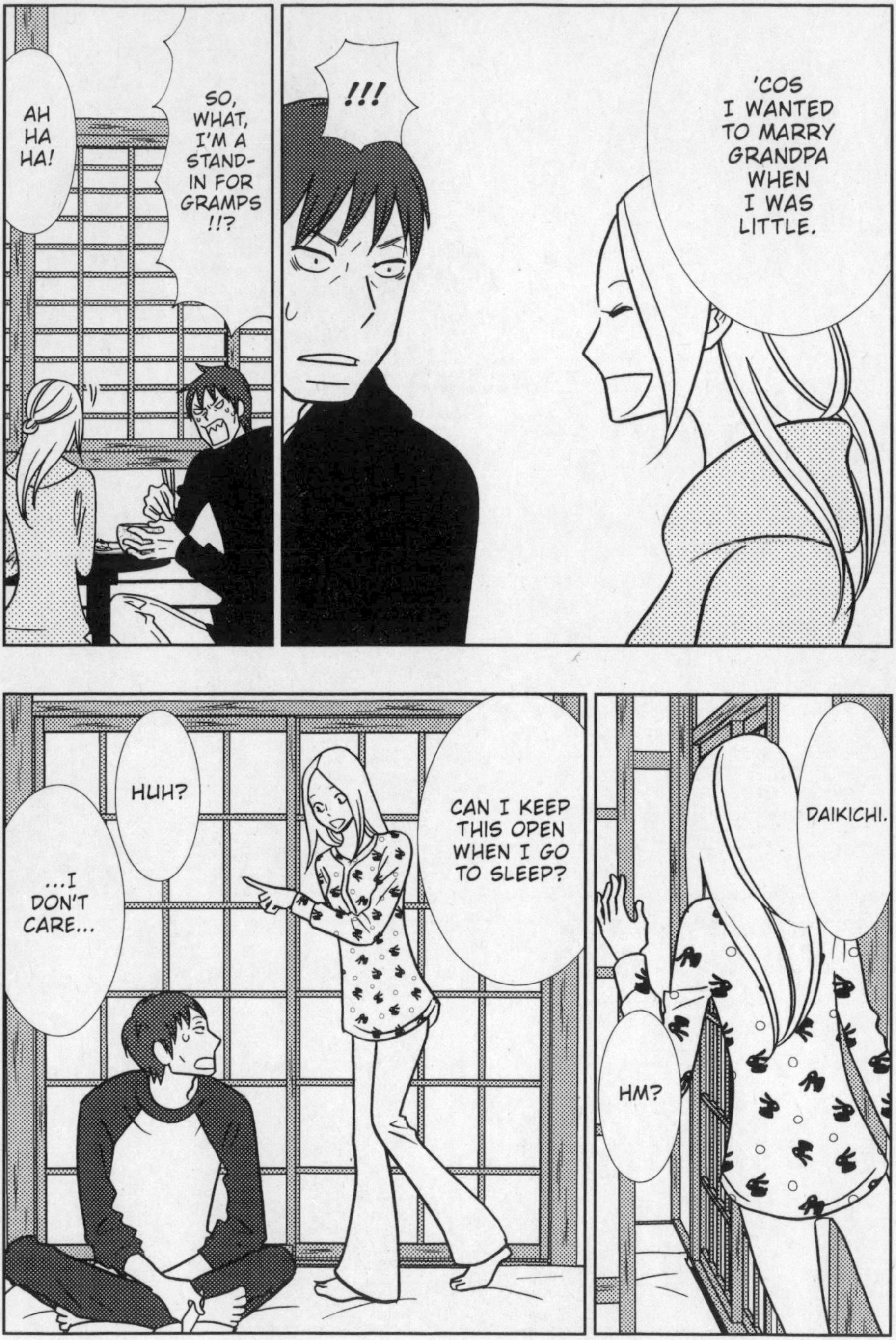
'COS I WANTED TO MARRY GRANDPA WHEN I WAS LITTLE.
!!!
SO, WHAT, I'M A STAND-IN FOR GRAMPS !!?
AH HA HA!
DAIKICHI.
HM?
CAN I KEEP THIS OPEN WHEN I GO TO SLEEP?
HUH?
...I DON'T CARE...

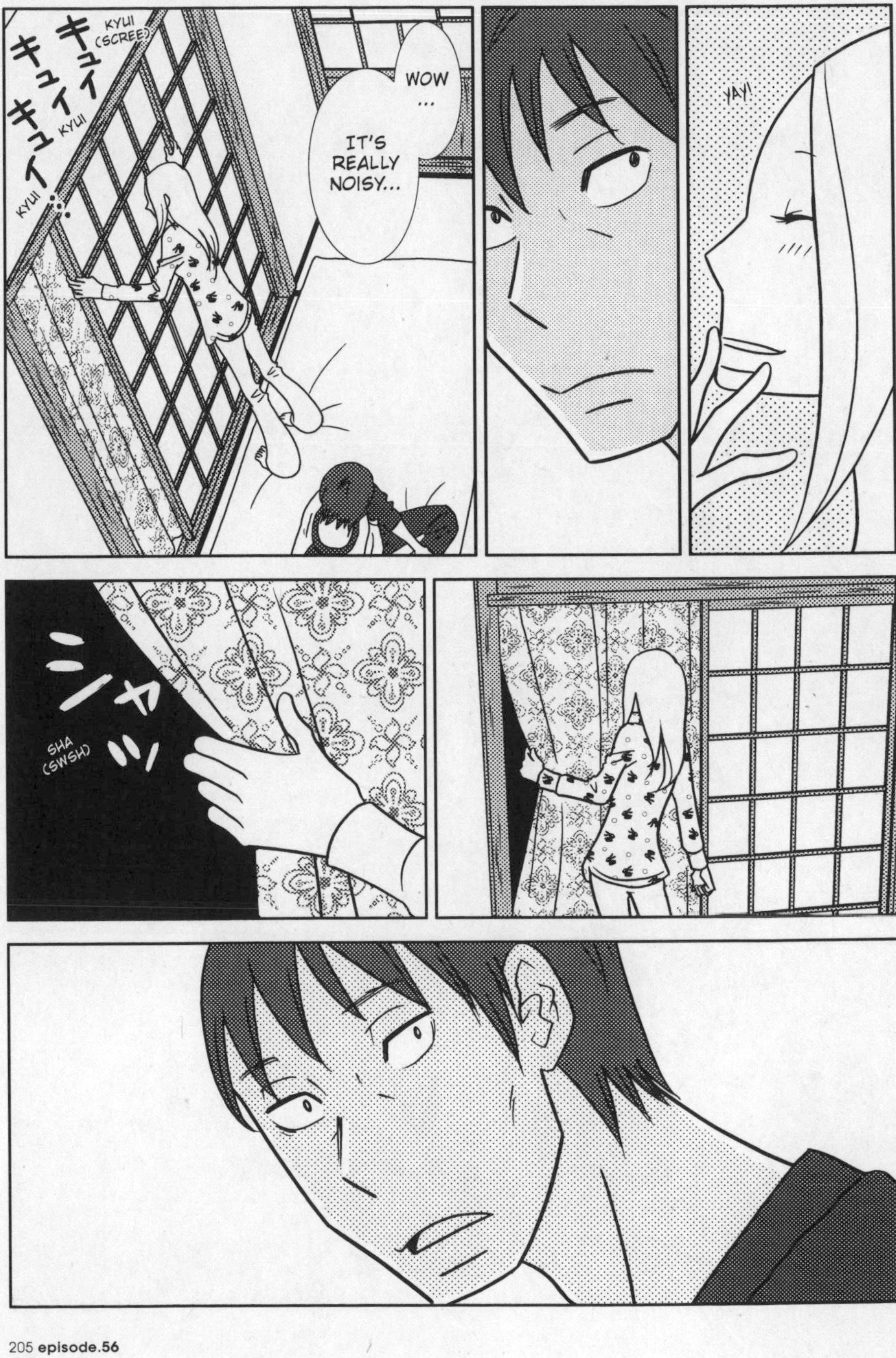
YAY!
WOW ...
IT'S REALLY NOISY...
キュイ
KYUI (SCREE)
キュイ
KYUI
キュイ
KYUI
シャッ
SHA (SWSH)

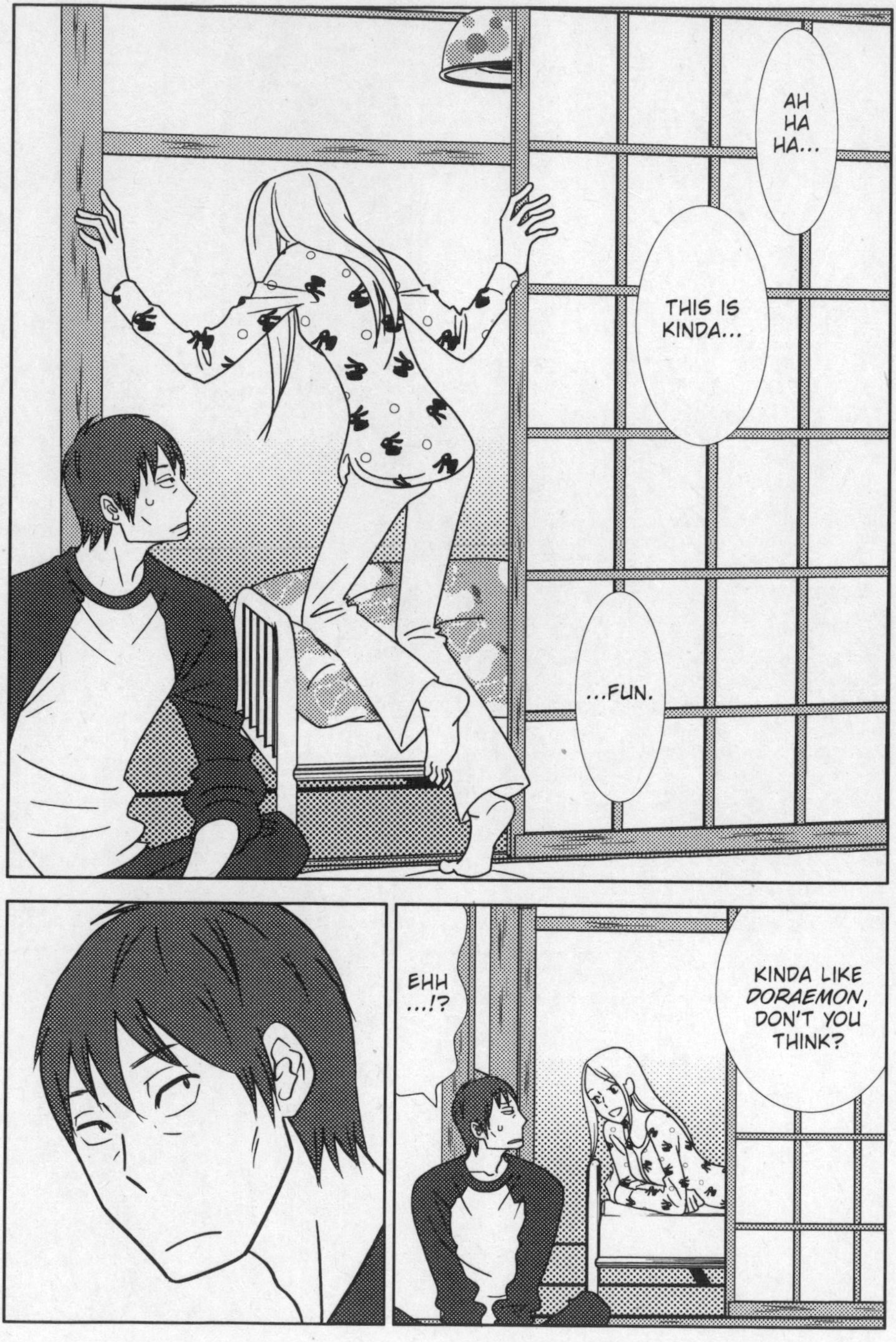

AH HA HA...
THIS IS KINDA...
...FUN.
KINDA LIKE *DORAEMON*, DON'T YOU THINK?
EHH ...!?

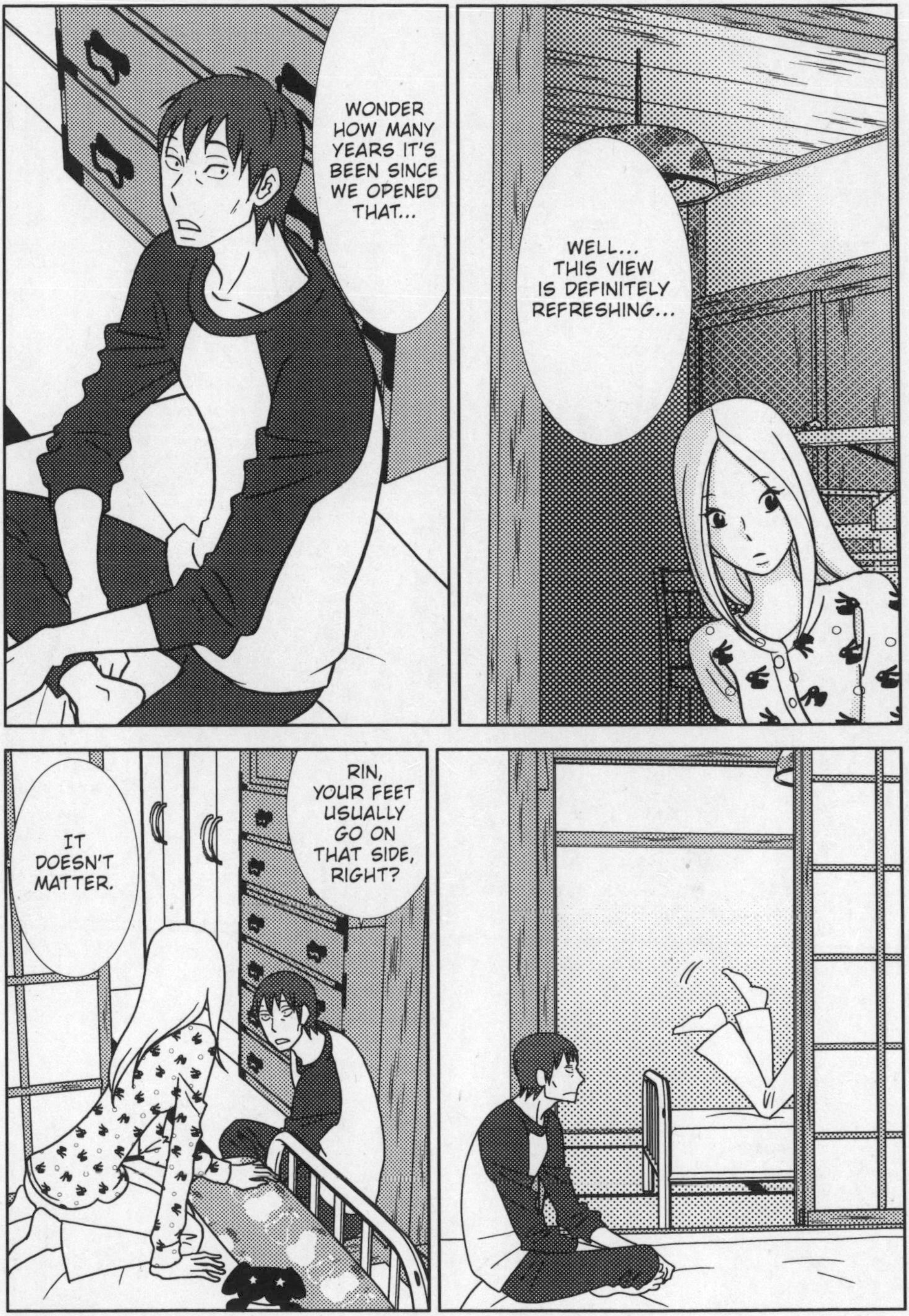
WELL... THIS VIEW IS DEFINITELY REFRESHING...
WONDER HOW MANY YEARS IT'S BEEN SINCE WE OPENED THAT...
RIN, YOUR FEET USUALLY GO ON THAT SIDE, RIGHT?
IT DOESN'T MATTER.

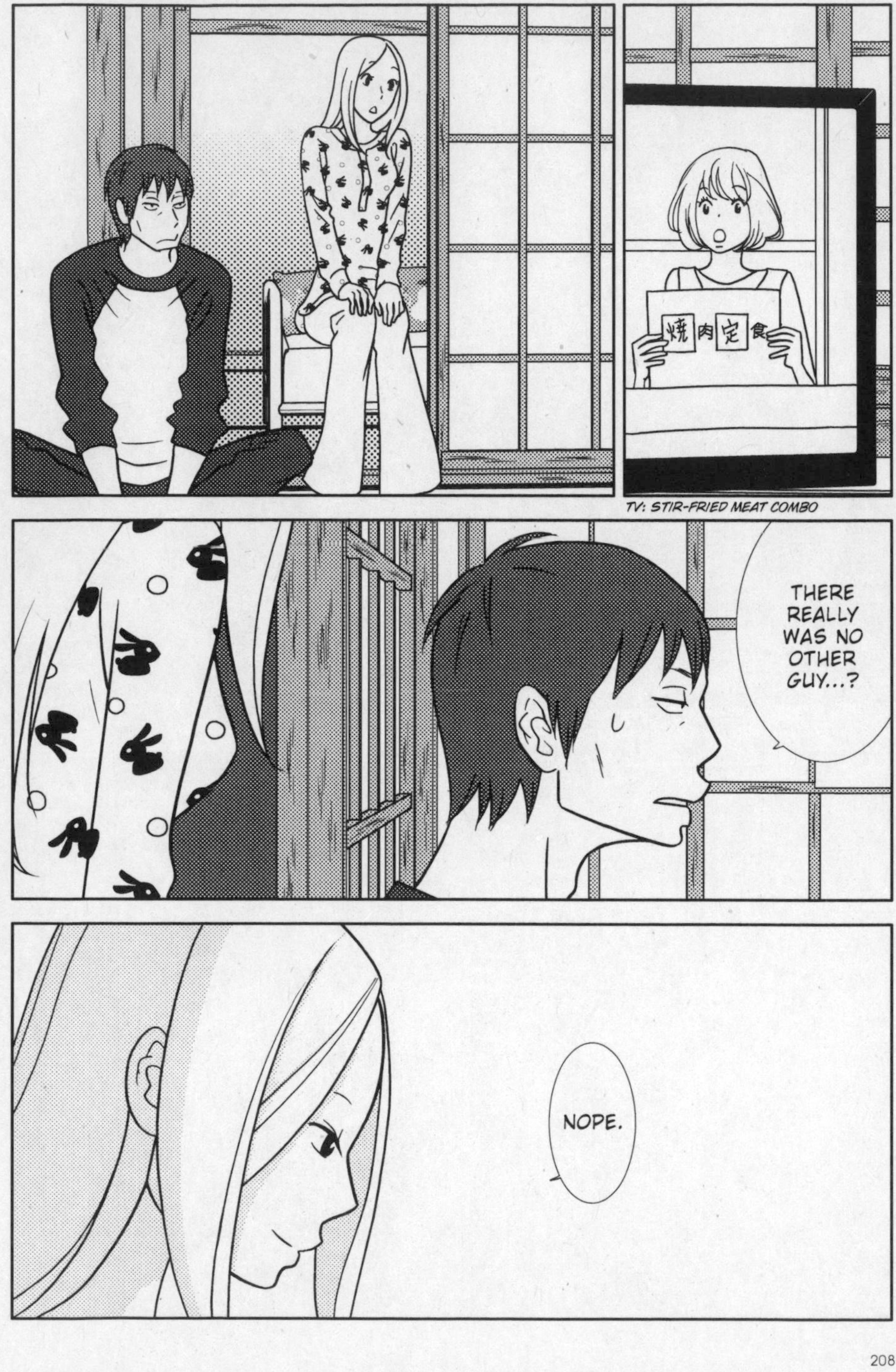
焼肉定食
TV: STIR-FRIED MEAT COMBO
THERE REALLY WAS NO OTHER GUY...?
NOPE.

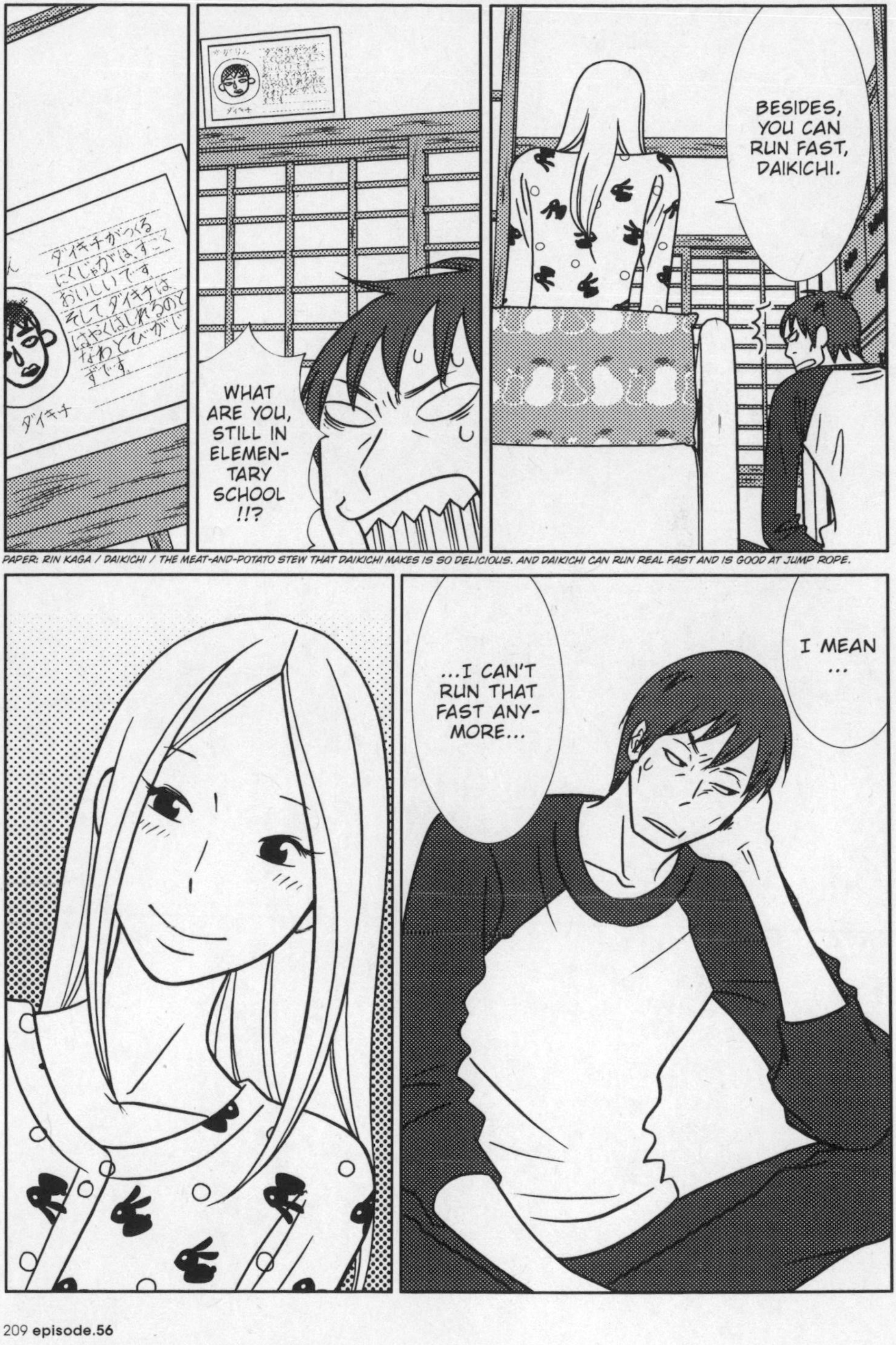
BESIDES, YOU CAN RUN FAST, DAIKICHI.
WHAT ARE YOU, STILL IN ELEMENTARY SCHOOL!!?
ダイキチがつくる
にくじゃがは、すごく
おいしいです
そしてダイキチは
はやくはしれるのと
なわとびがじ
ずです。
ダイキチ
PAPER: RIN KAGA / DAIKICHI / THE MEAT-AND-POTATO STEW THAT DAIKICHI MAKES IS SO DELICIOUS. AND DAIKICHI CAN RUN REAL FAST AND IS GOOD AT JUMP ROPE.
I MEAN...
...I CAN'T RUN THAT FAST ANYMORE...

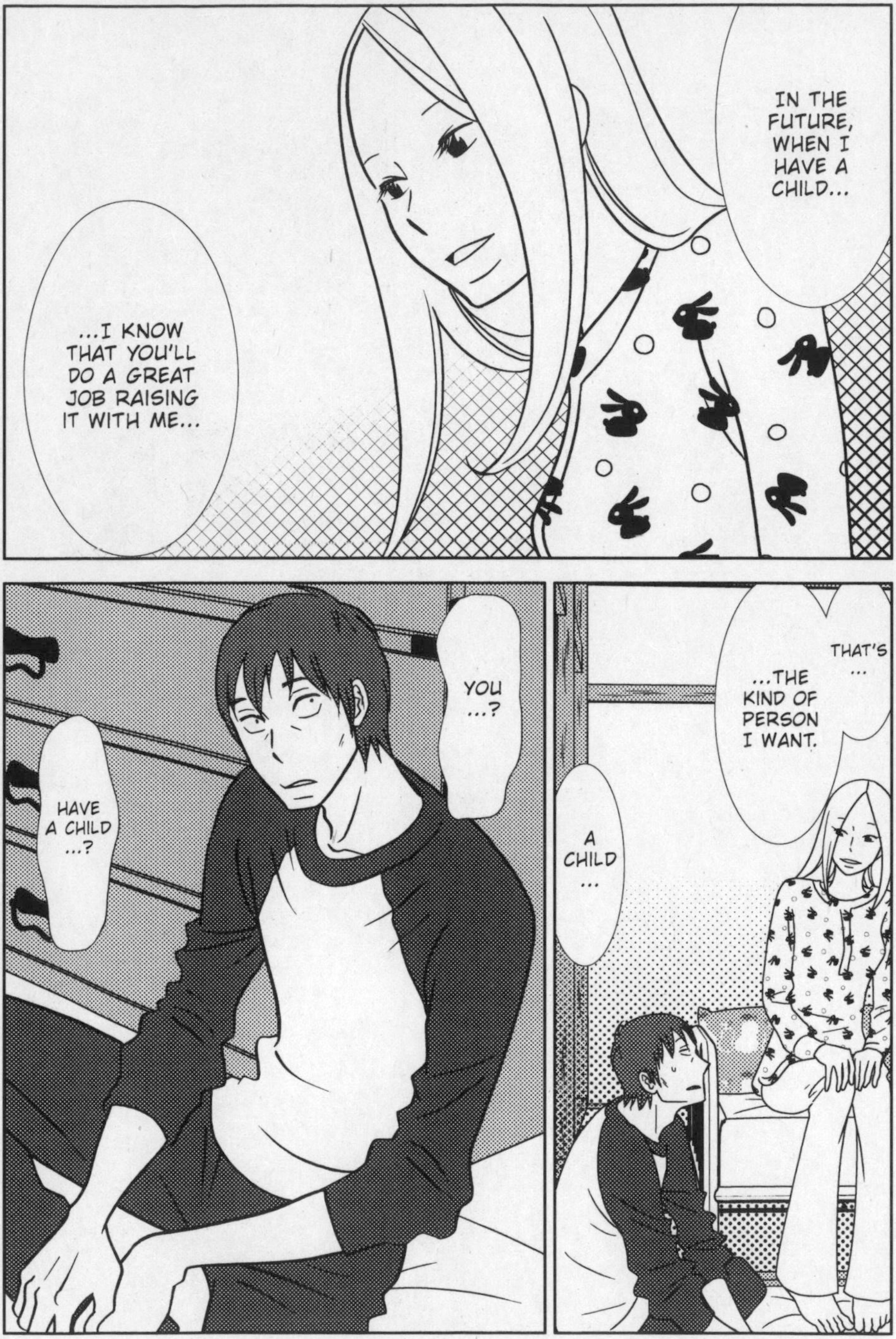
IN THE FUTURE, WHEN I HAVE A CHILD...
...I KNOW THAT YOU'LL DO A GREAT JOB RAISING IT WITH ME...
THAT'S ...
...THE KIND OF PERSON I WANT.
A CHILD ...
YOU ...?
HAVE A CHILD ...?

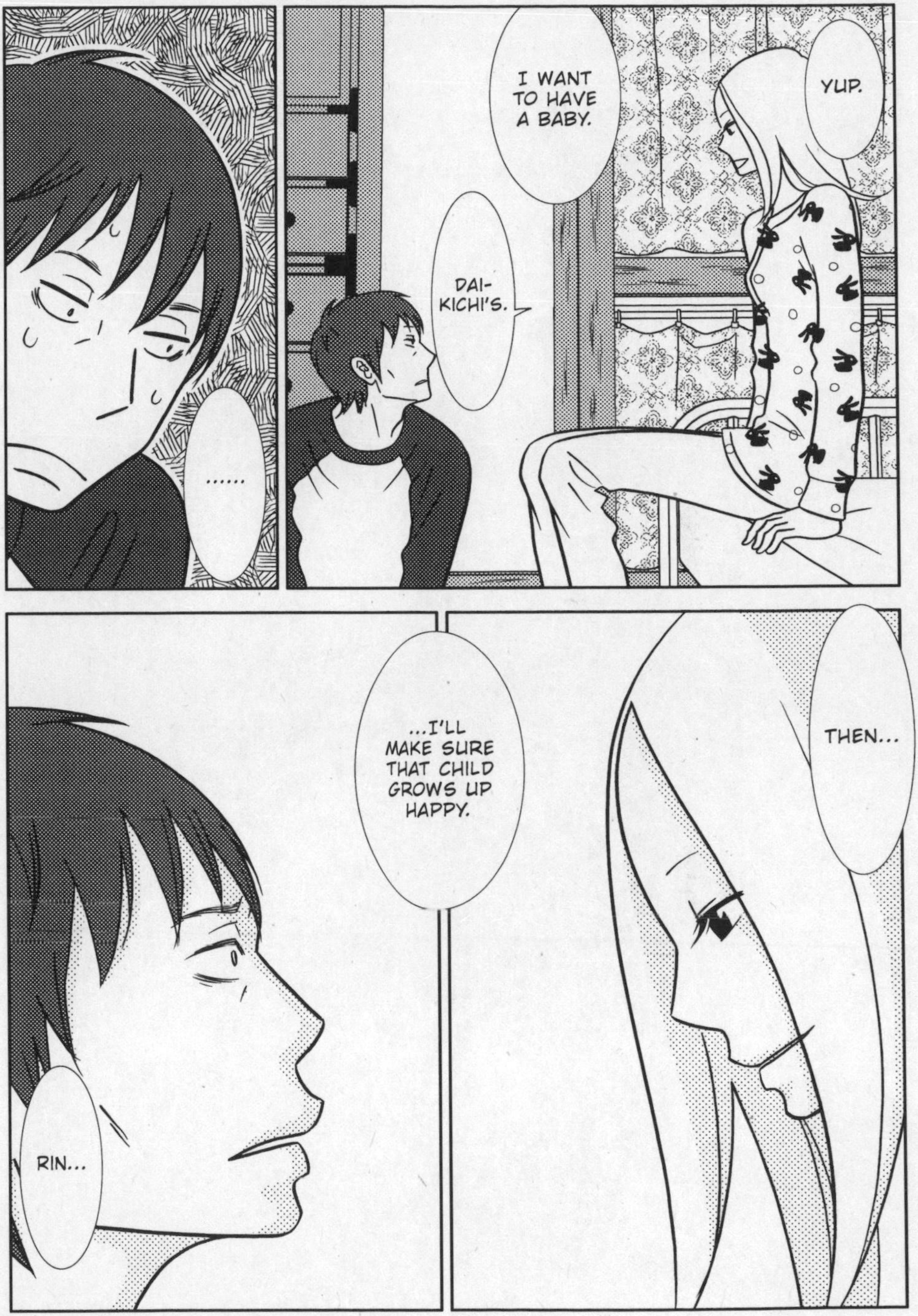
YUP.
I WANT TO HAVE A BABY.
DAI-KICHI'S.
......
THEN...
...I'LL MAKE SURE THAT CHILD GROWS UP HAPPY.
RIN...

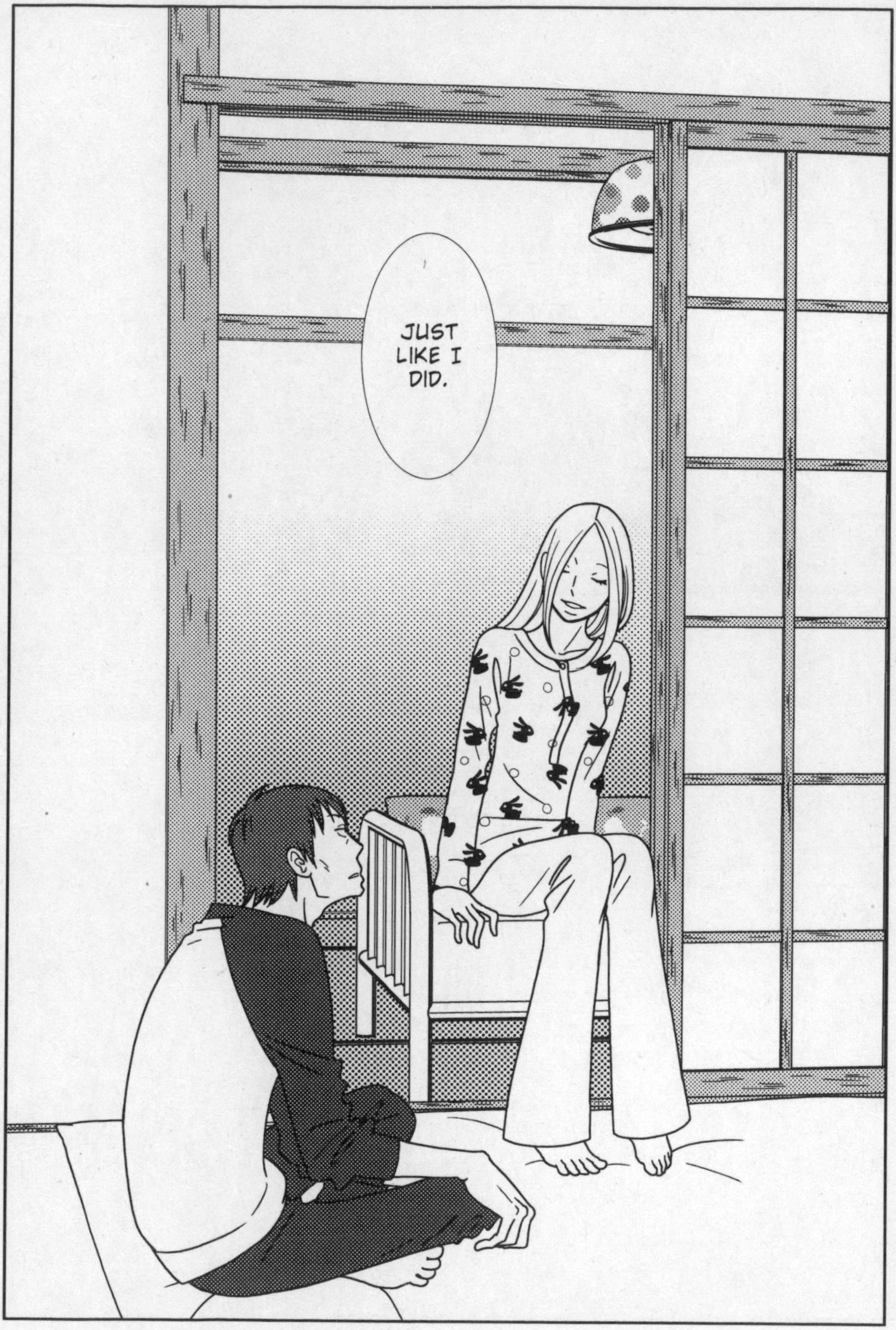
JUST LIKE I DID.

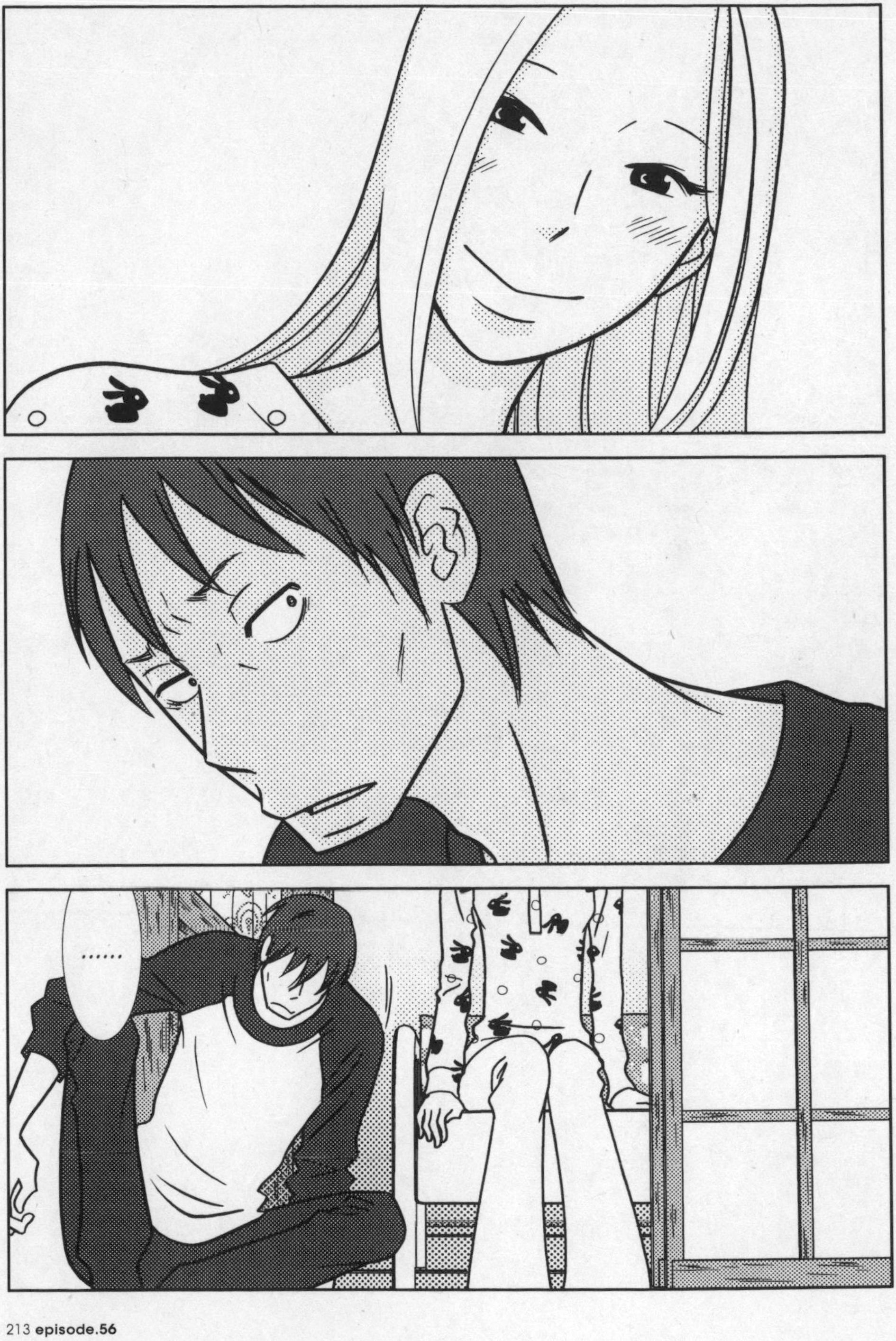
......

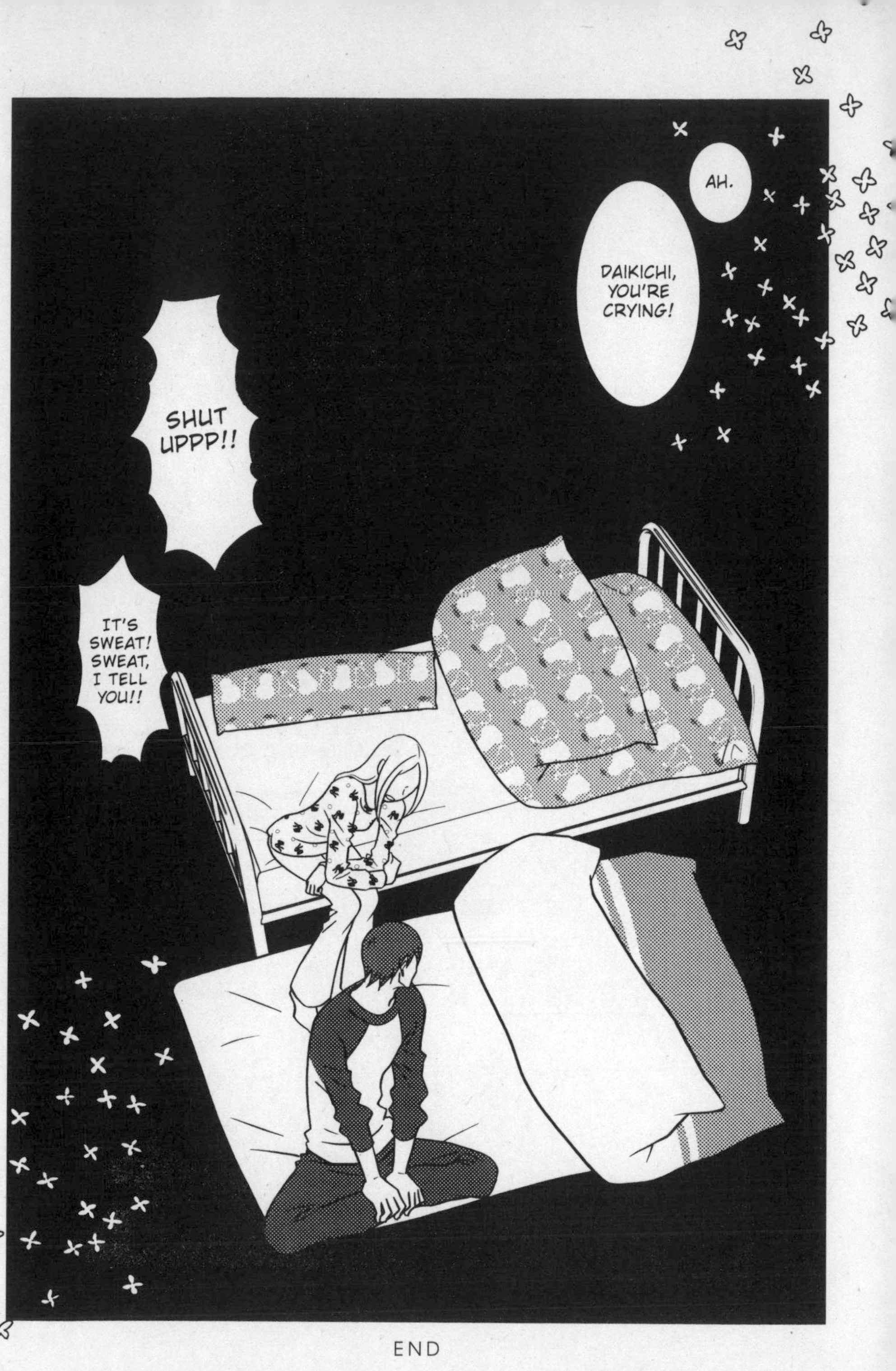
AH.
DAIKICHI, YOU'RE CRYING!
SHUT UPPP!!
IT'S SWEAT! SWEAT, I TELL YOU!!

END

Thank you so much to all the readers
who stuck with *Bunny Drop* till the end.

Initially this was going to be a one-volume
story, but it grew into a surprisingly lengthy
journey as it slowly got longer and longer.

This has been my longest serialization to
date, and I'm still in the middle of the journey
since I'm working on the extra volume...

I'll never forget this series.

The only reason why little old me was able to
work so hard and come this far is because of
everyone's support. Thank you so very much.

Hope you'll enjoy the extra edition...

2011.5

Yumi Unita

TRANSLATION NOTES
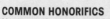

COMMON HONORIFICS

No honorific: Indicates familiarity or closeness; if used without permission or reason, addressing someone in this manner would constitute an insult.

-san: The Japanese equivalent of Mr./Mrs./Miss. If a situation calls for politeness, this is the fail-safe honorific.

-kun: Used most often when referring to boys (though it can be applied to girls as well), this indicates affection or familiarity. Occasionally used by older men among their peers, but it may also be used by anyone referring to a person of lower standing.

-chan: An affectionate honorific indicating familiarity used mostly in reference to girls; also used in reference to cute persons or animals of either gender.

Page 70
Katsudon: A rice bowl topped with a deep-fried pork cutlet and egg.

Page 107
Egg roll: *Tamagoyaki* in Japanese, these mildly sweet egg rolls are made of thin, cooked layers of beaten egg.

Page 125
Meat-and-potato stew: Called *nikujaga* in Japanese, this dish is a bit different from a Western dish that might have the same name. In Japan, it is a common comfort food dish of thinly-sliced meat, potatoes, onions, and other vegetables in a sweetened soy sauce-flavored broth.

Page 130
"Thank you for the food.": *Gochisousama* in Japanese. This is said after every meal. At the beginning of the meal, the phrase would be *itadakimasu*, or "Thank you for the food we are about to eat."

Page 155
Family registry (koseki): An official document under the Law of the Family Register that records names, dates of records (birth, marriage, death, adoption, etc.), and places. Typically each household has a *koseki*.

Page 158
Mochibana: A Japanese New Year's decoration that mimics cherry blossom branches and is made by putting white and pink colored *mochi* ("sticky rice cake") balls on willow branches.

Page 184
Golden Week: This week spanning the end of April to the beginning of May is the longest vacation period for Japanese people. Many employees get paid time off, and some companies shut down completely. The holidays included in this week are: the Emperor's Birthday, Green Day, Showa Day, Constitution Memorial Day, Citizen's Day, and Children's Day.

Page 198
"...quite the prize on a pedestal.": In the original edition, Daikichi calls Rin a *takane no hana*, or "a flower on a high peak."

Page 203
Old man smell: Many Japanese girls and women describe this "old man smell" as unpleasant, so much so that companies in Japan have released items to reduce this "old man smell." Shiseido released a study attributing this odor to the chemical called nonenal being produced in greater quantity in the bodies of men over forty.

Page 206
Doraemon: A Japanese manga series by Fujiko Fujio about a boy, Nobita, and his friend, Doraemon, a robotic cat from the future with a magic pocket that can produce various items such as the Dokodemo Door ("Door to Anywhere").

BUNNY**DROP**

Can't wait for the next volume? You don't have to!

Keep up with the latest chapters of some of your favorite manga every month online in the pages of YEN PLUS!

SOUL EATER NOT!

READ IT THE SAME DAY AS JAPAN!

MAXIMUM RIDE

SOULLESS

WITCH & WIZARD

THE INFERNAL DEVICES
CLOCKWORK ANGEL

Visit us at
www.yenplus.com
for details!

SOUL EATER NOT! © Atsushi Ohkubo / SQUARE-ENIX • Maximum Ride © James Patterson, Illustrations © Hachette Book Group • Soulless © Tofa Borregaard, Illustrations © Hachette Book Group • Witch & Wizard © James Patterson, Illustrations © Hachette Book Group • The Infernal Devices: Clockwork Angel © Cassandra Clare, Illustrations © Hachette Book Group.

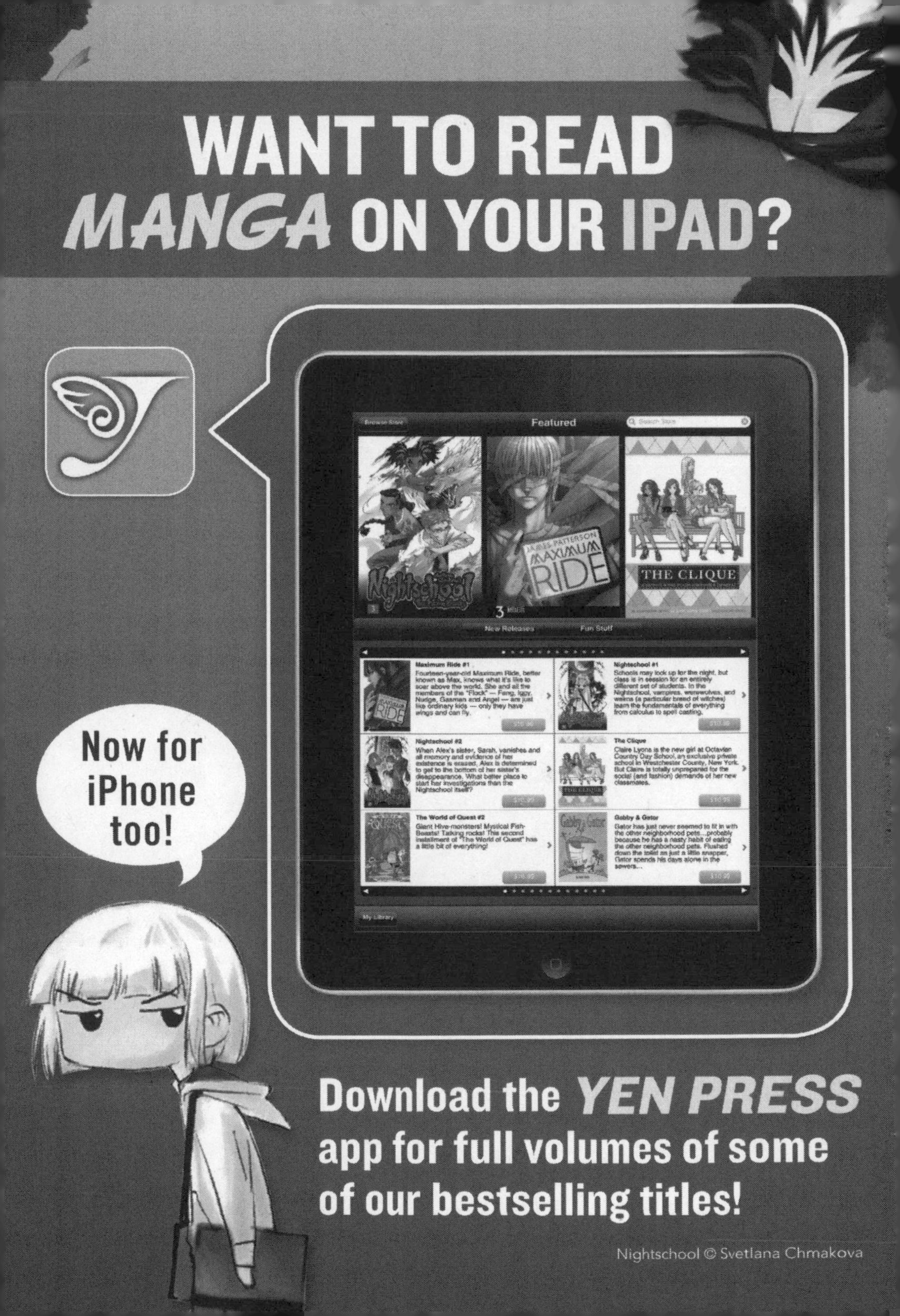
WANT TO READ
MANGA ON YOUR IPAD?
Featured
MAXIMUM RIDE
THE CLIQUE
New Releases
Fun Stuff
Now for iPhone too!
Download the YEN PRESS app for full volumes of some of our bestselling titles!

Hello! This is YOTSUBA!

Guess what? Guess what?
Yotsuba and Daddy just moved here from waaaay over there!

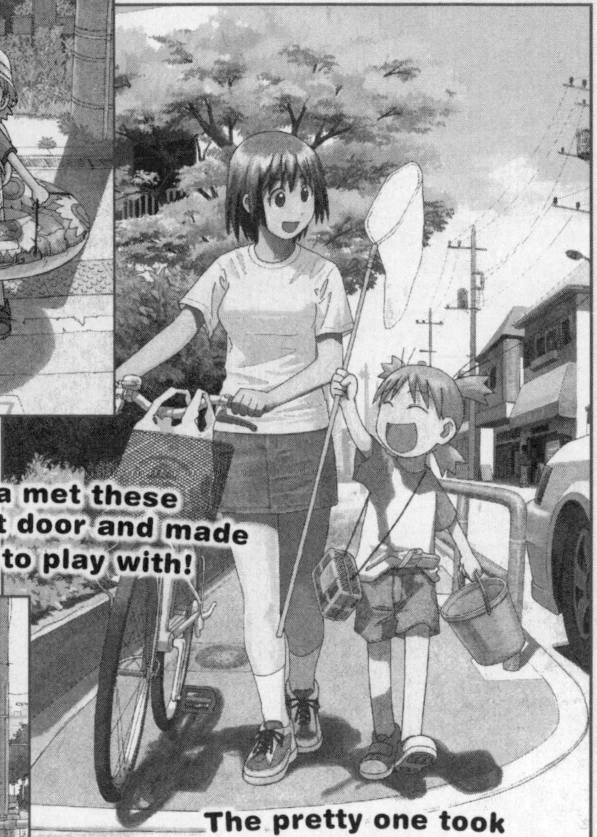

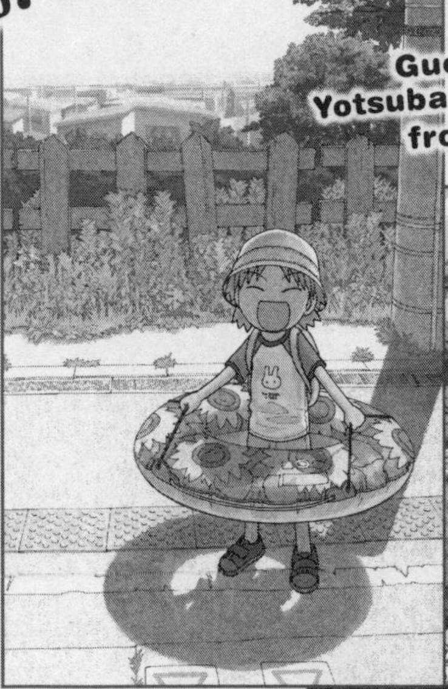

And Yotsuba met these nice people next door and made new friends to play with!

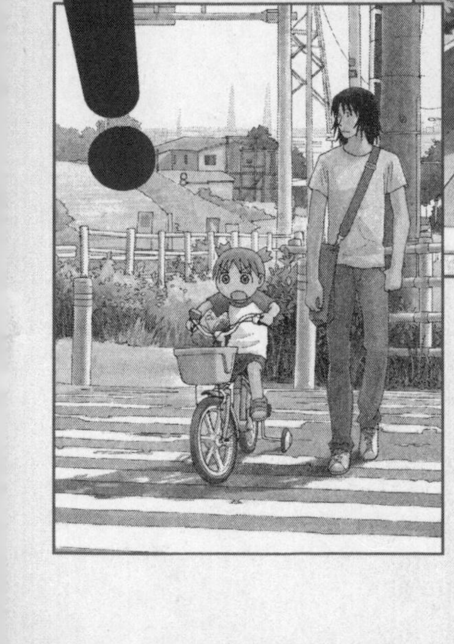

The pretty one took Yotsuba on a bike ride!
(Whoooa! There was a big hill!)

And Ena's a good drawer!
(Almost as good as Yotsuba!)

And their mom always gives Yotsuba ice cream!
(Yummy!)

And...
And...
OHHHH!

ENJOY EVERYTHING.

YOU SHOULD COME PLAY WITH YOTSUBA TOO!

Join Yotsuba as she delights in the things many of us take for granted in this Eisner-nominated series.

VOLUMES 1-11 AVAILABLE NOW!

Visit our website at www.yenpress.com.

Yotsuba&! © Kiyohiko Azuma / YOTUBA SUTAZIO

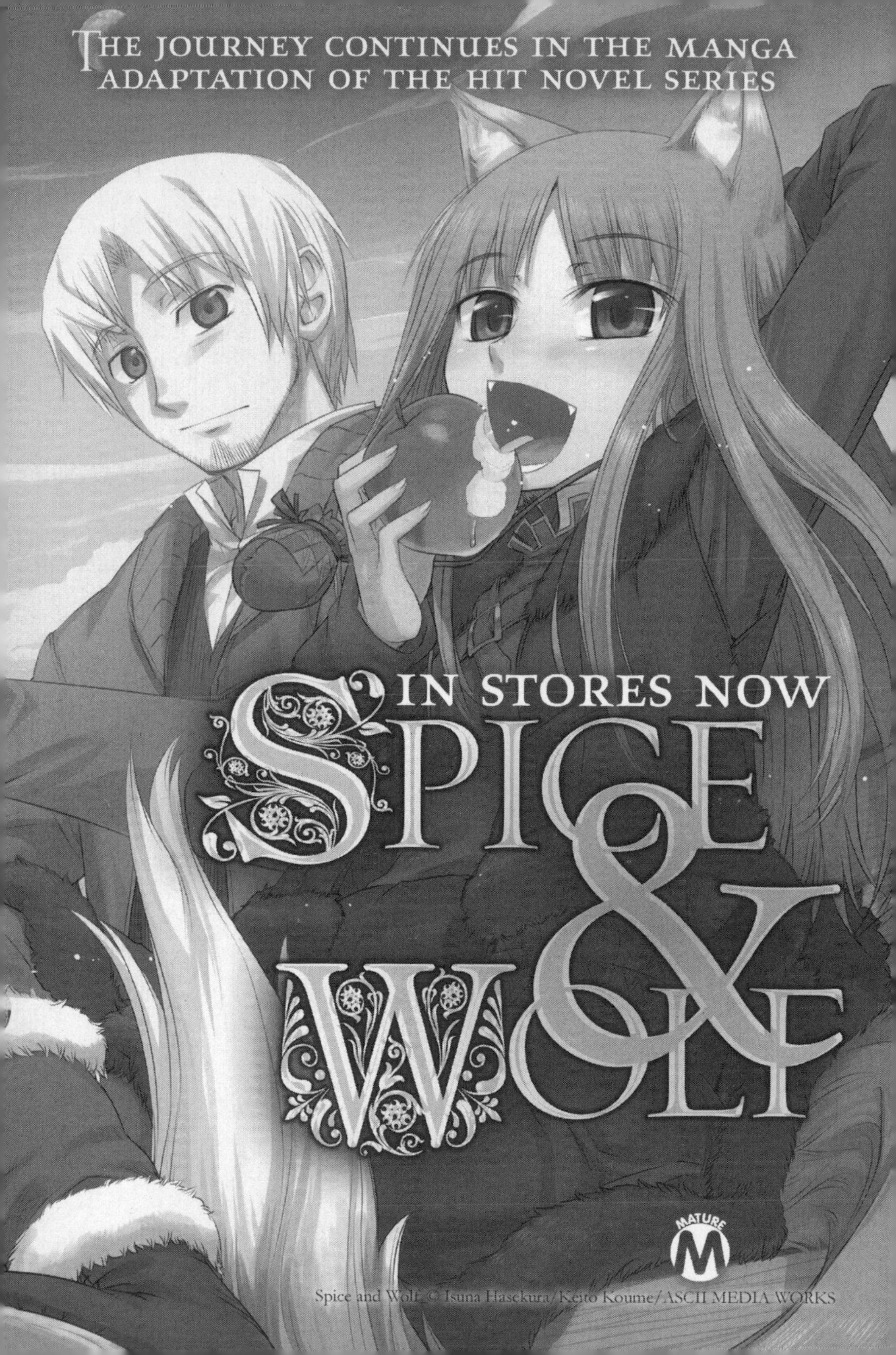
THE JOURNEY CONTINUES IN THE MANGA
ADAPTATION OF THE HIT NOVEL SERIES
IN STORES NOW
SPICE & WOLF
MATURE
M
Spice and Wolf © Isuna Hasekura/Keito Koume/ASCII MEDIA WORKS